THE ESSENTIAL GUIDE TO
EMBROIDERY

THE ESSENTIAL GUIDE TO
EMBROIDERY

MURDOCH
BOOKS

DISCOVER EMBROIDERY

Introduction

The art of embroidery embraces many different techniques, each with its own distinctive character. This book provides a comprehensive guide to sixteen of the most popular styles of embroidery, from counted techniques such as cross stitch to methods of embellishment such as goldwork. Each technique's history is related, followed by detailed instructions on how to work it, guidance on design and step-by-step projects for you to make or adapt. Whatever your level of skill, this book will help you experience the thrill of transforming a fresh piece of fabric into an object of beauty, and the satisfaction of watching a design come to life under your fingers.

The art of decorating textiles is almost as old as the human race, and the study of its history affords a fascinating insight into the social, economic and religious aspects of art and design throughout the centuries. Embroidery has been used in countless ways and for many different purposes: to embellish elaborate trousseaux and funerary wrappings, to proclaim the glory of God and the majesty of kings and queens, to display great wealth or simply to add a little colour to the homes of peasants.

Luxury and labour

For many non-stitchers, embroidery is an activity from the past. They imagine a refined pastime enjoyed by aristocratic ladies, as depicted in formal portraits by court painters. Of course, there is a great deal of truth in this. Many images confirm it: Queen Elizabeth I in her extraordinary blackwork ruffs; Madame Pompadour at her elaborate tambour frame *circa* 1764; or one of the Ladies Waldegrave stitching white sprigs on muslin in Joshua Reynolds' painting of 1780. To the people depicted in these paintings, embroidery was a pleasure and an accomplishment.

However, embroidery was not just a pastime for wealthy women; it was also a way of earning a living for those at the other end of the social spectrum. The privileged lives of the purchasers of embroidered goods, whose rapidly changing fashions and foibles ensured constant innovations in designs and techniques, stand in stark contrast to the hardship and drudgery of the people who laboured to produce the work. Embroidery may have represented incredible luxury and finery, but it also equated with hard labour. Early nineteenth-century descriptions tell of Irish women working fine whitework collars in only ten days. They had little choice in their work at a time when Ireland was in the grip of famine. Paid a pittance and

working against harsh deadlines, they saved time by using children to thread their needles, and were reputed to splash whiskey into their eyes to help them keep going. For them, embroidery must have been an arduous chore, undertaken to feed themselves and their family.

Small children would often spend hours at their own embroidery. They would master their sewing skills and perhaps their alphabet by working detailed samplers. The aim of their painstaking work was to gain a job as a lady's maid, when they would spend long hours stitching the family linen.

Exploring new techniques

There has been a great upsurge of interest and innovation in the art of embroidery in recent years. Modern embroiderers often have a new, experimental attitude to their art and use a wide variety of fabrics and threads, some of them far from conventional. You will find both the traditional and modern techniques of embroidery explained in this book.

If you are already well versed in the art of embroidery, you will no doubt be keen to explore some of the more difficult techniques. However,

even if you are a novice embroiderer, don't be afraid to try them. Each section of the book clearly explains how to work the stitches required and you will soon discover that many techniques share certain stitches. Familiar and adaptable, old friends such as back stitch, cross stitch, French knots, satin stitch and couching are used in many different techniques, blurring the boundaries between different styles of embroidery. As a result, techniques that are generally considered difficult are in fact quite closely linked to traditionally easy forms by common stitches. So, if you can master those stitches on a counted fabric such as Aida or canvas, there is nothing to stop you from trying them in stumpwork, crewel work, silk shading or free surface embroidery. Once you see the connections, the mystery of these many different techniques is exploded, and you are back to what you know – needle, thread and fabric.

The same applies to that apparently magical group of techniques that can turn ordinary fabric into something resembling lace: pulled work, drawn threadwork, Hardanger and cutwork. It is hard to imagine being confident enough to pull, cut and remove threads of the fabric. However, once again you will come across reassuring names for stitches you already know – and what could be frightening about buttonhole and running stitch?

Inspirational projects

Within each technique section there are step-by-step projects created by talented embroiderers that you can make yourself. Browse through the following pages and you will be enticed by the prospect of creating the beautiful designs on offer – just imagine the delicate cutwork Lavender Pillow (page 131) or the pretty pulled work Flower Cushion (page 100) adorning your own home and you will be eager to begin.

Some of the projects, such as the canvas work Indian Panel (page 84), rely on bold colours and added embellishments (in this case tassels and shisha glass). A completely different kind of splendour is offered by the goldwork Art Nouveau Panel (page 276), stitched on silk and inspired by enamelled jewellery. While you are working this project, imagine the goldworkers of the medieval period, working with real gold and silver, pearls and garnets. They were prohibited from using inferior materials; if they did, their work could be burned. In contrast, blackwork restricts itself to one colour (though modern pieces often break this tradition). As you can see from the blackwork cushion project on page 68, finely detailed stitching and an elegant design can be enhanced by this colour restraint.

Perhaps you are inspired by the three-dimensional effects of beadwork, stumpwork or ribbon embroidery? You could make the stumpwork beetle on page 238, padding its gold-leather body and conjuring its wings in simple needlelace. The beadwork Star Pin Cushion on page 290 combines the contrasting textures of velvet and beads, in a design reminiscent of the Victorian age. One of the ribbon embroidery projects, the Spring Flower Panel (page 260), begins with a painted background – another idea that can be combined with many different stitching techniques, such as free embroidery (see Poppy Panel, page 210). Or why not try the contemporary three-dimensional technique of machine embroidery on dissolvable fabric? When the fabric disappears, you are left with a filigree network of stitching, perfect for making the sophisticated Evening Purse on page 225.

Other techniques depend on subtle shading for their impact. The crewel work Glamis Stag (page 190) and Tree of Life Panel (page 196) at first seem to have little in common with the silk shading brooches on page 172, but you will soon discover how in both techniques the stitching and colours follow the contours of animals and plants to create realistic effects. Then the two techniques seem to be separated by little more than the difference between their respective wool and silk threads.

Whitework, on the other hand, depends purely on the skill of the embroiderer to produce perfectly even stitches in white thread on a white background fabric. This white-on-white look has many forms, but throughout the centuries women have loved to use it for baby clothes and bedlinen. You could follow in this tradition by making the Mountmellick Bedspread on page 147 or the Ayrshire work Christening Robe on page 150, which provides ladybird, daisy and butterfly motifs fit for any family heirloom.

Rich rewards

Every one of the projects in this book will richly repay the work involved – by the satisfaction of seeing the finished piece and the knowledge of new techniques acquired. Don't let anyone look down on your work because it is not your own design. Embroiderers have been using professional designers since the very earliest days. Even most of those aristocratic ladies in previous centuries paid designers to outline their motifs for them. However,

if you would like to branch out to designing your own projects, there are many useful guidelines. You could start by changing the colour scheme of an existing design, perhaps, then move on to seek out your own sources of inspiration.

Whichever route you choose, you have many pleasures ahead. You can look forward to picking up your embroidery and feeling the fabric and thread in your hands. The addiction will grow as you watch colour and pattern filling your blank 'canvas'. With friends and fellow stitchers, you will visit embroidery shops and shows and revel in the ravishing display of threads – jewel colours and textures that cry out to be handled. Perhaps you will enjoy the sociability of a group or workshops. You may be convinced that your embroidery provides the perfect therapy for a busy, technology filled life – even an escape from family and work. No doubt you will long for more time to stitch, and probably you will start a few projects that never reach completion. But that won't matter, because the whole point is the joy of the stitching itself.

GETTING
STARTED

Needles

The type of needle you should use depends on the technique you have chosen. Sharp, pointed needles are used for techniques that pierce the fabric and blunt-tipped tapestry needles for counted techniques, in order to avoid splitting the fabric threads.

Types of needles

Sharp needle
A general sewing needle, with a short, round eye to give the needle extra strength.

Quilting / between needle
Designed for fast, even stitching, this needle has a short, round eye.

Tapestry needle
Its blunt point can pass through canvas or evenweave without splitting the fabric threads, but would damage other fabrics.

Chenille needle
Similar to a tapestry needle, but with a sharp point to pierce the fabric, a chenille needle is useful for stitching with textured yarns.

Embroidery / crewel needle
This pointed needle suits work on plain weave and the long eye lets you thread many strands.

Bodkin needle
Round or flat, this needle's large eye threads cords and ribbons.

Ballpoint needle
This needle has a small eye, ideal for needlelace and stumpwork.

Beading needle
This fine, flexible needle goes through tiny beads and holds several beads at once.

Curved needle
Used for stitching rigid surfaces together.

Gold-plated needle
Available as quilting, crewel and tapestry needle. Useful for anyone who suffers from a nickel allergy.

Double-ended needle
With a middle eye, this needle is ideal for cross stitch and tapestry.

Threading the needle

Loop method
Loop the end of the thread over the eye of the needle and pinch it tightly together. Slip the pinched loop off the needle and push the fold of the thread through the eye of the needle.

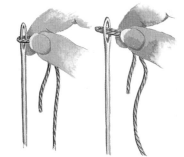

Loop the thread over and then through the eye of the needle.

Needle threader method
Slip the wire loop of the threader through the eye of the needle. Then, place the thread through the loop and draw the threader out through the eye.

Put the thread through the loop and draw out the threader.

Paper method
Cut a strip of paper narrow enough to fit through the needle eye. Fold in half on the end of the thread. Push the paper through the eye, pulling the thread with it.

Slip the folded paper through the eye.

Method for metallic threads
Loop the end of the thread and push through the eye of the needle. Pass over the needle point and pull in order to tighten the loop and secure the thread.

Attach metallic threads with a loop to prevent them from shredding.

Sewing machines

A sewing machine is one of the most creative embroidery tools at your disposal. You do not need to spend a fortune on the latest model as even a basic machine can produce a wide range of wonderful effects.

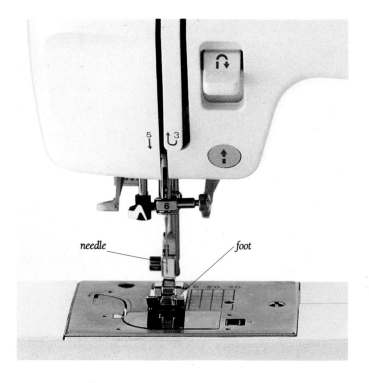

needle   foot

To ensure successful machine embroidery, your sewing machine must have the following:
• straight and zigzag stitches
• feed dogs (the teeth feeding the material under the needle), which can be lowered or covered
• adjustable lower tension.
You may also wish to have:
• built-in stitch patterns
• computerized pattern design, but these are not compulsory.

Before you begin to stitch, it is worth spending a little time getting to know your machine. You will need to consult the manufacturer's manual to verify the settings, so keep the manual handy. Make sure your machine is clean and warm – it should be stored at room temperature, so that the oil lubricates well. Clean the bobbin regularly to remove any fluff and bits of thread that may build up. If your manual advises it, oil your machine when needed.

Make sure your machine is threaded correctly, and test the stitching on a scrap of fabric. If the quality of the stitching is poor, the tension may need to be adjusted following the manual. If the machine has been oiled, this stitch test will also remove any surplus oil that could otherwise damage your work. You will need to replace needles on a regular basis, as a needle that has become blunt may result in either uneven or skipped stitches.

Choosing a model
Most manufacturers produce sewing machines ranging from the basic straight/zigzag-stitch models to the most sophisticated, computerized machines. Before purchasing a machine, establish your needs. Although machine embroidery does not require all the features provided by the top-of-the-range models, you may find a machine with a good range to be more cost effective.

Bobbins
Extra bobbins are quite cheap and always useful. Different machines use different bobbins, so use those recommended for your machine rather than universal ones.

Bobbin and case

Needles
When using a machine, the thread creates a groove in the eye of the needle that is unique to that type of thread. If you then change to another type of thread, the groove will not match and the thread may snap or shred. In order to avoid this, stick a label on the needlebox to identify which needle was used with which thread.

Use a universal needle for machine embroidery. Large needles, size 90/100, are ideal for most threads as they cause less wear-and-tear on the threads, but for metallic threads use a needle with an extra-large eye in order to prevent shredding. Spring needles will allow you to work free machine embroidery without the need for a foot. Use twin needles to stitch with two threads simultaneously, checking that the hole in the base plate of the machine is wide enough to fit both needles.

Basic needle

Twin needle

Spring needle

Feet
Use a standard foot when working general stitching and automatic patterns with the presser foot on and the feed dogs up. Darning feet are used with the feed dogs down for free machine embroidery. Use a zip foot to insert zips, make piping and for general making-up techniques.

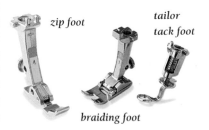

zip foot   *tailor tack foot*

braiding foot

Frames

A frame will keep the background fabric taut and maintain an even tension when stitching. It is possible to work some techniques without a frame, but this may result in uneven stitches and a poor finish, the fabric may wrinkle and pucker, and some stitches may even distort the fabric.

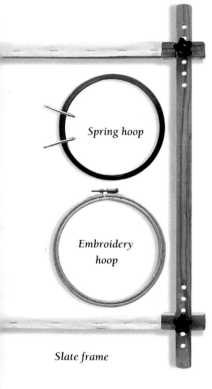

Slate frame

Types of frames

Embroidery hoop
Also known as a ring or tambour frame, this hoop is made from wood or plastic. It is suitable for small projects, as the design needs to be smaller than the hoop.

Slate frame
The most rigid of frames, its adjustable peg or screw fittings are tightened to hold the fabric taut. The bars at the top and bottom have a webbing strip onto which the fabric is sewn.

Hand-rotating frame
This frame, also called a tapestry or roller frame, is available in various widths. The depth of the frame is less important as the excess fabric can be rolled onto the top and bottom rollers. Keep tightening the wing-nuts, which hold the rollers in place, to maintain an even tension.

Stretcher frame
Consisting of two pairs of canvas stretchers slotted together, the fabric is fixed with pins or staples.

Spring hoop
Popular in machine embroidery, it can be slipped under the needle of the machine. To reposition this hoop without removing your work from the machine, leave the needle in the work, release the inner frame and move the frame to the new area to be worked.

No-sew frame
With this frame, there is no need to sew the fabric into the frame as you attach it by means of clips, drawing pins or staples.

Seat frame
On this height-adjustable stand, the flat base is placed under your leg when seated. Some may have a fixed embroidery hoop or a clamp to attach your own.

Table clamp
The height-adjustable embroidery hoop is attached to a clamp that can be fixed to a tabletop.

Floor stand
A stand that can be adjusted and will hold a variety of frames.

Using a frame
The fabric must be stretched tight for most techniques, except where stitches need to be scooped. On rectangular frames, the straight grain of the fabric must align with the sides of the frame. To leave hands free for stitching, support the frame on the edge of a table, on the arm of a chair or in a stand.

If the fabric is too small to fit the frame, add extra fabric by sewing strips of cheap or waste fabric onto the sides.

Add extra strips of fabric if needed.

You can also sew the main fabric onto a larger piece of fabric, then cut away the extra fabric from the back behind the area to be stitched.

Cut the extra fabric behind the work.

Seat frame

No-sew frame

Hand-rotating frame

*Floor stand
and frame*

*Stretcher
frame*

Using an embroidery hoop

1 To prevent your fabric from slipping, bind the inner hoop with fabric strips or bias binding, securing the end with stitches. For fine or delicate fabric, also bind the outer hoop in this way.

Bind the hoop with extra fabric.

2 Place the fabric over the inner hoop. Using the screw on the outer hoop, adjust so it fits snugly over the inner hoop and fabric. Ease the outer hoop down, pulling the fabric taut. Tighten the screw.

Tighten once the fabric is taut.

3 Protect fine fabric with tissue paper or another layer of fine fabric before placing the outer hoop. Cut away the tissue or fabric inside the loop.

Cut away the paper or fine fabric.

Using a slate frame

1 Turn your fabric over 12mm (½in) at the top and bottom edges. Measure and mark the centre of the roller bar on the webbing. Mark the centre at the top and bottom edges of the fabric. Matching the centre points of the fabric to the centre of each bar, pin the fabric to the webbing, starting at the centre and working out. With small stitches, oversew the fabric to the webbing, starting at the centre and working out.

Oversew the fabric to the webbing.

2 Roll excess fabric around one or both bars. Insert the side bars into the slots in the top and bottom bars. Insert the pegs (or tighten screw sides) so the fabric is taut. Attach strips of webbing to the side edges of the fabric. Lace through the webbing and around each side bar with fine, strong string, leaving 45cm (18in) at each end. Pull the string to stretch the fabric. Fasten with a slip knot.

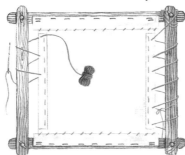

Lace around each side bar.

Using a stretcher frame

1 Place the fabric face down and lay the frame on top. Allow enough fabric to wrap over the edge of the frame except for canvas, which can be pinned to the top of the stretchers. Pull the fabric over the frame and secure in the centre with a pin. Pin opposite sides first, working from the centre out. Secure the other sides. To stop threads catching, cover the heads of the drawing pins with masking tape. Use silk pins for fine fabrics.

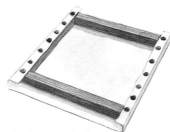

Pin the fabric to the frame.

Using backing cloth

A fine fabric or one that is too small to fit into a frame should be stabilized by applying it to a backing cloth before mounting.

If using an embroidery hoop, first tack the fabric to the backing cloth, place into the hoop and pull the fabrics to an even tension.

On a slate frame, mount the backing as described. Starting at the centre top edge and working outwards, pin down the main fabric. Smooth the fabric and pin the lower edge. Pin the sides so it is wrinkle-free and long-and-short stitch in place, removing the pins.

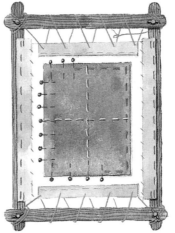

Pin down the fabric onto the frame.

On a stretcher frame, mount the backing to the frame, then attach the fabric with drawing pins in the gaps between the ones holding the backing in place.

Tips

• By repositioning the frame as you work, you can use an embroidery hoop on larger projects. However, take care when doing this, as the hoop can flatten the stitching.

• You will need to be able to turn the frame over to start and finish threads.

• Unless the frame is well outside the area being stitched, remove it when you are not working to avoid damage to the embroidery.

Beeswax

Booboo stick

Daylight bulbs

Paper scissors

Embroidery scissors

Dressmaking scissors

Specialist scissors

Tools

You do not need a vast array of special equipment for embroidery, but it will make your life easier if you have the right tool for the job. A pair of fine-pointed, sharp embroidery scissors, needles and an embroidery hoop or frame are essential – the other tools may be acquired as and when you need them.

Beading wire
Used in stumpwork, choose the coloured or brass, 34-gauge type.

Beeswax
Used to strengthen thread for goldwork or beading.

Blocking board
This is a softwood board used for stretching and re-aligning work that has become distorted while being stitched.

Booboo stick
Useful for careful unpicking, the brush drags the snipped threads out to the back of the fabric so the surface is not damaged.

Clip-on magnifier
Used either to read a chart or for fine stitching.

Coloured pencils
You can create your own design on canvas using coloured pencils. You can then embroider in the details over the top.

Cosmetic sponge
Use the dampened sponge to smooth rayon threads.

Daylight bulb
Makes it easy to see colours in poor lighting conditions.

Drawing pins
Used for blocking (see page 29), make sure that you buy the rustproof variety.

Dressmakers' carbon
This specific type of carbon paper is available in a variety of colours.

Dressmakers' marking pencil
Mark the fabric with the pencil, then use the brush on the other end to remove the marks when no longer needed.

Dressmaking scissors
Used for cutting fabric.

Embroidery scissors
These scissors must be sharp, fine-pointed and able to cut right to the tip of the blades.

Fray-check product
Used around the outer edge of fine fabrics to prevent them from fraying as you work.

Ruler

Set square

Masking tape

Pointed tweezers

Pins

Glass-headed pins

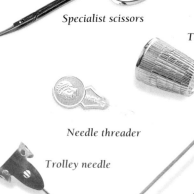

Needle threader

Trolley needle

Thimble

Tacking thread

Stiletto

Tailors' chalk

Graph paper
Used when altering the size of a design or to plan your own.

Hard pencil
Used to trace a fine outline onto light-coloured fabric. Take care when using pale threads as the pencil may make them grubby.

Iron
A steam iron can be used for steam or dry ironing.

Lamp
Good lighting will help to prevent eye strain and many mistakes.

Light box
Not a necessity, but very useful when transferring a design onto fine or pale-coloured fabric.

Magnifier with built-in light
Make sure to choose one that takes a daylight bulb.

Masking tape
Multi-purpose, including holding fabric in position temporarily and binding raw edges.

Needle threader
This makes it easy to thread the finest of needles.

Paper-covered wire
Used mainly in stumpwork and available from sugarcraft suppliers.

Paper scissors
To be used for cutting paper.

Pillowcase
To protect and store your work.

Pins
Use standard dressmaking pins or longer, glass-headed pins.

Pounce
Made from crushed charcoal tablets (black), or powdered cuttlefish (white), you can mix the two to create grey.

Ruler
Essential for drawing straight lines and grids and also for checking the count of an evenweave fabric.

Screwdriver
Used for tightening the screw on an embroidery hoop.

Set square
Used to check that corners are square when blocking embroidery (see page 29).

Silk pins
Used to attach silk or fine fabrics to a stretcher frame.

Specialist scissors
The curved design of the blades makes it easy to cut threads with the hoop in place. These are available for different techniques.

Stiletto
Used for easing bulky threads and wrapped wires through the fabric, and for shaping eyelets in cutwork and Hardanger.

Tacking thread
General-purpose sewing thread.

Tailor's chalk
Used to make temporary marks on fabric.

Tape measure
Useful for measuring fabric.

Thimble
When stitching on heavy fabrics, wear a thimble on your finger to push the needle through the fabric.

Toolbox
A large, plastic toolbox, with its numerous separate compartments, will provide excellent storage for your materials.

Tracing paper
Choose good-quality paper for more precise copying.

Paper-covered wires

Beading wires

Tracing wheel
Used with dressmakers' carbon paper. Roll the wheel around the outline of the design.

Transfer pencil
Useful for transferring an image onto fabric (see page 31).

Trolley needle
Used for laying multiple strands of thread, it gives a smooth finish.

Tweezers
Useful for techniques that involve withdrawing threads, such as drawn threadwork.

Vanishing pen
Light sensitive, the line will fade in time. Unsuitable for large projects as it will need to be re-applied.

Water-soluble pen
For use on washable fabrics.

Tracing wheel

Tape measure

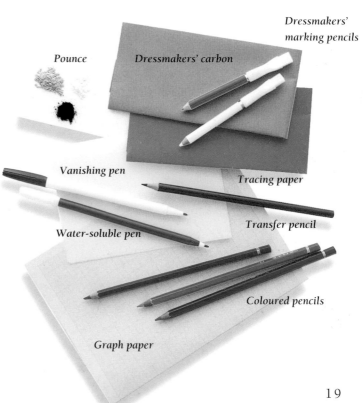

Dressmakers' marking pencils

Pounce

Dressmakers' carbon

Vanishing pen

Tracing paper

Water-soluble pen

Transfer pencil

Coloured pencils

Graph paper

Linen

Cotton

Aida and linen bands

Hardanger

Silk gauze

Aida

Perforated paper

Fabrics for counted thread embroidery

Quality fabrics are an essential part of your embroidery. In some cases, the background fabric will show as much as the stitches. For counted techniques, choose an evenweave such as linen, a blockweave such as Aida, or canvas. They are woven with the same number of warp and weft threads within a given measurement.

Warp threads run along the length of a piece of fabric and weft threads are woven across the warp.

The number of threads per inch in a fabric, or *tpi*, is also known as the count. To check the count of the fabric, lay a ruler on the fabric and place pins 2.5cm (1in) apart; count the number of threads (or blocks on Aida) between the pins.

Count the blocks on Aida (left) and the threads on linen (right).

The count of the fabric governs the size of the stitches, so a fabric with a high count will result in small stitches and reduce the overall size of the finished design. The size of a design can be varied simply by stitching on a coarser or finer fabric, or by working the stitches over a different number of fabric threads. The type of thread or number of strands of stranded cotton may also have to be adjusted if you choose to use a different count of fabric.

The same design is smaller on 32 count (left) than 27 count (right).

Made from cotton, linen, wool or mixed fibres, most counted fabrics are available in a variety of colours, especially in the most popular counts. Individual fabric names refer to products from different manufacturers, but it is the count and the fibre content that affect the embroidery work.

Most counted fabrics are available by the metre, with the most popular counts and colours also available as pre-cut pieces. Pre-cut pieces may be folded or rolled in a tube. When buying fabric, it is not necessary to buy a full metre as it is generally sold to the nearest 10cm (4in). Some fabrics are sold as 'fat quarters'. A standard quarter of a metre will give a piece of fabric measuring 25cm the width of the fabric, whereas a 'fat quarter' will provide a piece measuring 50cm (20in) deep x half the width of the fabric from selvedge to selvedge, which is often a much more useful size.

A coloured background fabric can transform the look of a finished piece. However, holes in dark-coloured fabrics do not show clearly, so mount the fabric in a frame and work in such a way that there is light behind the fabric. Alternatively, place a white cloth on your knee.

To fold fabrics for storage, iron them first then store them rolled onto a cardboard tube so the folded edges do not get grubby.

Aida

The threads in Aida fabrics are woven into clearly defined blocks with easy-to-see holes. The count

of Aida refers to the number of blocks per inch. Popular for cross stitch where one stitch is worked over one block, it is less suitable if your design includes half or quarter stitches as you will have to stitch through the middle of a block. Aida is also not suitable for drawn threadwork and Hardanger embroidery.

More unusual fabrics are also available, such as Aida with lurex threads going through the fabric or Aida with a rustic finish.

Evenweave linen

This single-thread fabric has more threads to the inch than Aida, but stitching is generally worked over two fabric threads, so that a design worked on 28-count linen will be the same finished size when stitched on 14-count Aida. This fabric is perfect for working more complex counted stitches.

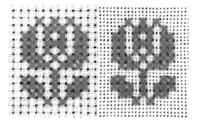

14-count Aida (left) and 28-count linen (right) give the same finished size.

Evenweave cotton

A reasonably priced alternative to pure linen, this is easy to stitch on and has an even finish.

Fabric bands

Linen and Aida bands with pre-finished edges are available in various widths, colours and counts. Many ready-made items have an Aida insert, but check that it is of good quality or you may end up with uneven stitches.

Hardanger

The threads in Hardanger fabric are arranged in pairs, but each pair is treated as one thread. As its name suggests, it is generally used for Hardanger embroidery.

Silk gauze

Silk gauze is used for small-scale embroideries, particularly for dolls' house miniatures. Too small and fine to fit in a conventional embroidery frame, the gauze is usually taped behind an aperture cut into a cardboard mount.

Choose a needle that will go through the fine mesh without distorting it. On 18- to 30-count gauze, use a fine tapestry needle and on 30-count or finer, use a sharp crewel or between needle, making sure the needle does not pierce the threads of the gauze.

The mesh is so fine that a half cross stitch worked over one thread of gauze with a single strand of cotton gives good coverage. Never carry a thread across the back of an area that is not solidly stitched as it will show through the translucent gauze.

Perforated paper

Punched with regularly spaced holes, perforated paper is ideal for counted techniques. This type of paper (sometimes called stitching paper) has a rough and a smooth side, and the stitching should be worked on the smooth side. The holes in the paper are larger than those in 14-count Aida. So, to obtain a better coverage, use three strands of stranded cotton.

When stitching, take care not to pull the thread too tight, or the paper may pucker or even tear.

Perforated paper cannot be mounted into an embroidery hoop so use masking tape to attach it to a cardboard frame.

Canvas

Much firmer than the other fabrics, canvas can support close-worked, heavy stitching such as tent stitch. Canvas is also often measured in threads per inch. It is worth spending a little extra for a good-quality (deluxe) canvas as it will have a smoother finish and cause much less wear-and-tear to the working threads. There are various types of canvas.

Single-thread (mono-) canvas

This canvas has a simple, plain weave. Some stitches may slip at the points where the threads of the canvas intersect.

Interlock canvas

Mono-canvas is constructed so that the threads of the canvas are locked in place. It is suitable for all canvas work stitches.

Double-thread canvas

The mesh is formed by pairs of vertical and horizontal threads. A pair of threads can be treated as a single thread, or the threads can be separated to allow smaller stitches to be worked – useful if your design includes some finely worked areas.

The gauge of a double canvas is expressed using two numbers: in a 14/28 canvas, the 14 is the number of double meshes per inch and the 28 is the count if the threads are separated.

Congress cloth

At 24 threads to the inch, this is one of the finest canvases. It is sometimes referred to as 'coin net'.

Plastic canvas

This is a moulded, medium-gauge canvas. It is sold either by the metre, or as pre-cut shapes.

Waste canvas

This canvas allows counted thread techniques to be worked on non-counted fabrics.

To use, cut a piece slightly larger than the design area. Position and tack it onto the area.

Work the design, stitching into the centre of the canvas squares. Do not pierce the threads of the canvas or they will be difficult to remove. Once the stitching is complete, remove the tacking thread, dampen the canvas (this softens the glue that holds the canvas threads together) and use tweezers to remove the canvas one thread at a time.

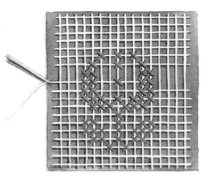

Ease out stubborn threads with tweezers, then remove.

Repairing canvas

To repair ripped canvas, remove stitches from around the damaged area to allow for a patch. From the same gauge of canvas, cut a patch a few threads bigger than the area. Place the patch behind the ripped canvas and tack. Work stitching, sewing through both layers.

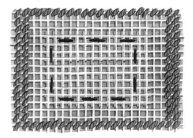

Tack the patch onto the canvas.

Rug canvas

This coarse canvas is generally used for knotted rugs. It can also be woven with ribbons or pliable material to create a textured surface that can be embellished with surface stitching.

Single-thread canvas

Interlock canvas

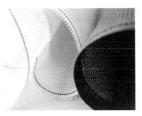

Double-thread canvas

Congress cloth

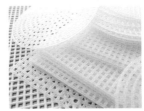

Plastic canvas

Waste canvas

Rug canvas

Calico

Cotton

Felt

Furnishing fabric

Lamés

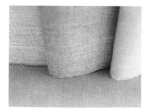

Linen twill

Muslin

Plain weave fabrics and foundations for surface embroidery

Plain weave fabrics have a tightly woven surface and are used for surface embroidery techniques, such as crewel work, goldwork and freestyle embroidery. From simple cottons to the finest of silks, furnishing fabrics to handmade papers – you can stitch on almost anything as long as it is pliable enough to allow the needle to pierce it.

Generally, heavier embroidery techniques need to be supported by a more robust background fabric. You can use a finer fabric, but it should be backed with a firmer cloth for added support. If you are using a backing cloth for your stitching, wash both fabrics before use in case they shrink at different rates.

Decorative fabrics

Your choice of main fabric is very important to the appearance of the finished needlework. Plain weave fabric does not have to be a plain colour. As a matter of fact, stripes, checks or self-patterns can add an extra dimension to your stitching. In all cases, when you are unsure whether a fabric is at all suitable for your chosen technique, you should always work a test sample first.

Calico

Calico is a plain cotton fabric that is often sold unbleached. It takes colour well and may be dyed or painted in order to add extra interest or to create a background image before the stitching is begun.

Cotton

This natural fabric is available in a variety of weights, from fine lawns to the heavier poplins and piqués. There is a comprehensive range of plain and patterned finishes available, and patchwork and most quilting suppliers will often offer a range of space-dyed cotton fabrics.

Felt

The fibres in this non-woven fabric are matted together, and the edges will not fray when cut. Felt is especially useful for padding, in techniques such as stumpwork and goldwork. You can actually make your own felt or dye a ready-made piece in the colour of your choice.

Furnishing fabrics

Plain colours or self-patterns (such as damask) provide an excellent background fabric for embroideries. Be aware though that very strong patterns may overwhelm the embroidery. These fabrics are quite robust and are therefore suitable for use as soft furnishings once they have been embroidered.

Lamés

These fine metallic tissues fray very readily and are easier to work with if they are backed with an iron-on interfacing.

Linen twill

A closely woven fabric with a distinctive diagonal weave, linen twill supports heavy embroidery, such as crewel work. Because of the density of the weave, the threads of the fabric close up around the stitches, leaving no holes. It is available in only one colour: a natural creamy-beige.

Muslin

Muslin is a fine, soft cotton fabric with a fairly open weave, which gives it quite a gauzy appearance.

Silk

Silk is available in a wide variety of both weights and finishes. Medium-weight Habotai silk frays easily and should therefore be applied to a backing cloth before stitching starts. Silk noil has a more textured finish, while the heavier silk dupion has a certain amount of dressing, which gives it a crisp feel. In shot-silk, the warp and weft threads are of a different colour, resulting in a play of colour. Silk is available in a huge spectrum of rich, vibrant shades, but it is also very easy to colour it with silk dyes and paints to create your own unique fabric.

Silk paper

A comprehensive range of colours and finishes is available from a number of specialist suppliers. Alternatively, you can also make your own. Silk papers are quite versatile and can be moulded into three-dimensional shapes.

Sheer fabrics

These see-through fabrics include organza, voile, tulle, chiffon, etc. Sheers can be used to create layers, add a hint of colour or to entrap decorative threads, sequins and fabric motifs. They are also often used for techniques such as shadow work.

Many sheer fabrics fray easily. This characteristic can be seen as an attribute, as the frayed edges can be used to add texture to a piece of work or, when used in an embroidered landscape, to create the impression of grass.

Synthetic fabrics

Manmade fabrics such as polyester, nylon and rayon are available in a wide choice of finishes, but try to avoid knits and other stretchy fabrics as they may distort when stitched, causing the finished embroidery to pucker.

Velvet

Velvet encompasses a wide range of fabrics with a raised pile. It is available in a variety of weights, from a heavy plush-pile cotton velvet to the finer silk or synthetic fibres. Silk velvet has a silk backing with a viscose pile and is used for dévoré, a technique that involves dissolving areas of the pile to create a design.

When working with velvet, be aware that the direction of the pile can affect the look of the fabric, therefore the pile is usually laid in the same direction. To prevent flattening the pile, velvet should always be ironed on the wrong side into another piece of velvet or other soft surface.

Wool

Choose a firmly woven wool fabric such as blanketing wool or doctor's flannel. Blanketing wool is popular for wool embroidery in Australia and can be found elsewhere, although a ready-made blanket may be easier to source.

Backing cloth

Both calico and fine cotton make excellent backing cloths as they are quite firm. A non-woven backing cloth, such as an iron-on interfacing, can also be used to back fine, smooth fabrics.

Refer to page 17 for how to use the backing cloth within a frame. If not using an embroidery frame, rows of diagonal tacking stitches should be worked to hold the backing cloth and the main fabric together, or they may slip and cause puckering. You should always make sure that the straight grains of the backing cloth and those of the main fabric align perfectly.

Other fabrics

Paper-backed fusible web

This product, which is sold under a variety of trade names, consists of a fusible web of glue attached to silicone paper, and it is generally used to apply or bond one or more fabrics to another fabric.

To use, place a piece of the paper-backed web glue side (which feels slightly rougher than the paper side) down onto the back of the fabric to be applied and then iron in place. You may find it easier to draw or trace the shape of the required motif onto the paper side of the bonding product before it is ironed onto the fabric, but bear in mind that this will result in a mirror image of the motif. In order to avoid this, copy the design onto tracing paper and then flip the tracing over and trace the flipped design onto the paper backing. Leave the paper backing in place, as it adds stiffness to the fabric, which makes it much easier to cut out small or intricate shapes, especially when using soft or slippery fabrics.

Once you have cut out all the required shapes, peel off the paper backing and position the shapes glue side down on the fabric. Finally, place a sheet of silicone paper between the iron and the motif to be ironed in order to prevent the glue from adhering to the iron, then iron to bond in place.

Self-adhesive paper backing is also available, which helps to prevent any distortion if you are using a sewing machine.

Dissolvable fabrics

These fabrics include a range of fabrics that can be used for both hand and machine stitching.

Stitches worked onto the fabric must interconnect or they will unravel when the supporting fabric is removed. The fabrics are dissolved in a variety of ways, including by immersion in hot or cold water, or by heat (ironing). Whichever product you finally decide upon, you should always follow the manufacturer's instructions carefully.

Non-woven backing

This fabric is a soft, supple interfacing, suitable for backing delicate fabrics. The iron-on interfacing will support stitching on fine fabrics and also help to prevent fraying. It is available in white, charcoal and black in a variety of weights and should be chosen to complement the fabric you wish to back.

Both sew-in and iron-on interfacings remain in place to give the fabric body and to provide support for the surface stitching. Tear-away backings give stability to the fabric and stitching while it is being worked but are torn away once the stitching is complete.

Pelmet-weight interfacing is sold for soft furnishings and crafts. It is also useful for padding stumpwork and creating three-dimensional embroideries, such as book covers or jewellery. Pelmet interfacing is quite thick and firm and therefore lacks the suppleness of the lighter-weight interfacings. It is often used in stumpwork, particularly for creating both hands and faces. An excellent choice for beginners to machine embroidery, pelmet interfacing does not need to be mounted into a frame and it will provide a stable base for free machine embroidery.

Wadding is used behind the surface fabric. Stitching can be worked through the fabric and wadding, or it can be placed behind a finished embroidery in order to give it a lift.

Silk

Silk paper

Sheer fabric

Synthetic fabrics

Velvet

Woollen fabric

Interfacings and waddings

Stranded cotton threads

Coton perlé threads

Coton à broder threads

Soft embroidery threads

Rayon threads

Silk threads

Wool threads

Threads

Embroidery threads are available in a wonderful array of colours and in a wide variety of weights and textures. Cotton and wool are the most well known types of thread but silk, viscose, rayon, metallic and synthetic threads are also widely available.

The colour is identified by the number on the thread band or label. However, even standard ranges of threads may have slight variations in dye lots, so make sure to buy enough of each shade of thread to complete your work. This is particularly important if working a large area in a single colour. To substitute threads from a different manufacturer, use a thread conversion chart in order to obtain corresponding colour numbers. These shades will not always be exactly the same – just the nearest match.

Cotton threads
Stranded cotton
A lustrous thread made up of six strands twisted loosely together. The strands must be separated and then recombined as required.

Coton perlé
A twisted thread with a lovely sheen, coton perlé cannot be divided and is used as a single thread. It is available in skeins or balls, in up to four weights: 3, 5, 8 and 12. The lower the number, the thicker the thread.

Coton à broder
This 'cotton for embroidery' is available in a range of weights: 12, 16, 20, 25 and 30. A smooth thread, it has a gentle sheen.

Soft embroidery thread
A fairly thick, soft cotton thread with a matt finish, it cannot be divided and is used as a single strand. Soft embroidery thread can be used instead of tapestry wool, particularly for long-stitch designs.

Flower thread
Flower thread, sometimes called Danish flower thread, is a soft, fine embroidery thread with a matt finish. It is perfect for country-style projects and a good choice if you want to give a sampler a traditional, antique look. It works well on cotton or fine linen fabrics, but is a little too fine for cross stitch on a 14-count fabric.

Rayon threads
Stranded rayon can be substituted in any design that is suitable for stranded cotton. However, it is best used for flat stitches such as satin stitch, which show off its brilliant shine.

Often described as a 'lively' thread, the strands have a tendency to kink, but this can be controlled by moistening the thread with a damp cosmetic sponge. It is preferable to work with short lengths to a maximum of 30cm (12in).

Silk threads
Floss silk
Also known as Japanese silk, floss silk is an untwisted thread with a high sheen. It can be divided in order to suit the finest work, or several strands may be used together. The fine filaments are very delicate and may catch on rough fingertips or nails, so handle with care.

Twisted silk
Made from several strands of thread twisted together, twisted silk can be used as a single thread and some types can be separated into individual strands.

Stranded silk
Easily divided into individual strands, stranded silks have a lustrous sheen.

Wool threads
Available in a wide range of colours and weights, embroidery wools are packaged in skeins or, for larger areas, in hanks.

Persian wool
This three-stranded wool can be used as a single thread or separated into strands, depending on the coverage required.

Tapestry wool
Slightly finer than three strands of Persian wool, it cannot be divided and is used as a single thread.

Crewel wool
This fine, single-stranded wool is used for crewel embroidery and is similar to one strand of Persian wool. For canvas work, several strands may be used together to give better coverage.

Silk ribbons
Available in a variety of widths, pure silk ribbons are the preferred choice for ribbon embroidery (see pages 252–255).

Metallic threads
Available in a variety of weights and finishes, from the finest blending filaments to the more robust braids, cords and ribbons.

Designer threads
These include a wide range of threads – stranded cottons, silks, rayons and ribbons – and a host of types and textures.

Space-dyed
Also called random-dyed, the colour of this thread may be shaded from light to dark. Or, it may combine various colours.

Variegated thread
Usually mass-produced, the different shades of variegated threads are evenly repeated along the length of the thread.

Machine threads
Cotton, rayon, polyester and metallic threads are all suitable for machine embroidery. They are packaged on reels, cops or cones.

Variegated and space-dyed
Different shades are repeated along the length of these threads.

Bobbin thread
A cheap alternative for use on the bobbin, this is compatible with most machine threads.

Metal threads
Used for goldwork, these should not be confused with metallic threads. Available in colours including silver, copper and shades of gold, metal threads are applied (couched) to the fabric surface (see pages 270–273).

Japan thread
When using fine gold threads such as Japan or passing thread, you will usually need to couch two threads together.

Twist thread
The couching stitches should be placed at the same angle as the twist so the stitches are hidden.

Pearl purl
The couching stitches should be hidden in the 'bobbles' of the pearl purl.

Purl thread
Hollow, purl can be cut into short lengths, threaded onto a needle and sewn down like a bead.

Preparing the threads
Always ensure that the threads are colourfast. If this information is not on the manufacturer's label, do a test first. To do this, snip off a short length of each thread, wet it and press between kitchen paper or tissues. If the colour 'bleeds', it is not colourfast. Very few hand-dyed threads will be guaranteed colourfast.

Work with a length of thread no longer than 50cm (20in). For the weaker threads, a maximum length of 25–30cm (10–12in) is recommended. Longer threads may become thin and the surface dulled as the yarn is repeatedly drawn through the fabric.

Using a looped skein
Leave the paper bands on and pull out the end of the thread from the centre of the skein. Cut the length required and then separate the strands.

Draw out the required length.

Using a twisted skein
Remove the bands, untwist the skein and cut all threads once at one end. Tie loosely with a slip knot. To remove a thread, pull out a strand from the loose knot.

Tie the threads with a loose slip knot.

Separating strands
Separate the ends of the strands you require, hold the divided strands in each hand and allow the skein to hang down, gently pulling the strands apart as they untwist. For twisted yarns such as Persian wool or twisted rayon, hold the yarn lightly between the thumb and forefinger and draw out the strand to be separated. In order to prevent tangling, straighten the remaining strands as you go. Continue until the required length has been separated.

Hold the required number of strands and push the others back up the length.

Thread organizer
Threads should be arranged in numerical order so the correct colour is easy to locate. Thread organizer boxes are useful, as the threads are wound onto card or plastic bobbins, which can be marked with the shade number and thread type. Or, you can organize and label threads for a project onto a card organizer.

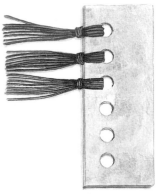

Secure threads onto a card organizer.

Silk ribbons

Metallic threads

Designer threads

Machine embroidery threads

Japan threads

Purl threads

Pearl purl threads

Beads

Buttons

Tassels

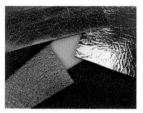

Metallic leather

Flotsam and jetsam

Handmade paper

Ribbons

Embellishments

Adding some carefully chosen embellishments such as buttons, beads, ribbons, mirror glass or feathers can add texture as well as providing an extra dimension to your work. In fact, with such a wide choice of embellishments available, the only restriction is your imagination…

When attaching embellishments such as buttons, beads or charms, use a strong thread that matches the embellishment rather than the background fabric.

Beads

The jewel-like colours of beads can be used to add richness and texture to embroidery. Seed beads and bugle beads are the types that are most commonly used for embroidery (see pages 282–296). They are available in a variety of finishes, including iridescent, opaque, transparent and metallic. Packaged in small quantities, they can be bought from needlework shops and departments. If you require larger quantities, it is more economical to buy them directly from a specialist supplier.

Glass beads

Small round glass beads are also known as rocailles or seed beads. They come in many finishes, colours and sizes. The most common sizes for embroidery are 8, 10 and 11 – the higher the number, the smaller the bead.

Bugle beads are also made of glass. They look like tubes and are available in many lengths – the longer lengths are generally used for fringing. Bear in mind that these beads have very sharp edges and can cut threads.

Metal beads

These beads are generally gold, silver, pewter and bronze. Metal beads come in a large number of sizes and novelty shapes. The small drops and balls are mostly used for embroidery.

Buttons

An increasing number of novelty buttons are readily available. Make sure that the buttons you use are in proportion to the scale of your embroidery or they may be overpowering.

Self-cover buttons (which are available from most haberdashery departments) can be used on garments and soft furnishings, such as cushions.

Place the buttons on your chosen fabric and trace around the shape. Embroider a small motif in the centre of each circle if desired, keeping it within the diameter of the actual button. When the stitching is complete, trim the circles to size, allowing enough to gather around the button, and run a gathering stitch around the edge. Then, pull up the thread so the circle curves to fit over the button shape. Insert the backing, following the manufacturer's instructions.

Gather the edge of the fabric to fit around the button.

Tassels

Made from the threads used in the embroidery, or from ribbons, wool or even strings of beads, the swishing 'skirt' of a simple tassel can add both colour and movement to a finished piece. Add them to soft furnishings or panel designs. Tiny tassels can even be added to three-dimensional embroidery techniques, such as stumpwork.

To make a tassel, cut a piece of card to the length you want the finished tassel to be, allowing an extra 1.5cm (⅝in). Cut a tying thread about 20cm (8in) long and lay this along the top of the card. Wrap your chosen yarn around the card and the tying thread to give the desired thickness of tassel. Next, tie the ends of the tying thread together with a double knot so the wrapped thread is held firmly. Do not cut the ends of the tying thread as this can be used to attach the finished tassel to the embroidery. Slide the wrapped threads off the card and then, using a sharp pair of scissors, cut through the loops at the lower edge to form the tassel and remove the card.

To bind the tassel, wrap a length of matching or contrasting thread around it a little way down from the top. Fasten off with a knot, then thread the ends of the binding thread into a needle and take the needle down into the centre of the tassel. To neaten the tassel, trim the ends off so they are the same length.

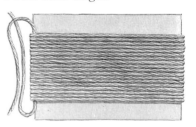

Wrap the yarn around the card until you reach the required thickness, then tie together with the tying thread.

Tassels can be embellished in many ways. For example, a collar of beads may be added on top of the binding thread. To do this, thread beads onto a length of thread, ensuring that the threaded beads encircle the tassel neatly, then tie in place.

Metallic leather

Used to accent goldwork, leather is available in a variety of metallic finishes. It can be applied either flat or over padding using a sharp, pointed needle. Gold thread is often couched around the edge of the leather in order to cover the stitching.

Flotsam and jetsam

Tiny shells, feathers, driftwood or pieces of smooth, sea-washed glass can all be used in order to add texture and interest to the work. Attach them with stitches or use PVA glue, which will dry clear. Stones and shells can also be drilled so they can be attached in the same way as beads.

Handmade paper

Handmade papers are available in various colours and finishes, from the lightest tissues to the more robust card-weight papers. Most handmade papers are made from organic fibres such as silk, mulberry, banana leaves, bark and papyrus. Straw, seeds, grasses, flowers, fragments of fabric or snippets of thread are also often added to give texture and pattern.

These papers are available from a number of specialist suppliers, many of whom will also stock the materials and equipment you need to make your own.

You can either hand- or machine-stitch into the papers and they can also be moulded into three-dimensional shapes.

Ribbons and braids

Available in various widths, colours and finishes, ribbons and decorative braids can be used in many ways. Some can be threaded on a needle for stitching. Some can be used as a background fabric. They can make borders, disguise raw edges and create woven patterns.

Singlefaced satin ribbons are shiny on one side and dull on the other, and are often printed with a pattern. On the other hand, doublefaced satin ribbons are shiny on both sides.

With their distinctive crosswise rib, grosgrain ribbons are very firm and hard wearing, while Jacquard ribbons have a raised pattern woven into them.

Sequins

Available with a flat or faceted surface, round sequins are sometimes referred to as spangles. Whether they are flat or faceted, the light-reflecting qualities of sequins will certainly add a touch of glitz to a piece of embroidery. Also available in a variety of novelty shapes such as shells, birds, moons, etc., sequins may be applied to the fabric with a stitch in a matching thread or, alternatively, held in place with a stitch through a bead.

Gems

Fake gemstones (usually glass or plastic) can add an opulent touch to embroideries worked in richly coloured fabrics and threads. Attach them to the fabric in the same way as shisha glass. Some gems are available with holes so you can thread and stitch them in the same way as beads.

Metals and foils

These can be attached to the fabric with either hand or machine stitching. You could use the blunt point of a knitting needle to make a pattern in the foil before you sew it in place. Marks made from the front will create an indented pattern, while working from the back will give a raised pattern.

Charms

Available in a vast array of shapes, metal charms should be good-quality and used rather sparingly. To achieve a more natural look, choose charms that have been carved from natural materials, such as wood or even bone. To attach a charm to your work, use a thread that matches the charm, not the background.

If the needlework is exposed to damp, the chemical residues on charms could damage the fabric. In order to avoid this, you should rub the charm on a paper towel, then coat on the back with clear nail polish before attaching it to the embroidery.

Shisha glass

Small pieces of shisha glass were originally used in order to create eye-catching designs on richly patterned Indian textiles. Now available in many different sizes and shapes, shisha glass is held in place with simple straight stitches over which decorative stitching is worked.

Cords

Twisted cords and fringes in matching colours add a finishing touch to many projects. You can also apply cords to the fabric to be embroidered and stitch with the narrower ones.

All types of cord are available ready-made in the furnishing department of most large stores. Alternatively, you can make your own from the same threads you used to stitch the embroidery.

Sequin waste

As the name suggests, this is a by-product of sequin production. It can be cut to shape and applied in strips or blocks, but be aware that the effect can be rather ostentatious so it is best used sparingly. Sequin waste is available in a huge range of metallic colours and, sometimes, with an iridescent finish.

Braids

Sequins

Gems

Metals and foils

Charms

Shisha glass

Sequin waste

Basic techniques

There are some basic techniques, explained here, which are used in most types of embroidery. More specific methods are explained in the appropriate embroidery sections.

Preparing the fabric

To determine the size of the fabric you need, measure the design and add an allowance of 5–8cm (2–3¼in) all around for stretching in a frame and finishing. Cut, following the straight grain of the fabric. The materials list will usually stipulate the size of the fabric, including the allowance.

To ensure the design is placed on the fabric correctly, tack the centre lines both vertically and horizontally. To find these lines, fold the fabric vertically and press firmly along the crease. Open out and tack along the crease. Repeat horizontally. The centre of the fabric is where the two lines cross. On evenweaves, tacking stitches should be of even length, under and over five threads, to make it easier to work counted designs.

You can now transfer your design onto the fabric (see pages 30–31). Then mount your fabric into a frame, if using one (see pages 16–17).

Starting to stitch

Stitching should be worked in a logical order. Some techniques have a specific sequence, but generally work background elements first then areas that lie over them, allowing the two to overlap. This will give a more realistic, three-dimensional effect and ensure that the design lines do not show. Avoid stretching across stitched areas or you will wear the threads if you rub them.

Starting with a waste knot
Knot the end of the thread then insert the needle on the right side of the fabric 5cm (2in) from where you will start stitching, so

the thread lies in the path of the stitching. Come up to the starting point. Work the first stitches over the thread with the knot. Snip off the knot and weave the end into the stitches on the back.

Stitch over the thread to secure.

Starting without a waste knot
Leave a thread tail on the reverse of the fabric. Hold it in place and work the first stitches over it to secure it. Cut off the excess so it is not pulled up to the surface.

Oversew the thread to secure it.

Loop method
Fold one strand in half and thread the ends into the needle. Bring the needle through at the point where you will start stitching, leaving the loop at the back.

Pull the needle through to the surface, leaving the loop on the reverse side.

On the first stitch, take the needle through to the back then through the loop to secure.

The needle goes through the loop.

Back and running stitches
If an area is to be covered with stitching, you can begin with a few small back stitches under the area to be worked or work small running stitches on the design line.

Small running stitches can be covered by the subsequent stitching.

Joining threads

The new thread should be woven behind same-coloured threads, as darker colours may show through if woven in behind a light-coloured thread. This is not always possible when changing colour and you may need to begin a new thread using one of the methods described on page 28.

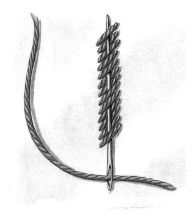

Weave through the last stitches.

Working the stitches

Always keep the tension of your stitches even. They should not be too loose but lie firmly on the surface without pulling the fabric.

Working with a supported embroidery hoop or frame will let you use both hands as you stitch. Work with one hand above the frame and the other below it, using a stabbing motion to push the needle straight down through the fabric and pull it back up.

To work scoop stitches, where the needle goes through the fabric with an in-and-out motion, the fabric should not be too taut within the frame. You can also work this type of stitching in the hand without a frame.

When you are working counted techniques, try to bring the needle up through an empty hole or space and then go down through one shared with a previous stitch. This will avoid splitting the threads of the earlier stitch and also take any wispy ends to the back of the work.

To work with many different colours, thread up a number of needles with the different shades before you begin so you are not constantly re-threading needles. If working on several small areas of different colours close together, do not start and finish a new thread each time. Instead, 'park' the threaded needle away from the area being stitched until it is required, then work the needle through the back of the last few stitches to the new area.

When stitching is complete, hold it up to the light to check you have not missed any stitches.

Finishing the stitching

On the reverse side of the work, weave the needle through the back of the last few stitches, pull the thread through and snip off close to the work. Or, work a few small stitches where they will be hidden by future stitching.

Weave through the last few stitches on the wrong side of the work.

Goldwork threads

Use a needle with a large eye, such as a chenille needle, to plunge goldwork threads to the reverse of the work. Oversew the ends to the fabric and snip off the excess.

Finishing the work

If using an embroidery frame, your work should not need to be pressed. If it does, lay the piece face down on a soft surface and press lightly on the back to avoid flattening the stitches. Never press wool threads.

Blocking

Blocking is a method for squaring up distorted work, especially on canvas or linen twill, but it is not suitable for non-washable fabrics, non-colourfast threads or where non-waterproof media have been used. Place pieces worked in tent stitch face down on the blocking board, and more textural stitching face up to avoid flattening stitches.

Blocking embroidery

1 Dampen the work with a water mist spray or by rolling it in a wet towel. Pull the four corners in the opposite directions and then along the edges to square it up. Place the fabric on the board and pin at the centre top. Using the grid as a guide, stretch the fabric until straight, holding it in place with rust-free pins starting at the centre of the top edge, working to the corners.

Hold the fabric in place with pins.

2 Pin the bottom edge then the sides. Check the corners are square and the sides straight. Dry, then remove from the board.

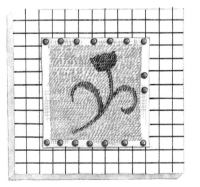

Always pin starting from the centre.

Working from charts and diagrams

The instructions for working different embroidery techniques may be presented in a number of ways. Some designs are printed directly onto the fabric while others are worked from a chart, or may need to be transferred onto the fabric.

Designs on canvas

The design can be printed onto the canvas and stitching is worked over the image. Small squares of the colours to use are printed at the side of the canvas. To prevent confusion when working with similar colours, tie a short length of the correct shade of yarn to the coloured square.

The design may also be 'trammed' in long stitches across the canvas. Tent stitch is worked over the tramming. Finer details in 'petit point' (stitched over a single canvas thread) may already have been worked.

Charted designs

Designs for counted techniques are printed on a square grid or chart. For most techniques, each small square represents a single stitch. The squares are filled with symbols, colours or both and indicate, by cross reference to the key, the colour, type of thread and sometimes stitch to use. Every tenth line on the grid is darker, so it is easier to count.

Working with keys

Patterns for freestyle and counted techniques have a key giving details of the threads, colours and possibly the stitches used. For working the more complex techniques, written instructions and illustrations may also be given.

Transferring designs

Freestyle designs are usually given as a diagram with a key. The outline must be transferred onto the fabric. There are several ways to do this, depending on the fabric and techniques to be used.

Enlarging and reducing designs

The simplest way to alter the size of a design is by using a photocopier. Printed designs will often need to be enlarged, and the size of the enlargement is usually provided. If you increase or decrease the size of the design by more than the stated amount, it may alter the amount of thread you need and you may have to adjust the thickness of the thread and possibly alter the stitch.

Grid method

Draw a small grid with equal squares over a tracing of the design, then draw an extended diagonal line through the corners of the grid to create an enlarged box of the same proportions. Draw a grid with the same number of squares in the enlarged box, then copy the design as accurately as possible from the small grid to the large grid.

Copy the design from the small grid to the enlarged grid.

Tracing the design

If using a fine, light-coloured fabric, place the fabric over the outline of the design and then secure with masking tape. With a fine-tipped, waterproof pen, trace the outline directly onto the fabric.

Tracing on a light box or window

Photocopy or trace the design outline and tape it onto a light box or window. Tape the fabric over the tracing and trace the design onto the fabric with a fine-tipped, waterproof pen.

Trace the design onto the fabric.

Soluble transfer pens

Do a test sample on an off-cut of the fabric before you start. These pens are not suitable for all fabrics and they may 'bleed' on silk, resulting in an indistinct outline. They also do not always disappear as completely as they should. Do not use water-soluble pens on non-washable fabrics. Air- or light-soluble pens are not suitable for large projects, as the design will fade and vanish over time – especially in strong light. To use the pens, first trace the design on a light box or window as described above, using a transfer pen in place of the waterproof pen.

*Dressmakers' carbon
transfer paper*
This is the easiest way to transfer a design onto a dark or heavy fabric. Tape the fabric onto a flat, smooth board or working surface. Place the transfer paper face down onto the fabric and tape the design on top. Using a firm, even pressure, trace over the design with a ballpoint pen, taking care not to puncture the paper. This transfer paper is available in many colours so use one that will show best on your fabric.

Apply firm pressure on the pen so the outline on the fabric is clear.

Transfer pencils
This pencil will give a permanent image that will not wash out. You need to hot-iron the design onto the fabric, making this method unsuitable for some synthetic fabrics. To use, trace the design, flip the tracing and trace over the image with the pencil. The pencil must be sharp-pointed to draw thin lines. Place the pencilled image face down onto the fabric and iron firmly on the design to transfer the image.

Tacking through tissue paper
This method leaves no permanent marks and is suitable for use on all types of fabric.

1 Carefully trace the design onto the tissue paper, then position the tracing on top of the fabric and pin in place around the edge. Tack around the outline, with a thread that shows up on the fabric, starting and finishing the thread securely.

Make sure the stitches are not too small, or they will be quite difficult to remove, and not too big, missing parts of the design. Remove the pins.

Work small stitches along the design.

2 Once the stitching is done, carefully tear away the tissue, leaving the tacking on the fabric. If working on a light or delicate fabric, tear the paper gradually to reveal the area being worked. The tacking stitch outline can be removed as you progress, or after the embroidery is completed.

Carefully tear away the tissue paper to reveal the stitching.

Prick and pounce
Use the prick and pounce method when you want to re-use a design or to re-position and repeat a particular motif.

1 In order to make a pad to apply the pounce, roll up and secure the end of a 6 x 15cm (2⅓ x 6in) piece of felt. Then, trace the design onto tracing paper and lay the tracing on a folded cloth or ironing board. With a hatpin, prick a series of small holes closely together all along the design lines.

Prick small holes close together along the design lines.

2 Tape the fabric onto a flat board or working surface and then tape the tracing paper onto the fabric. Dip the felt pad into the pounce (see page 19) and, using a circular movement, gently rub the pounce over the design. Remove the pricked tracing paper and use a soft cloth to clean the pounce from the tracing so it can be used again.

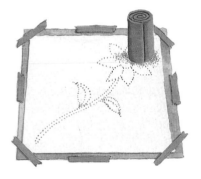

Dip the felt pad into the pounce and rub the pounce over the design.

3 Following the pounce outline, paint a fine line along all the outlines on the fabric with a fine paintbrush and watercolour paint. Then, shake the fabric to remove the pounce.

Use a fine paintbrush to paint over the outlines.

Tips

• With any of the methods described here (apart from tacking through tissue), do not transfer very fine lines or details that will be difficult to cover with stitching. The stitching must cover the transferred design lines entirely.

• If the original or traced design is hard to see through the fabric, you may need to strengthen the outline by going over it with a black felt-tip pen.

• Test out a pencil on spare fabric to make sure that it will not bleed when damp and spoil the finished design.

31

Making up

After all the hours of hard work spent on your embroidery piece, it is well worth taking the time to make sure that it is immaculately finished and presented. Here are some ideas and techniques to make the most of your finished masterpiece.

Cleaning your work

If your embroidery has been handled and stored correctly, it should not need to be cleaned. However, if it is dirty or stained, it should be cleaned prior to being made up into a finished piece. The method used for cleaning must be suitable for all the elements used in the embroidery, including the fabric, threads, backing material and any embellishments you have added.

Framing

The frame is very important to the appearance of the finished work. For a custom-made frame, you will need to go to a professional framer. Many framers will offer a stretching and lacing service, but this will be quite expensive. If you decide to stretch it yourself, choose the frame before cutting the card over which the work will be stretched to ensure that the work fits the frame.

You can also use a ready-made frame but check it has a rebate that is deep enough to take the embroidery as well as the mount. For three-dimensional techniques such as stumpwork or ribbon work, you should use a deeper box frame.

While glass will protect the work, needlework is traditionally framed without glass in order to reveal the tactile, textured surface. If you are using glass, make sure it does not rest directly on the needlework. It may be distanced from the glass by using a mount, or inserting spacers (narrow strips of card) around the edge of the frame between the glass and the work.

You can use either reflective or non-reflective glass, but be warned that non-reflective glass may dull the work slightly.

Stretching and lacing the fabric

Before framing your work, you must stretch and lace it over rigid card using an acid-free board that will not discolour or degrade it.

Cut the card to size. Put the work face down on a flat surface and place the card on top. In the centre of the longest side, pin through the fabric into the edge of the card. Pull the fabric towards the opposite side and pin the centre of that edge. From the centre working out, pin along both edges. When the first two sides are secured, check that the grain of the fabric (as well as the edges) is straight and pin the other sides. Using a strong thread and working from the centre out, lace the long sides of the fabric. Mitre (see Stitching the hems) and pin each corner before lacing the short sides together.

Mitre and pin the corners of the fabric.

To stretch your work over an oval or round card, work a running stitch around the outer edge of the embroidery, place the card on the embroidery and pull up the thread to draw the edges over the card. Check that the work is positioned correctly then tie off as tightly as possible. With a strong thread, lace across the work, working around the shape.

Using craft cards

Mount small works onto a plain craft card with clear craft glue or double-sided tape. If using a card with a pre-cut aperture, place the adhesive on the back around the aperture. Trim the work so it fits neatly over the aperture. Press it onto the adhesive. To give the work a lift, place wadding behind the work. Add tape to the top, bottom and right edges of the left panel of the card, fold it over and finally press into place.

Using flexi-frames

To use flexi-frames, secure the embroidery around the inner frame as around an oval or round card. Tie the thread as tightly as possible. Cut a small piece of felt for backing, slip stitch it in place to hide the edges and clip the outer frame in place.

Making cushions

In order to give a small piece of needlework greater presence on a cushion, it can be applied to a suitable fabric. Simply turn in the edges of the work and then stitch it to the cover with invisible stitches. As a finishing touch, sew a matching ribbon or braid over the join for added definition. Also, try adding a contrasting fabric border to the embroidery (see pages 100–102).

Simple cushion cover

1 First, trim the work to size, including a 1.5cm (⅝in) seam allowance. Place the embroidery on the fabric for the back with right sides facing. Pin and tack together. Stitch along the seam lines, leaving an opening on one side. Trim across the seam at the corners to remove excess fabric. Turn the cover to the right side through the opening, easing it into shape and pulling the corners into neat points.

Stitch around the seam line.

2 Insert either a cushion pad or cushion filling. Then, turn in the open edges and finally slip stitch them together.

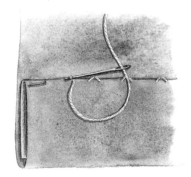

Slip stitch the edges together.

Envelope cushion cover

The back of this type of cover is made in two sections. Cut two pieces of backing fabric each measuring the same width as the fabric for the front and three quarters of the length. Turn over and hem 1.5cm (⅝in) along one

edge of the width of each piece. Place the fabric for the front and one backing piece right sides together. Lay the second piece face down on top. Pin and tack the layers together, then stitch around the seam lines. Turn right side out, easing the corners into neat points.

Stitch around the seam line to secure the layers of fabric together.

Button-fastened cushion cover

Follow the instructions for the envelope cushion, but create buttonholes in the back section that is positioned first. Turn the cushion cover right sides out and add decorative buttons to line up with the buttonholes.

Cushion cover with zip

Cut two pieces of fabric for the back, allowing for an extra seam. Mark the opening needed for the zip and then stitch the seam on either side of the marks. Press the seam open and pin the zip in position. Stitch around the zip in order to secure it. Finish the cover as above.

Stitch the zip in place.

Stitching the hems

Hand-stitched hems with mitred corners will ensure your work is beautifully finished.

1 Neaten the edges of the fabric and decide how wide you want the hem to be. Measure three times the width of the hem in from each edge and work a row of tacking stitches at that distance along each edge. This marks the position for the stitching that will be done later. Now, press the fabric to give two folds along each edge: the first, one hem width and the second, two hem widths .

2 Unfold the fabric. Trim the fabric to 5mm (¼in) beyond the outer fold to reduce bulk in the hem or leave untrimmed for a fuller look. Trim across the corners in a diagonal line from the ends of the inner fold.

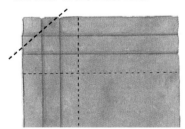

Work lines of tacking before trimming the fabric.

3 Fold the trimmed corners over on the diagonal from the ends of the tacked lines. Then, fold each edge along first the outer, then the inner fold. Pin and tack the hem in place. Slip stitch the mitred corners. Either hem stitch along the edges (see page 98) or slip stitch them in place.

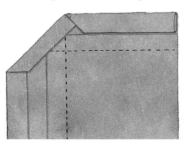

Fold the trimmed corners.

Care of embroidery

• *Avoid damp environments or excessive heat.*

• *Do not place in bright sunshine as it will fade the colours.*

• *Store wrapped in acid-free tissue paper.*

• *Store in a moth-free environment. Use herbal sachets rather than moth balls.*

• *If the fabric and threads are washable, the work should be gently swished around in cool water with a little mild detergent, making sure not to rub. Rinse thoroughly then lay the work on a towel and roll to squeeze out any excess water. Leave to dry away from direct sunlight.*

• *In order to remove stubborn stains, use a proprietary stain remover, but test it first on a scrap of the fabric and/or threads. Alternatively, take the embroidery to a reliable dry-cleaner.*

Inspiration for embroidery designs

This book is full of designs, carefully selected to give you the opportunity to learn different techniques and to practise your skills. As your confidence grows, you could experiment by choosing different colours, threads, or even stitches. Eventually you may want to create your own designs – this is not difficult and you will find guidance on the next eight pages and in the sections on the individual embroidery techniques.

Being inspired

The process of designing your own pieces of embroidery may start with deciding on a particular project you want to make, such as a panel, a bag or an item of clothing, or grow out of a design idea from something you have seen that was inspirational. The main thing is that it is a glorious adventure that will bring you hours of pleasure and a sense of achievement, not something to worry about or feel daunted by. Get excited by the sources of inspiration around you and with a bit of practice you will be developing design ideas that really please you. The world is overflowing with an infinite number of exciting images that provide sources of inspiration for every embroiderer's needs.

Good design is difficult to define and is ultimately a matter of personal taste. However, it is generally recognized that the components of colour, line and texture and the way they are used in a composition play an important role in the overall success of a completed piece. Remember, no design can be intrinsically wrong – it may be unusual and maybe next time you would do it differently, but if you like it, it has a value and the characteristics of its style make it unique to your work. Even if you do not like it, it still has a value, as part of the learning process, and will contribute to the success of the next piece.

The idea of actively looking for inspiration can seem rather intimidating, but be satisfied with keeping it on a simple and enjoyable level – remember that no one ever starts out as a great artist or designer. Everything and anything can be a source of inspiration, from products on the supermarket shelves to the flowers and insects in the hedgerow. The sheer wealth of choice may be the main problem you encounter.

Sources of inspiration

Inspiration does not come out of thin air. The essence is to observe closely – this will help you to focus on your subject, understand how it is constructed and see all the possibilities. Through this type of observation you will begin to understand the form and structure of the subject: for instance, how petals are attached to a stem or how the branches of a tree curl towards the sky. This appreciation of your source of inspiration will help you to record your impressions more clearly and will eventually show through in your finished design.

Nature has been a source of inspiration for creative work since time began. Try looking at individual flowers, petals or leaves, bunches or styled groupings of flowers, or whole hedgerows or meadows. You may find trees appeal to you, whether in full leaf in the summer or in skeletal starkness against a winter sky. Rock contours and geology are another possibility – on a small scale even pebbles, whether lichen-encrusted or smoothed by erosion, provide a vast array of contrasting textures.

Landscapes are awe-inspiring. Pause to enjoy the broad expanse of the sky and far-off hills. Pathways through woodlands will keep you busy for hours observing all the intricacies of nature. If you are lucky enough to live by the sea, marvel at the seascapes, whether they are cool and flat or dark and stormy. Be sure to benefit from all the seasons – for example, garden borders provide an all-year-round source of inspiration, full of flowers in the spring or bare with frost in the winter.

However endless the inspiration drawn from nature, make sure you also think about man-made structures. Buildings and skylines offer a geometric treat to the eye whereas individual artefacts, jewellery and textiles provide more random patterns. Keep an eye out for any interesting exhibitions and take the time to rediscover your local museums.

Man-made objects are all around us and demonstrate how others have interpreted original source material. For example, a comparison of how the same type of flower is treated by the Dutch masters or in pop art will help you develop your design skills.

Colour, line and texture

Whatever subject you choose to observe, examine all the subtleties of its colours and textures, its structure and the lines that give it definition. The understanding of these core elements will help you build the confidence needed to develop your design ideas.

The same colour can appear in many guises – it might be dark or light, or in a myriad of subtle shades. We all experience colour in different ways and it can evoke particular feelings and emotions. For instance, ice blue might suggest cold and red, passion.

The main lines and shape outline of a composition will contribute to its success or failure. They can give a sense of movement, balance and stability. In your own designs, try to avoid lines that confuse or lead the eye away from the composition.

Embroidery is a great chance to experiment with texture. Contrast different textures, from smooth to knobbly, to make them work to best effect.

Organizing your ideas

This is a crucial part of the process that should not be overlooked. You need a method of keeping a record of visual ideas and notes to yourself, as well as somewhere to keep printed materials and other sources of inspiration you have found. Keeping everything well organized will help you to develop your observational skills, find your ideas easily later and provide the best record from which to start work on designing.

A simple notebook or sketchbook is ideal for keeping everything together, but you could use plastic files of cuttings or put together an artistically arranged portfolio. Choose the system that suits you and the nature of your source material best, so that everything is meaningful as well as accessible. A jumble of ideas and cuttings might be stimulating, but will not necessarily help you to observe and study.

A small, cartridge paper, spiral-bound sketchbook is a good start. The spiral binding allows you to stick cuttings and samples into the book without putting it under strain and to sketch and make notes on a firm, flat surface. Make sure the book you choose is small enough to fit into your bag so it is available at any time you want to make notes.

Collecting ideas

You may want to sketch straight from your source of inspiration, but do not feel that you have to or that it needs to be a very accomplished attempt. There are other ways to gather ideas together. Your notebook is very personal so there is no need to feel embarrassed by its contents. As it progresses, it will become a colourful diary, full of ideas and samples to give you some source material.

You may want to include postcards, either inspirational or factual, in your book – for example, of favourite paintings or sculptures. Pages torn from magazines can also be inspiring, particularly as a reference for the way colours are used together. Scraps of paper of different types – tissue, gift wrap or handmade – will suggest colours and textures. Paste layers of tissue paper into your book to build up the intensity of tones and colours. Try pressing flowers and leaves. Your own photographs are also an excellent means of recording your impressions. Make sure that you understand all the functions of your camera so you can fully exploit the quality of the images you take. Zoom in as close to the subject as possible and then take a wider perspective, so you have as much information as possible.

If you do fancy trying your hand at sketching, don't try to be too ambitious. Even unsophisticated diagrammatic sketches can convey plenty of information from your original source to help your inspiration. You will find that the more you persevere, the more confidence you will gain. The sketching will get easier and more of a pleasure. Start with basic outlines and add hand-written notes to explain the forms and colours you can see. For instance, if you happen to see a beautiful tree, note down what type it is and the exact shades of green the leaves are or what they remind you of – the difference between lime and khaki green has all sorts of connotations.

There are various ways of sketching. Pencil can be very effective, but try other materials as well. Fine-tipped, black pens give clear, crisp outlines so they create bold impressions and are ideal to trace afterwards. Crayons and watercolour pencils will allow you to merge lines and colours. Pastels are soft and you can rub them with your fingers, but they need to be sealed to prevent smudging.

However you decide to record your sources of inspiration and put them all together over the months, your notebook will build up a record to help you focus on the ideas you have seen. The process of putting it together will become a personal journey full of ideas, a reminder of precious moments in time and an inspiration for the future. You may not use all your ideas and some of them will develop into something entirely different, but this does not matter. It is the journey that matters and a successful design, beautifully worked, is the bonus.

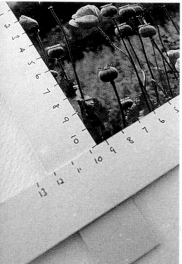

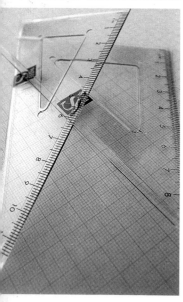

Developing design ideas

There are many methods you could use for developing ideas from your source materials into a successful design. Different methods will suit different projects and may be an exploration in themselves – so don't worry if your first effects are not so inspiring.

Equipment

In order to help you follow the design process through in a clear and simple way, you will need the following materials: a range of fine to wide black felt-tip and rollerball-type pens, a notebook (see pages 34–35), A3 cartridge paper, a ruler, an eraser, sharp pencils, tracing paper and finally two 20cm (8in) square pieces of plain card.

Choosing the image

1 Cut the two pieces of plain card in an L shape, keeping both sides at a 20cm (8in) length. Mark each 1cm (⅜in) interval along the two inside lengths. These L shapes will help you select which section of the sketch or photograph you want to use for your stitched design. Place the L shapes over each other in a square or rectangle, and re-position them over various areas of the design in order to isolate them.

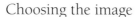

Position the L shapes to limit the area of the design you want to use.

2 Once you have selected a pleasing composition, remove the L shapes and place a sheet of tracing paper over the design. With a fine black pen, trace the framed area, making sure to mark in the boundary.

Secure the tracing paper then trace over the design with a fine pen.

3 Evaluate the design. Look at whether the components are well spaced and the areas are pleasingly filled. If you find there is a lack of balance, re-position some of the components or transfer some from another area.

Re-position the flowers as necessary to correct a lack of balance.

4 Also examine whether any of the elements compete with each other or are overcrowded. Parts of flowers, for example, can be omitted or some whole flowers can be left out altogether. Remember to make sure both the left and right sides of the design are equally interesting.

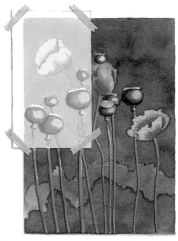

Re-trace some areas to make sure the spacing is accurate.

5 Take time to evaluate how busy the design is. Are some elements competing with each other? Are there any areas that lack interest? If an area is too busy, you need to simplify it.

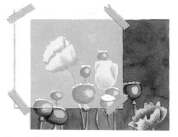

Simplify a busy area to make the stitching easier.

Distorting the image

You may wish to enlarge or reduce the size of the composition or fit it into a different shape. To distort the image, place tracing paper over the first composition and trace the perimeter. Divide the area into equal sections. On blank paper, make a grid to the new shape, keeping the same number of divisions. Re-draw the shapes box-by-box.

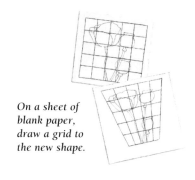

On a sheet of blank paper, draw a grid to the new shape.

Considering size and shape

The actual size and stitching technique of the finished piece are elements to consider throughout. For example, if the design is to be worked on canvas, the smallest design unit is one tent stitch but, by contrast, very small elements will be too difficult to interpret into appliqué. You should consider the size of the design in relation to the finished project.

Always consider the overall shape of the finished piece in relation to how it will be framed. Frames are not just restricted to wooden picture frames, as the borders of a cushion, the side of a bag or the shape of a garment will all frame the embroidery in some way. The design should fill the frame in an appropriate way. In simple terms, tall and long designs look better in rectangular frames, whereas round or square ones fit a square frame better. Use the L shapes throughout the design process in order to decide on the best final shape.

Creating patterns

A design can be developed in many ways, but using patterns is a reassuring place to start. Patterns are composed of design elements that are repeated to create an overall design. The repeating element in the pattern can be thought of as one unit. Select units that will create an interesting background when repeated. Asymmetric images give greater potential for pleasing mirror images.

Ideas for patterns

Trace simple elements from your source material. Re-trace or photocopy the units several times and cut around them quite roughly. Use these units to play with different pattern ideas.

Two basic patterns.

Repeat the same image along a horizontal line to create a border of alternate mirror images. Trace the image onto the back of the paper and flip the paper every time you position another unit.

Mirror images.

It is more difficult to get a well-balanced scattered effect. Here pencil guidelines marking the vertical and horizontal, and a protractor, will help.

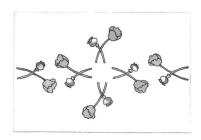

Scattering the poppy heads.

A half-drop pattern is also effective and here the images have been arranged on diagonal lines which form a trellis pattern.

Diagonal guidelines forming a trellis.

Mitring a pattern

When working a border pattern, it is often necessary to turn a corner and you should consider the best way to mitre the design at the corners to give the best effects. The placement of the design along the borders and at the corners might affect the overall size of the embroidery.

Draw out the basic border pattern on two pieces of paper. On one, mark a line at 45 degrees across the border where you think a mitred angle will work.

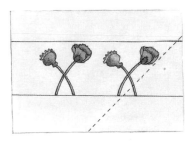

Mark the folding line at 45 degrees.

Draw a similar line on the other piece of paper at a corresponding position on the design and fold the paper under along the line. Butt the two borders together to check the effect. If you need to crop the image to mitre it into the corner effectively or the result is not as you anticipated, you will need to establish a new mitre line.

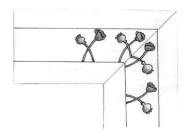

Make sure the two borders fit well.

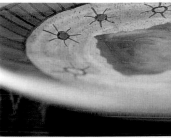

37

Exploring colour palettes

When you have decided on the composition of your design, you will need to start thinking about the colours to use, if you have not already been eagerly anticipating this stage. Colour will be brought to the design in all the threads and other materials you choose, but you can also paint the background fabric to bring depth to the finished piece. There are a few basic rules, but it is more important to experiment.

Inspiration for colour

Many of us have the opportunity to travel more than ever before and we are surrounded by media images from all around the world, so there is no shortage of familiar and exotic colour combinations to choose from. We can have just as good an understanding of the hot colours of India and the cold blues of the Arctic, as of the colours around our own homes.

Understanding colour

The colour wheel is used to explain the relationship between colours. In the colour wheel, the three primary colours – red, yellow and blue – are equally spaced around a circle. Mixing these colours produces secondary colours, shown between the primaries on the colour wheel. For example, if you mix red and yellow, you obtain orange. Yellow and blue make green, and blue and red make purple. By mixing the primary and secondary colours together in different proportions, you obtain a full range of colours such as olive green, magenta, ochre and so on.

Complementary colours

These colours lie opposite each other on the colour wheel, as do blue and orange for instance. They provide the greatest contrast and are frequently used to enliven each other.

Nature offers many examples of complementary colours. For instance, the purple iris appears to be even brighter and bolder because it is set off with a splash of yellow. Other examples are the red berries of holly against the green leaves and yellow daisies with their deep purple centres. The invigorating effect of complementaries works best when one colour dominates. Used in equal amounts they tend to cancel each other out.

Analogous colours

These colours are found next to each other on the colour wheel between the primaries and therefore groups can extend no further than a third of the colour wheel. Such a range would be the colours and shades from orange to red. Analogous colours sit comfortably together – pinks and purples, greens and blues, yellows and greens. When used together, a set of analogous colours will form a pleasing and soothing composition.

Neutral colours

The more black that is added to any colour, the closer that colour tends towards black, graduating through shades along the way. Adding more and more white to a colour takes it closer to pure white, but with several shades in between. Experimenting with these processes clearly shows the subtleties obtainable and that there are infinite shades of white, grey and black – the colours we recognize as neutral colours. They add subtlety and texture to a piece as well as providing a necessary foil to many other colour schemes. Experiment with different shades of white, varying from soft to brilliant varieties, in order to highlight and add texture. Explore the range of blue and greeny greys that can be found in the most ordinary of objects and then translated into fabric and thread.

Colour relationships

Colours affect one another. A colour placed on white will be perceived totally differently if it is then placed on another colour or black.

When planning a project, it is useful to gather together all the colours that are to be used, ideally in the same proportions as in the finished piece, in order to see how well they work together. Substitutions and alterations to the proportions are much easier at this stage. Try wrapping your chosen threads around a piece of card wrapped in a piece of the background fabric and you will quickly see the effects you can anticipate.

Fabric paint and tools

There are many fabric paints and dyes available for colouring fabric. Do not feel intimidated by this exhaustive range. The following information will introduce you to simple ways to get colour onto fabric, but enjoy the rest as you come across them because they all open up lots of possibilities.

Start by using the same types of paint together and avoid mixing them until you are confident of their properties.

There are also numerous methods of transferring the paint to the fabric and tools designed for the job. However, the tools you make yourself or find around the house can be just as good, so do not forget to improvise.

Brushes

It is useful to have brushes of different sizes, whether they are fine quality artists' brushes or household paint brushes. Household brushes in 1.25cm (½in) and 2.5cm (1in) widths are quite useful for painting larger background areas, artists' brushes are best saved for any finer details. Stencil brushes have short, firm bristles and enable you to get into small corners.

Other applicators

As well as brushes, you will find sponge applicators in craft stores, but you could also use a cosmetic or natural sponge. Small rollers can also be used to apply paint to large areas

Printing blocks

These can be bought ready-made as a firm rubber stamp or as a wooden block. You can also make them yourself in a variety of ways. You could simply cut a shape out of half a potato or slice a firm vegetable to transfer its own image. Or, you can cut an image into a piece of lino with specialist tools. Another idea is to cut shapes out of cork tiles or make patterns out of string and glue them to a piece of card.

Stencils

Ready-made stencils are easy to use and can be ideal to start with, but you can design your own, developing images from magazines and photographs. The traditional brown stencil card is coated in order to make it waterproof and resilient enough for repeated use. Cut the card carefully with a craft knife and work on a cutting mat. Cut into tight corners of the design from both directions to achieve a sharp point. Clear stencil film, which is also waterproof, can be spray-glued to a surface and removed repeatedly, in order to allow you to see where you are positioning the stencilled image. Cut this in the same way as the card. Take care, as the film cuts very easily. You will need a stencil brush or a small sponge to apply the paint.

Acrylic paints

These come in pots and tubes in an extensive range of colours, metallics and special effects. They have a thick consistency, are water-soluble and can be diluted and mixed together. They are ideal for stencilling and painting when used straight from the pot and for washes when diluted. They are light and colourfast, versatile and can be used on most fabrics.

Silk paints

These can be used on all fabrics, although they work best on natural fabrics. They consist of a free-flowing liquid that gives clear colours. The paint flows across fabric such as silk freely and will merge unless held back by a water-resistant medium such as gutta.

Gutta

This is available transparent and in a range of colours. It can be applied straight from the tube or the colours can be mixed and used from a clean dispenser with a special nozzle available from craft stores. Gutta acts as a resist to the paint, creating areas that do not accept colour, either as isolated patches or defining outlines. Remember that if you want to restrict the paint to a particular area, the line of gutta must be continuous and of a consistent width.

Paint sticks

These are large oil crayons wrapped in a cardboard roll and are available in a wide range of plain, metallic and pearlized colours. A skin forms around the outside of the stick and needs to be peeled off at the rounded end before use. The colours must be fixed onto fabric so they will withstand laundering and strong light. After applying the paint, iron the fabric with a warm iron. Allow the colour to set for 48 hours before developing the design.

Transfer crayons and paints

These work best on synthetic fabrics. Draw or paint your design onto lightweight paper. Turn the paper design side down onto your chosen fabric and iron over the paper with a cool iron to transfer it. You can use the same design for a few repeats after which it will start to deteriorate.

Fabric pens

Available in a variety of colours and thicknesses, these are ideal for adding delicate details to a design. Fix the colours according to manufacturer's instructions.

Metallic media

As well as metallic paints and sticks, you can also create a metallic effect by using bronze powders. These are ideal for printing and stencilling and are available in a range of metallic colours. They need to be mixed with a fabric medium to form a paste before applying them to fabric. It is advisable to wear a mask and to work in a well-ventilated environment. The colours must be fixed in the same way and for the same reasons as paint sticks (above).

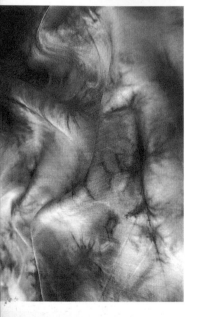

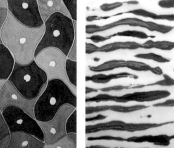

Painting fabrics

You can paint on most fabrics, but calico and habutai silk accept dye particularly well and will make excellent backgrounds. Make sure you always paint a larger piece than you require for your project, so you can choose the painted area that suits your needs.

Painting backgrounds

Before beginning to use any of the methods below, lay down some newspaper, put on a waterproof apron and wear surgical gloves.

For most painting methods, it is good practice to tape the fabric down with masking tape in order to prevent it moving and blurring the painted image. After painting, you should always allow the fabric to dry thoroughly and then fix the colour according to the manufacturer's instructions.

Basic method

Tape the fabric down and use a household brush to apply the paint in long strokes across the fabric. You can use either acrylic paint diluted with water or silk paint direct from the pot. Merge different colours together, making sure you keep to smooth strokes, as overworking the areas will create muddy colours. Alternatively, you can use a sponge to apply the paint to obtain a different effect. Allow to dry thoroughly and then fix the colour as appropriate.

Tape the fabric down with masking tape then start to paint.

Textured effects

Fabric can take on soft folds and shapes, and this can be a means of creating interest. Try scrunching up a piece of silk with a sheet of polythene. Then, lay unflattened polythene on the work surface with the silk on top. Gently apply silk paint to the ridges of the fabric so it seeps into other areas in an irregular way. Apply one or two colours as desired. Allow to dry thoroughly, iron the fabric and fix the colour.

Salt resist

Stretch lightweight silk over a simple frame so it is drum-tight. Paint the fabric with two colours of silk paint, allowing them to merge. While the paint is still wet, scatter sea-salt granules over the fabric. The salt will soak up some of the paint and create beautiful patterns. When the fabric is dry, shake off the salt and fix the colour before washing to remove any remaining salt.

Gathered patterns

Sew rows of gathering stitches along a piece of silk at 2.5cm (1in) intervals. Pull the gathering stitches together and tie off. Gently apply silk paint along the ridges of the fabric so it seeps into the folds in an irregular way. Allow to dry thoroughly, then iron the fabric flat and finally fix the colour.

Gather the silk fabric and then apply silk paint.

Tie-dye

This method will result in surprising random patterns. A simple method of tie-dying is to fold a piece of silk or calico lengthways into concertina folds. Then, fold the resulting shape into triangles from one end to the other, to end up with one bulky triangular shape.

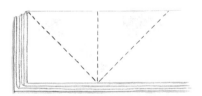

Loosely fold the piece of silk.

Tie sewing thread tightly around different parts of the triangular shape. Either apply the paint with a brush or submerge the fabric in a container of diluted acrylic paint or fabric dye and then leave it to absorb the colour. If you submerge the fabric in different colours, use the palest one first and work through to the darkest last, altering the ties and the time allowed for the colour to seep through. Allow to dry thoroughly, iron the fabric flat and then fix the colour.

Tie threads around the folded fabric.

Transferred images

This method is effective for building up layers of colours on a background. Draw a pattern on a piece of lightweight paper using transfer paint or crayons. When dry, place the paper face down on top of synthetic fabric. Iron the paper, following the manufacturer's instructions, always using smooth strokes. Make sure the image has transferred properly by peeling back just a section of the paper. Replace the paper if necessary.

Check the patterns have transferred properly before removing the paper.

Painting details

Once you have finished painting a background, you may wish to add some details before starting to stitch your embroidery. The following will give you some ideas that you can use for very simple, but effective, results or develop into sophisticated techniques.

Silk painting

This method can be used to create a whole design or to add details to a previously painted background.

Stretch a piece of lightweight silk over a simple frame so it is drum-tight. If the fabric is too loose, the paint will collect in pools and spoil the effect. Make sure your selected design encloses all the spaces where you wish colours to remain separate. Place the design under the frame and trace it through onto the fabric using gutta. Allow the gutta to dry. Then, examine the fabric to make sure the gutta has penetrated it and there are no breaks in the line. Fill in any gaps and allow to dry again.

Using an artists' brush, gently feed silk paint into the different areas of the design. The paint will bleed into the fabric up to the gutta outline freely, so do not flood the area. Finish painting, allow to dry then remove from the frame. Remove transparent gutta by ironing it between sheets of kitchen paper. Fix the colours.

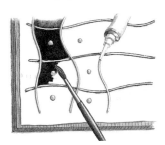

With an artists' brush, fill each design unit with silk paint.

Stencilling

Stencilling images is an ideal way to create single motifs or repeated patterns. Trace a design motif onto thin paper. Tape a piece of stencil card onto a cutting board and then tape the tracing centrally onto the card. Using a craft knife, cut around the stencil outline through both layers.

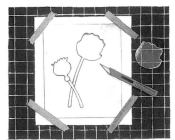

Tape the design onto the card and cut the shape through the two layers.

Make sure the stencil is cut cleanly and then spray it on the reverse side with temporary adhesive. Place it in position on the fabric. To stencil the image, use undiluted acrylic paint or paint sticks. Place a small amount of acrylic paint on a plate or paint palette. Use a damp sponge or a stencil brush to pick up the paint and blot on kitchen paper to remove excess. Dab the sponge

or brush inside the stencil. Alternatively, rub colour from paint sticks on the card outside the stencil outline. Use a stencil brush, blot the paint as before and apply the colour to the design. With either method, always build up the colour gradually. Finally, fix the colours.

Rub the paint stick around the shape then drag the colour into the stencil.

Block printing

Images from a printing block can give you single motifs and quick patterns, but you could also experiment, allowing the images to break up and create more subtle effects.

Place some paper on your work surface to absorb the pressure from the printing and then cover with polythene. Tape your fabric on top. Mix acrylic paints with bronze powder and arrange the colours on an old plate or palette. Dab the printing block into the paint and press it down firmly onto the fabric. Allow to dry and then fix the colours.

Calligraphy

More delicate details such as calligraphy or tiny patterns can be added by using fabric pens. Copy any script onto paper, so you can copy the lettering accurately or trace it through the fabric over a light box. Secure the fabric carefully then fix the colours.

Rubbings

Paint sticks are ideal for taking rubbings off everyday items and printing blocks. Experiment with building up a large area of colour using multiple rubbings.

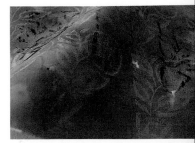
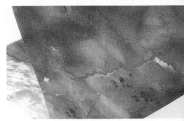
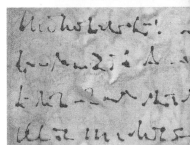
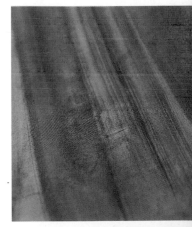

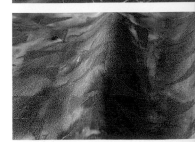

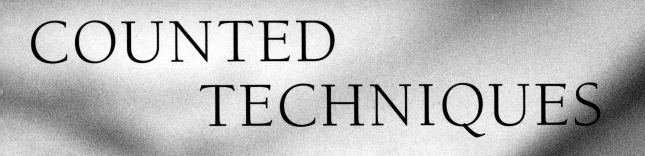

COUNTED
TECHNIQUES

Cross stitch

Counted thread embroidery (including cross stitch) creates a decorative pattern on an evenly woven fabric, where each warp and weft thread (along and across the fabric respectively) occupies the same amount of space. The stitches are positioned by counting the fabric threads. Often a simple cross stitch is used, one diagonal stitch crossed over another in the opposite direction, but there is a wide range of variations such as long-armed, Greek, double cross and star stitch. Another interesting variation is marking cross stitch, also known as 'brave bred stitch', which was used for marking clothes and household linen to ensure that the stitch was the same on both sides.

Cross stitch is probably the oldest form of needlework, and appears in every society throughout the world. However, its history is often difficult to determine, particularly in folk traditions. One of the earliest books of cross stitch designs was published in 1728 in Augsburg by Martin Gottfried Crophius. These designs are mainly small motifs, like those found on samplers. In 19th-century Britain, cross stitch was also known as sampler stitch and still to this day is most widely associated with samplers. In the 18th and 19th centuries, learning cross stitch was an indispensable part of a girl's education, combining needlework tuition with lessons in spelling, arithmetic or geography. Typical works, of which very many survive, are stitched with alphabets, numerals and small motifs, which include peacocks, lions, coronets, dogs, flowers, birds, trees, strawberries and of course mottoes and moralizing verses warning of imminent death and encouraging the virtue of obedience. Castles and buildings were also used and occasionally these can be identified as schools or orphanages. Cross stitch was also found in multiplication tables and on maps, very popular between 1770 and 1820. Some of these were worked in minute black silk cross stitch on outline maps printed on white satin. Earlier samplers often include other stitches. However, those of a later date are most usually worked entirely in cross stitch in red and green wools on a coarse mesh canvas. There has been a recent revival of interest in cross stitch samplers but, in contrast to earlier times, these are now made by adults, often using kits.

Assisi work

One of the most distinctive forms of cross stitch is known as Assisi work. In this technique, stitches are closely related to the fabric on which they are worked to the extent that the background of these single-colour designs is as important as the stitched pattern. Assisi work is named after and originates from the small town of Assisi, in the central Italian province of Umbria. Today, the work consists of a plain motif outlined in double running stitch either in black or dark brown thread, with the background filled in with cross stitch in either blue or red. Originally, the linen background was filled with silk threads in long-armed cross stitch, or whipped stitch on drawn threads. As early as the 14th century, the designs comprised simple animal shapes, often of a heraldic nature, worked in pairs facing each other, similar to woven silk and woodcarving designs. This work was carried out for church furnishings only and had declined by the 19th century, but there was a revival after the new state of Italy was founded in 1861. As in other countries during the late 19th century, including Britain, there was a general interest in reviving traditional crafts, which was also intended to help poor women to supplement their families' incomes with paid work.

On 4 October 1902, St Francis's Day, St Anne's Convent in Assisi established a handicraft workshop for poor girls who wanted to learn embroidery. The original colours were retained but traditional techniques and designs were simplified.

Opposite page: Detail of a 19th-century bed curtain from the island of Cos in Greece. This piece of silk on linen is worked with vertical rows of the spitha pattern bordered by stars.

Below: Detail of a 19th-century Assisi work border – red silk on linen.

Above: Tea cosy linen with peacocks and floral motifs in cross stitch, Switzerland, 1948.

Cotton thread was used and the outlines were no longer drawn freely on the cloth, but counted out one stitch at a time and the background filled with cross stitch. The designs were taken from old embroideries, but sometimes also from complex intertwining stone and wood carvings in the local churches, reduced to simple scrollwork patterns. As befits St Francis, bird motifs were the most common. These designs were no longer confined to religious furnishings but were transferred to more commercial tablecloths and napkins and sold to visitors and tourists. This technique quickly became popular and spread throughout the region and to other parts of Europe and overseas. In the early 20th century, albums of colour plates with Assisi work designs for borders, corners and large squares were published in France in English, French, Italian and German. Until the 1930s, articles worked in Assisi itself were marked in the bottom right-hand corner with the cross of St Francis and the arms of the town.

Greek embroidery

Cross stitch is common to many peasant cultures, where it is used to embroider textiles for the home and often worked by girls preparing their dower chests. Greek island embroidery, unlike Assisi work, combines cross stitch with other embroidery stitches including back, chain, ladder, herringbone and satin stitches, as well as French knots. Monochrome work is almost always carried out using red thread in the Greek islands, except in Crete where dark blue and dark red threads are occasionally used. However, the finest red embroidery is carried out to the north on the islands of Melos, Patmos and Naxos, where cross stitch in red often forms a solid filling for repeated flower or bird motifs that are outlined in green. The designs in Cretan embroideries often show an Italian influence. This is no surprise considering Crete was under Venetian jurisdiction from the early 13th century until 1669, when the Turks conquered it. In Rhodes, cross stitch is worked in a thick, loosely twisted floss silk thread, giving a curly astrakhan surface on which it is quite difficult to detect individual stitches. The cross stitch is often worked randomly, and is used in conjunction with step stitch in a diagonal line with the direction of the stitch being either vertical or horizontal. Heavy linen is the normal ground fabric, and a light brick red thread is often used alternately with a green one.

Right: Linen sampler with brown and pink wool. The inscription reads: 'A Token of Love 1811, M Pollard'.

Popular embroidery motifs include pairs of leaves known as 'king' designs and leaves and flowers known as 'queen' designs, which are worked next to or framing the 'king'. These motifs are particularly effective on the bed tents produced on Cos, where kings and queens are worked alternately with hexagon, diamond and other geometric patterns, and the spaces filled with a profusion of animals, birds, flowers, ships and figures in a range of colours and stitches, including cross stitch. The bed tents are similar to those used in 16th-century Italy and are circular, made of strips of linen, narrower at the top than the bottom and suspended from a wooden ring. Bed tents provided a little privacy in homes that usually consisted of a single room. The most elaborate versions were made on the islands of Cos and Rhodes and, as the bed was the most dominant piece of furniture, they were also important for their decorative and status values.

Other favourite motifs are pairs of animals or birds, double-headed eagles and peacocks. In some works, pairs of birds are placed on either side of a tree of life represented as a large vase of flowers. These probably originated in ancient Mesopotamia and came to the Greek islands from Byzantium and Persia. However, both the bright colours – typical of Crete – and the richness of design owe more to the Italian influence. This is certainly true of the popular double-tailed mermaid, who features in the legend that Alexander the Great condemned his sister to live in the sea and become half fish. Some of the best work is also used to decorate traditional dresses, but throughout the island, embroidery is more commonly used to decorate household textiles such as cushion covers and wall hangings.

Swedish embroidery

Other distinctive forms of peasant embroidery using cross stitch come from southern and central Sweden. The town of Skane, in south-west Sweden, has long produced interesting embroidery and weaving. A large majority of the items made in the 18th and early 19th centuries illustrated bible stories and included naively drawn figures such as Adam and Eve. These were worked in multi-colours in blocks of chain stitch, cross stitch and seeding on a linen and wool ground. Other popular motifs included angels, lions, stars, flowers, plants, tulips and acorns. Individual motifs were often worked in square compartments as borders for household linen. In central Sweden, in the region of Svealand, there are several forms of cross stitch embroidery. Delsbo work is distinctive because of its use of star and heart motifs worked in blue and red on white linen. It is usually used to decorate tablecloths, cushion covers and small items such as collars and cuffs. Jarvso work uses similar motifs but these are worked in rose-coloured threads on white or natural linen, often with additional small tassels of thread. On the east coast of Svealand, around the port of Gavle, similar cross stitch embroidery in blue, white or rose-coloured threads is worked in repeated geometric motifs.

There was great interest in peasant embroideries during the 1920s and 1930s, and many of the embroidery magazines, such as *The Needlewoman*, featured articles explaining the background history, design and technique. Swedish, Assisi, Spanish as well as Balkan designs were soon adapted for simple furnishings such as cushions and table linen, and were accompanied by instructions that were suitable for the amateur enthusiast in many countries.

Above: A modern cross stitch design of a beautiful sunset using a mix of pink and ochre threads. Designed by Thea Gouverneur, 2001.

Cross stitch stitches and techniques

Cross stitch is probably one of the easiest forms of embroidery to learn. Attractive geometric patterns are very simple to do, but the same simple stitch also gives you the ability to create intricately shaded images. Cross stitch is often worked as a counted technique, on evenweave fabric such as linen, or blockweave fabric such as Aida. However, it can also be used in free embroidery.

Design your own

• *Use graph paper and coloured pencils to create simple motifs and geometric patterns.*

• *Convert pictures into charts by placing special grid tracing paper, which is available in different counts, over the image and colouring over it.*

• *Use one of the numerous services that will convert your favourite photograph into a chart.*

• *Investigate computer programs that are specially designed to create cross stitch charts.*

Fabrics

Counted cross stitch must be worked on an evenweave fabric, either natural or synthetic fibre, or on Aida fabric (or any other Aida-based product). Popular counts are 14-count Aida or 28-count evenweave, which work out at the same scale. The higher the count, the finer the finished work will be (see pages 20–21). Cross stitch is usually worked over one Aida block or two threads of evenweave fabric.

Needles

Tapestry needles are best for cross stitch as this minimizes the risk of the fabric threads being pierced unintentionally. The size of needle will depend on the thread and fabric used. You will need a size 26 tapestry needle for 14-count Aida or 28-count evenweave. On a finer scale, a size 28 needle will suit work with one strand of cotton on finest evenweave, and on a larger scale, a size 24 needle will be fine with an 11-count Aida.

Threads

Six-stranded cotton is probably the most widely used embroidery thread for cross stitch. Two strands are usually recommended to obtain the best coverage and work well on 14-count Aida or 28-count evenweave (see pages 20–21). However, very fine work will often require just one strand. The colours are popularly used on their own, but you can also blend two strands of harmonious shades together in the needle in order to create subtle effects.

Other types of threads can be used to add different qualities to the cross stitch. Try using stranded metallic, iridescent or rayon threads, or add a metallic blending filament to a single strand of cotton.

Cross stitch techniques

Cross stitch is both simple and versatile. It is formed by two diagonal stitches, with one made across the other to form a cross. Whole stitches can be used to make geometric patterns or to fill in blocks of colour on motifs and more sophisticated images. For this type of design, the stitches can be worked in horizontal rows or vertical columns. More subtly shaded images are created using various colours, so one colour may be used for just a few stitches. The most important technique to bear in mind is to keep all the stitches going in the same direction.

Blocks of whole cross stitches result in a stepped outline, which is fine for geometric shapes but may be less appropriate for other designs. Smoother outlines are therefore achieved by using half and three-quarter cross stitches, which can also give a softer effect.

The use of back stitch can enhance the design further, by defining outlines and the lines of internal shapes. It can be worked in any direction across the threads of fabric, including diagonally at different angles.

It is most important with any cross stitch design to keep an even tension. Therefore, you should use an embroidery hoop or tapestry frame to keep the fabric taut and the tension even. You will find this will also help to keep the stitches regular and neat.

Samplers are an excellent learning tool for cross stitch. They enable you to practise the stitch in bands without too many colour changes, as each motif is usually worked in single colours. Both the tulip place mat and napkin designs on page 50 use just two colours, so you can practise on these simple projects and make something very pretty for your dining table.

Following a chart

Counted cross stitch designs are provided on a grid-like chart, which is divided into small squares. Each square represents the area taken up by one cross stitch, either one Aida block or two threads in each direction of evenweave fabric. Always start from the centre of the design and work outwards unless otherwise instructed, to ensure that the design is correctly positioned on the fabric. The centre lines of the design are usually indicated on the chart and the centre point is where they cross. In order to find the corresponding point on the fabric, fold the fabric in half first width- and then lengthways. Press creases along these lines to find the centre (see page 28). Mark the centre lines with tacking stitches for ease of working, particularly on large designs.

Starting and finishing

It is very important not to leave knots in your embroidery, as they create lumps and will eventually work loose or catch. To start, take both the needle and thread from the front to the back of the fabric, leaving a short length on top. Then, bring the needle up again 4cm (1½in) to one side of the starting point. Start stitching the first row of cross stitch, working over the thread at the back. Once it is secure, pull the end through to the wrong side, thread it through the needle and then weave the end under a few stitches. To finish off, leave enough thread and weave it under a few stitches.

Embellishing the design

Cross stitch is very effective on its own, but you may wish to add texture and extra interest by incorporating other stitches such as back stitch (below) and French knots (see page 205), or decorating with beads and charms (see pages 26–27).

CROSS STITCH, ROW BY ROW

USES: filling

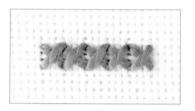

The instructions for all the stitches in this table are illustrated on evenweave, where each stitch is worked over two fabric threads. If you are working on Aida, bear in mind that one stitch is worked across one Aida block. Cross stitch is usually worked either in horizontal rows, from either left to right or right to left, or in vertical columns starting from the top or the bottom. It can also be worked as single stitches (shown below) when the need arises.

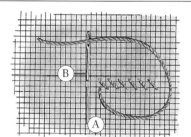

1 Bring the needle up at A, bottom right, and insert it at B, top left, to make a diagonal stitch. Repeat to fill the row with the first part of all the cross stitches.

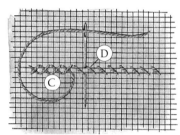

2 Bring the needle up at C, directly below B, and insert it at D to finish the cross. Repeat to complete the top part of all the cross stitches worked in the row.

INDIVIDUAL CROSS STITCH

USES: filling

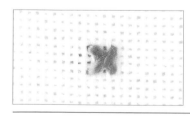

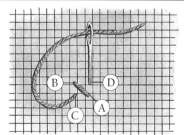

To work one stitch at a time, bring the needle up A and insert it at B to make a diagonal stitch. Bring the needle up at C, directly below B, and insert it at D to complete the cross.

BACK STITCH

USES: outline

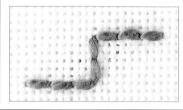

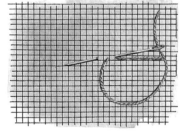

Bring the needle up and work one stitch length to the right. Bring the needle up one stitch length left of the start. Take each back stitch into the same hole as the previous one.

HALF CROSS STITCH

USES: filling

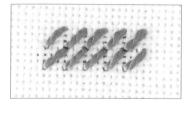

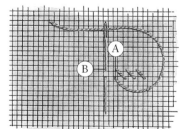

Bring the needle up at A and down at B. Repeat until you reach the end of the row. These stitches must always lie in the same direction as the top part of a whole cross stitch.

THREE-QUARTER CROSS STITCH

USES: filling

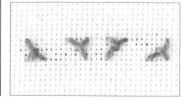

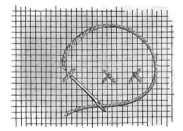

Stitch the first part of a cross stitch. Take the needle up as for a whole cross stitch but insert it in the central hole of the square. This stitch works better on evenweave than Aida.

Tulip place mat and napkin

Tulip motifs were common in early cross stitch embroidery and have been used as the inspiration for the following two projects. Variegated stranded cotton has been chosen to create a clean and contemporary border to the place mat and a simple circular motif on the napkin. Blue thread is used for the flowers here, but you could easily choose a shade to match your own colour scheme. Design by Maria Diaz

Design area

Place mat: 40 x 26.5cm
  (15¾ x 10⅜in)

Napkin: 7cm (2¾in)
  square

Materials

56 x 42cm (22 x 16½in)
  14-count white Aida
  (for the place mat)

41cm (16in) square
  14-count white Aida
  (for the napkin)

Embroidery threads
  (see chart key)

Equipment

Tacking thread

Embroidery hoop

Size 26 tapestry needle

Embroidery scissors

Needle, pins and matching
  thread for making up

Place mat

1 Tack a 41 x 26cm (16 x 10¼in) rectangle centrally onto the fabric. Then, fold the fabric in half vertically and tack a short line along the fold to mark the centre point on the bottom edge.

2 Place the fabric in the embroidery hoop and, starting with the blue thread, work from the centre out. Use two lengths of stranded cotton. As a variegated colour is being used, it is best to work the design stitch by stitch to create an even and gradual colour change.

3 Note that the pattern repeat on the chart is indicated by dotted red lines. Start stitching the bottom row of cross stitch from the centre point on the bottom edge, one block up from the tacked outline. Centre one whole tulip motif at this point and then work two more repeats on each side. Then continue stitching the pattern into the corner.

4 Turn the fabric and continue the corner pattern along the side edge. Then, work two repeats. Stitch the other side in the same way. Complete the final two corners and stitch the top edge to match the bottom one.

5 When stitching is finished, remove the tacking thread and, with a warm iron, press gently from the wrong side to iron out any creases. Put a towel beneath the fabric to avoid crushing the stitches.

6 Turn the edges over to the front of the embroidery, first by 0.75cm (¼in) and then 3cm (1¼in) to make a hem all round. Pin and then slip stitch in place. Mitre the corners and finally slip stitch these in place (see pages 32–33).

Napkin

1 Mark the centre of the design by stitching two lines of tacking 10cm (4in) in from one corner of the fabric.

2 Place the fabric in the embroidery hoop and, starting with the blue thread, work from the centre out. The centre is indicated by arrows on the chart. Use two lengths of stranded cotton. As a variegated colour is being used, it is best to work the design stitch by stitch to create an even and gradual colour change.

3 Once all the blue is completed, fill in the leaves and stems with two strands of the green thread.

4 Remove the tacking thread and press. To finish the napkin, turn the hems and mitre the corners as for the place mat.

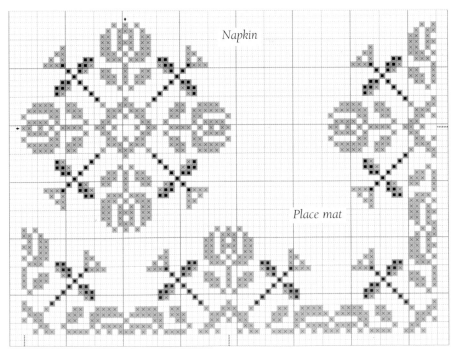

Napkin

Place mat

TULIP KEY	
DMC stranded cotton	Note: You will need
☒ 121	4 skeins of 121 and
■ 3816	1 skein of 3816.

Iris tablecloth

Modern cross stitch is probably one of the simplest forms of embroidery and yet it is possible to create very sophisticated designs using just the one stitch. Cross stitch is similar to painting by numbers in that you build a picture with blocks of colour. The design for this tablecloth was inspired by the Art Nouveau style and is positioned around the borders of the cloth in a very dramatic way. Design by Maria Diaz

This particular tablecloth has been designed to fit a rectangular dining table, measuring 92 x 155cm (36 x 60in), with seven motifs along each long side and four motifs across each short side. You could alter the dimensions of the cloth in order to fit a different-sized table. However, you must remember to calculate the exact size of the fabric you will need very carefully, by working out how many motifs will fit best, making sure to include the spaces in between them.

1 Measure the tabletop carefully and then add an extra 39.5cm (15½in) all around, in order to allow for the drop, with the motifs and hem. You could also use a ready-made cloth provided it is of a good-quality evenweave fabric and if its measurements are suitable.

2 Bind the two raw edges of the fabric and leave the selvedges on the other two. Work a line of tacking stitches 7.5cm (3in) in from the edge on all four sides. Next, fold the fabric in half both widthways and lengthways, and then finally tack a short line of stitches across the outline stitches in order to mark the centre points on each side.

3 Start with the centre motif from the centre point on one of the long sides of the fabric, positioning the bottom row of stitches two threads up from the tacked outline. Then, place the fabric in the embroidery hoop.

4 Using two lengths of stranded cotton, start stitching the iris stem and leaves working up towards the flowerhead. When stitching, bear in mind that it is easier to work in blocks of colour and, as a single colour thread is being used here, it will actually be quicker and tidier to work the cross stitch in rows.

5 Once you have completed stitching all the green areas of the iris design, proceed on to the stitching of the blue shades on both the flowerhead and bud. Once all these areas have been completed, finish with the golden centre of the iris flower.

6 When all the cross stitch has been worked, start outlining the design using one strand of the dark violet in order to back stitch the iris flower and one strand of the dark green to work the foliage.

7 The motifs along each side of the cloth are positioned with 60 unstitched threads of fabric between them. Count the gap of 60 threads out to one side of the first motif and then proceed on to counting another 30 threads in order to find the centre point of the next motif. Complete that motif.

8 Count out the position of each motif from its completed neighbour, until you have completed seven motifs along both long sides of the fabric.

9 There are four iris motifs that need to be positioned on the short sides of the fabric. To position the first one, you must count 30 threads of fabric out from the centre point for half the central gap. Then, continue counting the threads in order to find the centre point for the first motif. Complete the embroidery on both short sides of the fabric.

10 When all 18 motifs have been completed, carefully remove all the tacking threads. Then, with a warm iron, press gently from the wrong side in order to iron out any creases, placing a towel underneath the fabric to avoid crushing the stitches.

11 Finish the tablecloth by turning the edges under by 1cm (½in) and then turning a hem of 2.5cm (1in) all around. Finally, mitre the corners and then slip stitch in place (see pages 32–33).

Design area
16.5 x 31.5cm
(6½ x 12½in)

Materials
2.3 x 1.70m (2½ x 1⅚yd) wide 28-count white evenweave fabric

Embroidery threads (see chart key)

Equipment
Tacking thread

Embroidery hoop

Size 26 tapestry needle

Embroidery scissors

Needles, pins and matching thread for making up

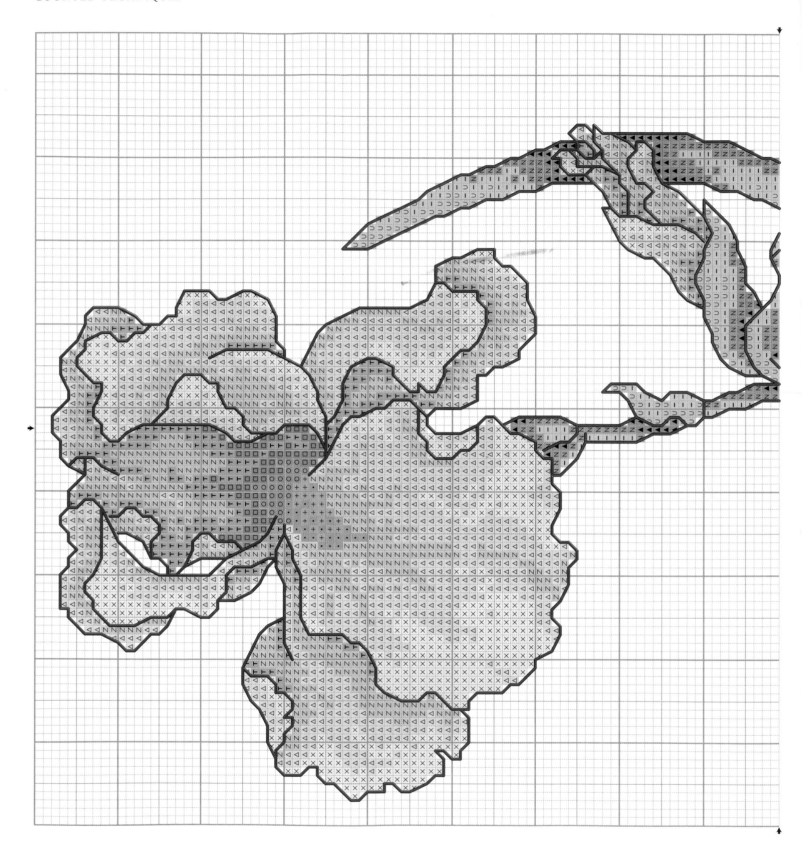

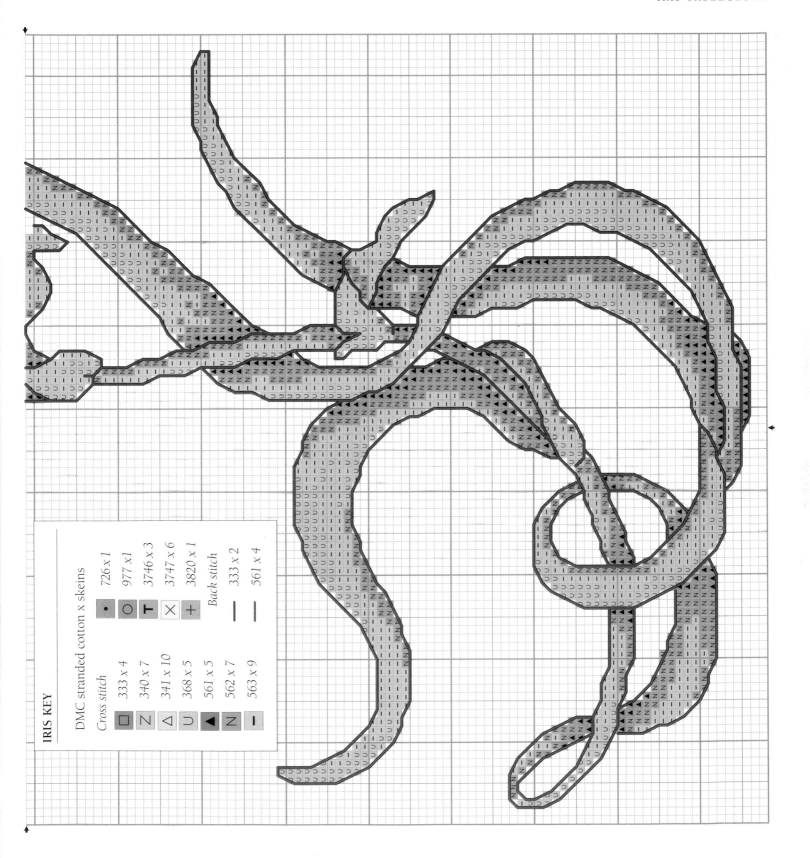

IRIS KEY

DMC stranded cotton x skeins

Cross stitch

●	726 x 1	
○	977 x 1	
T	3746 x 3	
X	3747 x 6	
+	3820 x 1	

☐	333 x 4	
Z	340 x 7	
△	341 x 10	
∪	368 x 5	
◄	561 x 5	
N	562 x 7	
I	563 x 9	

Back stitch

—	333 x 2	
—	561 x 4	

Blackwork

Blackwork has enjoyed a long period of popularity. It was a favourite throughout Europe during the Renaissance and continued to be popular in America until the late 18th century. It was certainly known in England at the end of the 14th century when Chaucer, in the Canterbury Tales, described a smock worn by the carpenter's wife as having a collar embroidered with 'cole blak silk'. Blackwork has evolved throughout the years, and has been used on household linen as well as clothing. Today, it is a style of embroidery that is still proving popular with many modern embroiderers adapting it to more contemporary designs.

In the 14th century, blackwork was known as Spanish work. The technique, being of Arabic origin, was widely used in Spain as a formal geometric edging. Spanish work edgings on handkerchiefs and the collars and cuffs of men's shirts and women's smocks were based on interlacing knot patterns like those used in the garden design of the period. These edgings and more elaborate designs can frequently be seen in 16th century portraits.

Blackwork was usually worked in monochrome on white or natural-coloured evenweave linen, which best showed the clear definition of the

stitches and pattern. Although frequently black, this technique was also traditionally worked in blue, red or dark green. The black or sable silk was available in two different qualities and occasionally a third thread was used, which was made by spinning a black and white thread together. A single thickness of thread was used to work a wide variety of stitches including double running or Holbein, back, stem, buttonhole, chain, closed herringbone and seeding, which was also known as speckling. Originally, these stitches would have been worked with a Spanish steel needle. The Spaniards had learned the highly skilled art of tempering steel from the Arabs and needles and scissors imported to England were expensive and highly prized.

Traditional uses

During the course of the 16th century, formal geometric blackwork border patterns were also used as decorative elements on household linen such as towels, sheets and pillow covers, which were known as 'pillow beres'. However, in England, as there was an increasing interest and delight in plants, another form of blackwork embroidery developed, which had quite a distinctive form of naturalistic twining stems, fruit, flowers and leaves. The designs were no longer confined to borders, but instead became all-over designs of boldly outlined shapes filled with a variety of intricate geometric patterns. These particular filling patterns were made by repeating small, straight stitches vertically, horizontally or diagonally over the threads of the linen fabric. Another method was to fill shapes such as leaves with tiny speckling stitches in order to obtain a shaded effect. These fillings gave pattern and texture to the work and frequently gold or silver sequins or spangles were added as a means of catching the light and contrasting with both the black silk and the matt white ground.

Above: Decorative border of a pillow case, English early 17th century.

Opposite page: Portrait of Mary Cornwallis, Countess of Bath, by George Gower circa 1575.

Left: Black silk on linen, English, late 16th century.

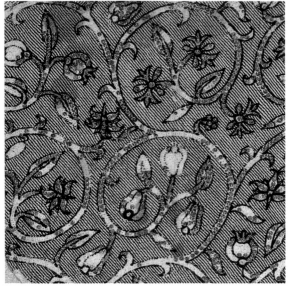

This informal style of blackwork embellished both men's and women's clothing, where it was sometimes combined with gold or silver thread embroidery. Men's caps were often embroidered with flowers such as roses, honeysuckle, pinks or pea pods, with stems and berries or acorns worked in plaited gold. According to Frances, Countess of Hereford, the best embroiderer of nightcaps was 'Mrs Price in the Strand'. She wrote to her steward in London in 1603 instructing him to buy one in 'black silk and gold and silver' and expected to pay about £3. William Freke, an Oxford student, is recorded as having bought a 'black-work and gold cappe' for 17s and 6d in 1629. This price difference may reflect that either his was less elaborate, was of poorer quality or simply that the style was going out of favour. Such caps, although they were known as bedchamber or night caps, were not actually worn in bed, but indoors with informal garments. Some were quilted and occasionally had lavender or rosemary stitched inside the lining. John Gerard, in *Herbal First*, published in 1597, recommended these 'to comfort the brain' and help recovery from a head cold. Women's caps, also called coifs, were similarly decorated.

Lavishly embroidered clothes

During the late 16th and early 17th centuries, women's fashionable large puffed sleeves provided a good opportunity to display blackwork and these were sometimes worn with gauze oversleeves. Skirts and jackets were also lavishly embroidered with blackwork. Examples can be seen in portraits from that particular period and several shirts decorated with bands of pattern have survived. One surviving shirt is decorated with bands of pale lilac silk. It belonged to Dorothy Wadham, deceased in 1610,

and is now displayed at Wadham College, in Oxford. The Victoria and Albert Museum in London features a boy's shirt, worn in about 1540 and embroidered in blue silk with columbines in an interlacing pattern. Also at the Victoria and Albert Museum is possibly the best example of a late 16th-century blackwork jacket, which is known as the 'Falkland jacket'. It is adorned with an all-over floral design of leaves, flowers, fruit, animals, insects and several emblem designs taken from *Whitney's Choice of Emblems and Other Devices*. This book was first published in 1586 and the designs became so popular that they were widely copied. Unfortunately, like so many early blackwork pieces, this jacket is in poor condition. The black dye caused the silk thread to deteriorate and decay, and in many instances the only indication of the original embroidery is the pattern of holes remaining.

Blackwork embroidery demonstrates Elizabethan style and sense of design at its very best. Its lively flowing patterns were worn with white cutwork and reticella lace, both of which are restrained and geometric. Such contrast was enjoyed by the Elizabethans and the courtiers of James I of England (James VI of Scotland). However, with the introduction of the French taste for plainer silks and satins by Henrietta Maria, wife of Charles I, blackwork had fallen out of favour by the 1630s.

Modern use of blackwork

During the late 19th and early 20th centuries, there was a revival of interest in blackwork embroidery. This was part of a rediscovery and renewed appreciation of historic needlework, particularly the work from the late 16th century, when secular embroidery was at its finest. A large number of exhibitions were held featuring examples from

Above: Man's blackwork and silver gilt embroidered cap, early 17th century.

Top left: Detail of apron sampler, 1930s. The linen fabric is embroidered with silk threads in blackwork, cross stitch and drawn and pulled threadwork.

Top right: Woman's cap with voided designs and sequins, early 17th century.

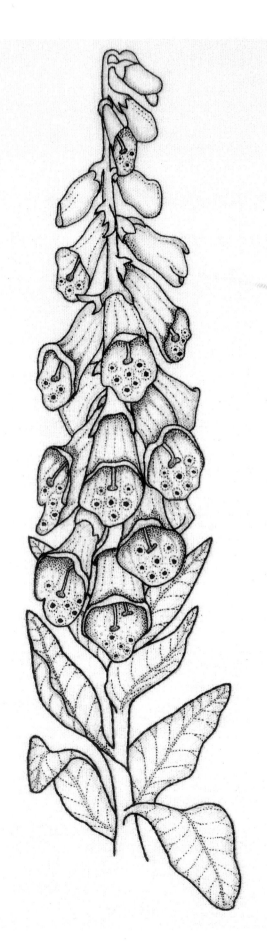

old families and historic houses, which were seen by the public for the first time. These stirred considerable interest among both private collectors and museums. Mrs Grace Christie (1872–1938), who taught at the Royal College of Art, was an authority on historic embroidery and, as was usual at that time, encouraged her students to study historic examples of all kinds in order to understand the techniques fully before actually creating their own designs.

Although some embroiderers continued to be fascinated by traditional intricate blackwork, by the late 1950s new attitudes to embroidery, as well as new sources of design, were being sought. Patterns for blackwork, based on wrought iron work, mosaic pavements as well as architectural details, were used to fill designs inspired by nature, such as cross sections of fruit and vegetables. The density of pattern was varied and different weights and thicknesses of threads were used to vary the texture. As design became much freer and more abstract, the individual parts of the design were no longer enclosed by a solid line, nor was it considered necessary to work the filling patterns in fine thread. Embroiderers were encouraged to create their own designs and to make imaginative use of traditional techniques to produce work that was both modern and of its own age. Therefore today, blackwork embroidery is not limited to a practical role, but is one amongst a wide range of techniques available to the embroiderer as a means of expressing personal and contemporary ideas.

Blackwork stitches and techniques

Blackwork filling patterns are built up of the simplest element – a straight line – so the more complex patterns are easier to work than you may think. Even, regular stitches are the key, so work them with precision and you will always get the best results from this technique. An extra dimension can be created by using reversible stitches, allowing a design to be viewed from either the front or the reverse side.

Design your own

• *In general, strong contrasts work best – white threads on a navy or black fabric produce a wonderful lacy effect.*

• *Although effective in Hardanger or whitework, threads and fabrics of the same colour family – antique white, ivory or ecru used together – tend not to work as well for blackwork.*

• *Moorish or Islamic patterns can provide strong geometric spaces within which you can place various filling patterns.*

• *Stencils, stained glass designs, ironwork, metalwork and jewellery are other good sources of design material for blackwork projects.*

Fabrics

Blackwork patterns are counted, so the finer the fabric, the more detail that can be achieved. For a more traditional look, choose an evenweave with single warp and weft threads. If you have never stitched on a non-blocked fabric before, you may like to try one of the lower fabric counts available. If you are used to stitching on blocked fabrics, such as Aida, you may find fine damask Aida or 22-count Hardanger fabrics easier to work on. For fine work, use evenweave fabrics with a count of around 60 or more.

For best results, choose a piece of fabric which is free of slubs and that is not misshapen. In non-reversible work, you may find it useful to back your fabric with a thin cotton batiste, or shirting fabric. When you stitch, stitch through both the surface and backing fabrics. This will help to prevent tiny stitches over a single fabric thread from slipping between the warp and weft threads. It will also help you position your stitches, give your work more regularity and make it less likely for any running threads at the back of your work to show through to the front once you have mounted your work in a frame.

Needles

A small, sharp needle will provide greater control over the positioning of stitches. Use a size 10 or 12 sharp or crewel needle with fine threads and a larger size with thicker threads. The sharp needle allows you to split the stitching or fabric threads discreetly to achieve smooth, continuous, flowing lines.

Threads

Silk thread is traditionally used for blackwork. However, this technique can be worked in other threads as well. When working traditional blackwork using black silk thread, try using high-quality silk threads in various thicknesses. Look for threads with a consistent twist. Although silk is one of the more expensive fibres on the market, you do not need to buy much to start off with.

Every thread is different, and an unusual thread can help achieve a particular effect. If you decide you would like to do more blackwork, you can then start building up a resource of different thicknesses and types of thread in order to experiment with the effects each one can provide.

Blackwork techniques

Blackwork filling patterns are made up of straight stitches that are placed vertically, horizontally or diagonally. These can be combined to create a wide range of linear patterns. The simplest straight line can be used as the basis for a border or a band on a sampler. Other patterns can be positioned within an outline so that they add to the sense of flow. Complex patterns add interest to an otherwise simple outline.

Starting and finishing
For blackwork, it is important to make sure the grain of the fabric is totally straight and, in non-reversible work, to align any backing cloth used with the top fabric. Always leave free a length of thread at least two to three times that of the needle at the start and finish.

In reversible blackwork, you should start with a waste knot (see page 28). You can use this method in non-reversible work as well, but you can also secure the starting thread with a few discreet seeding stitches.

In order to secure finishing threads, you can use the weaving method (see page 29). There are also other ways that are better suited to blackwork embroidery and ensure that stray threads are not visible.

One option is to stitch the working thread into the fabric threads, a method that works best along diagonal lines.

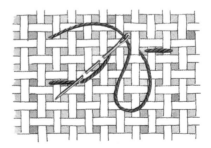

Secure a finishing thread by stitching into the back of the fabric threads.

You can also stitch into the back of the stitches that have already been worked.

RUNNING STI...

USES: pattern d...

STEM OUTLIN...

OTHER NAMES...

back stitch

USES: outline, s...

PEKINESE STI...

USES: outline

REVERSIBLE C...

USES: reversibl...

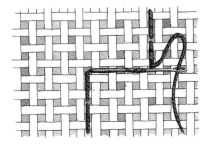

Stitch into the back of the stitches to fasten the working thread.

Aim to maintain a tight, but comfortable stitching tension at all times, especially when you are working back stitch. If the tension is too loose, then the stitches may appear looped – too tight and you may distort the surface fabric.

Make sure your tension is even (top), and not uneven (bottom).

Sharp points and angled corners

Whether stitching simple bands or intricate filling patterns, the way the stitches work into a point or corner is critical to the precision of blackwork.

To make a sharp point in stem outline stitch, work a line of stitches, up to where you want the point to be located. Stitch the second line, working towards the point again. Bring the needle down at a shallow angle where the stitched lines meet, to create the sharpest angle possible.

When stitching counted patterns in straight lines, work

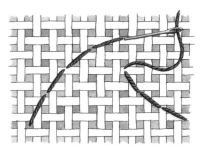

Make sure the second line of stitching meets the first.

---

discretely into embroidery or fabric threads already in place where necessary to create seamless joins wherever lines intersect.

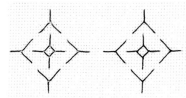

The stitches should meet at the intersections (right), rather than leave a hole (left).

Filling patterns

These are used to shade, decorate and stylize a blackwork design. Choose a filling pattern and then position it within an outline. The positioning of the filling pattern is crucial, as it will dictate how neat the finished design will look.

The type of filling pattern you choose will generally depend on considerations of scale; where the centre of an area falls in relation to the fabric threads as well as the density of shading you wish to achieve.

With a symmetrical outline, try positioning a complete motif at the centre of the shape to fill. On the other hand, if you are working with a non-symmetrical outline, position a complete motif at the top centre of the shape.

This same octagonal pattern is shown adapted to a vertical axis for the centre petal and on the diagonal for the side ones.

The direction in which a filling pattern is laid out – vertically, horizontally or diagonally – will give movement in that direction wherever it is placed in a design.

Filling patterns can be centred on fabric holes or thread intersections.

Shading

Most blackwork filling patterns can be altered by either adding or subtracting lines to or from the basic patterns in order to make them more or less dense. This can produce quite a wide range of gradations in shading.

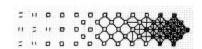

Lines are added or subtracted to make filling patterns more or less dense.

The filling patterns themselves can be superimposed on one another, thereby opening up a vast array of design potential. For example, superimposing a pattern in two different colourss can provide a rather interesting three-dimensional effect.

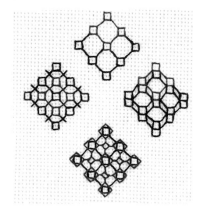

The basic pattern has been highlighted in red (top three), rotated and superimposed (bottom).

INSPIRATION AND DESIGN:
black and white contrasts

Blackwork by its very nature conjures up the contrasts of the 16th and early 17th centuries. This was an age when religion co-existed with magic and alchemy, sumptuous wealth, beautiful fabrics and laces with intrigue, hangings and assassinations.

While the objects of beauty created in this age have had the widest impact on embroiderers through the years, we must not forget the world from which they came. In that world of perplexing contrasts, people sought to dispel the chaos around them through the reassurance of a sense of order, the patterns of which symbolized the divine. Order in even the smallest pattern was seen as a metaphor for greater truths.

These themes are echoed in many of the filling patterns used in blackwork – the basic building blocks of stitches giving birth to triangles, octagons and squares which in turn combine into repeat patterns. These patterns can be seen simply as decorative shapes, yet each can also have a symbolic value. A circle can symbolize unity, a square growth and development, and a triangle consciousness, manifestation and the three aspects of divinity. The patterns derived from these basic forms and the properties ascribed to them were used symbolically and decoratively in medieval Christian and Islamic arts, both of which can claim to have influenced the style and development of blackwork embroidery.

It is not surprising that the stark contrast between black and white – each potentially uninspiring on its own – is characteristic of an earlier world so used to appreciating the balance between good and evil. Each needs the other to show its true character and through the wise use of simple shapes and forms, black and white can produce stunning results.

The idea of designing your own blackwork piece can seem daunting. However, you will find that it is one of the easiest techniques to use, as long as you follow some basic rules about the placement and scale of filling patterns and the importance of accurately transferring the design to fabric.

Inspiration can come in various ways. Some pieces are born from a sudden flash of inspiration while others develop over a long period of time. Whichever approach you take, let your starting point be something you feel strongly about – either as an idea you want to explore, or a pattern, text or image you find beautiful or moving. The cushion design, with its pearl embellishments, on pages 68–71 discreetly evokes the splendour of the Elizabethan era. It is indirectly inspired by the style typical of the blackwork revival in England in the 1930s. Design motifs in this period drew on the legacy of the Art Nouveau and Arts and Crafts movements in their use of flowing lines, natural curves, and a simpler, more naturalistic portrayal of plants and flowers.

Whether you decide to take a traditional approach or explore a more modern one is up to you. See what happens when you start to experiment. You will quickly develop the confidence to explore more possibilities. To start with, try out a few ideas on a 'doodle cloth'. Practise working the stitches described in this section, and see where they lead. Let the stitches and threads speak for themselves. If you feel something is not working, revisit the original idea, to make sure you have not deviated too far from your initial inspiration. Often, however, a project can develop just from a small stitch sample stitched as a doodle. Simply enjoy it and have fun!

Round the garden cushion

This sophisticated cushion design takes its elegance from the black on white colour scheme and the finely detailed patterns of stitches. It is not difficult to work, although it does take good light and plenty of patience. Real freshwater pearls have been chosen to complement the embroidery, although you could easily substitute similar beads and still be sure of compliments. Design by Leon Conrad

Stitching the design

1 Make five copies of the design from the diagram on page 71 on a photocopier. Cut four of these out along the broken lines from the outside to the inner circle, then around the inside of the right central leaf and the outside of the left one. Stick the copies on firm card, matching them over the repeat positioning shown on the diagram and up to the broken lines to form a circle.

2 Smooth out the linen and the backing fabrics, one on top of the other, on a flat surface, ensuring the warp and weft threads of both fabrics are perfectly aligned. Attach the linen evenly to the backing fabric along the edges by pinning the layers together and working herringbone stitches (see page 81) with matching thread.

3 Transfer the design to the fabric using the method of your choice (see pages 30–31). Use the guidelines given in the diagram to align the design with the grain of the fabric, without transferring these lines onto the fabric. Mount the fabrics onto the embroidery frame squarely and stretch to an even tension (see pages 16–17).

4 Stitch all the outlines in stem outline stitch using one strand of black silk.

5 Choose the filling patterns for the flowers from the chart. You will need one pattern labelled A for each flower centre. The flowers have six petals, in alternate light and dark patterns, so choose one pattern labelled B and one labelled C for each flower. Stitch the patterns in combinations of back (see page 49), running, double running and running back stitch, using one strand of black silk.

6 Still using one strand of black silk, work seeding stitch in one half of each central leaf motif then work the hatched pattern labelled D into the outer petal border. Whip the stem outline stitch (see page 206) on the stems and work Pekinese stitch on the inner circle around the leaves.

7 Attach the pearls using a beading needle (see page 286) and fine black thread. Place them on the inner and outer points on the outer petal border. Work at least three stitches to secure each pearl.

Making the cushion

8 Remove the embroidery from the frame and press it on the reverse side if necessary. Make a circular paper template with a radius of 36cm (14in), marking the centre clearly and precisely. Pin through the centre of the template and place in the centre of the embroidery. Pin the template to the embroidery and carefully cut the circle out of the fabric. Cut another circle to match the first and a 12 x 10cm (5 x 4in) strip from the furnishing fabric.

9 Machine sew the two short sides of the strip of cushion fabric together, leaving a seam allowance of 1cm (⅜in). Press the seam open. Pin this border for the cushion to the embroidery, right sides together, again allowing for a seam of 1cm (⅜in) and notching the edge of the fabric in order to ease it around the curve. Tack along the seam line when you are sure you have a perfect circle and then machine sew in place, leaving a very small opening to take in the piping later. Repeat this process to attach the back of the cushion, but leave a 15cm (6in) opening in the seam. Remove all the tacking thread.

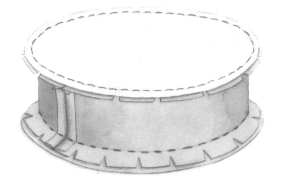

Notch the seam allowance to ease the border around the top and bottom of the cushion cover.

Design area

26cm (10¼in) in diameter

Materials

45cm (18in) square antique white 36-count linen

66 x 56cm (26 x 22in) fine cotton or polycotton shirting or lawn fabric for backing

Embroidery thread (see chart key)

Black freshwater pearls or similar beads (see chart key)

0.5 x 1.2m (½ x 1yd) grey furnishing fabric

2.2m (2½yd) black piping

35cm (14in) diameter cushion pad

Equipment

Paper scissors

Firm card 30cm (12in) square

Embroidery frame

Size 10 crewel needle

Embroidery and dressmakers' scissors

Beading needle and thread for beads

Pins

Matching sewing threads

Tacking thread

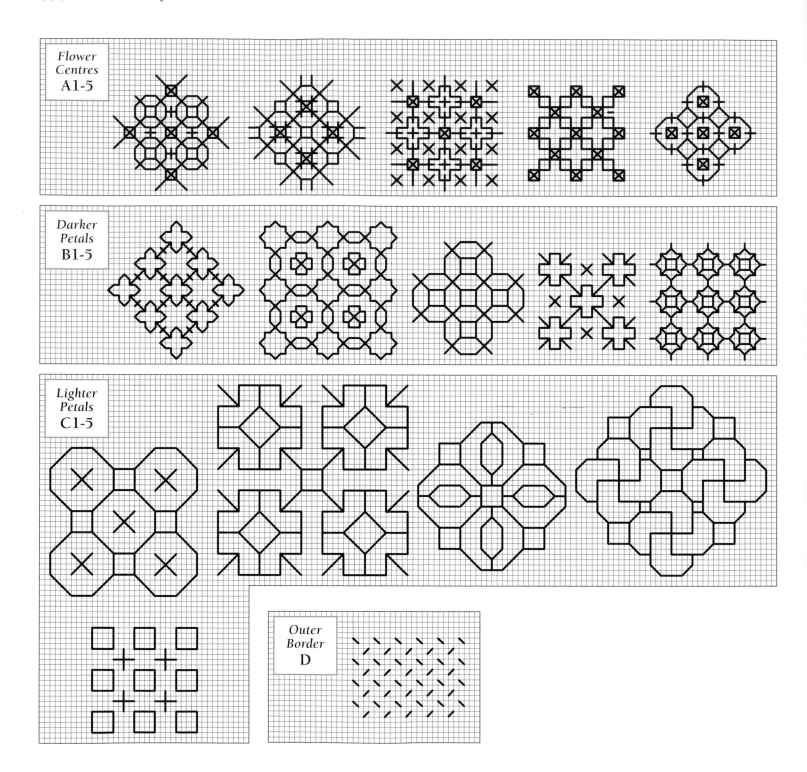

10 Turn the cover right side out and press the seams. Slip stitch the black piping around the top of the border, pushing the ends through the opening. Turn the cover inside out and machine sew across the opening, securing the piping ends.

11 Turn the cover right side out again, insert the cushion pad and close with slip stitches in a matching thread. Finally, slip stitch the black piping in place around the bottom of the border.

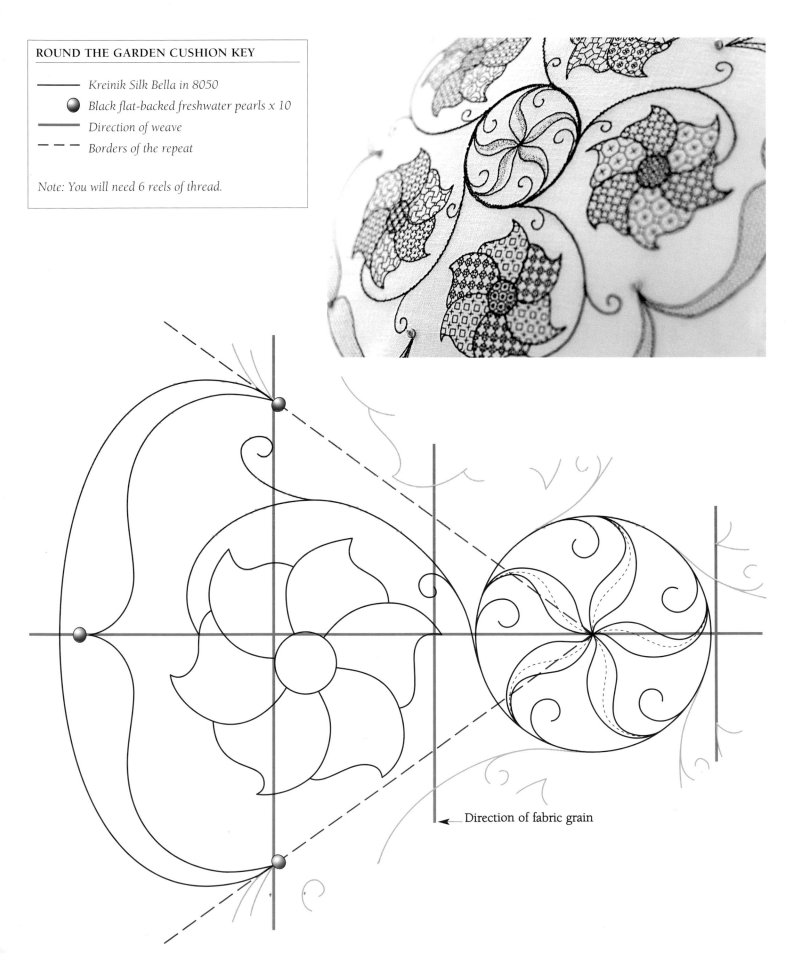

ROUND THE GARDEN CUSHION KEY

——————— *Kreinik Silk Bella in 8050*

⬤ *Black flat-backed freshwater pearls x 10*

——————— *Direction of weave*

— — — — *Borders of the repeat*

Note: You will need 6 reels of thread.

← Direction of fabric grain

Canvas work

Canvas work is any decorative embroidery stitched on an evenly woven canvas ground. The stitches most often found on old work are tent, Gobelin and cross stitch. There are now many types of canvas, but until the 1840s only single canvas was available. Canvas work results in a durable textile, especially suitable for furnishings and upholstery. In the 16th century, wealthy families often moved from one house to another, taking their furnishings with them as tapestries, table carpets, cushions and hangings were status symbols. Embroidery provided warmth, comfort and privacy as well as colour and decoration.

The bed was the largest and most imposing piece of furniture. The hangings would consist of curtains and two sets of valances: three valances hanging around the tester (canopy) and three narrower ones for the part of the bed below the counterpane. Often decorative canvas work borders in designs of leaves or twisted cords were applied to the silk or velvet curtains. Few curtains survive because of their constant use. However, many valances, made in professional workshops and worked on fine linen canvas in tent stitch in wool with silk highlights, survive in surprisingly good condition.

Similar to these valances are canvas work wall hangings, covers and carpets for chests and tables. Floors were usually strewn with sweet rushes or matting. The most outstanding examples of embroidery of this type are the Gifford and Bradford table carpets, worked in the mid and late 16th century respectively, now to be found in the Victoria and Albert Museum.

Perhaps the most famous amateur needlewoman of the time was Mary, Queen of Scots (1542–1587). During her captivity, she worked with Bess of Hardwick, the wife of her jailer, the Earl of Shrewsbury. Together with their ladies, they produced dozens of small canvas work panels. Worked in tent and cross stitch in multicoloured silks these might have been intended as the decoration for walls or bed hangings. The majority are at Oxburgh Hall, Norfolk, some at the Victoria and Albert Museum, Hardwick Hall, Derbyshire and Holyrood Palace, Edinburgh.

The virtues of embroidery
Making household furnishings was labour-intensive and in keeping with the Protestant work ethic, in which embroidery was regarded as a virtuous pastime. For example, Oliver Cromwell's wife was said to have maintained at her own expense six clergymen's daughters whom she employed at needlework.

By this time, in the early 17th century, wood panelling had become a popular feature in interiors, allowing less space to display large hangings, and so smaller pictures became fashionable. Although tapestries were still very prestigious, they could only be afforded by the rich, whereas needlework hangings were less expensive to produce. Small canvas work pictures, made in imitation of woven tapestries, were therefore introduced in the 1630s and were to remain popular throughout the 17th and 18th centuries. It is this stage in its history that has given rise to the inaccurate use of the word 'tapestry' for canvas work, or needlepoint as it later came to be known in the United States.

The designs for these pictures were copied from new pattern books such as Richard Shorleyker's *A Schoole-house for the Needle*, published in 1624, or adapted from woodcuts and engravings of classical, mythological or biblical stories. Designs could be purchased from print sellers, or drawn specially to

Above: Bed hangings in Florentine work, England, late 17th century.

Opposite page: Detail from a panel of canvas work motifs embroidered with wool and silk threads in tent stitch on canvas, mid-17th century.

*Left: Octagon by Mary, Queen of Scots in tent and cross stitch, circa 1570–1584. The marigolds are turning to the sun with the motto **Non Inferiora Secutus** (Not Following Lower Things). Mary's cipher is visible on the right.*

Above: Panel depicting Hagar and Ishmael, England 1630–1660. Sarah and Isaac watch as Abraham banishes his son Ishmael with the Egyptian servant Hagar, his mother, into the desert. This subject was popular in canvas work and also common in 17th-century Dutch and Italian art.

order, and in effect became the first embroidery kits, although the choice of stitch and colours and the interpretation of the design was an individual matter.

By the late 17th and early 18th centuries, idealized rural scenes appear in painting and in embroidery: shepherds playing flutes, fishermen, milkmaids, and farmers ploughing indicate a new interest in nature and advances in agriculture. These pastoral scenes depict a Golden Age, when man lived in harmony with his fellow man and nature. Therefore country scenes and especially floral designs became predominant. Canvas work made a durable and decorative covering for upholstered chairs. Those dating from the early 18th century, often in matching sets with settees and day beds, usually have bold floral designs with naturalistic shading. Firescreens, footstools and cards table covers were also worked.

Berlin woolwork: the new craze
A new form of canvas work known as Berlin wool work became synonymous with Victorian interiors. This derives its name from the soft, untwisted silky wool, dyed in a wide range of shades, that was ideal for filling the holes in canvas and gave a smooth, even surface. This wool was used along with designs printed on point paper where one square represented one stitch. Introduced in about 1810 by L.W. Wittich in Berlin, it was imported in small quantities to Britain. It was not until 1832, when Mr Wilks of Regent Street, London, began offering the patterns and materials for sale that it became widely known. Although not particularly popular in France, Berlin woolwork became a craze throughout Europe, Scandinavia, Britain and America by the mid-19th century when designs were widely available and reproduced in women's magazines.

Requiring only the ability to work simple tent and cross stitches and to count, Berlin work became the pastime of leisured women who produced cushions, chair and table covers, carpets, firescreens, stool tops, mantel borders, pelmets, bell pulls and even men's waistcoat fronts and slippers. Canvas work copies of paintings by artists such as Landseer were also stitched, some almost 2m (6½ ft) long. Biblical and sentimental subjects were popular as were historical subjects such as the works *Mary Queen of Scots with the Dying Douglas after the Battle of Langside* and *Washington Crossing the Delaware*.

Furnishings had flamboyant floral or animal and bird designs, sometimes with highlights worked in silk threads or glass or steel beads, and during the 1850s, three-dimensional effects were introduced by means of padding and plush or velvet stitch. Plush stitch was made by loops worked over the finger and carefully clipped to the required shape. Occasionally, chenille thread was used for added texture and there were stitch variations such as leviathan stitch, also known as railway stitch because it covered the ground so quickly. With the discovery of synthetic, aniline dyes in 1856, new vivid colours such as mauve, magenta and a bright blue were introduced. The lack of individuality and subtlety in the work and the excess to which Berlin work was produced led to an inevitable reaction against it. Essays in the *Art Journal* of 1855 'On Design as Applied to Ladies' Work' attacked the vulgarity of Berlin work, and it eventually went out of fashion during the 1870s.

Texture, colour and variation

Canvas work has never lost its appeal even into the 20th century, perhaps because it has so many practical applications and it is easily worked by the inexperienced. It is also a technique that many men enjoy. Wounded soldiers were taught various embroidery techniques as a form of occupational therapy during the First World War. Among those involved in this activity were Ann Macbeth, her students and Ernest Thesiger, an influential champion of embroidery. D.H. Lawrence and his wife Frieda also enjoyed embroidery and Queen Mary was a keen advocate of canvas work, and taught all her children including the Duke of Windsor, who later referred to it as his 'secret vice'.

Since the 1930s, canvas work has been widely used for church kneelers. These were inspired by the Winchester Cathedral project, in which Louisa Pesel, first President of the Embroiderer's Guild, organized 200 embroiderers to make kneelers and seat cushions. Canvas work was also used for picture panels during the 1930s. Original designs for screens and mirror panels were produced by painters such as Paul Nash, Duncan Grant and Vanessa Bell who, despite having a basic knowledge of the simplest canvas work stitches, encouraged more subtle colour effects by crossing one colour over another. In these works, the stitch is secondary to the pictorial image.

Today, traditional tent stitch canvas work designs happily run alongside the more adventurous contemporary and experimental work. Texture and innovation are crucial to modern canvas work – paint-sprayed backgrounds may be used to show through the work as part of a design and texture may be created from the huge choice of stitches and threads now available including metal threads, braids, ribbons or scraps of shredded silk. Variations of stitch in scale and proportion add another dimension to experimental work. Contemporary canvas work often incorporates techniques such as pulled thread, Hardanger, blackwork and goldwork, as well as wire mesh, sheers, leather, beads or tassels.

Left: Pair of slipper fronts, England, mid-19th century. Designs such as this would be made up by a shoemaker and were popular gifts.

Below: Gold on Canvas, by Pamela Watts, 2000. This piece is worked in couched metallic threads, metal and beads with textured canvas work stitches.

Canvas work stitches and techniques

There is a wealth of stitches to be used in canvas work, ranging from hardwearing (tent stitch) to very textured ornamental stitches. Some stitches may be reversed or have small variations added to them to become a different stitch. Experiment with a range of threads, ribbons, braids, colours and textures to achieve exciting effects.

Design your own

• *Incorporate objects such as stones, shells and shisha glass. Secure them in place with suitable embroidery stitches.*

• *Use thick and thin textures to show painted backgrounds.*

• *Utilize surface stitches to create curves or special effects eg chain stitch, raised chain band, fly stitch, couching, etc.*

• *Combine other techniques with canvas work such as pulled and drawn threadwork and ribbon embroidery to create different textures and contrasts between filled and open stitchery.*

Fabrics

Canvas work is generally stitched on a stiffened, evenly woven cotton fabric called canvas. The quality of canvas varies, and it is worth buying the best that you can afford. It is important to choose the correct type and count of canvas for the project you are undertaking.

Working on a mono canvas will give you complete scope for using any canvas work stitch you wish and will suit most projects.

Interlock canvas is mono canvas, but with the threads locked together so stitches cannot slip through at the intersections. Double canvas is stronger and more durable, and the work may be trammed for wearability and coverage, but there are some limitations as to the choice of stitch other than tent stitch and smaller decorative stitches.

Plastic canvas lends itself to structured pieces such as boxes, book covers, bags, etc.

Threads

Traditionally, wool is the thread used in canvas work, whether it is tapestry or crewel. It is important to use the correct weight of wool for the canvas and stitches chosen. Use enough strands to cover the canvas background and also fill the holes of the mesh.

Depending on the project at hand, a huge variety of threads may also be included from cotton, silk and rayon to ribbon, machine embroidery and metallics (see pages 24–25). Always buy enough yarn to complete the project – and bear in mind that sometimes dyes vary.

If you branch out into space dyed/shaded threads, make sure that the colours are fast and will not bleed when the work is dampened and stretched.

Needles

Tapestry needles are used for canvas work, as they have blunt points and long eyes. The size of the needle to use is governed by the size of the canvas mesh and thread. You should be able to pull the needle through the work without a struggle. Equally, the needle should not drop through the canvas holes. The thread should also go through the eye easily, without falling out.

Additional tools

It is always best to use a frame for canvas work, and there are many types (see pages 16–17). Framing will help prevent your work from distorting, and once you are in the rhythm of stabbing the needle from top to bottom and back again, your tension will become more uniform and the result more professional.

A stand to hold the frame is a valuable extra, as it will help with posture and also leaves both hands free with which to sew.

A stiletto is useful for running across the canvas to check lines of stitches, counting threads or enlarging eyelet holes. It can also be used to help stroke and lay the threads as you stitch.

You may also wish to use tweezers to pull out unwanted threads from the canvas.

Canvas work techniques

The wide variety of interesting stitches that are used in canvas work is a significant contributory factor in making this embroidery technique universally popular. The constraints of an essentially geometric technique can be overcome with the clever use of both surface embroidery and canvas work stitches.

The choice of a stitch for your design depends on the effect you are trying to achieve as well as the suitability for the project itself. Smaller, flat background stitches will wear better on upholstered items. Definition and detail within a given shape will be achieved using the smallest of stitches such as tent stitch. Sensitive shading moving from one colour to the next or sharp contrasts are also easily accomplished with this small stitch.

Florentine canvas work is often used for upholstery and soft furnishings and, as long as the canvas is not too large and the wool is thick enough to give a good coverage, your project should last for years. To fit Florentine patterns into a given space, work up to the design outline and, keeping the basic pattern correct, complete as much of it as possible in the space. Sometimes, these cropped compensating stitches may only be over one thread.

With constant use, surface threads of textured ornamental stitches will rub away quicker than a flat background stitch. Likewise, some stitches do not cover the canvas as well as others and are therefore not as practical.

Decorative stitches offer varying textures and patterns, but less scope for intricate detail. Designs will be completed more quickly and there are endless possibilities for stitch and colour combinations.

Although the aim of canvas work is to cover the canvas so the background fabric is not visible, there are also situations when ornamental stitches, and even background stitches, are specifically used with finer thread to create open lacy effects. In these instances, the colour of the background, whether painted or natural, shows through and plays a crucial part in the design. This is most apparent when combining canvas work with other techniques such as goldwork, pulled threadwork or Hardanger.

Starting and finishing

All canvas work should be started and finished with the wool brought to the surface of the work. The resulting knots and 'tails' may be cut off, as later stitches will cover these up and secure the waste thread. Avoid weaving the starting and finishing threads through the back of tent stitches, as this can cause ridges to show up on the front and spoil the look of the work. If there is no alternative, split the wool strands and take them carefully through the stitches in different directions.

If using crewel strands, keep the wool flat as you sew. In order to prevent the wool from crossing over itself, untwist the needle and thread when necessary, or lay the thread over a stroking needle or stiletto as you sew the stitch.

Florentine

Florentine is a particular type of canvas work that is also called Bargello or Hungarian point. It is characterized by the use of straight stitches worked up and down in steps across the canvas. Both the stitch length and step dimensions can vary, giving Florentine distinctive zigzags, wavy lines or geometric shapes.

Patterns are often described in numerals – for instance 4.1, 4.2 or 6.1. The first number refers to the number of canvas threads over which the straight Gobelin stitch is made and the second refers to the number of threads that form the step between stitches.

Even zigzag patterns are accomplished by working stitches of the same length in order to create equal highs and lows of pattern steps.

Uneven zigzags are formed by combining different length stitches or steps so the height and depth of pattern is altered.

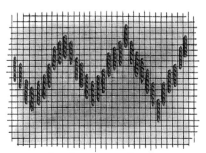

Using the Florentine technique, you can work irregular zigzag lines.

Curves are achieved by using blocks of a given number of straight stitches between the single stitches, at the top or bottom or on the way up or down a design. Single stitches create a steep climb of steps. The gradual introduction and mirror image of blocks of two, three or four stitches alternating with the single stitches creates a curve. The combinations of blocks and number of stitches in each block will determine the shape of the curve. The position of the first block in the climb will also have a bearing on the final arch shape.

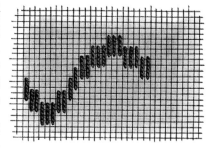

You can also work work curved lines with the Florentine technique.

Colour is the enduring and significant element of this technique and is used to identify rows. Colour tones are used to add movement and depth.

Tent stitch

This is the smallest, probably the most familiar of all canvas stitches and certainly the most useful for hardwearing backgrounds and fine work. When used on a double canvas, it is possible to make four small stitches ('petit point') to pick out detail in the same space as one normal-sized ('gros point'). Tent stitch can also be defined as petit point when worked on a mesh of 18 threads per inch or more. Tent stitch should cover the canvas. It can be worked horizontally, vertically or diagonally, and each method will influence the look of the work.

Ornamental stitches

Ornamental stitches offer an exciting variety of choices. Some are practical, some are decorative and some are representational; but all of them may be used to great effect to create a specific effect or texture and utilize the play of light on a piece.

The following stitches are some of the most popular and many of them are used in the projects (see also fly stitch on page 205 and back stitch on page 49).

GOBELIN STITCH
OTHER NAME: satin stitch

USES: border

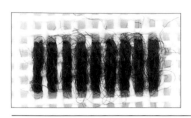

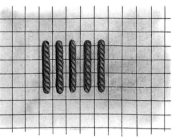

Work a line of straight stitches over two canvas threads or more, either vertically or horizontally. Work from left to right or right to left, stitching with an even tension.

FLORENTINE STITCH
OTHER NAMES: Bargello, Hungarian point

USES: filling, background

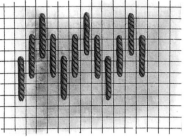

Work straight Gobelin stitches in steps up and down to form zigzags, wavy lines or geometric shapes. Stitches vary from two to six threads high.

TENT STITCH
OTHER NAME: continental stitch

USES: background, fine work, definition

1 Tent stitch works in any direction. To work from left to right, make a diagonal stitch over one thread A to B. Repeat to complete the row. Make long, slanting stitches on the back.

2 To work from right to left, make the same diagonal stitch over one thread following the A–D sequence above. Repeat to complete a whole row, keeping the tension even.

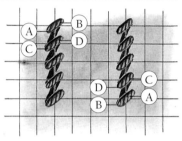

3 To work downwards, follow the sequence on the left; to work upwards, the one on the right. Do not work half cross stitches (see page 49). Keep a long, slanting coverage on the back.

DIAGONAL TENT STITCH
OTHER NAME: basketweave

USES: background

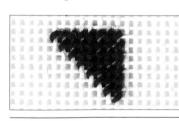

1 Work a diagonal tent stitch upwards on the rows where the horizontal canvas thread lies over the vertical one. Go behind two vertical threads of canvas between stitches.

2 Stitch downwards on the rows where the vertical canvas thread lies over the top of the horizontal one. Go behind two horizontal threads of canvas between tent stitches.

This stitch minimizes distortion and the basketweave pattern on the reverse makes it very hardwearing. Beaded tent stitch is usually done on double canvas so the beads fit snugly in the intersections. Canvas count governs the bead size. They must sit close together. Use tent or half cross stitch (see page 49), threading the beads before each stitch and making a small back stitch over the vertical stitch on the reverse every five stitches for strength.

BRICK STITCH

USES: background

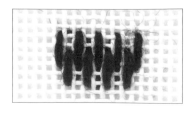

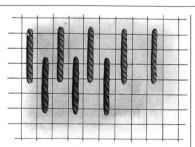

Work vertical stitches from left or right over two, four or six threads, leaving a one-hole gap between each. Work the next row of stitches in the gaps one, two or three threads down.

PARISIAN STITCH

USES: background

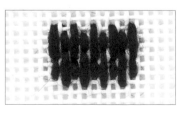

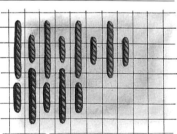

Work a row of alternating long and short stitches from left or right over four and two threads respectively. Make sure each row slots into the row above.

HUNGARIAN STITCH

USES: background, pattern

Work a unit of three stitches over two, four, and then two threads. Leave a one-hole gap and repeat. Each subsequent row must fit into the spaces created in the row above.

CUSHION STITCH

OTHER NAMES: Scotch stitch, diagonal satin stitch, flat stitch

USES: background, border

Work diagonal stitches over one, two, three, then four threads. Reverse the process to complete the square unit. This stitch can be oriented in any direction and the size varied.

MOSAIC STITCH

USES: background, border, detail

This is a small version of the cushion stitch. Work three diagonal stitches to form a square unit over two threads of canvas. You can work it in any direction.

MILANESE STITCH

USES: filling

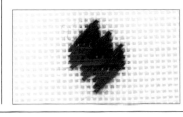

Work four stitches as cushion stitch. Repeat, placing the fifth stitch in the middle of the fourth. Reverse each subsequent row so the longest and shortest stitches touch.

BYZANTINE STITCH

USES: filling, background, diagonal line

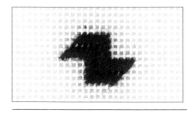

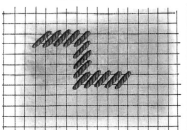

Work diagonal stitches over two threads in steps of five stitches. The last stitch on each step becomes the first on the next. Work upwards or downwards. Stitch length can vary.

DOUBLE STRAIGHT CROSS

USES: filling, texture, border

Work an upright cross stitch over four threads, then a diagonal cross over two threads on top. Complete the row across. Slot the next rows into the gaps made by previous rows.

RICE STITCH

OTHER NAME: crossed corners stitch

USES: filling, texture, border

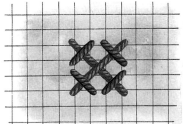

First, work a diagonal cross stitch over two or four threads. Then, cross each arm of the unit with a back stitch over one or two threads.

SMYRNA CROSS

OTHER NAME: double cross

USES: filling, outline, border, texture

Work a diagonal cross over four threads. Overlay it with an upright cross. This stitch can be worked over two or four threads, or varied for creative work.

DIAMOND EYELET WITH BACK STITCH

OTHER NAMES: diagonal eyelet with back stitch

USES: filling, single motif

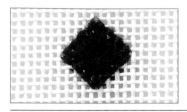

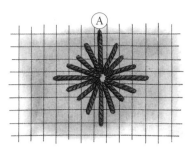

1 Starting at A, work the first stitch vertically down four threads into the centre hole. Continue clockwise around the unit. Take the last stitch slightly behind the first for a neat fit.

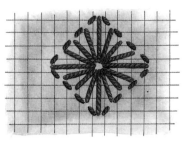

2 Complete the unit by working a line of back stitch (see page 49). Each back stitch sits over one canvas thread and is positioned around the outer edge of the unit.

By altering the dimensions and shape of the stitch, eyelets can be worked on canvas as diamonds or squares with varying numbers of spokes. The more spokes there are, the more times the thread will have to go through the centre hole, so make sure it is of a thickness that works well in this situation. Other variations can be created by working just one quarter or half of the eyelet and repeating this to form a repeating ray-like pattern.

RHODES STITCH

USES: filling, texture, single motif

Work the first diagonal stitch across the required number of threads. Work the next stitches anti-clockwise around the square, crossing the first stitch at the centre.

LEAF STITCH

USES: filling, texture, border

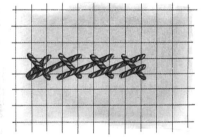

Work the first diagonal stitch over three threads at the bottom left-hand side of the shape. Repeat, working into the centre in a clockwise progression. Add a vein if desired.

LONG-ARMED CROSS STITCH

USES: filling, outline, texture, border

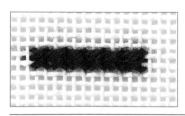

1 To start the row, work a small cross stitch over two threads. Bring the needle up again at A and take it down at B, making a long diagonal arm across four and up two threads.

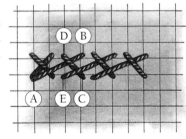

2 Bring the needle up at C, two threads below B. Take the needle back down at D, working diagonally backwards over two threads to form a cross. Repeat, starting at E.

3 Make the final stitch a small, compensating cross stitch instead of a long-armed cross stitch to finish the row neatly. The dimensions of the stitches can be varied.

SQUARED HERRINGBONE STITCH

USES: single motif, texture, border

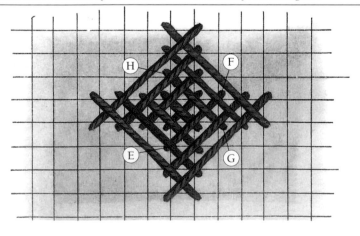

Work a cross stitch over two threads. Come up in the hole directly below the first stitch at E and, working anti-clockwise, take the thread down at F. Take the needle behind two threads and come up at G. Take the thread down at H. Continue around the diamond shape. When you reach the last stitch in each round, take it back underneath the first stitch in the round to keep the crosses in sequence. Repeat rounds as desired.

NORWICH STITCH

OTHER NAME: waffle stitch

USES: border

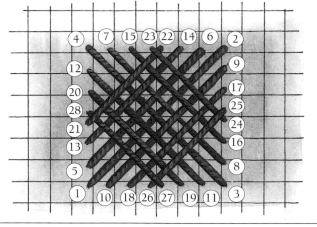

Working over an uneven number of canvas threads, make a diagonal cross stitch from 1 to 2 and 3 to 4. Follow the sequence shown around the square, crossing each previous stitch as you proceed. The last stitch of each round goes underneath the first stitch of that round to keep the crossing sequence accurate. On the reverse, straight stitches outline the square. You can work this stitch over an even number of threads, but the effect will be slightly different.

JESSICA STITCH

USES: decorative motif

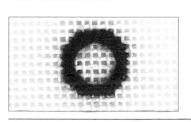

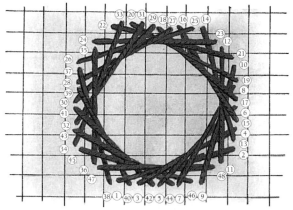

Work the first diagonal stitch from 1 to 2, across six and up two threads. Follow the sequence anti-clockwise around the shape. When you reach the stitch 39–40, complete it by taking the thread under 1–2. Complete the unit by doing the same with the remaining four stitches, 41–42, 43–44, 45–46 and 47–48. The dimensions of this stitch can be varied and the centre can be filled with foil, beads, tent stitch, French knots or a spider's web.

GHIORDES KNOT

OTHER NAME: Rya

USES: pile, texture

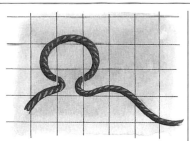

1 Take the needle under one thread then over two in the opposite direction. Bring the needle up in the centre hole. Do not tighten the stitch until you form the loop to the next stitch.

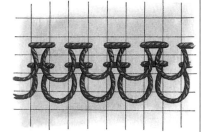

2 Take the needle across two threads to start the next stitch. Repeat to form a row, working from the bottom line upwards so the loops lie over the row below.

3 Loops may be left as they are or cut to size. To keep them uniform in size, work them over a knitting needle. Vary the weight of thread to produce different effects.

Above: A beautiful rendering of canvas work stitches.

Exotic red box

The lattice pattern for this box is inspired by the window designs of Indian temples and palaces. The repeating shape, use of simple stitches and mixture of threads in different textures make this an ideal starting point for learning canvas work. The tent stitch is mitred in each of the diamond shapes to maximize the play of light with the colour combinations. It is finished off with small beads at all junctions. Design by Jill Carter

Design area

16cm (6¼in) square

Materials

25cm (10in) square
  antique 14-count
  mono canvas

Embroidery threads and
  braids (see chart key)

12 red beads
  (see chart key)

Stiff card or board for
  stretching embroidery

16cm (6¼in) square
  wooden box with recess

Equipment

Embroidery frame

Tacking thread

Size 22 tapestry needle

Needle and thread for
  sewing on beads

EXOTIC RED BOX KEY

Tent stitch in Appletons
crewel wool in 995

Tent stitch in Appletons
crewel wool in 505

Diamond eyelet in Anchor stranded
cotton in 47 and backstitch in Kreinik
metallic fine braid #8 in 003HL

Diagonal mosaic stitch in Anchor
stranded cotton in 47

Single tent stitch line in Kreinik
metallic medium braid #16 in 003HL

Red beads size 11

Smyrna cross stitch in Appletons
crewel wool in 502

Long-armed cross stitch in Appletons
crewel wool in 502

Back stitch in Appletons crewel wool
in 505

Centre line

Note: You will need 2 skeins/reels of Appletons 505 and
Anchor 47, 3 of Appletons 995 and 1 of all other shades.

1 Prepare the canvas and mount it on the frame (see pages 16–17), then tack in the vertical and horizontal centre lines.

2 Following the chart, establish the basic lattice pattern with diagonal mosaic stitch. Using the stranded cotton, start from the centre of the work. Remember to count the number of stitches on each side of the diamond carefully and end each side with a short stitch so the lines mitre at each 'junction' and criss-cross successfully.

3 Still using the stranded cotton, work a diamond eyelet in the centre of each unit, making sure that the threads lie smoothly on the surface of the fabric.

4 Following the changing directions of the stitch and pattern, work a tent stitch on either side of the diagonal mosaic. Work the tent stitch, using the medium braid to highlight the lattice outline. Fill each diamond-shaped unit with tent stitch worked in four directions mitred on the vertical and horizontal centre lines as shown in the chart. First, stitch seven rows with two strands of the

no. 995 crewel wool. Then, using two strands of the no. 505 crewel wool, complete the final four rows until you reach the eyelet shape.

5 Using the fine metallic braid, back stitch an outline around the eyelet shape. Repeat this process in order to delineate all the diamond eyelet shapes. Finish off this section by sewing red beads at each lattice 'junction' as well as in the centres of the eyelets.

6 Following the chart, work a border of Smyrna crosses, followed by two borders of long-armed cross stitch using two strands of the no. 502 wool. Back stitch over two threads between the inner two borders, using two threads of the no. 505 wool. It is worth working an extra line of tent stitches around the design to cover the canvas so that it does not show when it has been made up.

7 To finish this lattice design, block the work (see page 29), stretching it over a piece of card or board to fit snugly into the recess of your chosen box. Alternatively, you can make up the embroidery as a pin cushion.

Indian panel

Vibrant and unique, Indian textile designs are a continual source of inspiration. This particular project capitalizes on colourful patterns and their appealing lack of uniformity. Designed to be more challenging, there is scope to re-interpret the project using your own mix of 'hot' colours, threads and textures. Shisha glass and small tassels are added for embellishment and a touch of authenticity. Design by Jill Carter

Design area

16 x 23.5cm (6⅛ x 9¼in)

Materials

26 x 33cm (10¼ x 13¼in) antique 14-count mono canvas

Red, copper and gold acrylic spray paint

Embroidery threads and braids (see chart key)

22 x 11mm (½in) diameter circles of Shisha glass (or copper and aluminium shim)

Purple, pink and copper beads

Equipment

46cm (18in) embroidery frame

Tacking thread

Needle and thread for sewing beads

Stiff card or board for stretching embroidery

Strong thread for lacing

Mounting board and frame of your choice

1 Following safety instructions and health warnings on the cans of paint, spray the canvas with a layer of red paint, then copper and finally apply a light dusting of gold to create a burnished red background colour. This will enable the colour to show through when some of the stitches are worked using the finer threads. Prepare the canvas and mount into the frame (see pages 16–17).

2 Following the chart, establish the bottom line of long-armed cross stitch using the coton perlé 915 and starting 5cm (2in) in from the side and bottom edges. Count 45 threads to find the centre of the work and tack in the vertical centre line for reference. Stitch the next two lines of long-armed crosses, the first in coton perlé 911 and the second in crewel wool 435. Note that lines of long-armed cross stitch are repeated throughout the design.

3 Work a row of fly stitch (see page 205) over four threads, taking the vertical end over all three bands of long-armed cross stitch, in coton perlé 718. Overlap this row with a second one, slotting the fly stitches in between the first.

4 Stitch the main green zigzag in band 4 with crewel wool 435 and coton perlé 911. Fill in the coloured triangles of varying dimensions above and below the main zigzag, using the colours and threads shown on the chart. Use three strands of wool and one of perlé throughout.

5 Create circles to enclose the Shisha glass or shim with Jessica stitch, using one strand of wool in colours 864, 866 and 504. Start on the left-hand side of the work. Remember to leave the first thread spare as shown on the chart. Make up your own sequence of colours or follow the colours in the chart. Complete three sides of a Jessica 'circle' before slipping either the Shisha or shim into the centre of the stitch. If necessary, stabilize the Shisha or shim in position with a small piece of double-sided sellotape. Carefully pierce a hole with a sharp needle in the middle of some of the Jessica stitches and fill in with either a French knot (see page 205), a single medium bead or a few smaller beads. Some of the Jessica stitches enclose a background tent stitch or you could use a stitch of your choice. Complete the background with straight stitches in a mixture of the mauve and pink threads. Work the back stitch detail on the top and bottom of the band with the fine braid 024HL.

6 Form vertical lines of 'arrowheads' as the basis of the main design in band 8 by stitching two halves of a cushion stitch, reversed and over five threads. Use two strands of crewel wools 455, 607 and 804 and one strand of coton perlé 915 as shown on the chart. Alternatively, develop your own bands of colour.

7 Using coton perlé 915 and 552, braids 024HL, 012 and 027, metallic thread 5289 and shiny floss 30915, fill in the other half of the triangles with a random mixture of tent, straight and diagonal stitches. Use just one colour in each triangle. Bear in mind that part of the charm of this piece is the uninhibited nature of the stitching. Complete the band by randomly working half a cushion stitch on top of some of the first ones but this time in the opposite direction, and using a varied selection of the metallic, shiny floss and coton perlé threads.

8 The next three bands work together. Stitch the first line of long-armed crosses in crewel wool 435 first, then the band of Gobelin in wool 607 and then repeat the line of crosses. Stitch the back stitch detail above and below the Gobelin in braid 024HL. Soften the straight line and decorate the surface with fly stitch in coton perlé 552. Work one row of fly stitch over four threads across the bottom crosses and the Gobelin stitch. Then, work a second row over the top crosses and the Gobelin stitch, alternating between the first row of stitches.

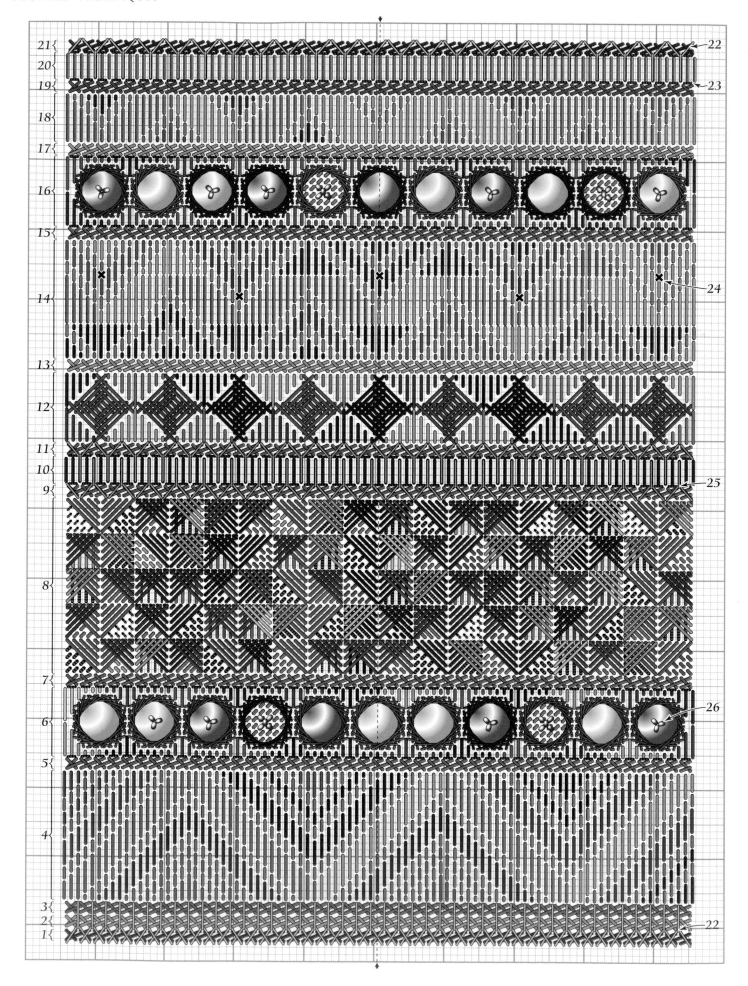

INDIAN PANEL KEY

- ▬ *DMC coton perlé no. 5 in 911*
- ▬ *Appletons crewel wool in 435*
- ▬ *Kreinik fine braid #8 in 024HL*
- ▬ *Kreinik medium braid #16 in 027*
- ▬ *DMC coton perlé no. 8 in 552*
- ▬ *Appletons crewel wool in 455*
- ▬ *Appletons crewel wool in 607*
- ▬ *Appletons crewel wool in 864*
- ▬ *Appletons crewel wool in 866*
- ▬ *Appletons crewel wool in 504*
- ▬ *Appletons crewel wool in 804*
- ▬ *DMC coton perlé no. 8 in 718*
- ▬ *DMC coton perlé no. 5 in 915*
- ▬ *DMC metallic in 5289*
- ▬ *DMC rayon in 30552*
- ▬ *Kreinik fine braid #8 in 012*
- ▬ *DMC rayon in 30915*
- 0 0 0 *Beads size 11*
- ----- *Centre line*

 *Shisha or shim 11mm (½in) diameter x 22*

1 *Long-armed cross stitch in DMC 915*
2 *Long-armed cross stitch in DMC 911*
3 *Long-armed cross stitch in Appletons 435*
4 *Gobelin stitch outline in Kreinik 027 – zigzag in Appletons 435 and DMC 911 – other shapes in Appletons 804, 455, 864, 504, 607 and DMC 915*
5 *Long-armed cross stitch in Appletons 435*
6 *Jessica stitch in Appletons 864, 866, 504 – gobelin stitch surround in Appletons 804, 455, 607 and DMC 915, 552, 718*
7 *Long-armed cross stitch in Appletons 435*
8 *½ cushion stitch in DMC 915 and Appletons 455, 607, 804; complete with tent, gobelin and ½ cushion stitches in a mix of Kreinik 024HL, 012, 027 and DMC 915, 718, 552, 5289, 30552, 30915*
9 *Long-armed cross stitch in Appletons 435*
10 *Gobelin stitch in Appletons 607*
11 *Long-armed cross stitch in Appletons 435*
12 *Squared herringbone stitch in Appletons 864, 866, 504 – triangles in Kreinik 027, DMC 915, 552 and Appletons 804, 455, 607*
13 *Long-armed cross stitch in DMC 911*
14 *Gobelin stitch outline in Kreinik 027 – main band in Appletons 435 and DMC 911 – other shapes in Appletons 804, 455, 607 and DMC 915, 552*
15 *Long-armed cross stitch in Appletons 435*
16 *Jessica stitch in Appletons 804, 455, 607 and DMC 915 – gobelin stitch surround in Appletons 864, 866, 504*
17 *Long-armed cross stitch in DMC 911*
18 *Gobelin stitch outline in Kreinik 027 – zigzag in Appletons 435 and DMC 911 – small triangles in Appletons 864, 866, 504, 455, 804, 607*
19 *Long-armed cross stitch in Appletons 866*
20 *Gobelin stitch in Appletons 435*
21 *Long-armed cross stitch in DMC 915*
22 *Fly stitch in DMC 718*
23 *Back stitch in Kreinik 024HL*
24 *Marks the anchored positions of tassels*
25 *Fly stitch in DMC 552*
26 *Positions of beads stitched through coloured foils and tent stitch fills*

Note: You will need 2 skeins/reels of Appletons 435 and Kreinik 027, and 1 skein/reel of all other threads.

9 Using one strand of crewel wools 864, 866 and 504, work a row of squared herringbone stitches in your own colour sequence. Fill in the triangular spaces with straight stitches in two strands of wools 455, 607, 804, coton perlé 552, 915 and braid 027.

10 Having worked the next line of long-armed crosses, start from the centre of band 14, consisting of triangles or 'prairie points'. Refer to the chart for the length of stitches in each triangle as they vary. Use the medium braid 027 to outline each point. Then fill in with coton perlé 915 and 552 and two strands of crewel wools 455, 607 and 804. Work the band of green Gobelin stitches in perlé 911 and three strands of wool 435.

11 The top band of Shisha or shim circles is a repeat of the first set with a row of long-armed cross stitches above and below. Work the Jessica stitches with coton perlé 915 and crewel wools 455, 607 and 804. Fill in behind the Jessica stitches with a combination of wools 864, 866 and 504. Finish this band with the back stitch detail, which is worked using the fine braid 024HL.

12 Band 18 is a smaller version of the previous band of triangles or 'prairie points'. Work the main green zigzag in coton perlé 911 and three strands of crewel wool 435, and use braid 027 to outline each point as before. Fill in the triangles with perlé 915 and 552, and wools 864, 866, 504, 804, 455 and 607, either referring to the chart or in your own sequence.

13 Finish off the design with a series of straight Gobelin stitches. Then, work two rows of long-armed cross stitch in crewel wool 866 below and coton perlé 915 above the Gobelin stitches. Overlay with a single-spaced row of fly stitches over four threads in coton perlé 718, as a means of embellishing the surface of the Gobelin stitches and long-armed crosses.

14 Make the tassels to sew on the triangle points in matching colours (see pages 26–27). You can use the threads you have been working with or fine machine embroidery threads. Make the tassels as fat or as thin as you wish. It is best to make them a little longer than you think is necessary and trim them once they are sewn on. Add a few small beads onto the sewing thread as you attach the tassels, to ensure that they hang downwards properly.

15 Block the work (see page 29). Then, frame it with a mount (see page 32) or make it up as the centre panel for an exotic cushion.

Tips

- *Substitute your favourite stitches, but make sure they fit in the same spaces and design to retain the overall balance.*
- *Fill the Jessica stitches with spider's webs (page 99) or tent, double straight cross or eyelet stitches if you wish.*
- *Repeat your favourite bands to lengthen the embroidery into a wall hanging.*
- *Substitute threads you already have as only small quantities are needed except for the bronze braid.*

OPEN WORK

Pulled and drawn work

Open work techniques change the structure of the fabric and a great variety of stitches enrich it with transparent effects and a lace-like quality. One of the oldest types of embroidery and originally known as opus tiratum, *drawn threadwork is the basis of many embroidery techniques where some of the fabric threads are drawn out. As this weakens the ground, the remaining threads are strengthened and decorated with overcasting, needleweaving and lace filling stitches. These techniques form the link between cutwork and pulled fabric work, in which no fabric threads are withdrawn but are pulled together with filling stitches in order to produce delicate lacy effects.*

Drawn threadwork did not appear in England until the 16th century, when it was used to decorate household linen and clothing. It can be found on many samplers surviving from the 17th century, where it is often used with other techniques. It is common to many countries such as Armenia, Ukraine, Portugal and Sicily, but is most often associated with Scandinavian embroidery, where it has been used on clothing and church linen since the 17th century. In mid-18th century Denmark, this technique, known as Hedebo, began to the west of Copenhagen as a peasant embroidery worked on coarse, hand-woven linen. In most surviving examples until about 1820, it consisted of only a little cut and drawn threadwork combined with a greater amount of surface stitches. Between 1820 and the middle of the 19th century, more cutwork fillings based on Italian reticella work were added and later, elaborate lace stitches were added to the drawn threadwork, by which time little surface stitchery remained. In Hedebo embroidery, the geometric motifs of squares, triangles or stars are outlined with small blocks of satin stitch known as kloster blocks, then some of the threads within the motif are cut and drawn out. The remaining threads are then decorated with either overcasting, needleweaving or lace filling stitches. This particular type of embroidery was used for linen shirt collars, fronts and wristbands and for wall hangings and friezes. In Sweden, drawn threadwork is known as Naversom or 'birchbark embroidery', after the original method of using a piece of birchbark as a frame on which to stretch the fabric.

Pulled fabric work

This technique is effective both in geometric and curved floral designs. It is best worked on a frame with a thick needle such as a blunt tapestry needle and a fine thread. The stitches are pulled tight, drawing the fabric together and leaving a hole. A larger needle than usual effectively enlarges the holes. Outlines of the motifs can be worked in suitable stitches, such as four-sided, satin and back stitch, and infilled with a wide variety of stitches, which can be drawn together. These include diagonal chevron, eyelet, faggot, honeycomb, three-sided, sheaf and wave stitches. Self colours are most effective and pulled work is often combined with other types of white embroidery and quilting. It is seen at its best in Dresden work (see page 154).

Opposite page: Darning sampler, England, late 18th century. The fine linen fabric is worked with pink silk thread and white linen thread in buttonhole, darned fillings, double running and drawn thread stitches.

Below: Detail of a table cover, Mityline, Greek Islands, 19th century. The counted satin and pulled stitches are worked on a white linen, backed with red silk.

Top right: Detail of pulled work in a baby robe, possibly 1830s–1850s, Irish (see page 141).

Right: Detail of Hedebo embroidery. Traditional work on linen with drawn thread, satin and chain stitches in a stylized flower and plant form.

Below: British Royal Arms by Lady Evelyn Stuart Murray, 1912. Worked on white cotton on cambric in satin and stem stitch with drawn fabric fillings.

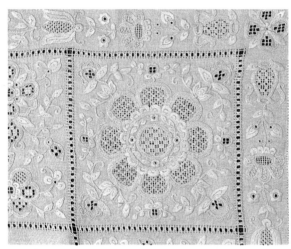

We know that pulled fabric was widely used in the Middle East during the 13th and 14th centuries, as examples with geometric patterns have been found in Egypt. In Europe, it was worked in the flax-growing countries such as Germany and Denmark, where varieties of linen were woven. Those linens woven with a loose mesh were suitable for creating open work effects without cutting the threads. With the development of mechanization, new materials such as organdie, organza, net and voile became available and were used for pulled work. Such a diversity of ground fabric ensures a wide variation in quality of the finished embroidery. For instance, in some Italian and Spanish pieces from the 16th century, the linen ground forms the motifs or pattern while the background and details are of pulled fabric worked to resemble 'lacis' (darned net). Other examples worked on the finest linen had great delicacy and were worn as 'lappets' attached to a woman's cap or sleeve ruffles as an alternative to bobbin lace.

18th-century waistcoats and aprons

In Britain during the early 18th century, men wore long waistcoats under full-skirted, knee-length, dark-coloured coats and during the 1730s, there was a fashion for waistcoats in white linen. These were frequently enriched with a combination of pulled fabric, quilting and surface stitches. Only the two front panels were worked, usually in a floral or leaf design. French knots were used extensively to add variety to the texture of the work and some of the motifs have a raised outline in cord and buttonhole stitch. Occasionally, the pulled work formed the background to the motifs rather than the motifs themselves. The buttons were also a decorative feature, and these were made of linen embroidered in patterns of either tiny stitches or French knots.

During the middle of the 18th century, women's aprons were similarly embroidered. These were not functional garments, but a decorative feature made from the finest fabric. The most usual design was an overall sprig with more elaborate embroidery concentrated at the hem and corners. Sometimes, exotic birds were included. Some may have originated in India, where fine, open-textured muslin was used rather than linen for pulled work. Similar work was used to decorate handkerchiefs throughout the 18th and 19th centuries, but it was at the start of the 20th century that one of the most outstanding examples of drawn work was made.

Outstanding work

In 1905 in the Belgian lace town of Malines, Lady Evelyn Stuart Murray, younger daughter of John, seventh Duke of Atholl, and an accomplished needlewoman, decided to work a panel depicting the British Royal Arms. She had the design drawn by a draughtswoman in Vienna. The British Arms are enclosed in a scroll border with thistles, roses and shamrocks with the Prince of Wales's feathers and motto 'Ich dein' (I serve). It is worked in soft white cotton on the finest glass cambric in satin, padded satin and stem stitch with delicate drawn fabric fillings. Lady Evelyn was interested in lace and this is reflected in the pulled work, which is reminiscent of 'Brussels Point de Gaze'. The piece was completed in 1912, but before it was finished, it was sent to the Royal School of Needlework for appraisal.

European contrasts

Most of the pulled work done in northern Europe is monochrome, usually white, whereas in the eastern Mediterranean, in areas such as Turkey and Greece, they use pulled work as a foil for colourful silk and metal thread embroidery. In Armenia, cream hand-woven cotton and muslin shawls and scarves have colourful silk embroidery with areas of pulled work in mauve threads.

During the 1920s, European embroidery was of a much higher standard of design and was more adventurous than in Britain. In Austria, decorative pulled work on voile, linen lawn and net was used to work abstract designs or depictions of peasants and saints in a modern style. Britain saw the beginning of more experimental work by embroiderers such as Marion Stoll who, in 1926, used pulled fabric stitches as a background to her whitework panel entitled 'Dancer'. This angular design gives the impression of a single female figure caught in a spotlight against a lacy background, and strong diagonal lines add a sense of movement.

During the 1930s, 40s and early 50s, pulled work continued to be used for more practical applications. In France and Belgium, fine lawn blouses and crêpe de chine lingerie were decorated with delicate pulled work, but it was most often seen on household linen. Swiss sheets and pillow cases were embroidered with simple flower shapes, with satin stitch outlines and the centres in pulled work. In France, table linen was produced with motifs outlined in stem stitch or couched thread and with pulled fabric centres. In Sweden, traditional bird, leaf and geometric forms were worked on both tablecloths and mats in linen thread to match the ground fabric. These could be bought with the pulled stitches partially worked as a guide for the amateur embroiderer. With the growing use of washing machines, tumble driers and easy-care fabrics, pulled and drawn work techniques are now less popular for household linen. However, as with so many embroidery techniques, they are now used

Left: Sycamore leaf, 1999 by Jenny L. Adin. *This piece includes a variety of pulled threadwork stitches worked on linen using white flower thread. The outlines are worked in whipped stem stitch and back stitch.*

Below: Detail of a table runner by Kathleen Whyte, early 1950s. The pale golden Finnish linen has been worked in white linen and silk threads, with the insertion of drawn fabric with sheaf stitches.

93

Pulled and drawn work stitches and techniques

Both pulled fabric and drawn threadwork alter the structure of the fabric. In drawn threadwork, fabric threads are withdrawn altogether to create open spaces, which are then decorated with stitches in order to produce a geometric effect. In pulled fabric work, the stitches pull the fabric threads together to make fine lace-like patterns that can be used to fill geometric or free-flowing shapes.

Fabrics

Make sure you choose a slightly open evenweave to work pulled fabric work so the lace-like patterns are emphasized. Drawn threadwork should be worked on a strong evenweave fabric, which can be of a heavier weight if necessary.

Both techniques work well on household linens and drawn threadwork makes particularly effective borders for napkins and tablecloths.

Needles

For both techniques, use the largest tapestry needle that will go easily through the holes of the evenweave fabric. Use the same needles for withdrawing the threads of the fabric.

Threads

Choose a thread that is of a similar weight to a single thread of the fabric. A strong linen or cotton thread will be suitable for pulled work, and use a perlé or a stranded cotton thread for drawn threadwork.

Additional tools

Pulled work can be stitched in an embroidery hoop or a slate frame, although the fabric should not be stretched too tightly to allow the stitches to pull the threads of the fabric effectively. However, for drawn threadwork, you should start with the fabric in your hands while withdrawing the threads and hem stitching. Transfer the fabric to a hoop, bound on both the inner and outer rings, or a frame to work decorative stitches.

Pulled work techniques

Pulled fabric work relies on the choice of stitches to make particular patterns as well as on areas of different density to bring out the design. It is important to count the threads of the fabric meticulously, as the stitches need to be absolutely regular to show off the textures to best effect.

There is a large number of stitches suitable for pulled work, some of which appear on pages 96–99, and your choice will depend on whether the stitches fit into the shapes of your design and if they provide the density, direction and texture you are looking for. Note that delicate stitches work best on a fine fabric with a higher count, whereas a large-scale work will need a bolder design.

Transferring the design

Firstly, you must find the centre lines of the fabric and mark them with tacking stitches as described on page 28. Then, mark the centre lines on your design and trace it onto tissue paper. Pin the tissue paper design to the fabric, matching up the centre lines, and then transfer the design using tacking stitches as explained on page 31. Pull the tissue paper away to reveal the tacking stitches and insert the fabric into a frame, ready to start the embroidery.

Starting and finishing

Start the working thread with a waste knot. Leave a 10cm (4in) length to weave into the back of stitches later, in such a way that it does not show through the lacy patterns (see page 28). Start working the first row of stitches in the middle of the area to be filled. Then, centre the pattern and work a long row of stitches before working a partial stitch to fit in at each end of the row. Work all rows in the same way. Finish off by weaving the working thread into the back of stitches.

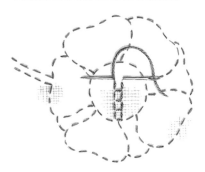

Start working the first row of stitches in the middle of the area to be filled.

Sequence of work

You should stitch the top elements of the design first and the background elements last. For example, if your design is a flower, work the centre first, the top petals next, then the underlying petals and finally the background. This will help to define the shapes in the overall design.

When all pulled work stitches have been done, remove all the tacking threads and work any outline stitching such as stem stitch where appropriate.

Remove the tacking threads and stitch around the outline.

Drawn threadwork techniques

In drawn work, warp threads are withdrawn along the length of the fabric whereas weft threads are withdrawn across the width. This results in characteristic open borders and square holes where the borders meet.

Hem stitches are used to bind the edges of borders and gather the remaining fabric threads into bundles of two, three or four.

Needlewoven stitches are then worked on the borders, by grouping the bundles into set multiples, and into the square holes at the corners.

These techniques all require careful planning and meticulous counting out onto the fabric to make sure the design works.

Planning the design

First, you should decide on the stitches you want to use. Each stitch is worked over a regular number of bundles of fabric threads, so count the design out in multiples appropriate to each stitch. Practise the stitches and borders on paper to determine how well they work together as well as the required dimensions for the fabric. Remember to plan for any hems too.

Transferring the design

Using a tapestry needle and a contrasting thread, tack all the borders and corners onto the fabric. If counting a long run, mark the fabric with pins every tenth thread of the fabric to avoid having to re-count from the start if you make a mistake. Remove the pins once the tacking is complete.

Withdrawing threads

Take a tapestry needle and lift one of the threads to be withdrawn from the centre point along the length of the border. Cut the thread and start removing it from the centre point. Withdraw the thread to within a short distance of the corner and cut it off, leaving a long enough end to weave it back into the fabric.

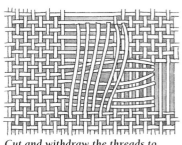

Cut and withdraw the threads to the required length.

Withdraw the threads one at a time to avoid distorting the fabric. Weave each one back into the fabric with a tapestry needle and then weave them back onto themselves, over and under the threads they cross in basketweave fashion to prevent unravelling. Keep the tension even so the edges of the corners stay straight.

Reweave back into the withdrawn threads with a tapestry needle.

Binding the edges

Hem stitch along the edges of the borders, bundling fabric threads into the required multiples. Weave the ends of the working thread under the hem stitches.

Bind the two outer edges of the rewoven corners, starting with a few back stitches then proceeding with buttonhole stitch. Finish by weaving the working thread into the back of the stitches.

Working decorative stitches

Put the fabric into an embroidery frame and then start weaving the working thread into the back of the buttonhole stitches at the end of the border. Next, bring the thread out in the required position, which is often the centre of the buttonholed edge. Work the stitches with an even tension. Finish by weaving the thread into the buttonhole stitches at the other end of the border.

Finishing the embroidery

When all the decorative stitching is complete, turn up the hems and pin them in place. Hem stitch them in position then mitre the corners.

On the following pages, you will find a selection of stitches for both pulled fabric and drawn work. You will find other useful stitches for outlines such as stem stitch on page 206 and fillings such as dove's eye filling on page 115 and throughout the book.

CHAINED
BORDER STITCH

USES: filling

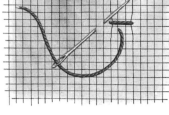

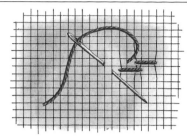

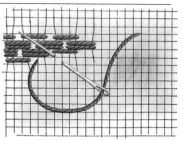

1 Work a stitch across four fabric threads. Go diagonally down behind two threads and make a second stitch over four threads, starting below and halfway along the first.

2 For the third stitch, come up in the same hole as the end of the first stitch and work a stitch over four threads. Make the fourth stitch as the second and continue to the end of the row.

3 Work the next row in the opposite direction, placing the top stitches in the same holes as the bottom stitches of the previous row, to form pairs. Keep the tension taut throughout.

FOUR-SIDED STITCH

USES: filling

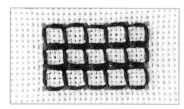

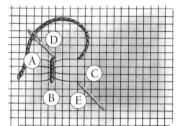

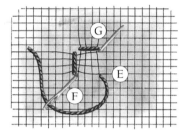

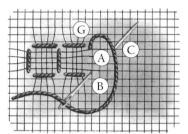

1 Make a vertical stitch down from A to B. Bring the needle up at C diagonally to the right. Make a horizontal stitch to D and come up at E diagonally to the right.

2 Make a horizontal stitch to the left at F and then bring the needle up at G diagonally up to the right, ready to start again.

3 Repeat the stitching sequence from the beginning in order to work a row of joined squares. Make sure you keep the tension taut at all times.

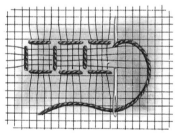

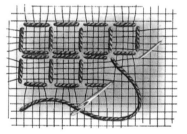

4 At the end of the row, stitch the fourth side of the square then bring the needle up again in the same hole from which that last stitch was started ready to work the next row.

5 Stitch the row below, reversing the instructions to work in the opposite direction or turn the work so the stitches can be made in exactly the same way as before.

Filling stitches like four-sided stitch are worked in rows to fill a shape. The rows can run up and down, diagonally or side to side, one row in one direction and the next in the opposite direction. On the return rows reverse the sequence, or turn the work so the stitches can always be worked in the same way. The sequence for each stitch makes the working thread, when taut, pull the fabric threads together and create the characteristic lacy patterns.

DIAGONAL
RAISED BAND

USES: filling

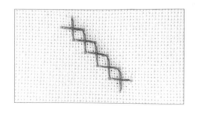

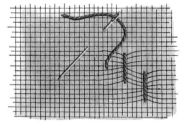

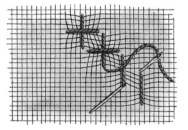

1 Work a vertical stitch down over eight threads. Start the next halfway down and four threads across from the previous one. Continue working vertical stitches in a diagonal line.

2 Turn the work and return along the same line, adding horizontal stitches across eight threads over each vertical stitch. Keep the tension taut throughout.

When the first row is complete, turn the embroidery again to work the next row. Position the first vertical stitch eight fabric threads across from the first vertical stitch on the previous row. Complete the row as before, so that eventually the ends of each cross stitch use the same holes as the neighbouring cross stitch. Although the stitch is worked over eight threads of fabric in this example, it can also be worked over four or six threads.

DIAGONAL SATIN FILLING STITCH

USES: filling

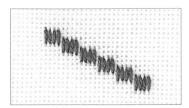

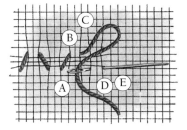

Working from left to right, make four satin stitches vertically down over four threads. Start each new unit of four across one thread and down two threads from the last unit.

HONEYCOMB STITCH

USES: filling

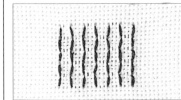

Make one vertical stitch from A to B. Bring the needle up at C three threads to the right. Make a vertical stitch down to D. Come up at E and repeat, keeping the tension taut.

FAGGOT STITCH

USES: filling

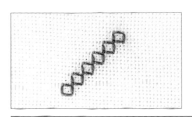

Faggot stitch is worked on a diagonal line from top right to bottom left. The stitches are always diagonal on the reverse side so that the threads of the fabric are pulled together. The stitch is worked over three threads of fabric in each direction in the following example, but could equally well be worked over four threads.

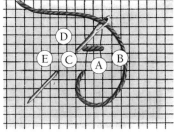

1 Work a horizontal stitch from A to B. Bring the needle up at C and make the second stitch, taking the needle down at D. Bring the needle up at E and repeat from the start.

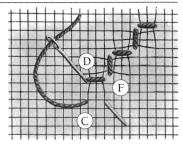

2 At the end of the row, complete stitch C to D. Then, bring the needle up at F. Work along the return row, reversing the sequence or turning the embroidery to work in the same way.

COIL FILLING STITCH

USES: filling

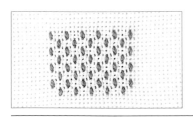

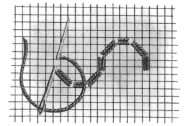

1 Work two vertical satin stitches in the same holes over two threads. Work the next pair of stitches on the same row four threads to the left. Continue to the end of the row.

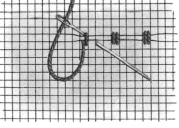

2 For the next row, bring the needle up two threads across and stitch the first pair of satin stitches. Continue, centring the pairs between those on the previous row.

Design your own

• *Choose an appropriate count of fabric for the scale of the stitches and design.*
• *Experiment with different directional filling stitches to give a sense of movement to a design.*
• *Use graph paper to plan your drawn threadwork.*

RINGED BACK STITCH

USES: filling

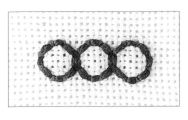

1 Work two vertical stitches over two threads then pairs of back stitch (see page 49) over two threads around the top of the first ring. Continue at the bottom of the next.

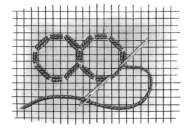

2 At the end of the row, stitch around the last ring and work back along the row completing the rings. Work the pairs of stitches where the lines cross, to give four stitches.

HEM STITCH

USES: binding edges, hems

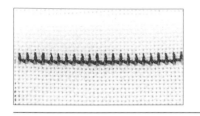

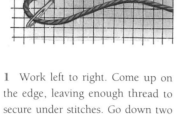

1 Work left to right. Come up on the edge, leaving enough thread to secure under stitches. Go down two fabric threads below then up on the edge two threads to the right.

2 Work clockwise around the two fabric threads to the left, keeping the tension tight and bundling them together. Repeat from the vertical stitch, working along the border.

Hem stitch is used to secure both edges of a drawn border and bundle the threads, in twos, threes or fours. These can be left plain, but can also form the basis for many interlaced and needlewoven patterns. Here, the stitch is worked on the right side of the fabric. It can also be used to secure a hem, whether with a deep drawn border or with just one thread withdrawn. Turn the hem on the back of the work and catch it in with every vertical stitch.

BUTTONHOLE STITCH

USES: edges, outlines

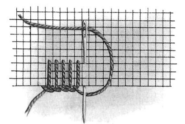

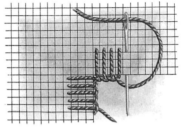

1 Secure the thread and bring it out on the edge being worked. Take the needle down through the fabric and up through the loop on the edge. Pull the needle through and repeat.

2 Turn an inside corner by working the first stitch around the corner at right angles to the previous ones. Then, pull the needle through, keeping an even tension.

Repeat the sequence of stitches close together along the edge, always making sure that they are exactly the same length and also evenly spaced.

Buttonhole stitch is popular for finishing an edge of fabric, in both counted and non-counted techniques, because it is extremely hard wearing. When buttonhole stitch is worked with wider spacing between stitches, it is known as blanket stitch.

SIMPLE INTERLACED BORDER
OTHER NAME:twisted border

USES: border

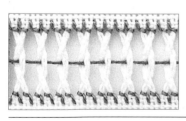

Before the interlacing process can actually start, you must secure the working thread under the stitches of the buttonhole or needlewoven bar at the right hand end of the border. Once this has been done, bring the working thread out halfway up the edge or bar. you can now proceed on to the interlacing.

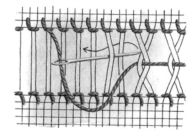

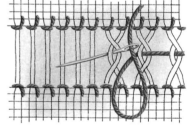

1 Working from right to left, take the working thread over the first two bundles of fabric threads. Take the needle back underneath the second bundle and over the first.

2 With the needle still between the bundles, rotate it anti-clockwise so the point faces left and the bundles twist. Pull the needle through and repeat, keeping an even tension.

SIMPLE KNOTTED BORDER

USES: border

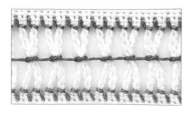

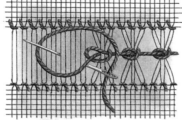

Bring the working thread out halfway up the edge or bar. Take the needle behind the first three bundles. Wrap the thread anti-clockwise around the point of the needle. Draw the needle

through the loop, pulling the bundles together and the knot tight. Repeat, knotting three bundles together each time to the end of the border and keeping an even tension.

This simple knotted border is most effective when worked over three or four bundles of fabric threads. Several variations are possible. For example, two rows of knots can be worked in a deep border in order to create a pattern of diamond shapes. The rows must

be equally spaced, one above the other. On the bottom row, make knots around four bundles of threads. On the top row, start by making a knot around the first two bundles from the bottom row. Then, continue to knot around four bundles along the border, splitting the bundles up from the row below. Finish with the last knot around two bundles. This principle can also be used to vary the simple interlaced border.

OVERCAST BARS

USES: border, bars

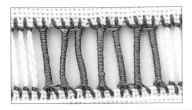

Needleweaving is an alternative to interlacing for decorating drawn borders. The simplest method is to overcast groups of two, three or four of the hem-stitched bundles to make vertical bars. Overcast bars are also very useful in Hardanger (see pages 112–115). Overcasting can be worked on plain weave fabrics as well, piercing the fabric to bind a cut edge such as around an eyelet in cutwork (see page 130) or Ayrshire embroidery (see page 145).

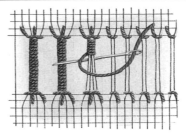

1 Wrap the thread closely in a single layer around four fabric threads, keeping it taut. Take it across the back to start the next group and wrap in the opposite direction.

Instead of working single vertical bars, try the following simple variation. Overcast one bar, but just before you reach the edge of the border, overcast twice as many threads of fabric. Then, work back across the border, reverting to half as many threads to create the second bar. Repeat, joining the bars at the top and bottom of the border to create a V-shaped pattern.

DARNED BARS
OTHER NAME: needleweaving

USES: border, bars

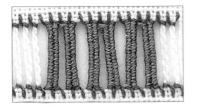

Darned bars involve weaving the needle under and over two bundles of threads in order to create a basketweave effect. They are very effective in Hardanger and cutwork, as well as drawn threadwork. They can also be embellished with picots (see pages 114–115 and 130).

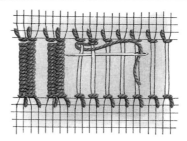

1 Go behind two bundles of threads, then in front of the two bundles to the left. Return the needle behind the left bundles and in front of the ones on the right. Weave to the bottom.

Darned bars can also be worked in many different variations and also in combination with overcast bars. Try overcasting one bundle of threads to halfway across the border from the top to the bottom. Then, pick up the next bundle and work a darned bar across them both for the rest of the distance. Finally, thread the needle discreetly along the darned bar and overcast the remaining unworked bundle of fabric threads.

SPIDER'S WEB

USES: filling

Needlewoven fillings like spider's web can be used to embellish the open squares that are formed where two lines of withdrawn threads meet, typically in drawn threadwork and Hardanger (see pages 112–115 for similar fillings). The squares must be bounded by overcast, needlewoven or buttonholed bars on all sides and these bars provide the anchor for the filling stitch. They can also be used in non-counted techniques such as Ayrshire and cutwork.

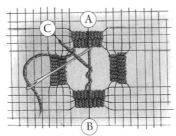

1 Secure the working thread and come up at A in the middle of the top bar. Go down at B and wind the thread around the spoke to the centre. Go down at C and repeat.

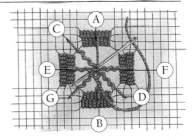

2 Follow the sequence, winding back to the centre on B to G. Then, cross the centre to the back, pull the spokes together with a looped knot and come out between E and G.

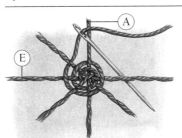

3 Weave the thread over spoke E then under and over each alternate spoke in a clockwise direction. When the web is the desired size, finish weaving after spoke A.

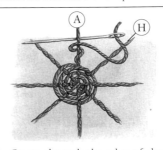

4 Go up through the edge of the web and take the last spoke out to H. Wind the working thread back to the web. Take the needle behind the web and up to wind the thread out to A.

This method shows the spider's web wound around six spokes before the last one is made and the first is wound to finish the unit. A simpler web can be made on four spokes crossed diagonally. Take the working thread right across one diagonal and wind back to the centre. Take the thread out to the third spoke, wind back and then repeat for the fourth spoke. Weave the spider's web. Finally, wind the thread along the first spoke.

Flower cushion

This lovely cushion design combines the fresh appeal of creamy, daisy-like flowers and the subtle, subdued colours of the leaves and background. The stitches pull the fabric into exquisite detail, providing different textures, which enliven the design and give it a three-dimensional quality, and are enhanced by the stem stitch outlining each flower. Design by Tracy A. Franklin

1 Trace the design overleaf, including the centre lines, onto tissue paper. Find the centre lines of the linen fabric. Pin the paper on the fabric, matching up the centre lines. Tack the paper in position along the centre lines and remove the pins.

2 Starting from the centre, tack around all the shapes using the sewing thread and securing it well. Remove the tacking threads along the centre lines. Tear the tissue paper away from the fabric, leaving just the tacked outline. Stretch the fabric onto an embroidery frame.

3 You will need a tapestry needle and two strands of stranded cotton for all the pulled fabric stitches. Stitch the flowers starting with the first one on the top right of the design, complete most of the leaves for that flower and then proceed to the flowers according to the numbers on the diagram.

4 Stitch the centre of each flower first. Each centre is worked in one of three different stitches in stranded cottons 3033 and 3782, and two centres are left unstitched.

5 Stitch the petals, starting with the one that most overlaps the others and finishing with the one most underneath. All the petals are worked in one of four different stitches in stranded cottons 3033 and 3782, with some areas of the petals left unstitched. Finish the final stitch on each row that touches the blank area, giving an uneven and softer edge.

6 Stitch the leaves for each flower before you proceed to the next flower. They are all worked in four-sided stitch over two threads of fabric in stranded cotton 832.

7 When all the flowers and their main leaves are complete, finish the rest. The very dark leaves are worked in four-sided stitch over two threads of fabric in stranded cotton 830. Work the rest of the background in chained border stitch over four threads of fabric in stranded cotton 3802.

8 Remove all the tacking stitches. Finish the design by working the stem stitch outlines (see page 206) around all the flower centres, using four strands of embroidery thread.

9 Take the embroidery out of the hoop and press. Lay the work face up on the backing cloth and, working from the centre outwards, tack the two layers together. When they are perfectly flat, tack around the edges of the embroidery through the two layers. Trim the edges to 1cm (½in).

Design area

21.5cm (8½in) square

Materials

50cm (20in) square
    25-count antique white
    evenweave linen

Embroidery threads
    (see diagram key)

50cm (½yd) square
    beige fabric

50cm (20in) square cream
    backing cloth

38cm (15in) square
    cushion pad

Equipment

Tissue paper and hard pencil

Pins

Pale sewing thread

Embroidery frame

Embroidery scissors

Size 24 tapestry needle

Needle and matching
    thread for making up

10 To make the cushion cover, cut four strips of the beige fabric each measuring 8.5cm (3½in) wide and 40cm (16in) long. With right sides together and matching the edges, pin one strip to the work along the tacking line. Then, sew along the line to make a 1cm (½in) seam, starting and finishing 1cm (½in) in from the edges of the embroidered fabric. Attach the remaining three borders in the same way, making sure that the seams meet perfectly in the corners. Oversew the edges to bind together and press the borders open.

11 Place the bordered embroidery face down on a flat surface. Arrange the borders so they lay one over the other at each corner. Draw a line from where the seams meet to where the outer edges of the borders meet on each corner. Then, re-arrange the top borders, laying them underneath their partners. Draw a second line on each corner in the same way.

Mark a diagonal line at 45 degrees from the corner of the inner seam across each border.

12 Pick the fabric up and then mitre one corner, with the right sides together, matching the pencil lines. Next, pin in position and carefully stitch the seam, starting right at the corner of the seam around the embroidery. Repeat the mitring process on the other four corners. Then, proceed on to trimming the mitred seams. Oversew the edges and finally press the seams open.

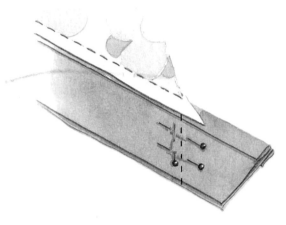

Pin the borders together, making sure that you match the diagonal lines.

13 You are now ready to complete the cushion cover in your preferred style. Detailed instructions on how to make a simple, envelope, button-fastened and zipped cover are to be found on pages 32–33. This particular design has been planned to allow for borders that are 6.5cm (2½in) wide with a 1cm (½in) seam, giving a 34.5cm (13⅜in) square cushion cover. Finally, insert the slightly larger cushion pad into the cover.

FLOWER CUSHION KEY

DMC stranded cotton

A	*Four-sided stitch in 830 over 2 fabric threads*
B	*Four-sided stitch in 832 over 2 fabric threads*
C	*Chained border stitch in 3802*
D	*Faggot stitch in 3782 over 3 fabric threads*
E	*Faggot stitch in 3782 over 5 fabric threads*
F	*Diagonal satin stitch in 3782 over 4 fabric threads*
G	*Diagonal satin stitch in 3782 over 6 fabric threads*
H	*Diagonal raised band in 3033*
I	*Honeycomb stitch in 3033 over 3 fabric threads*
J	*Honeycomb stitch in 3033 over 5 fabric threads*

K	*Unstitched fabric*
——	*Stem stitch in 3782*
≈≈≈	*Stem stitch in 3033*
– – –	*Broken fill pattern*

Note: You will need 2 skeins of 3033 and 3782 and 1 skein of 830 and 832.

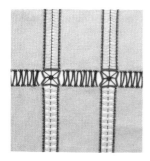

Table runner

The drawn thread design on this table runner is really stunning and the patience needed to plan and count it out accurately will be well rewarded. It is designed to fit a dining table for six, but can be reduced or extended to fit different-sized tables by simply cutting out or adding parts of the design. The colours of the fabric and threads used are warm and earthy, but can also be changed to complement any interior. Design by Tracy A. Franklin

Materials

2.5 x 1.5m (2¾ x 1⅔yd) 19-count bone-coloured evenweave fabric

Embroidery threads (see diagram key)

Equipment

Pins

Contrasting sewing thread

Size 22 tapestry needle

Embroidery hoop

Size 22 chenille needle

Size 7 embroidery needle

Very sharp embroidery scissors

1 Take time to study the diagram on pages 106–107. It shows one quarter of the design, so it must be flipped over along the horizontal and the vertical fold lines to repeat the design and create the whole table runner.

2 Following the diagram and key, sew a row of tacking stitches all along one long side of the fabric to establish the edge of the finished cloth. Leave a generous allowance for the hem and for binding the edges later. Now repeat, to establish the base line of the short right-hand edge.

3 Start to count and tack out the design from this first corner. Count each group of threads out twice and mark with a pin before you tack and then count them again. It is easy to miscount and time spent in checking now will avoid cutting holes in the wrong place later. Count eight threads for the face of the hem and the thread to be withdrawn and sew a row of tacking stitches along each line for the long and the short edge.

4 Establish the outer drawn thread border on this corner. Start by counting out a band of 18 threads along each of the two sides and tack this side of the border out. Count out the 20 threads for the other side of the border and tack that in place.

5 The next pair of borders on this corner are some distance away and the counting starts in earnest. Note the gap between the outer border and the next one along the long side of the fabric is 92 threads wide, but the corresponding one on the short side is 52 threads wide. Mark every tenth thread with a pin as you are counting, until you are sure have counted correctly. Then tack out the outer edges of these borders and remove the pins. Count out 20 threads for the width of the borders and tack out the inner edges of them.

6 Now progress along the length of the long side of the fabric. The next border is 352 threads further on and needs counting out with the utmost

care. Use pins to help you as before and tack out the next border when you are confident it is in the correct place on the fabric.

7 Continue to count the gaps and the next two borders as shown on the diagram. Now continue to map out the design for the rest of the long side by working back across the diagram in the opposite direction. Note that the gap between the middle two borders is 124 threads wide in total.

8 Now you have established the total length of the table runner, so make an allowance for the hem and for binding the side edge later.

9 You now need to map out the other side of the design to complete the symmetrical pattern. From the inner border already tacked out on the long side of the fabric count 26 threads across the short side to find the centre point. Continue counting another 26 threads to establish the next inner border.

10 Tack out this border and then the final one in the same way as before along the whole length of the fabric. Complete the counting to tack out the final 18 threads along the edge and the eight threads for the hem.

11 Check all your tacking lines and make sure that the whole design fits together correctly. Trim the excess fabric off the inner long edge to make it more manageable, but leaving a generous allowance for the hem and binding. Bind all the raw edges of the fabric to stop them fraying while you are stitching.

12 Now withdraw the threads along the length of each border and along the hem line. Cut the threads in the middle of the borders and withdraw them one at a time. Cut them again at the ends of the borders, allowing enough to re-weave them into the fabric using the embroidery needle.

13 Hem stitch along the edges of all the borders, using the tapestry needle. Start and finish the stitching four threads of fabric in from the totally withdrawn squares and bundle the threads into pairs. The borders along the length of the runner are worked in coton perlé 221 and those across the width are worked in coton perlé 434.

14 Put the fabric into the embroidery hoop to proceed with the rest of the stitching. Start with the buttonhole across the ends of each border, which is worked over three threads in coton perlé 3041 with the chenille needle.

15 Work the remaining sides of the withdrawn squares by needleweaving over the four unstitched threads of fabric, using coton perlé 3041 and the chenille needle. This will strengthen the edges of the square and provide a firm foundation for the spider's web later.

16 Now, work the stitches to decorate the borders, using the embroidery needle to pass the coton perlé through the woven bars to start and finish, but using the chenille needle to work the stitches. A simple knotted border is worked over two bundles and a simple interlaced border is worked over four bundles of threads along the long borders in coton perlé 420 and 333. Overcast bars are worked over two bundles of fabric threads across the short borders, using coton perlé 327.

17 Finally work the spider's webs with the chenille needle in coton perlé 333 and 420, alternating the colours across the table runner.

18 Once all the decorative stitching is complete, remove the embroidery hoop. Turn and pin the hem into place, mitre the corners and hem stitch. Press the table runner with an iron at the appropriate setting.

TABLE RUNNER KEY

DMC coton perlé no. 5

① ————— Hem stitch in 3041

② ————— Hem stitch in 434

③ ————— Hem stitch in 221

④ Spider's web in 333

⑤ Spider's web in 420

————— Overcast bar in 327

•••••• Simple knotted border in 420

————— Needleweaving in 3041

– – Simple interlaced border in 333

▬ Buttonhole stitch in 3041

Note: You will need 5 skeins of each shade.

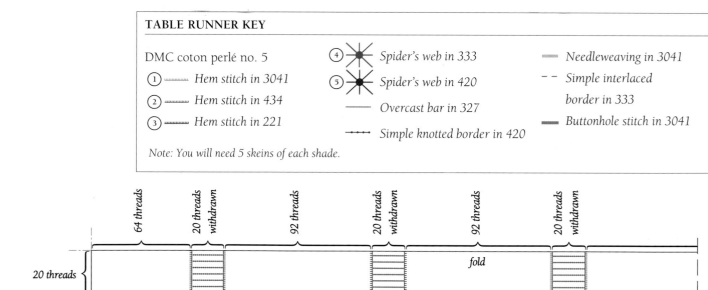

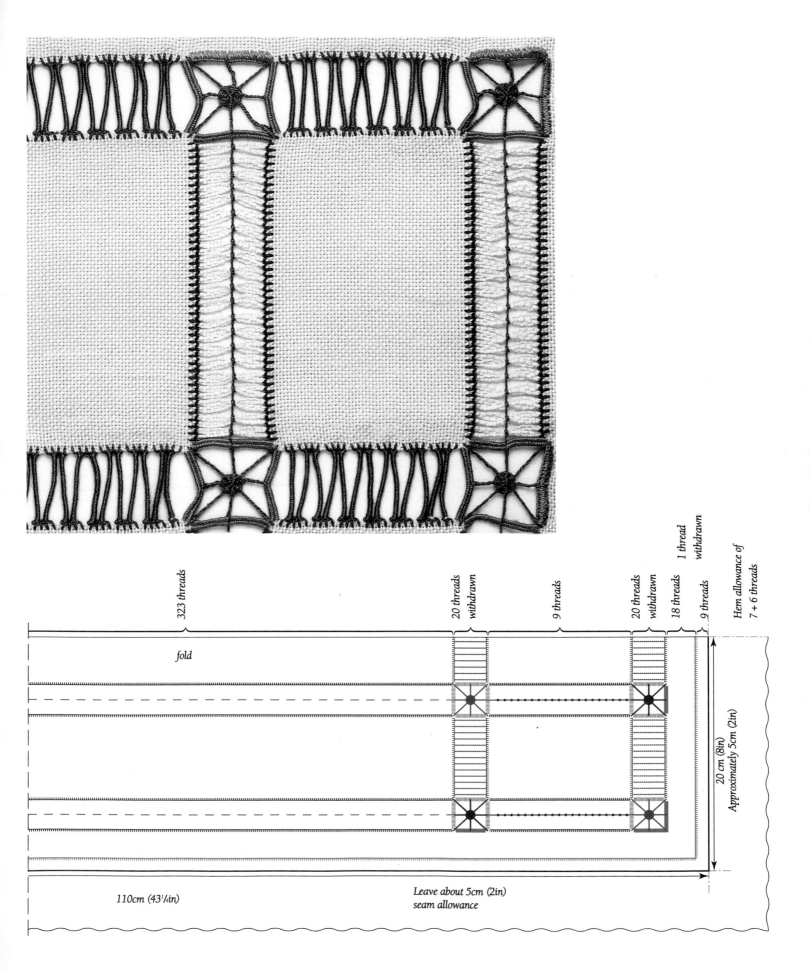

323 threads

fold

20 threads withdrawn

9 threads

20 threads withdrawn

18 threads

9 threads

1 thread withdrawn

Hem allowance of 7 + 6 threads

20 cm (8in)
Approximately 5cm (2in)

110cm (43¼in)

Leave about 5cm (2in) seam allowance

Hardanger

Since Viking times, Norwegians have been great travellers and in this way Norwegian embroidery, like all folk art, shows influences of the art and style of other countries and follows a process of evolution corresponding to the development of European design. Folk embroideries are characterized by a particular combination of stitch, pattern and colour repeated through succeeding generations. They become incorporated into national dress which, in turn, has an impact on the form of the embroidery. Above all, new patterns from external sources are adapted to the local materials and colour combinations, giving the embroidery its distinctive national character.

In different parts of Norway there are different embroidery traditions. East and west Telemark are noted for their colourful embroidery in wool, while in southern Norway and in the districts of Gudbrandstalen, Sunnmøre and Trøndelag distinctive, 'rosesaum' (rose embroidery) was popular. However, on the west coast in the Hardanger region, whitework embroidery on linen was most popular.

Earliest traditions

It is unlikely that Hardanger is of Nordic origin. From surviving 17th-century altar cloths with exquisite cutwork, the influence of Italian reticella embroidery is clear, therefore it seems likely that designs spread north from Europe through examples of work and German and Italian pattern books. Few early embroideries can be accurately dated and little survives before the 16th and 17th centuries. However, from extant examples it is evident that the finest folk embroidery appears to have been worked between the mid-18th and mid-19th centuries.

The various rural communities in Norway were entirely self-supporting: the women grew their own flax, sheared their own sheep for their wool and collected their own vegetables and herbs for dyeing. They converted these raw textile materials, spinning the thread, dyeing the yarn and weaving the material to suit the purpose for which it was intended. This understanding of materials was the foundation on which their embroidery tradition was built. Decorated textiles were an important part of local life and festivities. Young girls were expected to make and embroider their own and their bridegroom's wedding shirts. As part of their dowry they would provide embroidered household linen of sheets, pillow cases, tablecloths and towels as well as their own shirts, smocks, aprons,

Left: Table runner, Hardanger, Norway, 20th century. The border is in traditional design with an edging of a double row of buttonholed scalloped picots.

handkerchiefs, shawls and linen caps. Later, they would embroider for their husbands and children, although it is known from documented pieces that some women also sold their embroidery to supplement the family income. In some districts, there were other rituals involving embroideries, for example the bride gave gifts of embroideries to her mother-in-law and, at christenings, godmothers to godchildren. These occasions also called for specially embroidered clothes.

Hardanger was worked on linen, home-woven with a characteristic double thread in both the warp and weft, and the embroidery was worked with a thick home-spun flax yarn. Bold patterns of

Opposite page: Traditional Norwegian costume from Voss in the Hardanger region. The inherited bib insert has similar patterns to those on traditional Hardanger embroidery, but is worked in bugle and seed beads. The blouse is embroidered in cross stitch with black thread. This folk costume is worn with a white apron with a wide band of Hardanger embroidery on the bottom.

Right: Table runner, by Else Paulsson, Oslo, 1939. Dark brown, mixed grey and brown woollen threads and white mercerized cotton threads are worked on an orange-red linen fabric. The stitches used are buttonhole, chain, couched filling, cross, Romanian and stem stitches with French knots. The band uses symmetrical conventional motifs (birds on flowering branches) on either side.

Below: Tablecloth, Hardanger, Norway, 1934. The linen fabric is worked with a white linen thread in eyelet, double faggot, four-sided satin and drawn thread stitches and cutwork. The geometric border is comprised of squares, lozenges and triangles.

lozenges, triangles, cross and ladder formations are characteristic of this work. Cutwork, drawn threadwork and various kinds of hem stitch alternate with satin stitches, the latter often forming eight-petal roses and triangular figures, with faggot stitch used to divide the patterns. In old examples, a combination of satin stitch and eye stitch is found. Today, Hardanger work is characterized by the geometric open work designs stitched on evenweave fabric using cotton or linen threads. It is traditionally used in bands to decorate long aprons, head-dresses, the front panel covering the buttons of blouses, cuffs and collars, worn with red waistcoats and gathered black skirts. Some of the bib inserts, which slip under the waistcoats, have patterns similar to those in Hardanger whitework embroidery, but are worked in beads, stones and pieces of metal. Being both hard wearing and decorative, Hardanger embroidery continues to be used on household linen.

Whitework was also done in other western areas of Norway and in Trøndelag. For example, in Nordmøre geometric cut and drawn work is also used, but combined with patterns of stems, flowers and leaves known as 'labsom'. However, Hardanger embroidery remains the most popular and best known, although in the mid-19th century, its survival was threatened

by industrialization and the introduction of cheap but inferior machine-made fabrics and industrially produced aniline dyed threads. This coincided with the decline in daily use of traditional folk dress.

Revival of interest

The romantic revival of interest in rural life by artists throughout Europe during the 1870s and 1880s brought about a recognition of the importance of traditional crafts to national identity and led to a revival of interest in traditional textile arts. Inspired by William Morris and the Arts and Crafts Movement, various home craft organizations were set up in Norway, Sweden and Denmark in an effort to halt the decline. This led to a revival of interest in Hardanger work and, by the 1930s, more people were producing hand-embroidered items for the growing tourist industry. An increased interest in modern design by architects in Scandinavia, including Finland, led to the introduction of more original embroidery design, much of it based on traditional folk art. The idea, particularly in Sweden, was to design articles that were suited to their own time but also rooted in old traditions.

Similar moves to encourage greater interest in embroidery and raise the standard of design began in Scotland in 1934. Funded by J&P Coats, in collaboration with the four art schools, the Needlework Development Scheme (NDS) was

Above: Cushion cover with Hardanger embroidery. From a 1950s magazine on Hardanger, published by Coats Sewing Group.

Left: Early 20th-century Hardanger apron band insert, showing a traditional diamond design with an unusually wide variety of decorative fillings. It has a needlewoven drawn thread border.

established. A collection of foreign and British embroidery was made for circulation to domestic science and training colleges, women's institutes and schools, as well as art schools. During the 1950s, access was extended to organizations in the rest of Britain, with additional touring exhibitions and regular freely available leaflets. By 1961, the NDS collection consisted of over 3,500 embroideries by which time it was recognized that the Scheme had achieved its fundamental aims and the collection was dispersed to various colleges, museums and organizations.

Beautifully designed examples of modern European and Scandinavian work had a profound impact on the NDS collection and reflected an interest extended to all areas of Scandinavian decorative arts during the 1950s. Throughout the decade, pulled work was very popular and the preponderance of birds in embroidery design indicates this strong Scandinavian influence. Several pieces of Norwegian embroidery were purchased for the NDS collection, including a traditional Hardanger tablecloth in 1934, which reflects the renewed interest in whitework of all types, but especially Hardanger. Many leaflets were published by commercial firms with photographs of contemporary Hardanger pieces that were given names such as 'Viking', 'Stavanger' and 'Fiord', together with instructions for the designs. But

embroiderers were also encouraged to extend their efforts beyond technical knowledge of stitch, to be more adventurous by exploring the technique to discover its potential and limitations and to create their own designs as a means of personal expression.

The relative simplicity of the Kloster block and other elements of the design of traditional patterns is deceptive and belies the fundamental control and understanding of the basic technique. Hardanger still thrives, not only in Norway, but also especially in northern Europe and America, where modern interpretations retain the character of traditional designs, but often use shaded threads and the addition of beads to good effect.

Due to the surge of interest in traditional dress during the past ten years, Hardanger embroidery has flourished in Norway too. On Constitution Day, many people express their national pride by wearing traditional costume and today there is a thriving industry in making and embroidering 'bunad', the revived folk dress. Hardanger embroidery on collar, cuffs, blouse panel and apron is now often made as a matching set, whereas in the past there was more spontaneity with combinations of different patterns and treasured family heirlooms combined with new pieces. That the craft survives in such a healthy state is to the credit of those women who expressed their creativity through embroidery and kept their skills alive, passing them on to succeeding generations.

Hardanger stitches and techniques

Hardanger is a structured geometric technique with very specific disciplines that give the embroidery a serene and understated beauty. It is not difficult to master if you can count accurately, and taking pride in high standards of workmanship will produce crisp results. Choose to work in colour if you like, but with discretion, as the true nature of Hardanger comes through a restrained colour scheme.

Design your own

- *Try adding beads or space-dyed threads to break up your design and add interest.*
- *Use picots with the filling stitches to soften the framework of the grid.*
- *Try eyelets and a variety of pulled thread stitches to lighten and contrast with the motifs and filled-in areas.*
- *Use perlé 5 or 8 for 24-count fabrics or less; perlé 5, 8 or 12 for 25- and 26-count; and perlé 8 or 12 for 27- to 32-count.*

Fabrics

Hardanger embroidery is worked on evenweave fabrics in order for the finished design to be square and the threads to be cut and withdrawn easily, all an integral part of this technique. With such a wide variety of suitable fabrics now available, you can use any good-quality fabric that enables you to count the threads properly, including Hardanger fabric or mono canvas. Make sure you use a magnifying glass with a finer fabric if you feel it is required. Linen and a cotton/rayon mix (Lugana) were used for the projects in this chapter, but both designs may be adapted to other fabrics and counts.

Needles

Use blunt-ended tapestry needles in sizes that suit the thickness of the thread and do not split the threads or enlarge the holes of the background fabric. Sizes 22, 24 or 26 are most appropriate.

Threads

Cotton or linen threads are recommended. Two different weights of thread are used, depending on the count of the fabric. You will need a thicker thread for the Kloster blocks (which outline the design), all surface motifs and certain edgings so the stitches merge together. Needleweaving, filling stitches, pulled thread stitches and other edgings will require a finer thread to emphasize the delicate effects.

If using colours, make sure they either match or contrast with your background fabric. Remember the importance of showing off the delicate filling patterns and try not to let the colours overshadow and distract from the technique.

Available in an array of colours, metallic threads will add sparkle to your work. Choose a thread that is flexible and not so bulky it distorts the stitching. Use a slightly shorter thread to prevent 'shredding'. To create a discreet glistening effect and 'lift' the design, use a blending filament, which is very fine and has to be combined with an embroidery thread.

Additional tools

Use a sharp pair of embroidery scissors that cut right to the point for cutting the threads, to ensure that they are trimmed close to the Kloster blocks.

A stiletto is useful for separating threads, producing uniform eyelet shapes or simply for counting stitches or threads.

Using an embroidery hoop is not essential in Hardanger. However, if you prefer to work on a frame, only use it for stitching the Kloster blocks. You will need to control the work in your hands for the filling stitches and pulled thread techniques.

Hardanger techniques

It easier to understand Hardanger if you work methodically. First, Kloster blocks outline the design, binding and strengthening the edges of the open spaces, created by cutting and withdrawing threads. To finish, decorative fillings are worked on and around the remaining grids.

Planning out the design

Prepare the fabric (see page 28). It is helpful to tack in the centre lines in both directions in one colour and any other guidelines in another colour. Work bands of guideline tacking in multiples of four to correspond with the threads in the Kloster blocks. For large designs, tack in a grid of squares over the design area of the fabric to check the Kloster blocks are lined up in every direction. You will then easily find any miscounts. Make sure the Kloster blocks meet up in sequence all over the design. Any miscounts must be rectified at this stage, before any threads are cut and withdrawn.

Beginning to stitch

Start with the outline of the Kloster blocks, following a chart. Otherwise, start as near to the centre as you can and develop the design from there. The outlines can be at an angle, on a straight line or around a square. Complete any additional blocks, forming further detail to the design.

Start the stitching with a waste knot (see page 28). Then, finish off sewing the Kloster blocks by taking the thread to the back of the work and through the channels formed by the straight stitches. Take the thread through the first block and, in the second block, take a back stitch over the middle thread. Hold the stitch and give the thread a little pull to tighten the stitch. Repeat in the next block, run through one more block then cut off the thread.

Once all the blocks have been completed, stitch all the other surface shapes, lines or motifs.

Cutting threads

Now cut and withdraw threads in the designated areas of the design. Cut four threads against each block, unless the dimensions of the blocks have been changed. Always cut against the side of the blocks, never at the top or bottom 'open' end. Position the scissors to the left of the block, insert the tips into the fabric and pick up four threads onto the blade. Double check the number of threads you are about to cut. Cut them all together, as it is easy to cut an extra thread in error. Cut the threads on one side of the design, then turn the work to repeat on the other sides.

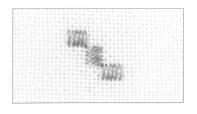

Cut four threads at a time.

Using the point of a needle or a pair of tweezers, ease out the threads one at a time so the grid does not distort.

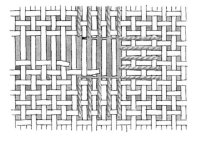

Withdraw the threads very carefully so the grid does not distort.

Making the bars

Now bind the remaining threads forming the grid. They can be overcast, woven using needle-weaving (see page 99) or buttonholed (see page 129). You can embellish the bars with knots or picots (see pages 114–115)

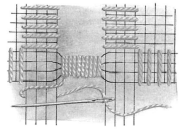

Moving from one overcast bar to the next.

Working filling stitches

Decorative or lacy filling stitches can also be used in order to enhance the grid. Filling stitches should always be worked in

sequence, either in conjunction with the sewing of the stitched bars or after all the bars have been completed.

You will find the stitches below and on the following two pages useful for a large number of Hardanger embroidery designs as well as the projects featured in this book. Note that the spider's web is another filling stitch (see page 99) that works well with Hardanger.

KLOSTER BLOCKS

USES: outline

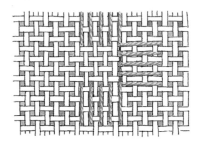

Kloster blocks form the outline of a design. They can be worked in straight rows or at right angles to each other along diagonal lines. Traditionally, each block has five stitches over four threads of the fabric, always stitched in thicker thread. Stitch through the holes of the fabric and do not split the fabric threads. Start and finish at one end of a block. The stitches should sit comfortably on the surface of the fabric. Check the blocks align with each other.

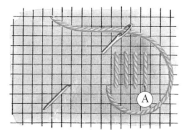

1 Come up at A. Make a vertical stitch over four threads. Make four more stitches, each one thread to the left. Move to the next block in a straight row, starting four threads to the left.

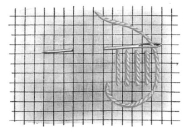

2 To work blocks diagonally, come up for the second block four threads to the left of the top of the first block. Stitch the block at right angles to the first. Continue alternating the blocks.

EIGHT-POINTED STAR

USES: single motif

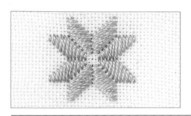

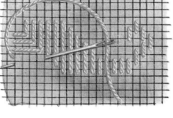

Start at A and work straight stitches to make one star petal. Finish at V and start the next mirror-imaged petal at W. Four or eight petals are worked to give a half or full star.

SHIP MOTIF

USES: single motif

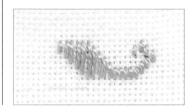

Work in the same sequence as the star, adding the curve to make a ship motif. Thread the needle through the back of the motif to stitch the second of a pair as a mirror image.

REVERSED DIAGONAL FAGGOTING

USES: outline, filling

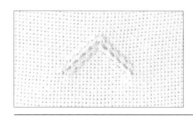

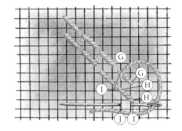

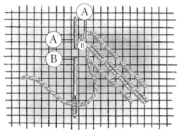

1 Bring the needle up at A and make a stitch diagonally down over two threads to A'. Come up at B and down at B'. Repeat, starting the next stitch at C, to the end of the line.

2 For a mitred end to the line, make the first stitch for the return journey from I to I', in the same holes as the previous stitch. Make the second stitch, coming up at J.

3 To turn a mitred corner, work the first stitch in the new line from A to A'. Start in the same hole as the first stitch on the previous row. The second stitch goes from B to B'. Follow the sequence.

SQUARED EYELETS

USES: single motif

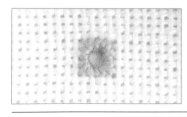

Take the needle up at A and down in the centre. Work each stitch over two threads around the square, going down in the centre and pulling the thread slightly to form a hole.

PICOT KNOT ON WOVEN BAR

USES: filling

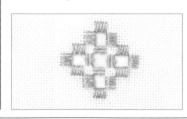

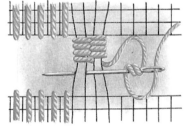

Needleweave to the centre of the bar. Wrap the thread, clockwise, twice around the needle. Take the needle down in the middle of the bar and complete the needleweaving.

SQUARE FILET

USES: filling

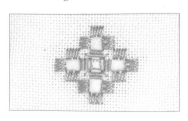

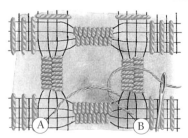

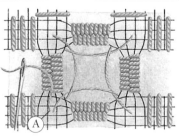

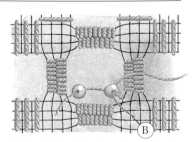

1 Work the bars first. Start the filling, coming up at A. Take it behind the fabric, up at B and under the loop formed. Repeat and adjust the loop to fit into the square as you proceed..

2 Repeat around the square. Bring the needle from the fourth corner over the first loop, under the fabric and out at A. Work a back stitch over a thread to stabilize the filling.

3 To add beads, thread two on the first loop. Come up at B and go through the second bead. Thread a third bead. Repeat. Finally, go through the first bead to complete.

DOVE'S EYE FILLING

USES: single motif, filling

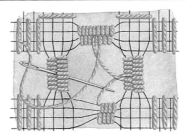

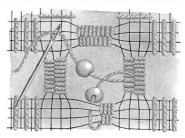

1 Bring the needle up from the middle of the fourth, unfinished, bar. Take it down into the bar to the right and over the first loop. Adjust the loop so it curves attractively.

2 Repeat around the square. Bring the needle from the last bar over the previous loop as before, but under the first loop. Go down in the middle of the bar and finish the weaving.

3 To incorporate beads, thread one on the first loop. Come out of the second bar and over the first loop, then thread the next bead. Repeat to add one bead to each separate loop.

GREEK CROSS SINGLE MOTIF

USES: single motif, filling

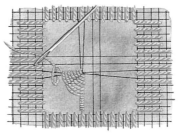

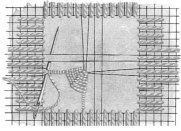

1 Wrap two threads in the first bar into the centre. Go under the first two threads to the left and come up. Pull the thread to the centre and start to weave the two bars together.

2 Weave a figure-of-eight pattern, loosening the tension as you work outwards to make a fan shape that fills half the shape. Wrap the threads on the second bar back to the edge.

3 Go under all four threads on the left and wrap the top two to the centre as from the start. Repeat to complete the cross. Wrap the ends of the last and first bar together.

GREEK CROSS DIAGONAL FILLING

USES: filling

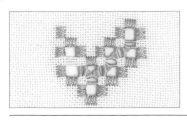

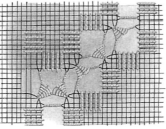

1 To work a diagonal line, make the fan-shaped units in one direction first. At a corner, work a fan, then weave a second, incorporating the wrapped bar between them to make a pair.

2 Turn the work to complete the opposite side, making a series of fan-shaped units on the unworked threads of fabric.

In wider open areas, the opposite half of the cross may be worked to form a whole cross. It is still necessary to stitch the opposite row on the diagonal as before, rather than form each unit individually.s

DIAGONAL TWISTED BARS AND PICOT KNOT FILLING STITCH

USES: single motif, filling

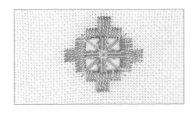

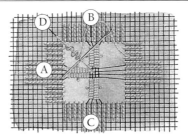

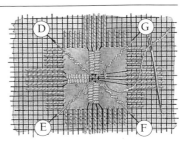

This simple combination filling stitch is the basis for a large number of complicated patterns traditionally found in Hardanger. It is worked to form a motif within a square bound by 13 satin stitches on each side – four stitches over four threads, on each side of five stitches over eight threads. Only the threads of the fabric bound by the short stitches are cut, leaving four fabric threads from each block of long stitches to form an upright cross formation.

1 Weave bar A, adding picots, from the edge, and bar B from the centre. Thread at the back to return. Repeat on bar C. Take a spoke from centre to D. Wind around it to return to centre.

2 Take spokes out to the remaining three corners in the sequence shown, winding the thread back along each one in turn. Come up in the centre and weave the final bar with its picots.

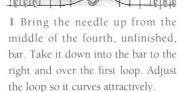

Duvet band

Give your duvet cover a makeover by trimming it with this embroidered band. Inspired by the fascinating patterns of ancient mosaics, three diagonal lines of Kloster blocks enclosing eyelets form a zigzag, alternating with open needleweaving. This minimalist design will be shown at its best placed on a crisp white or a contemporary colour. It may be adapted to fit any size of bed linen or pillow cases. Design by Jill Carter

Design area

136cm (54in) plus
10cm (4in) seam
allowance

Materials

160 x 5cm (64 x 2in)
28-count linen band

Embroidery threads
(see chart key)

Single duvet cover
136cm (54in) wide

Equipment

Pastel sewing thread

Size 24 tapestry needle

Embroidery scissors

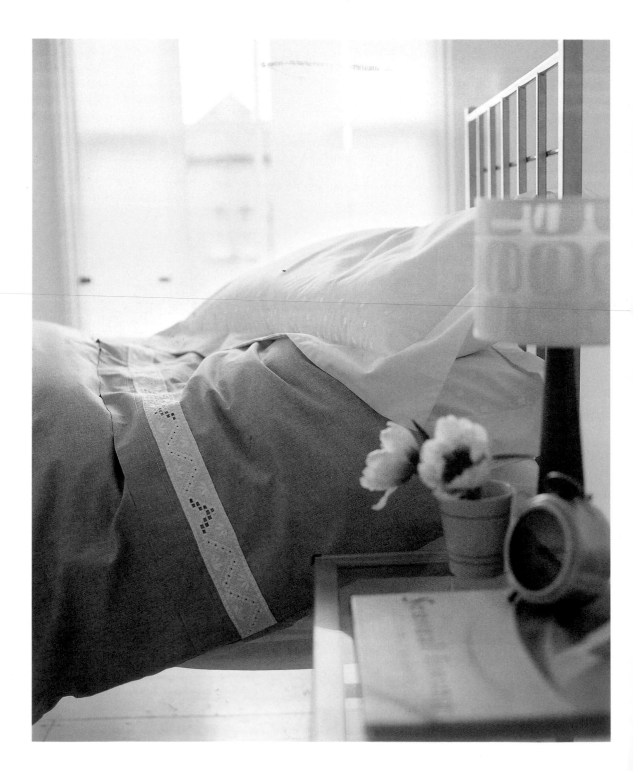

1 Prepare the linen band by tacking the horizontal and vertical centre lines using a pastel-coloured thread (see page 28).

2 Start stitching using the coton perlé no.8. Following the chart, start in the middle of the band. Position the first stitch of the Kloster block two threads to the right of the centre point and two threads down at A, astride the lengthways centre line. Work to the left, methodically building up the Kloster block design. Use one thread for one side of the design and another thread for the other side, which starts at B, located 16 threads below A. Work these lines in conjunction with one another so you can check the accuracy of your counting as you proceed.

3 Once you have established the first V shape, run a tacking line from the top and bottom Kloster blocks along the length of the band. This will serve as a further check to ensure your blocks are all in line lengthways. Complete all the Kloster blocks. Satin stitch (see page 78) the stars in coton perlé no. 8 and then change your thread to coton perlé no. 12 in order to work both the eyelets and the reversed diagonal faggot stitches.

4 Turn the band and work to the right from the centre in the same way and to the same length.

5 Cut and withdraw the threads from the single V shapes, ready for simple needleweaving. With coton perlé no. 12, needleweave the grid starting at C. You will have to turn the work so that the point of the V shape is to the left. If you are feeling adventurous, work some knots or picots on the bars for further embellishment or you can work them on alternate Vs. Complete the needleweaving.

6 Finish off the work with a border of Kloster blocks worked four threads away from the top and bottom Kloster blocks and using coton perlé no. 8 (not on the chart). Once the stitching is completed, wash and iron the band. Appliqué your finished band onto the duvet cover either by machine or with a hand slip stitch (see page 33).

If you prefer to use a band with a larger count, check that it is wide enough to take the design. You will need at least 44 threads in the width as the design uses 36 threads. When changing the dimensions of the design to suit a larger count fabric, work from the centre outwards as instructed above, and finish at an appropriate point in the design. You can also leave a small space at the end of the design blank if wanted.

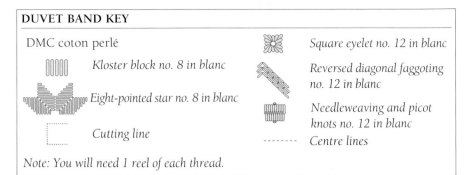

DUVET BAND KEY

DMC coton perlé

|||||| Kloster block no. 8 in blanc

Eight-pointed star no. 8 in blanc

⬚ Cutting line

Square eyelet no. 12 in blanc

Reversed diagonal faggoting no. 12 in blanc

Needleweaving and picot knots no. 12 in blanc

- - - - - - - Centre lines

Note: You will need 1 reel of each thread.

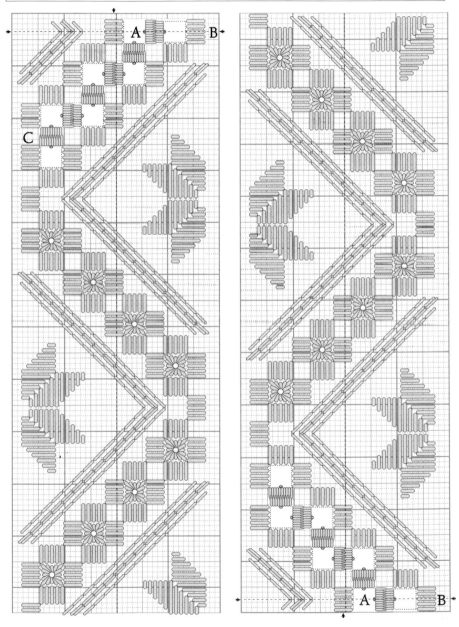

INSPIRATION AND DESIGN:
geometric precision

Glorious Venice with its superb buildings, vibrant atmosphere and warm shimmering colours, is an absolutely perfect place for dreamers, romance and embroiderers alike.

Inspiration for Hardanger is everywhere you look. On the outside of buildings, inside buildings or simply in structural outlines. Shape and pattern can be seen at every corner and none more so than on the breathtaking mosaic floor of St Mark's Basilica, which has been the inspiration for both pieces of Hardanger in this chapter. Divided into a myriad of patterned areas, these mosaics were laid between the 11th and 15th centuries.

Designing for Hardanger follows the same principles as any other type of embroidery even though the technique is essentially geometric in formation. Cut out, draw or trace a basic shape from your design source, keeping to simple lines. As Kloster blocks form the basic outline for Hardanger, interpret your drawing into Kloster blocks and onto squared paper, taking each square as a Kloster block. Use quick and simple scribbled strokes to indicate the direction of the blocks. On the diagonal, the blocks are connected, but on the straight the blocks are side by side separated by four threads.

If you are designing to fit a given size, dimensions are important and you need to check these as

you proceed. Multiplying the number of blocks you have drawn by four will give you the number of threads the design will take up (for example, 7 blocks x 4 threads = 28 threads). Divide this number by the fabric count (by 28 count = 2.5cm (1in)) to discover the width and length of the motif. Enlarge or reduce your motif accordingly by adding or subtracting blocks. It is also important to create spaces for surface motifs or patterns to contrast with the lacy effects of the embroidery. The solid satin-stitched areas give depth and maximize the play of light on the different stitch textures.

When you have established your outline of blocks, transfer the design onto plain paper and sketch in the lines that you would be left with once you have cut and withdrawn the appropriate threads. This will provide an overall impression of the finished shape and where filling stitches will fit in. Simple basic shapes may be reversed, mirror imaged, repeated and developed to form more complex designs.

The design for the band on the duvet cover (see pages 116–117), was based on a zigzag pattern found in the mosaics. To develop this design for a wider border, try a mirror image. Discard the Kloster blocks in the middle and you will now have a larger diamond shape for a lacy filling such as dove's eye or square filet and a complete eight-pointed star in the alternating spaces.

For the more advanced sampler (see pages 120–123), the bands have been developed from a variety of mosaic patterns and turned into a border, forming a more complex geometric design.

Working on a computer will definitely speed up your design process. Follow the same principles as you did when drawing with a pencil. Turning, reversing, mirror imaging, enlarging and reducing will all be achieved more quickly.

Although Venice is the design source for the two projects in this chapter, you may have a favourite city you would like to use as your starting point. Remember, inspiration is always at your fingertips.

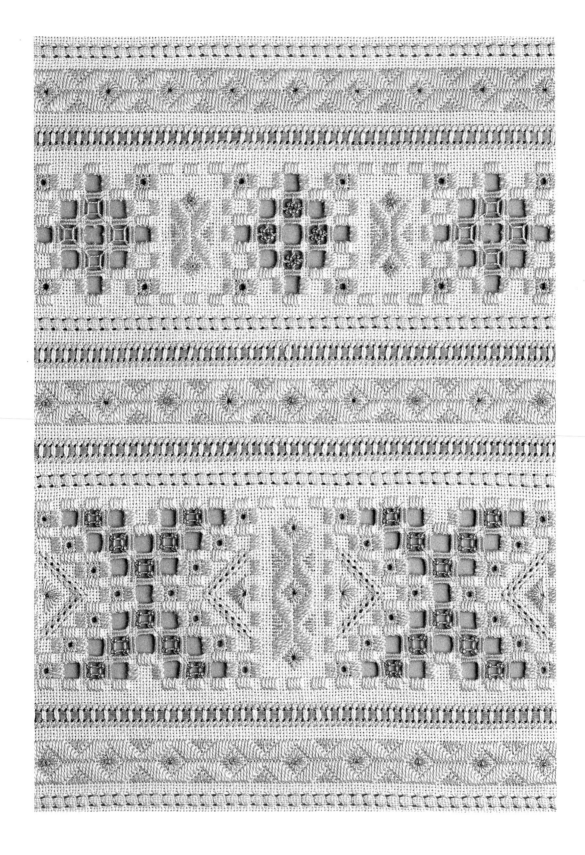

Blue sampler

This cool blue sampler captures the essence of the floor mosaics from St Mark's Basilica in Venice. The design has been developed from the tile patterns to give a series of banded effects. Stitched in pastel threads with glistening metallics, the technique of Hardanger is explored further by incorporating beads in the fillings. Although this design is worked in monochrome, you could also add more colour. Design by Jill Carter

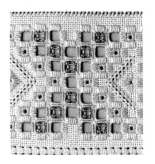

1 Bind the edges of the linen and then tack in the vertical centre line using a pastel-coloured thread (see page 28).

2 Following the chart overleaf, start at A on band 2. Work the first line of the lozenge shapes, which are formed by repeating one petal of the eight-pointed star. Place the first stitch of the first petal on the vertical centre line at A, 5.5cm (2¼in) down from the top edge of the fabric. Using the coton perlé no. 8, stitch the first line of petals in both directions, turning the work if necessary.

3 Complete the second line of petals underneath to form the lozenge shape band as shown in the chart. Work the small satin stitch triangles in the braid and fill the centres of the lozenge with diagonal eyelets in the same coton perlé thread as previously, but this time combined with the blending filament.

4 Still using the same mix of coton perlé thread and blending filament, stitch the four-sided stitch (see page 96) of band 1 above the line of lozenges and the two hem stitch borders (see page 98) below in band 3, starting on the right-hand side edge. Then, withdraw four threads between the two lines of hem stitching to act as casing for the ribbon. Work all the subsequent bands of four-sided stitch, hem stitch and lozenge shapes in the same manner and combination of threads as before, but in the sequence on the chart.

5 Outline the design of band 4 using coton perlé no. 8 for the Kloster blocks. Turn the work upside down to start at B, ensuring that this central Kloster block is lined up correctly on the tacking line. Work around the central diamond to establish the pattern, then radiate either side to complete the Kloster block outline. Do not cut any threads yet.

6 Now, complete all the square and diagonal eyelets, as well as the surface stitchery. Then, cut the threads of the fabric within the Kloster block outline as shown on the chart.

7 With coton perlé no. 12, finish the needlewoven bars, making sure to include the picots, square filet and dove's eye fillings in each diamond shape as shown on the chart. Start each diagonal line of needleweaving from the top right-hand corner and work in steps to the bottom left, to ensure that the sequence of any fillings is the same in each space.

8 If you wish to work four beads into the dove's eye filling, then select a short, size 10 tapestry needle in order to fit through the required bead. If you cannot get hold of this needle, you may substitute a fine embroidery needle that will take both the thread and the bead. Note that you will have to continue the needleweaving with a sharp, pointed needle so make sure not to split the threads. Make the fillings and ensure all beads are in the centre of the square on the looped part of the stitch.

9 Work the wider band 10 in the same way as band 4, starting from the middle Kloster block at C, working outwards in both directions in order to form the outline design of Kloster blocks. Fill in the surface stitchery as before, including the reversed diagonal faggoting and square eyelets, before cutting any threads. You can work the filling without beads if preferred.

10 Cut the threads of fabric within the Kloster block outline as before. Needleweave the bars and work the square filets. Add beads to the fillings or work without as preferred.

11 Attach some beads in the middle of the diagonal eyelets. Finally, thread the ribbon into a bodkin and through the hem-stitched borders. Secure with a few back stitches outside the design area.

12 When all the stitching has been completed, wash and iron the embroidery carefully. Gently pull the lines straight and lie the work flat to dry. Then, lace the embroidery onto acid-free board (see page 32) before framing it.

Design area

24 x 16.5cm (9½ x 6½in)

Materials

33 x 26cm (13 x 10½in) 25-count pale blue evenweave linen fabric

Embroidery threads and braid (see chart key)

Iridescent beads (see chart key)

1m x 2.5mm (1yd x ⅛in) silk or satin ribbon

Equipment

Pastel sewing thread

Size 24 tapestry needle

Embroidery scissors

Short size 10 tapestry needle

Bodkin

Acid-free board for stretching embroidery

Strong thread for lacing

Mount board and frame of your choice

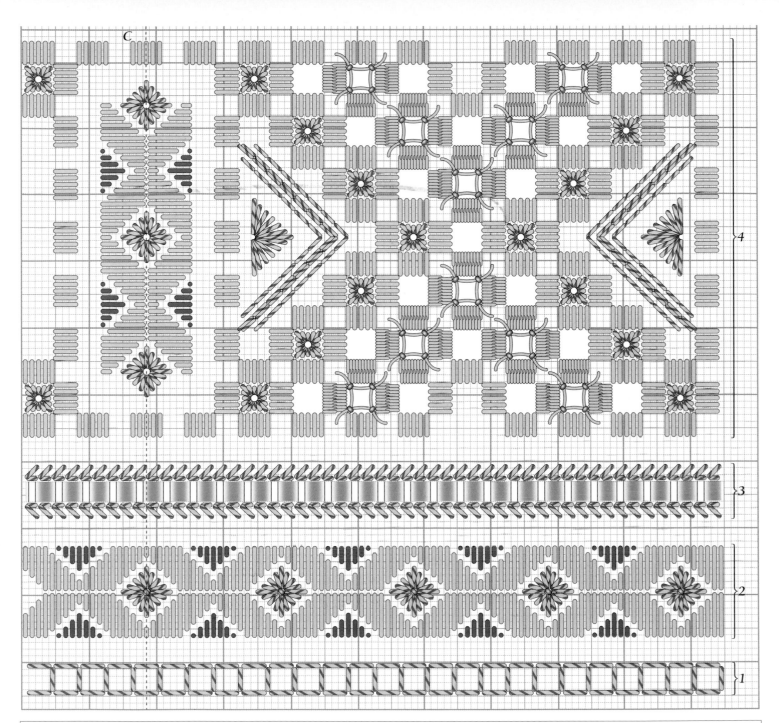

BLUE SAMPLER KEY

⬚ Four-sided stitch in DMC coton perlé no. 12 in 3753 with Kreinik blending filament in 094

Star petal border in DMC coton perlé no. 8 in 3753

✳ Diagonal eyelet in DMC coton perlé no. 12 in 3753 with Kreinik blending filament in 094

▪▫▪ Satin stitch triangle in Kreinik very fine braid #4 in 094

||||| Kloster blocks in DMC coton perlé no. 8 in 3753

Hem stitch (4 threads apart) in DMC coton perlé no. 12 in 3753 with Kreinik blending filament in 094

------ Centre line   ◦ DMC iridescent beads size 11 in 04 3761

Needleweaving with square filet filling and picot knots in DMC coton perlé no. 12 in 3753

Needleweaving with dove's eye filling and beads in DMC coton perlé no. 12 in 3753

Square eyelets in DMC coton perlé no. 12 in 3753 with Kreinik blending filament in 094

Reversed diagonal faggoting in DMC coton perlé no. 12 in 3753 with Kreinik blending filament in 094

Needleweaving with square filet filling and beads in DMC coton perlé no. 12 in 3753

Note: You will need 1 ball or skein of each thread.

123

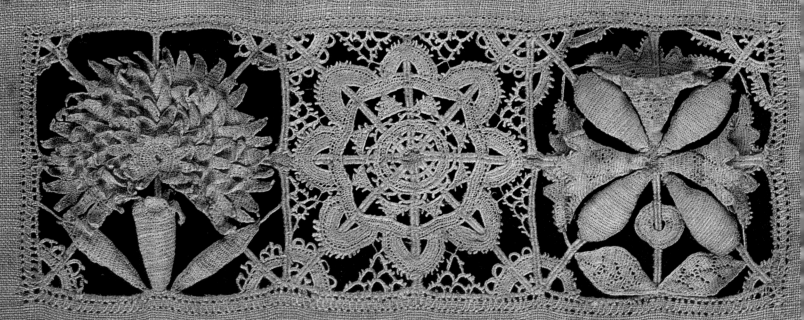

Cutwork

Originally known as opus scissum, *cutwork is a technique in which part of the fabric is cut away. In early work, a mesh of fabric threads is left as a foundation for the pattern. This embroidery also formed the beginnings of needle-made reticella lace in northern Italy and demonstrates how difficult it can be to see where embroidery ends and lace begins. Cutwork spread to northern Europe and, although initially worked mainly in convents for church use, became common on domestic linen and underclothes in the 16th and 17th centuries. In later cutwork, fabric is cut away to create open spaces, which are then encircled and crossed with buttonhole stitches.*

At first, cutwork was usually restricted to the border of the cloth and can be seen edging shirts, shifts and chemises in 16th-century portraits. However, with the introduction of parchment patterns, more complex scalloped, pointed and rounded shapes appeared. Elaborate cutwork became particularly popular for standing ruffs. These full, round shapes, tilted to frame the face, were of gathered linen supported on a variety of frameworks known as picadils or supportasses. Striking examples were worn by Elizabeth I – most would have been New Year gifts from her subjects.

Learning valued skills

Needlework was considered a desirable accomplishment for young women and they developed their skill by working samplers. Early examples had several uses, as they were also a record of stitches and patterns. They were stored in workboxes and used for reference at a time before pattern books were available. They were valuable to needlewomen and frequently mentioned in wills.

Training began at an early age, perhaps six or seven, when a simple sampler of border patterns would be worked. When the basic embroidery

Opposite page: Detail from whitework sampler by Frances Cheyney, English, dated 1664. Linen with linen thread in cut and drawn work with needlepoint fillings, detached buttonhole stitches, raised and padded work.

Left: Table mat, 1930s–1940s. Venetian lace worked in buttonhole stitch with figures dancing to Pan's pipes.

125

Right: Handkerchief, Carrickmacross, Co. Monahan, Ireland, 1880. Exhibited at the Glasgow International Exhibition of 1888.

Below: Poppy, by Jenny L. Adin, 1999. This piece is worked on fine Irish linen using stranded cotton. The techniques used are broderie anglaise and Richelieu cutwork with the addition of trailing and ladder stitches.

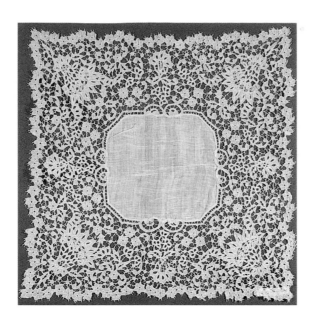

stitches were mastered, a girl would then make a more complex and technical cutwork sampler with white linen threads on white linen fabric. The first row was fairly straightforward, then each horizontal band was of increasing complexity until the final row had complete squares cut out. Paper or vellum was stitched to the back of the fabric to support the grid of foundation threads while the final row was being worked and was removed when the design was complete. The paper may also have had the pattern drawn on it to guide the young embroideress. The edges of the cut fabric were finished with overcast stitches and diagonal bridge threads added to the basic horizontal and vertical framework. Delicate, complicated geometric patterns were then built up on the framework using loops, picots and various buttonhole stitches.

By the late 16th century, cutwork was no longer strictly geometric but was often combined with drawn thread. Three-dimensional effects were incorporated by means of padding or by working individual pieces, such as flower petals, separately and then securing them to the sampler with only a few stitches. These samplers could have as few as six or as many as 24 rows but were normally about 50cm (20in) long and between 20.5 and 30.5cm (8 and 12in) wide. The most complex took up to two years to complete and later the technique and patterns would be used to decorate bed linen, caps, handkerchiefs, cravats and baby linen.

Regional specialities

After the famine in Ireland in 1846, a type of cutwork was revived in Carrickmacross as a means of poor relief, although it had failed to flourish in the 1820s. It takes its name from the area and in the finest form, guipure, the design was drawn on muslin, outlined with overcasting, cut out and joined with needlepoint bars. Often the edge is finished with needle-made loops. A school was set up where Brussels and guipure laces were used as sources for designs. They were mainly floral with leaves, shamrocks, scallops and scrolls. The work is still produced today.

One of the most popular forms of cutwork that developed in Britain during the mid-19th century was 'broderie anglaise' or eyelet embroidery. Simple, bold and repetitive patterns are worked with soft white mercerized cotton thread on white cotton fabric in a series of round or oval holes. The edges of the holes are tightly overcast or buttonholed and the remainder of the design is worked in padded and stem stitches. The work was used on petticoats and printed rows of pattern could be bought to work and use for trimmings. Patterns were available for collars and cuffs, some were quite elaborate.

However, the basic work was simple and eventually machine products pioneered in Switzerland and France became available. Despite this, handwork remained very popular and broderie anglaise continued as a favourite trimming on underwear. The magazine *Woman's Life*, issued on 4 August 1923, suggested that to be smart you had to be embroidered somewhere and that 'If you work broderie anglaise on your lingerie, and it is both modish and beautiful, then try the effect of doing the work in your favourite colours. You will be delighted with the result; the colours throw up your work so well.'

There were similar but more open forms such as Richelieu work that relied on cutwork, but, unlike broderie anglaise, the pattern was buttonholed around first before the background was cut away when the piece was complete. As well as buttonholed or woven bars, bridging the large background spaces are bullion or buttonhole picots and buttonhole wheels. In Hungary, cutwork was combined with black surface embroidery in bullion knots on women's dress and during the 19th century the technique was taught to peasant women in Madeira. Combined with surface embroidery, it became a thriving industry.

Revival and decline

As the industrial revolution gathered pace in Britain there were various efforts to develop cottage industries in rural areas to alleviate poverty and as an alternative to factory work in towns. John Ruskin, who lived at Lake Coniston in the Lake District, had strong views on social justice and, with Albert Fleming, revived the Langdale linen industry in Westmorland. This linen was most effectively used for cutwork embroidery in patterns similar to the geometric designs of old reticella lace. This was known as either Greek lace or punto-a-reticella and became the speciality of the area. The embroidery was worked in either silk or linen threads on linen quilts, cushions and wall panels and also became known as Ruskin lace. The success of the Langdale industry encouraged a similar craft revival at Fisherton-de-la-mere, Wiltshire, where a group of about 40 embroiderers produced work based on Italian embroidery including cutwork. The work was sold between 1890 and 1923, much of it through the Home Arts and Industries Association.

Cutwork continued to be used to decorate household linen and can be found featured in many early 20th-century embroidery magazines, but the technique was also exploited by some of the more innovative embroiderers. For example, in the exhibition Modern Embroidery held in 1932, and published in book form as a special edition of

Above: Sleeve, late 17th century, British. broderie anglaise design of circles and flowers.

The Studio, Rebecca Crompton showed a wall decoration entitled 'Simplicity'. The outline figure of an angel in a decorative border was worked on white linen in two tones of blue and cerise filoselle with additional areas of white. The edges were stitched with aluminium thread looped in small picots to catch the light. Herringbone was used to suggest hair and other small details. The panel was framed in silver-gilt with bands of fashionable Art Deco mirror glass between the mouldings.

More recently, the laborious process involved in working buttonhole stitch is often replaced by satin stitch worked on a swing-needle sewing machine. This has the advantage that the fabric can be cut away on both sides of the stitching to give delicate tracery effects. Cutwork is also now worked on layers of transparent fabrics that are cut, or on occasions burnt, away to reveal different colours and fabrics, and is combined with fabric paints and machine embroidery as well as hand stitching.

Cutwork stitches and techniques

Cutwork looks quite delicate and intricate, but it is surprisingly simple, and if you keep the stitches very neat, it is easy to achieve crisp, attractive results. The characteristic cut-away shapes give the work a light, open airiness and can also form pretty edges to the embroidery. Buttonholed edges, such an intrinsic part of the technique, make the work robust and ideal for decorating household linen.

Design your own

- *Look beyond traditional subjects such as flowers, leaves and butterflies – you may find shells, fossils, fish, lettering and geometric patterns equally inspirational.*
- *Keep the shapes simple with smooth lines and try to avoid complicated shapes that may not look effective.*
- *Try stencils as a design source.*
- *Add extra surface stitches in order to complement the cutwork, but do not overwork the design.*

Fabrics

It is important to choose a firm, closely woven fabric that will not fray easily. There are an increasing number of suitable fabrics, available in both natural and synthetic fibres, such as cotton and cotton lawn, linen and mixed fibres.

Some ready-made table linens would also be suitable, and they can save a considerable amount of work as they are already hemmed and available in a large number of shapes and sizes, usually with matching napkins.

Needles

Choose a sharp-pointed and large-eyed embroidery needle that will make a hole in the fabric that is just large enough for the thread to pass through smoothly without pulling or dragging.

Threads

Most cutwork projects require threads such as six-stranded embroidery cotton or coton à broder. However, other threads such as coton perlé, fine metallic threads, flower threads or even fine crewel wools may also be used if you are interested in more experimental work.

The thickness and type of thread must always be considered in relation to the fabric chosen. Therefore, stranded cotton is often the best choice as the number of strands can be varied, the colours can be mixed and the cottons can be combined with metallic stranded threads.

Additional tools

Use a pair of very sharp, pointed trimming or embroidery scissors for cutting away the fabric when stitching is complete. A pair of blunt scissors will 'chew' through the fabric and spoil the end result.

The use of a bound wooden embroidery hoop is strongly recommended to keep the fabric flat and prevent stretching or puckering that may occur when creating the cutwork bars. Always bind both rings of the hoop to give the fabric added protection.

Use coloured pencils to transfer the design onto the fabric, as these will leave the minimum of marks on the fabric and yet still be visible for working the design. Choose colours that are close to those of the threads used. Keep the pencils sharpened and do not press them down too hard.

Cutwork techniques

Key elements to successful cutwork are to plan the order of the work well and make sure all the cutting is done very precisely.

In its simplest form, cutwork is created by working a line of close buttonhole stitch around the design of a motif traced onto the fabric. The stitched lines must fully enclose any shapes to be cut away and the ridged ends of the buttonhole stitches, which provide the strong edging, should be next to the areas that are to be cut.

To embellish the simple lines of close buttonhole stitch and to give more interest to a design, add details made of double

buttonhole stitches, picots, bars and eyelets. These additional stitches may also include surface stitches such as seeding stitch (see page 189), to add textured patterns to the flat, close weave of the fabric. French and bullion knots (see pages 205 and 146) are always useful to echo and enhance the use of the various types of picots.

Reinforcing the edges

Start by working lines of running stitch (see page 63) in the chosen thread, around all the design lines to be edged by the ridges of the buttonhole stitch. For a more raised effect, running stitch can also be worked along the other design lines. These will strengthen the fabric that will later be cut.

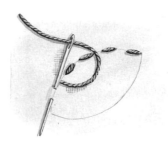

Work a series of running stitches to outline the shape.

Work a line of close buttonhole stitch around the shape (see page 98). Adapt the normal buttonhole stitch by keeping the stitches as close together as possible to form a solid line of stitching with no gaps to encourage fraying of the cut fabric. You will also notice that unlike some other techniques where the stitch is worked on an existing cut edge, in cutwork it is stitched first and the shape cut away later. Make sure you enclose the running stitch outline and also keep the ridged end of the buttonhole stitch next to the shape to be cut away.

A buttonhole stitch is usually worked from left to right. However, with a little practice, it can be worked in any direction. Start the stitching by making a waste knot on the surface. Always keep the stitches very even and close together.

Work a line of buttonhole stitch over the running stitches.

Adjacent cut areas

In some cases where the cut areas of a design lie side by side, you will need to work a line of double buttonhole stitch in order for both cut areas to have a neat, strong edge.

As the name suggests, a double buttonhole stitch is simply a double line of buttonhole stitch. The first line is worked along one edge of the design, with the stitches slightly apart so the stitches of the second line can fit neatly in the gaps. You may find it necessary to turn the work before starting to stitch the second row.

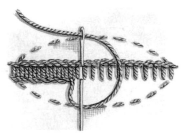

Work the second line of stitches in between those on the first line.

Adding bars

Bars embellish a design, but may also be required to hold and strengthen cut-away areas that need extra support when the fabric is cut. It is best to work bars after the running stitches but before the close buttonhole stitches, so the ends of the bars are securely and neatly hidden.

Insert the needle at one side of the shape requiring the bar, take the thread to the opposite side and catch it carefully in the fabric. Bring the thread back to the starting point and catch it again in the fabric. Repeat once more to have three threads laid over the fabric surface. These threads will form the foundation of the bar.

Run three threads across the shape to form the foundation of the bar.

Once the foundation has been laid out, work a neat, closely spaced line of buttonhole stitch over the three bar threads, taking much care not to catch the fabric underneath. When working a bar, be careful not to let the stitches twist around the bar.

Work a line of buttonhole stitch over the foundation of the bar.

Complex bar patterns

Once the technique for a single bar has been mastered, more complicated patterns can be

made by working more than one bar across an area to be cut away. These bars will intersect each other and may even be branched to form a web-like pattern.

To branch bars, start working a bar across the area to be cut away. Then, halfway through, pass the thread over the fabric to the edge of the shape and catch it securely to the fabric. Make the foundation between the first bar and the fabric as described before. Then, work buttonhole stitch along this bar. Continue along the first bar, working other branching bars in the same way as you reach them and finally, complete the first bar.

Branch bars to one another in order to obtain a web-like pattern.

A simple variation to working branched bars is to work more than one bar across an area to be cut away. These bars can then cross over each other as they do in the snowflake project design (see page 134–137).

Further embellishment

Once you have mastered close buttonhole stitch, you can go on to learn and practise stitching other features that will enrich and enhance simple designs. Try the various picots on the next page to decorate the bars or add the small eyelets traditionally associated with cutwork.

Other surface stitches, such as stem stitch (see page 206), feather stitch (see page 205) and seeding (see page 189) can also be used to complement the basic technique on the surrounding fabric, as shown in the next two projects.

LOOPED PICOT

USES: decorating bars and edges

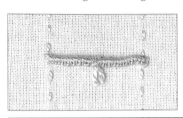

Various types of picot can be incorporated into the buttonhole stitch in cutwork, to provide a subtle decoration on bars or around cut edges breaking any severity of line on the design. Picots are traditionally placed in the middle of a bar or spaced evenly along a cut edge, but for free, experimental work, they can be worked randomly. Instructions for the buttonhole stitch are on page 98. Work the stitch after the picot firmly to hold the picot in place.

1 At the position for the picot, insert a pin in the fabric, under the bar, close to the previous stitch. Pass the thread under the pin, left to right and slip the needle under the bar, top to bottom.

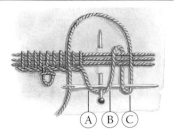

2 Slip the needle under the thread at A, over the pin and under the thread at B. Slip it under and over the loop of thread at C. Pull through. Tighten the thread to hold the little loop firmly.

BULLION PICOT

USES: decorating bars and edges

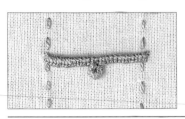

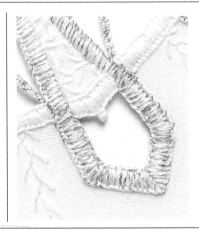

At the position for the picot, take the needle back into the loop of the last buttonhole stitch. Twist the working thread around the needle five or six times, then pull through.

Left: A beautiful example of a bullion picot as featured in the Snowflake table linen project (see pages 134–137).

BUTTONHOLE PICOT

USES: decorating bars and edges

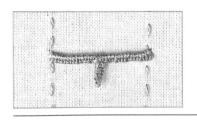

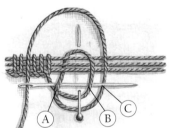

1 Insert a pin in the fabric, under the bar, where you want the picot. Pass the thread under the pin to the right then over the bar. Slip the needle under the bar, top to bottom.

2 Pull the needle through. Pass the thread under the pin again and loop upwards. Then, slip the needle under the thread at A, over the pin, under the thread at B and finally, over at C.

3 Pull the thread through and form a knot at the head of the picot. Work buttonhole stitches along the picot to meet the bar. Complete the bar and then remove the pin.

OVERCAST EYELET

USES: scattered open detail

Work tiny running stitches around a small circle. Push a hole in the fabric with a stiletto. Overcast the edges with tiny stitches, coming up outside the running stitches, down into the hole.

BUTTONHOLE EYELET

USES: scattered open detail

Work running stitches around a small circle and make a hole. Work tiny buttonhole stitches over the running stitches, so the ridged ends lay on the outer edge of the eyelet.

Lavender pillow

Create a touch of luxury in your bedroom with this charming bed pillow, which is embellished with very simple cutwork motifs. This project is ideal for a novice of the technique to practise. The softly coloured floral motif has been repeated three times across the watery moiré taffeta fabric and a simple satin ribbon border has been added to enclose the lavender motifs. Design by Jane Iles

1 Iron the taffeta fabric on an appropriate heat setting to remove any creases. Measure a 22 x 44cm (8½ x 17¼in) rectangle to indicate the exact position of the ribbon border. Tack along the border lines and bind the edges of the fabric with cream sewing thread to prevent fraying.

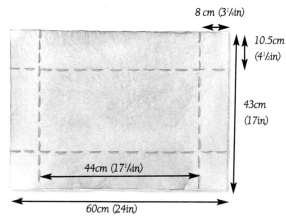

8 cm (3¼in)

10.5cm (4½in)

43cm (17in)

44cm (17¼in)

60cm (24in)

Using cream sewing thread, tack along the four border lines of the rectangle.

2 Trace the design pattern from the diagram (overleaf) and then make three photocopies. Arrange the photocopied patterns under the taffeta fabric so they are evenly spaced within the outline and pin to hold. The fabric is quite thin, so you can see through it. Using the green and mauve coloured pencils, trace the design lines onto the fabric.

3 Place one motif centrally within the embroidery hoop then gently pull until the fabric is taut, but not drum tight. Using three strands of stranded cotton, follow the diagram to work the design. Make sure you do not jump from one area of the design to another across the back of the fabric.

4 First, work the curved stems in neat back stitch. Then, work the lozenge-shaped leaves and lower petals in close buttonhole stitch with initial lines of running stitch to strengthen the areas to be cut away. Lengthen the buttonhole stitches at the points of the leaf and petal shapes.

5 Proceed on to the larger circular flowers, which are outlined first in running stitch and then worked as large buttonhole eyelets. Work the smaller flowers at the tips of the stems as simple overcast eyelets. Work the three motifs in the same way.

6 When the stitching is complete, remove the hoop and press the fabric carefully on the wrong side. Using the pair of very sharp scissors and working on the wrong side of the embroidery, carefully snip into the areas to be removed. Mark these areas on the wrong side if it is helpful. Take time and great care to cut away each small piece of fabric. It is easier to cut right next to the stitching from the wrong side than it is from the right side of the embroidery. Iron the fabric gently on the wrong side to remove any creases and to encourage the stitchery to stand out on the surface.

Design area

10 x 15cm (4 x 6in)

Materials

Two pieces of 43 x 60cm (17 x 24in) cream moiré taffeta furnishing fabric

Embroidery threads (see diagram key)

2.10m (2⅜yd) x 1cm (⅜in) wide cream satin ribbon

43 x 60cm (17 x 24in) pale green cotton polyester fabric

40 x 57cm (16 x 22½in) soft pillow pad

Equipment

Cream sewing thread

Tracing paper and pen

Pins

Pale green and pale mauve coloured pencils

20cm (8in) bound, wooden embroidery hoop

Small, sharp, pointed embroidery scissors

Stiletto or large, pointed bodkin

LAVENDER PILLOW KEY

DMC stranded cotton

- Small overcast eyelet in 211
- Small overcast eyelet in 3609
- Small overcast eyelet in 554
- Large buttonhole eyelet in 211
- Large buttonhole eyelet in 3609
- Close buttonhole stitch in 3364
- Close buttonhole stitch in 966
- Close buttonhole stitch in 3609
- Close buttonhole stitch in 554
- Close buttonhole stitch in 3836
- Back stitch in 3364
- Back stitch in 966

Note: You will need 1 skein of each shade.

7 Pin the satin ribbon along the previously tacked outlines to the edges of the fabric and tack into place. Then, machine-stitch the ribbon onto the fabric with cream sewing thread.

8 Place the layer of pale green fabric under the cutwork so the green shows up through the small cut shapes and pin to hold them together.

With the right sides together, place the second piece of moiré taffeta over the embroidered fabric. Allow a 1.5cm (⅝in) seam all around and machine-stitch the seams, leaving an opening of 20cm (8in) along one side. Clip the excess fabric at the corners. Turn to the right side, easing the corners into shape. Insert the pillow pad, fold in the open edges and slip stitch them together to close (see page 33).

Snowflake table linen

This beautiful snowflake design will demonstrate the skills of the more confident embroiderer. The strong open shapes let the light through and, with a blend of silver and white threads, evoke the icy feel of a wintery landscape. A tablecloth with a deeply scalloped edge has been chosen to enhance the cutwork snowflake and the table setting is completed with a small star design for napkins. Design by Jane Iles

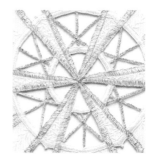

Tablecloth

1 Trace the pattern off the diagram using tracing paper. If you are creating your own design, it is a good idea to trace the design onto a spare sheet of paper first. Then, place it on a cutting mat and use a sharp knife to remove the cutwork areas. This will enable you to check if the design is going to work and also to assess which lines of stitching can be worked in close buttonhole stitch and which ones must be in double buttonhole stitch.

2 Position the traced pattern and tape it down on a clean, flat surface to secure in place. If desired, you can spray starch on the fabric to help stiffen it for working and also give it a crisp finish.

3 Position one corner of the tablecloth over the pattern, placing it approximately 10cm (4in) away from both cloth edges so you can work it in an embroidery hoop. Using a sharp, pale blue pencil, lightly transfer the design onto the fabric. Make sure that you do not transfer the lines of feather stitch or seeding stitches onto the fabric, as these are for reference only. In order to identify the areas on the fabric that will eventually be removed, lightly mark them with the coloured pencil. This will also help you to check that the positioning of the buttonhole stitching is correct.

4 Place the square piece of white fabric centrally on top of the traced design. Then, place both layers of fabric carefully in the large embroidery hoop and tighten both evenly. Using sharp embroidery scissors, carefully snip into the centre of the square of waste fabric and cut out a window that is large enough to work the snowflake in. This will prevent the white fabric of the tablecloth from becoming slightly soiled during handling.

5 Use two strands of white stranded cotton thread to work all the lines of running stitch, placing them just inside the double design lines on the sides next to the areas that are to be cut later. Make sure not to take the working thread across the back of the fabric from one area of stitching to another, as any trailed thread may show when the cutwork shapes are eventually removed.

6 Work the bars that criss-cross over one another, using a combination of two strands of white stranded cotton with one strand of silver metallic thread. Start at one corner of the pentagon shape, bringing the thread up in the adjoining area, where it will later be covered in close buttonhole stitch. Then, take the needle down in the opposite corner and work the bar in buttonhole stitch. Hold the bar of thread firmly to prevent the stitches from twisting around the bar. Work the other diagonal bar in the same way. Finally, work the third bar, looping the thread around the other two bars where they all meet to hold them together, before completing it.

7 Using the three strands of white stranded cotton, work the lines of double buttonhole stitch forming the inner and outer circular shapes. Space the first lines of stitching slightly apart so the second line of stitches fits snugly in between. This will give neat and solid bars, with the ridges of the stitches lying on each edge.

8 When working the outer line of double buttonhole stitch on the larger outer circle, make a single bullion picot at the six points, which will lie in the cut-away shapes.

9 Using the combination of one silver and two white strands of thread, work the six main stretched diamond shapes that branch out from the very centre of the snowflake in close buttonhole stitch. Starting at the centre point of the design, work the stitches so the ridged ends are around the outside of each diamond shape. You will have to alter the length of the tails of the stitches to fit into the pointed corners. Also, remember to space the stitches slightly apart around the outer section of each diamond to allow for the inner stitches making up the double buttonhole stitch that will eventually be worked there.

Design area

Tablecloth: 20.5cm (8in) square

Napkin: 6cm (2½in) square

Materials

White, closely woven evenweave ready-made tablecloth

Ready-made napkins to match tablecloth

40cm (15¾in) square white cotton fabric

Embroidery threads (see diagram key)

Equipment

Tracing paper and pen

Cutting mat

Craft knife

Masking tape

Pale blue coloured pencil

25cm (10in) and 15cm (6in) bound, wooden embroidery hoops

Stiletto or large, pointed bodkin

Small, sharp, pointed embroidery scissors

10 Using the same mix of silver and white threads, work the six outer spurs of the design. These are worked in a slightly different way to the previous lines of stitching. Start by working close buttonhole stitch from the white outer circle, out along the spur, until it broadens out into a hollow diamond shape. From this point, space the stitches slightly further apart until you have worked right around the diamond shape. Then, work down the other side of the spur back to where you started. Complete each spur by working a second row of stitches to form double buttonhole stitch around the inner edge of the diamond shape.

11 Fill in the solid areas of the stretched diamond shapes with randomly scattered seeding stitch (see page 189).

12 Then, using three strands of white stranded cotton, work lines of feather stitch (see page 205) on the outer edges of the design. Start at the outer end of each line and work back to meet the line of white double buttonhole stitches.

13 Work several tiny overcast eyelets scattered randomly around the snowflake design to complete the embroidery.

14 Remove the embroidery hoop as well as the protective piece of fabric. Always following the manufacturer's instructions, iron the table linen on the wrong side of the snowflake motif, so the stitching will look embossed on the right side.

15 Using a pair of sharp, pointed embroidery scissors, remove the appropriate areas of the design. Work with the wrong side of the design facing up, as it is easier to cut very close to the stitching on this side. Work slowly and with great care so none of the stitching is accidentally snipped. Take care when removing the five-sided shapes, especially close to the thin intersecting bars. If the buttonhole stitching is accidentally cut when the fabric shapes are being removed, carefully undo several of the stitches on either side of the cut thread. Neatly secure the cut threads with care. Then, using a new length of thread, re-work the missing stitches. Secure the starting and finishing threads within the stitches on either side of the repaired area.

16 Iron the design again carefully. If desired, work additional motifs in the same way in the remaining corners of the tablecloth.

Napkin

1 Map out the design by tacking a six-pointed star, centred attractively in one corner, on the napkin. Stretch the napkin in the small embroidery hoop.

2 Using three strands of white stranded cotton, work the lines of feather stitch, each one from the point into the centre. Finish the design with one French knot (see page 205) using the same thread.

3 Press the embroidery carefully as before. Complete as many napkins as you need for your family and guests.

SNOWFLAKE NAPKIN KEY

DMC stranded cotton

 Feather stitch in B5200

French knot in B5200

Note: You will need small amounts of thread.

SNOWFLAKE TABLECLOTH KEY

DMC stranded cotton

⬭ B5200

Seeding in B5200

Picot knot in B5200

⬭ B5200 with 5283
DMC stranded
metallic thread

Overcast eyelet in B5200

⬭ Cut-away areas

Feather stitch in B5200

① Double buttonhole stitch

② Intersecting bar

③ Buttonhole stitch

Note: You will need 3 skeins
of B5200 and 1 skein of 5283.

Enlarge by 110%

SURFACE
STITCHERY

Whitework

This term refers to any form of embroidery worked in white thread on a white ground and includes surface stitchery, cutwork, pulled and drawn threadwork. However, it is especially associated with fine cotton embroidery on muslin. The white on white embroidery requires a smooth fabric to emphasize the textures of the stitches and the contrasting areas of light and shade created by the stitches and different threads. Different types of whitework have been associated with ecclesiastical embroidery from earliest times, but fine work on muslin began to develop with tambouring. Elements of this work then became incorporated into delicate white embroidery such as Ayrshire.

Tambouring is the technique of making a continuous chain stitch on fine fabric or net using a small metal hook resembling a crochet hook. The fabric is first stretched over a frame, originally circular, hence the name, so it can be worked from the reverse side. The hook is held in one hand above the fabric while the other, below the frame, controls the thread. The hook is pushed through the fabric and picks up the thread which is pulled through in a loop. The process is repeated to form the chain. Tambouring was widely used in China and South Asia before the 18th century but only introduced to Britain around 1760. It became a fashionable occupation for young ladies and there is a famous portrait of Madame Pompadour working at her elaborate frame dated circa 1764. In Britain, the Ladies Waldegrave, the great nieces of

Horace Walpole, were painted in 1780 by Joshua Reynolds with one of them working white sprigs on muslin stretched on a tambour frame. Walpole is also known to have worn a tamboured waistcoat worked for him by Lady Ossary who may have found an appropriate design in one of the new ladies' magazines that began to appear in the 1760s and 1770s. However, at this time, professionals only used tambouring for coloured silks, cottons and gold embroidery and in the *Westminster Magazine* of 1774 we find the first British reference to 'waistcoats tamboured with coloured silks'.

At the end of the 18th century, the growing neo-classical taste for white muslin dresses and the import of fine embroidered muslins from India transformed tambouring muslin into an important industry, which was also known as flowering. As the mechanization of spinning in the factory system progressed in 1793 in Paisley the minister recorded that, 'Within this 12 month many women have laid aside the spinning wheel, that most useful instrument of domestic industry, and have applied themselves to the easier, more elegant and at present more profitable employment of flowering muslin.'

Schools were set up and the teaching of tambour was often combined with 'Dresden embroidery and Spanish flowering needlework'. Tambour workers were given three months' training which, when completed, enabled them to earn four shillings per week. They produced muslin delicately decorated with sprigs of flowers and leaves on trailing stems.

By the 1820s, open work stitches had been introduced in the centres of the flowers and these were gradually elaborated to include lace filling stitches. The outline of the motif was worked in satin stitch before the centre was enlarged with a stiletto, then a few threads were inserted to form the framework on which the pattern was worked, mainly in buttonhole stitch. It was not until the

Above: Front panel of a baby robe, possibly 1830s–1850s, possibly Irish. The design includes nursery rhyme images.

Opposite page: Baby's basinette cover, Ayrshire work, Messrs Macdonald, Glasgow 1851. Exhibited at the International Exhibition, London 1851.

Left: Crown of a baby cap, Ayrshire work, mid-19th century.

141

1830s, however, that this embroidery became known as Ayrshire work, by which time tambour work had gone out of fashion and the taste for white muslin gowns had given way to printed cotton and fine wools. In women's dress, the embroidered whitework was therefore confined to large collars, cuffs and accessories.

Exquisite Ayrshire work

Glasgow, the centre of cotton manufacturing in the west of Scotland, specialized in the production of fine, high-quality fabrics and became the main centre of the flowered muslin industry. Here, the designs were printed on the fabric, then, together with the needles and threads, were taken by an agent, of whom there were 400–500, to outworkers in the surrounding districts. Many of the workers were located in Ayrshire, but there were many more workers in Ireland where there was a plentiful supply of cheap female labour as a result of agricultural problems and the failure of the potato crop. Each design was stamped with the company name, design number and the number of hours allowed to work the piece. About ten days was allowed for a collar. The fine work was demanding and the women are reputed to have splashed their eyes with whisky to enable them to work long hours. To save time, children were pressed into service to thread the needles. Later the agent would collect the work and return it to Glasgow where it would be cut out, hemmed, washed and bleached to rid it of the 'peat reek', before being packed ready to be exported to America, France, Russia, Germany and London.

The workers produced collars, cuffs, caps and other small items that featured on the fashion plates of the day, but most notable at a time when child mortality was high, lavish attention was paid to babies among the middle classes and their clothing was expensively decorated. The bodice, cap sleeves and triangular front panel of baby robes were richly decorated and sometimes the design included peacocks and other exotic birds among roses. One of the most elaborate items produced was a baby's basinette cover specially made for the Great Exhibition by Messrs MacDonald, Glasgow. This was a virtuoso piece decorated with the national emblems of roses, thistles, daffodils and shamrocks, each with different filling stitches. It was probably originally backed with coloured silk to show the work to its best advantage. The complicated scalloped edging was worked in buttonhole stitch. A review of the exhibition described the company products as follows: 'A large proportion of the articles exhibited by this firm are for those small specimens of humanity upon whom mothers are frequently inclined to lavish very large sums and in truth, the robes, caps and especially the quilt, form a tempting display.'

Other types of whitework

However, through a combination of overproduction and the introduction of machine embroidered items, this fine whitework became available to a wider market and therefore lost its status and went out of fashion. The industry's decline was hastened by the American Civil War, which reduced the importing of raw cotton.

Other forms of white floral embroidery still flourished, and in Ireland, encouraged to help alleviate distress caused by the potato famines during the first half of the 19th century, Mountmellick was a much more robust embroidery in soft, thick white cotton thread on white cotton sateen. Unlike the other forms of whitework, Mountmellick has no drawn threads or open spaces. The embroidery mainly lies on the surface and usually consists of highly textured blackberries and flowers such as passion flowers, as well as local wild flowers and berries. These were worked in satin stitch with bullion, Gordian and French knots, as well as chain, thorn, coral, fern, feather, trellis and herringbone stitches. The designs were worked on bedspreads, but also on small items such as handkerchief sachets and were edged with buttonhole stitch and knitted fringing.

As bobbin lace was traditionally made in England, there were few forms of flowering embroideries made there during the course of the 19th century. The exception was Coggeshall work, which was named after the Essex village where it was introduced. This was worked in white cotton on a muslin ground and occasionally flower centres were worked with open work fillings and used to decorate costume items such as shawls, large cape collars and flounces. The floral designs were derived from woodland and hedgerow plants including bluebells, cow parsley and primroses. At its peak during the early 1850s, the industry provided employment for over three hundred outworkers, but it subsequently declined and ceased altogether in 1939.

Opposite page, left: Page from a book of tamboured muslin samples, Brown and Sharp, possibly late 18th century.

Opposite page, right: Baby cap, Ayrshire work, mid-19th century.

This page, left: Workbasket Treasures, designed and worked by Jenny L. Adin, English, 2000. The pulled and drawn threadwork is worked on single linen areas and the needlerun patterns on cotton net. The surface stitches include satin, buttonhole, trailing and ladder stitches as well as beading, French knots and eyelets, using stranded cotton.

This page, right: Handkerchief sachet, Mountmellick work.

Whitework stitches and techniques

Although Mountmellick and Ayrshire have some different qualities, they are both classic forms of whitework. Stitched in white on white, both rely on contrasting textures for interest. Mountmellick is easy for a beginner, is hardwearing and can be used on household linens. Ayrshire is much finer, requires more practice, and is better for items to be treasured such as a Christening robe or lace edgings for garments.

Design your own

- *Traditional inspiration comes from nature, so experiment with leaf, flower and insect shapes.*
- *Consider design ideas taken from wrought ironwork or architecture.*
- *Try designing in white paint or pastel-coloured paper.*
- *Cut out paper motifs and move them around within the design area to find the most effective arrangement.*

Fabrics

Mountmellick is worked on heavyweight matt cotton fabric. The Ayrshire technique should be worked on cotton lawn.

Needles

Use a crewel needle to take the thicker threads for Mountmellick and a fine embroidery needle for Ayrshire work.

Threads

Mountmellick embroidery is worked using thick and thin soft cotton threads to create the textures required. Ayrshire work uses finer threads, such as stranded cotton, as it relies on detail and delicate stitches.

Additional tools

To transfer the designs onto the fabric, use either pounce or a light box, and pale blue pencil or paint. You should avoid using a lead pencil, as it will make the thread look grey. For Ayrshire work, the stitching is so fine that you may require the use of a magnifying glass.

Mountmellick techniques

Mountmellick embroidery is a bold technique, showing texture to the full with its almost life-like quality. The surface stitches give textures from smooth and satiny to knotted and twisted.

Elaborate, three-dimensional sprays work well as independent designs, contrasting with the background fabric.

The original designs are best transferred by the prick and pounce method (see page 31), as fabrics tend to be too thick to be transparent. If you are embroidering a large project, you can work with a quilting ring frame, which is like an embroidery hoop but, being larger and deeper, holds a large, weighty piece of fabric more firmly. Smaller projects will require the use of a slate frame.

Ayrshire techniques

Ayrshire work is a fine, delicate technique with smaller areas of solid embroidery. These areas contrast with the filling stitches, which are situated in open areas and cut into the fabric, and the unworked spaces on the surface.

As the fabric used is fine and transparent, the design can be transferred by using pounce or tracing over a light box.

In order to obtain the best results, stretch a large piece of the fabric on a slate frame and only cut any pattern pieces for a garment after all the embroidery has been stitched. For small areas of work, you can also use an embroidery hoop, bound on both hoops in order to keep the fabric clean.

The following stitches include a selection of those typical of both Mountmellick and Ayrshire work. You will also find running stitch (see page 63) a useful complementary stitch.

CABLE STITCH

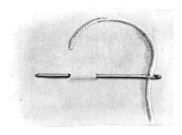

USES: lines

Work a straight stitch parallel to the design line. Start the next halfway along the first, the same length and parallel. Repeat, keeping alternate stitches on two parallel lines.

TRAILING STITCH

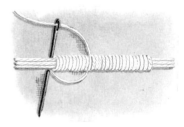

USES: lines

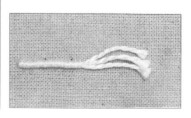

Lay three threads on the design line. Close straight stitch over the threads, up and back through the fabric on the design line. Take the couched threads at each end to the back and secure.

SATIN STITCH OVER SPLIT STITCH

USES: filling

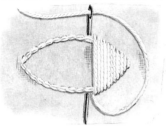

Bring the needle up at one end of the shape just outside the split stitch outline. Make a straight vertical stitch down. Repeat, keeping the stitches close and the tension even.

LARGE OVERCAST EYELETS

USES: edges

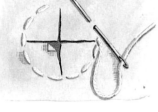

1 Work running stitch around the eyelet shape. Then, starting from the middle, cut the eyelet both vertically and horizontally until you reach the running stitch.

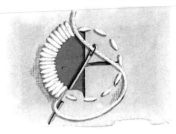

2 Fold the cut fabric under and then overcast to secure, coming up on the outside of the previously worked running stitch and then down into the hole.

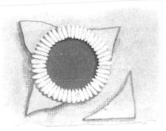

3 Trim any excess material away from the back once you have finished. To make a square eyelet, work in exactly the same way as the large eyelet but in a square shape.

BACK STITCH WHEEL

USES: filling

Large overcast eyelets of any shape provide the foundation for needlelace fillings which can be worked inside the eyelet and add lace-like detail. Start the fillings with a separate length of thread. Two of the easiest, the back stitch wheel and a simple needlelace filling, are shown here, but you could explore more intricate needlelace and drawn thread fillings, starting with the spider's web on page 99 and the square filets and dove's eye filling on pages 114–115.

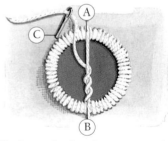

1 Secure the thread, come up at A. Make a vertical spoke down, going down at B. Wind the working thread back along B to the centre point and make another spoke, going down at C.

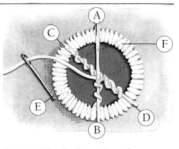

2 Wind back along C to the centre. Continue, winding spokes from D and E. Take the final spoke out to F and wind back to the centre. All the spokes should be evenly spaced.

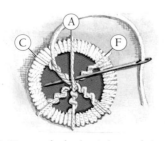

3 To start the back stitch part, bring the working thread up at the centre to the left of spoke A. Take the needle down to the right of spoke A and up to the left of spoke C.

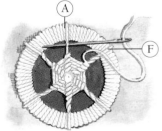

4 Weave around the spokes anti-clockwise, taking a back stitch over one and working forwards under two. Finish with a back stitch over spoke F and come up left of spoke A.

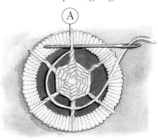

5 To finish the filling, wind the working thread back up spoke A to overcast the edge. Then, secure the thread on the back under the overcasting stitches.

NEEDLELACE FILLING

USES: filling

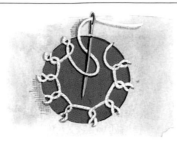

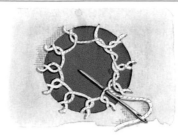

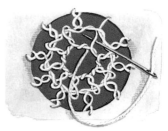

1 Secure the thread in the overcast edge. Take the needle down to the right, over and under the loop. Pull until the loop is 2mm (⅛in) deep. Work evenly spaced stitches.

2 When you reach the first loop, wind the working thread around the present circle of loops until you complete the first ring. Make a second ring inside the first in the same way.

3 Work more rings, tightening the tension to shape them in towards the centre, then wrap the thread back out along the line of unwrapped spokes to the overcast edge.

BULLION KNOT

USES: detail, filling

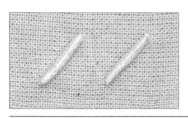

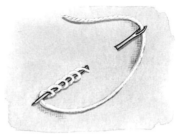

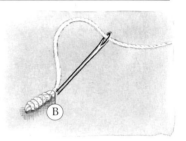

1 Bring the thread up to the surface at A, one end of the required bullion knot. Take it down into the fabric at B, the other end of the eventual knot, and up again in the first hole at A.

2 Before you pull the needle through, wrap the thread around the point of the needle a few times depending on the length of the knot. Pull the needle through the fabric and the thread.

3 Pull the thread towards B without distorting the twists. Pull the thread tight and use the point of the needle to regulate the twists closely along the knot. Re-insert the thread at B.

MOUNTMELLICK STITCH

USES: lines, outlines, borders

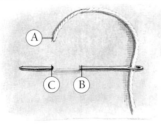

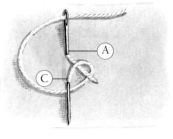

1 Bring the needle up at A and make a diagonal stitch down to B, allowing it to lie flat on the surface of the fabric. Bring the needle up at C, to the left of B and directly below A.

2 Pull the working thread through. Take the needle over the first stitch and slide it underneath, without penetrating the fabric. Pull the thread through, without pulling it too tight.

3 Take the needle back down at A and up again directly below at C. Loop the thread under the point of the needle. Pull the thread through so that the knot is not pulled tightly.

See also:
stem stitch (page 206)
satin stitch (page 188)
French knots (page 205)
buttonhole stitch (page 98)
long and short stitch (page 171)
tapestry shading (page 171)
split stitch (page 171)

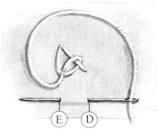

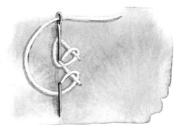

4 Continue the sequence, starting the next knot by making another diagonal stitch down to D. Bring the needle up again at E and then pull through.

5 Continue making the knots in the same way along a line, keeping the tension even and not too tight.

Above: Mountmellick stitch worked downwards the main stem line (see pages 147–149).

Mountmellick bedspread

This design for an elegant bedspread in shades of white is taken straight from nature, keeping faith with the inspiration for traditional Mountmellick work. The spray of wild rose, brambles and intertwining stems and leaves, worked in richly textured stitches, has a strong presence. The ordered spray design could be scattered more randomly across the bedspread if you prefer or used for other household linen. Design by Tracy A. Franklin

1 Photocopy the diagram of the spray on page 148. Make a pricking of the design, including the centre lines, as described on page 31.

2 Tack along the two centre lines of the bedspread. Decide on the position of the motifs along the vertical line, allowing enough space for borders of equal width at the top and bottom. Then, tack a line all around the bedspread to show the position of the border. Measure the distance between the top border line and the centre line below it, and then tack another line exactly between the two. Repeat, in order to tack a final line between the centre line and the bottom border line. Where the last two lines meet the border gives the position for the remaining four motifs. Adapt these positions to suit different sizes of bedspread.

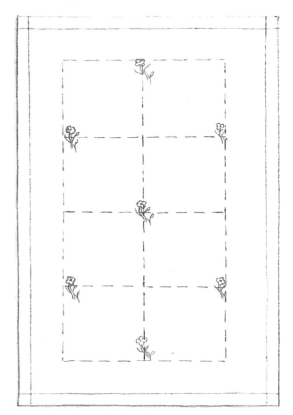

Position the motifs on the bedspread.

3 Pin the pricking over each position in turn, carefully matching up the appropriate centre lines and remembering that all except the central motif are set in from the border line. Pounce and paint the design in each position, before moving on to the next.

4 Place the area of the bedspread to be worked into a bound embroidery or quilting frame. Start to stitch using the white cotton thread and the chenille needle throughout. The design is worked from the background shapes to those on the top, to maximize the three-dimensional quality of the embroidery.

5 Work the stems on the back spray in stem stitch first, without omitting the little thorns, which are worked in satin stitch. Then, work the blackberries in satin stitch and French knots. Complete the back spray by working the leaves in satin stitch on one side and with bullion knots within a stem stitch outline on the other side of each leaf.

6 Next, work the Mountmellick stitch stem of the wild rose, with the thorns in satin stitch. Work the spray of leaves on this stem in stem and satin stitch with bullion knots as before.

7 Work the two leaves behind the wild rose petals next. They each have a buttonhole stitch outline with an unstitched centre.

8 Complete the motif by working the petals of the rose in long and short stitch over a split stitch edge, in the order shown on the diagram. Then, fill the centre of the rose with French knots.

9 When you have finished stitching all the motifs, launder the bedspread if necessary. Press the bedspread with the motifs face down on a soft surface so as not to flatten the embroidery. Whisk the bedspread over the bed and lie back in elegant splendour!

Design area

12 x 21cm (4¾ x 8¼in)

Materials

One single bedspread

Embroidery thread
  (see diagram key)

Equipment

Pale tacking thread

Tape measure

Grey pounce

Fine paintbrush

Pale blue paint

Embroidery frame at least
  25cm (10in) in diameter
  and 2.5cm (1in) deep

Size 20 chenille needle

MOUNTMELLICK BEDSPREAD KEY

Coats 50g/150m (25oz/1²⁄₃yd) Lyric 8/4 cotton

∞∞∞∞∞∞∞   *Mountmellick stitch in white*

- - - - - - -   *Buttonhole stitch in white*

- ⸱ - ⸱ - ⸱ -   *Long and short stitch over split stitch edge in white*

🌀   *French knot in white*

⋯⋯⋯⋯⋯   *Satin stitch in white*

— ⸱ — ⸱ —   *Stem stitch in white*

ıııııııııııı   *Bullion knot in white*

— — — —   *Centre lines*

Note: You will need 2 balls to complete seven motifs.

Christening robe

Three exquisite motifs – a ladybird, a daisy and a butterfly – decorate this charming Christening robe. The fine embroidery, using traditional techniques characteristic of Ayrshire work, is very delicate. The motifs can be arranged on any robe pattern, and are suitable for any other special outfits for a baby or small child. You could also break with tradition and try working the motifs in colour. Design by Tracy A. Franklin

1 Cut out the pattern pieces for your Christening robe and decide how you wish to arrange the embroidered ladybird, daisy and butterfly motifs.

2 Photocopy the templates for the motifs from pages 152–153, making separate copies for each repeat of each motif. You will see that you also have the option of a mirror image of the daisy. Carefully cut around each photocopied template. Place each template in position on the pattern pieces and tape them down securely.

3 Lay the cotton lawn on a flat, clean surface and pin the largest pattern piece to be embroidered on top, allowing enough fabric all around the pattern piece for that section to be bound and stretched on a slate frame. Tack around the shape of the pattern. Pin and tack around each pattern piece to be embroidered in the same way, always allowing enough fabric to work on a frame. Finally, before you cut any of the fabric, make sure the rest of the pattern pieces, that will not be embroidered, will fit on the remaining fabric. Only then, cut the fabric for the embroidered pieces, not around the pattern pieces, but as a block including the allowance for working on a frame.

4 Unpin the pattern pieces from the fabric. Replace them under the fabric, within the appropriate tacked outlines and pin them back in position. Place each piece of fabric to be embroidered on a light box and trace the outlines of the design onto it with a pale blue pencil.

5 Bind the edges of the section of the garment to be embroidered and stretch on a slate frame. If you decide to use an embroidery hoop instead, bind both hoops to give extra protection to the cotton lawn.

6 Stitch the motifs following the instructions on pages 152–153. When the embroidery is complete, make up the Christening robe according to the instructions for your chosen pattern.

Use the mirror effect on the top part of the garment as well as on the bottom part.

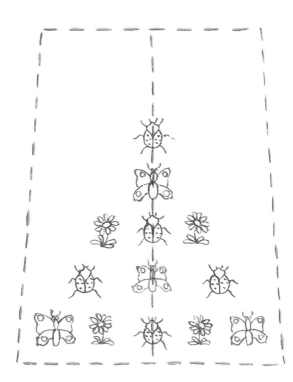

Draw centre lines onto the patterns so the motifs can be placed symmetrically.

Design area

Daisy: 3.5 x 5cm (1⅜ x 2in)

Ladybird: 2.5 x 3cm (1 x 1¼in)

Butterfly: 4.5 x 3cm (1¾ x 1¼in)

Materials

Cotton lawn fabric as required by garment pattern, plus extra allowance for working on a frame

Embroidery thread (see diagram key)

Equipment

Christening robe pattern

Masking tape

Contrasting tacking thread

Pale blue pencil

Slate frame or embroidery hoop

Size 8 and 10 embroidery needles

Fine, pointed embroidery scissors

Stiletto

Daisy template

Daisy stitch diagram

A

B

Daisy motif

7 Thread three strands of stranded cotton in the size 8 needle. Start with a waste knot in the centre of the daisy. Bring these threads, the foundation for the trailing stitch, to the surface at point A on the diagram. Thread one strand of stranded cotton in the size 10 needle and work the trailing stitch to the base of the stem.

8 Take all the threads through to the back. Bring them up again at B to work the bottom right leaf. Complete all the leaves in the same way,

adjusting the start points along so the leaves fit together attractively and the stitches do not stress the fabric.

9 Using one strand of stranded cotton, split stitch around the outlines of each petal. Satin stitch across each petal in the direction on the diagram.

10 Work plenty of French knots with one strand of stranded cotton in the centre of the daisy, so that none of the background fabric remains showing.

Ladybird template

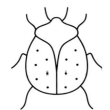

Butterfly template

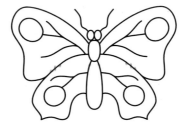

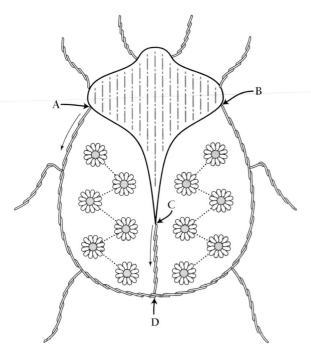

Ladybird stitch diagram

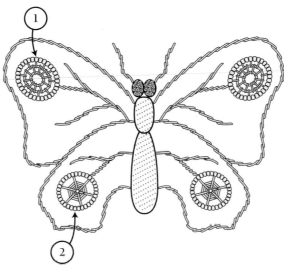

Butterfly stitch diagram

Ladybird motif

11 Stitch the ladybird using one strand of stranded cotton throughout. Start by making the eyelets. Pierce a small hole in the fabric with the stiletto for each eyelet as you come to work it and then overcast it before moving on to the next one. Stitch all six eyelets on each wing case with the same length of thread, trailing the thread just once from one eyelet to the next on the reverse. This avoids too many trailing threads and loose ends which would spoil this fine embroidery.

12 Stem stitch around the body and legs, starting at point A. Stitch each leg in turn, returning the thread neatly along the back of the stitches to the body. Finish at point B. Work split stitch around the ladybird's head, starting at point C and work stem stitch along the front legs and antennae as before.

13 Starting in the middle at the top of the head and going out to each side, work long and short stitch across that area. Come up just outside the split stitch outline and take each stitch down towards the wing cases, keeping the stitches absolutely vertical. Where the outer edges of the shape taper, the stitches will naturally become satin stitches worked from one outline to the other. When the head is complete, work along the centre line from points C to D as before.

Butterfly motif

14 Stitch the butterfly using one strand of stranded cotton throughout. Starting with the big circles on the top wings, overcast the large eyelets and then work the needlelace filling in each one. Overcast the large eyelets on the bottom wings and then work a back stitch wheel in each one.

15 Work stem stitch around the top wings and their veins and then complete the bottom wings in the same way.

16 Work split stitch around the bottom half of the body and then work satin stitch at an angle over the outline. Repeat for the top half of the body. Finally, stem stitch the two antennae and work lots of French knots in the two eye shapes.

Shadow work

Shadow work uses sheer fabric such as fine lawn, organdie or organza through which stitches or fabric pieces can be seen, forming a shadow effect. Traditionally white on white, modern shadow work often uses coloured fabric. Shadow work was combined with pulled embroidery in imitation of expensive bobbin lace. As well as being cheaper, it was also more durable. The most notable form was Dresden work from Saxony and in the first half of the 18th century, it was highly regarded enough to be remounted onto muslin when the original garment became worn through frequent wear.

Left: Border of a fichu, Dresden work, first half of the 18th century. Using white linen thread on a white lawn fabric, the shadow work is in herringbone on the wrong side and the filling stitches are in satin stitch, pulled work and counted threadwork. The beautiful scalloped edge is worked in buttonhole stitch.

Worked on fine muslin imported from India, Dresden work was a precise technique with floral motifs often outlined with shadow herringbone. A wide variety of other intricate stitches were also used, such as whipped stem, whipped chain, coral and embossed satin stitches, with numerous fillings such as faggot, four-sided honeycomb, three-sided, step, trellis and wave stitches. These were combined in rococo patterns with flowers, shells and ribbons using the same designs as lace, which often came from the brocaded silks woven in France.

Dresden work was copied in Britain, and in the 1750s prizes for good imitations of Dresden work were offered by the Art-Gallican Society in England, the Edinburgh Society and various Irish societies. It was often taught in small schools and workshops in many towns and cities where girls were given board, lodging and the various skills that would enable them to earn a living. The Glasgow Mercury of 9 January 1783 carried the following advertisement: 'Mrs Aird notifies that she is giving up her business and 'entreats the continuance of employment of her daughters. They intend to teach white and coloured seam, Dresden, working lace etc and continue the making and selling of Grave cloths.'

The Protestant Moravian emigrés who settled at Ballykennedy, Gracehill, County Antrim during the 1760s produced fine embroidery including Dresden work. Similarly most religious groups, including the Society of Friends and the Quakers, taught girls needlework and, although this was

Opposite page:
Ancestral Hearth *by* **Rosemary Campbell,** *detail, 1991. This large panel was inspired by an ancient Stone Age dwelling at Skara Brae in Orkney. It depicts the hearth, the heart of the home. Layers, including shadow work appliqué, are used to add a subtle depth of colour. Shadow work was also used to enhance the surface.*

155

*Above: Monkey panel,
Kathleen Mann, circa 1934.
Various stitches and shadow
appliqué are worked on this
organza fabric.*

mostly confined to plain sewing, some decorative work was produced. There are surviving samplers with Dresden work in Pennsylvania, for instance, where in the late 18th century whitework samplers depicting that typically American motif, a basket of flowers, were popular. The stems were in chain stitch and the flowers, leaves and details of the basket filled with drawn thread or Dresden work. Around the central motif squares or circles filled with floral motifs were also often included, giving a fine lacy quality to the work. These were worked in white silk or linen thread on fine linen or cotton.

Chikan work

Similar to Dresden is Chikan work, embroidered with untwisted white cotton threads on fine white muslin. It depends for its effect on the contrast of different thickness of threads to form opaque fillings and lace-like patterns. The main stitches used are simpler than those used in Dresden work and include stem and double back stitch forming shadow work, French knots, satin and buttonhole stitch with areas of pulled work. A particular characteristic of the work is long trailing stems worked in running stitch that lend a more flowing element to the design. Although the term Chikan as applied to whitework embroidery was not known before the early 19th century, there is a long tradition of embroidery on fine white muslin in India, recorded in documents

and paintings. However, it is likely that 18th-century European embroidery influenced the development of Chikan work, which may have developed as a cheaper alternative to more expensive woven fabric.

Although forms of Chikan work were carried out in Dacca and Calcutta, the best work was carried out in Lucknow, which had been an important artistic and cultural centre before the decline of the court of the Nawabs of Oudh and the Mutiny in 1857. However, the city recovered as a trade centre boosted by the building of the railway, and Chikan work appears to have flourished from about 1860. By the 1880s it had a fine reputation and won prizes at various international exhibitions. It became one of the most important industries of Lucknow and several of the original firms continue to flourish.

Today, Chikan work is done on industrially produced cotton, polyester and cotton, or sometimes silk with silk or rayon thread. Thick crewel needles with a small eye are used with fine stranded white cotton. For pulled work, a thread is drawn from the selvedge of the fabric as it is stronger and this is worked from the back of the fabric. Occasionally coloured threads are introduced, two colours being twisted together to give a shaded effect. The fabric is not worked on a frame but stretched tight around the index finger and held secure. The embroidery is carried out by Muslim women, with their children learning at a young age to carry on the tradition and the same profession. However, the embroiderers are invariably the most poorly paid of those involved in the industry and live in abject poverty.

Sheila Paine, an expert in this field, has observed that Chikan embroidery is unique in that each of the six basic stitches is used for only a single purpose. For example, chain stitch is never used to work a stem or a small leaf or flower, but confined to the final outline of a large leaf or petal. Similarly, the number of threads used never varies. It is also a peculiarity of Chikan work that some stitches are worked from the back of the fabric while others are worked from the front.

The designs are transferred to the fabric with carved woodblocks using dye from various gum trees. These designs usually consist of floral sprays, leaves, tendrils and large flowerheads, and only in the very finest quality work are birds, elephants, deer and fish sometimes found. Different embroiderers work different sections of the design, but their eyes can only sustain up to five hours' work each day. It has been calculated that today almost half a million inhabitants of Lucknow are Chikan workers. However, the finest master embroiderers died in the early 1980s and today, although some fine work is still done to commission, much of the Chikan work produced is of poor quality.

Experimental work

Most of the shadow work done in Britain in the 20th century was as decoration on clothing, mainly children's clothes and women's fine silk underwear. During the late 1920s and early 1930s, fashionable bias-cut dresses necessitated lighter-weight fabrics for women's underwear. Silk was popular but expensive, and new fabrics such as rayon provided a cheaper alternative. Underwear became more glamorous and matching sets were often embroidered with delicate floral motifs in shadow work appliqué. At the same time, a few embroiderers experimented with shadow work to create a new form suitable for picture panels. They combined different stitches and appliqué on gauze and the panels were mounted on about 1cm (⅜in) from the back of the frame so the shapes would throw shadows to enhance the overall effect.

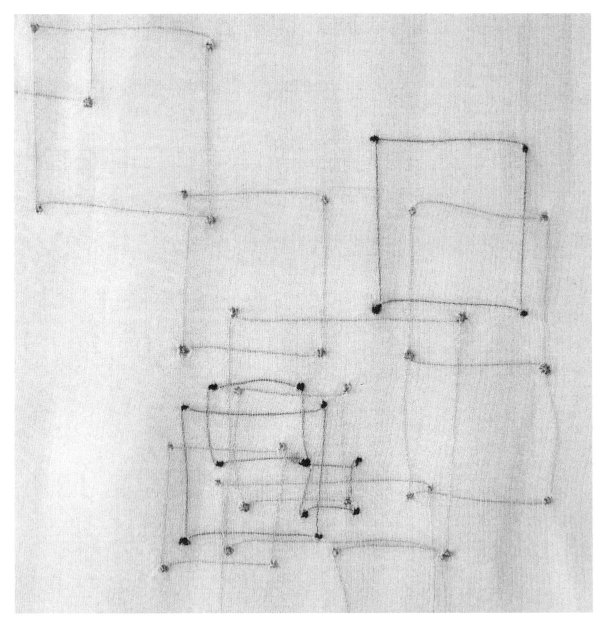

Top left: Fragment of shadow work, Britain, early 20th century. The motifs are typical of those worked on women's blouses and underwear.

Left: Modern piece by Rebecca Hogg, 2000. Silk fabric worked in satin stitch using silk threads.

Shadow work stitches and techniques

Modern shadow embroidery is created on very fine translucent fabric to give a delicate, airy effect of stitches that are floating upon the fabric. This effect is made entirely with one stitch, called either closed herringbone or double back stitch. This stitch creates an outline of back stitch around the shapes on the surface of the fabric, which are filled in with the criss-crossed herringbone pattern showing through from underneath.

Fabrics

In order to achieve the delicate translucent effect of shadow work, it is essential to choose your fabric carefully, so if in doubt, work a small sample first. The fabric must be very fine, almost transparent and yet strong enough to sustain intense lines of closed herringbone or double back stitching. A close weave fabric such as organdie, organza, voile, muslin, chiffon or very fine silk is suitable.

Needles

Select a sharp, pointed, large-eyed embroidery needle that will allow the thread to pass smoothly through the fine fabric without having to pull and spoil it.

Threads

Threads such as six-stranded embroidery cotton, coton à broder and coton perlé no.5 are suitable for this technique.

The thickness of the thread must be considered carefully, as a thread that is too thick may be too heavy and bulky to be used with a very fine fabric. The stranded threads are particularly good for this reason. With a little experimentation different types of threads may also be used, such as stranded metallic threads or even very fine flower threads.

White or soft colours, worked on white or pale fabrics, give a delicate effect. On the other hand, brightly coloured threads produce striking designs as the outlines show up in strong colours and the herringbone stitches can be seen as pastel shades on the right side of the fabric.

Additional tools

The use of a bound wooden hoop is highly recommended to achieve and retain an even tension. The combination of using a very delicate fabric and a technique that involves stitching backwards and forwards across the fabric could lead to puckering and distortion if the work is held loosely in the hand. However, do not overtighten a delicate fabric, as it may easily get damaged or stretch and lose shape.

Use coloured pencils to transfer the design outlines to the fabric. Draw the outlines as lightly as possible so they cannot be seen around the finished stitches.

Shadow work techniques

The stitch used for shadow work can be referred to by two different names depending on which way it is worked. It can be called a double back stitch when it is worked as two lines of back stitch on the surface of the fabric, which are joined by a criss-cross of stitches on the wrong side. It can also be called double herringbone stitch, taking its name from the criss-crossed herringbone pattern that is clearly visible through transparent fabrics.

It is best worked looking at it from the right side in order to ensure the lines of back stitch are neat and even, while at the

---

CLOSED HERRINGBONE STITCH

OTHER NAME: double back stitch

USES: outline, filling

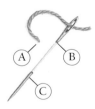

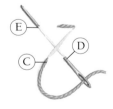

1 Bring the needle up at A. Make a short back stitch and take the needle down at B. Bring the needle up again diagonally across to the opposite side of the outline at C.

2 Work a short backstitch from C to D and cross the shape again to bring the needle up at E. Keep stitches to a maximum, even length of 2mm (⅙in) where the shape allows.

3 Work a stitch from E back to the first stitch and take the needle down in the same hole. Continue to fill the shape. It is usually more comfortable to work from right to left.

same time being able to see the pattern of herringbone stitches being created on the underside of the fabric.

Neatness really is the essence of this technique as any loose ends or untidy joins show through and cannot be hidden on the wrong side of the fabric.

Starting and finishing

Trace the design onto the translucent fabric and place the fabric carefully within a hoop.

Start with a waste knot (see page 28) on the right side within the design area and close to where you will start stitching. Snip and remove the knot from the right side of the fabric when the working thread is securely attached by the stitching. Finish off a thread by passing it through a few of the stitches on the wrong side of the work, close to a line of double back stitches rather than through the herringbone stitches. Then, trim the end. Check the stitching is neat on the right side.

When working the stitches, take care not to pull the thread too tightly as this can create holes in the fabric.

The wrong side and the thread secured with a waste knot.

Working different shapes

It is not always possible to keep the stitches of an even length, because the shapes of the design will often have fluid curves. It will therefore be necessary to vary the lengths of both the back and herringbone parts of the stitch in order to fill the shapes as they curve and come to points.

The size of the back stitches on the inner curve of a shape will be considerably smaller than those situated on the outer curve. This principle becomes clear when working around a ring shape. You will need to work the back stitches around the inner ring on a tiny scale, so the longer stitches that are located on the outer ring can keep pace without having to be too big.

Varying the length of stitches to fit around a ring.

When the shape eventually tapers to a point, you must keep the back stitches the exact same length. However, you will need to reduce the length of the herringbone part of the stitch in order to work it into the tapered points of the shape.

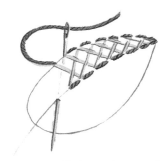

Tapering double herringbone stitch into a pointed shape.

A pointed shape may eventually taper into a single line as when a leaf joins a stem for instance. The herringbone part of the stitches will shrink in size, then disappear altogether. When this happens, the whole stitch can then be reduced to one line of back stitch.

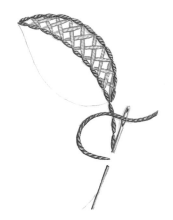

The double herringbone eventually becomes a simple back stitch.

Working two shapes close together will result in a double line of back stitches down the centre of the overall shape, which can be very effective when two different colours of thread are being used. It is important to make sure the length of the back stitches is the same in this situation, in order to keep the work looking as neat as possible.

Working two adjacent shapes creates a double row of back stitches.

To keep the intrinsic qualities of shadow work, there is no need to embellish the design with numerous other surface stitches. However, you may find a couple of surface embroidery stitches useful, such as back stitch (see page 49) to work any single lines and also add fluidity, and French knots (see page 205) to add tiny details to the design.

With both stitches, but especially the knots, you must secure the threads very neatly behind the worked stitches.

Design your own

- *Use simple shapes that can be filled in, such as leaves, petals, ribbons, lettering, simple geometric shapes and silhouettes.*
- *Keep the size and scale of the motifs small, so the stitches are not too big.*
- *Try design ideas out on tracing paper, working on both sides of the paper with coloured pencils as though they were threads.*

Flower spray drape

This exquisitely delicate transparent drape will enhance any room in the house and look very fresh wafting in the breeze from a window. It is an ideal project for anyone who is unfamiliar with the technique of shadow work to undertake. You need only six motifs to create a full-length drape, but you could always work just one motif or use fewer repeats for a smaller window. Design by Jane Iles

Design area

8 x 19cm (3¼ x 7½in)

Materials

Length of cream, organdie-type drape with a 2m (7½ft) drop (hemmed, headed and sides neatened)

Embroidery threads (see diagram key)

Equipment

Pins

Pale green and pale pink coloured pencils

20cm (8in) bound, wooden embroidery hoop

Size 6 embroidery needle

Sharp, pointed trimming or embroidery scissors

1 Make six photocopies of the motif. Iron the fabric carefully. Place the drape on a large, flat surface and arrange the motifs at least 8cm (3¼in) away from the edge so the embroidery can be worked in a hoop. Carefully slip the motifs under the fabric and temporarily pin them in position. Trace each motif accurately onto the fabric, using the pale green and pink pencils. Place one design motif centrally within the embroidery hoop.

2 Following the diagram, shadow stitch using three strands of stranded cotton. Start with a waste knot and secure the thread ends on the wrong side. Make sure the wrong side is neat as it will be seen on the right side. Work each leaf in two halves, from tip to stem or stem to tip. Work stems in back stitch. Keep the stitches on the right side even so it is impossible to tell where the back stitch becomes closed herringbone stitch (double back stitch). Work clusters of three French knots to make tiny flowers.

3 Re-position the hoop to work each repeat motif following the diagram. When complete, iron the fabric gently on the wrong side.

FLOWER SPRAY DRAPE KEY

DMC stranded cotton

Back stitch in 746
Closed herringbone stitch in 746

Back stitch in 369
Closed herringbone stitch in 369

Back stitch in 3813
Closed herringbone stitch in 3813

Back stitch in 503
Closed herringbone stitch in 503

Back stitch in 3348
Closed herringbone stitch in 3348

French knot in 819

Note: You will need 1 skein of each shade to complete six motifs.

Baby's patchwork blanket

This cosy blanket takes a fresh look at shadow work. The motifs have been stitched on a layer of fine cream dress fabric, similar to organdie but kind enough for a baby's skin, to make an enchanting design in pretty pastels. The blanket has been given a warm, snuggly backing of soft woollen flannel. You could easily adapt the design by choosing your favourite motifs and adding baby's name. Design by Jane Iles

1 Using a photocopier, enlarge each motif overleaf by 200 per cent so it measures 17.5cm (7in) square. Make four copies of each design. Trim around the edge of each square.

2 Tape together two sheets of A2 layout paper to obtain one 58 x 84cm (23 x 33in) sheet. Arrange the motifs centrally, allowing 1.5cm (⅝in) between each square, then tape the squares in position. Rearrange the motifs at this stage, if desired.

3 Place the pattern on a large, smooth surface, then position the transparent fabric centrally over it, aligning the grain of the fabric with the straight lines of the pattern. The fabric will extend beyond the edges of the pattern sheet. Use fine pins to secure in place, then trace each motif onto the fabric using the appropriate sharp, coloured pencils. Retain the pattern to trace the squares later.

Position the various motifs onto the sheet of paper, allowing space for the grid around each one.

4 Select a motif, then carefully place the fabric in the bound hoop. With the coton perlé threads, work each motif in closed herringbone stitch. Start with the heart shapes, which are probably the easiest to stitch, until you feel confident. Take care to shape the closed herringbone stitches around the inner and outer curves and into the points.

5 Next, work the leaves and straight stems of the green motif. Stitch the double back stitches around the inner circle of the ring in this motif much smaller than those around the outer circle.

6 Finally, work the ribbon motifs, which have quite a few shaped corners to fit the stitches into. To work the trimmed, pointed ends of the ribbon, start by stitching one point and finishing the thread off neatly when you reach the full-width part of the ribbon. Start again and stitch the other point of the ribbon, but this time continue stitching up the whole length of the ribbon, matching the stitches where the two sections meet so the join does not show.

7 When a motif is complete, carefully remove the delicate fabric from the hoop and re-position the hoop ready to stitch another motif.

8 When all the motifs have been worked, iron the fabric on the wrong side of the fabric in order to smooth away any creases and flatten it once more.

9 Place the transparent fabric over the paper pattern, aligning the shadow work motifs with those on the paper below. Pin to secure. With the tan coloured pencil and a long ruler or metre stick, carefully draw the straight lines onto the fabric, linking the lines from one square to another to obtain a grid of double lines extending to the edges of the fabric. Remove the fabric.

10 Trim the flannel fabric, removing the selvedges, to measure 67cm (26½in) wide by 86cm (34in) long. Then, place it on a smooth, flat surface.

Design area

67 x 86cm (26½ x 34in)

Materials

1m x 90cm (40 x 36in) cream, soft, transparent fabric such as voile or chiffon

Embroidery threads (see diagram key)

90 x 70cm (36 x 28in) cream doctor's flannel

Equipment

A2 layout paper

Clear adhesive tape

Pins

Pale blue, green, pink and tan coloured pencils

25cm (10in) bound, wooden embroidery hoop

Size 5 embroidery needle

Sharp-pointed trimming or embroidery scissors

Long ruler or metre stick

Tacking thread

11 Lay the embroidered fabric centrally, right side up, on top of the flannel. Then pin in place, working from the centre outwards. Keeping the layers flat and close to the work surface, work tacking stitches across the area.

12 Trim around the edges of the transparent fabric, leaving a 3cm (1¼in) hem allowance beyond the edges of the flannel. Using long lengths of coton perlé 437, work neat, even running stitches (see page 63) along the traced network of straight lines to embellish the design and join the two layers of fabric together. Start and finish each line of running stitches on the edge within the hem allowance. There is no need to secure the threads as they will be neatened when the fabric is hemmed.

13 Measure 1.5cm (⅝in) away from the outer line of running stitches on each edge of the blanket and stitch one more row to finish the grid

14 Fold a double hem all around the transparent fabric and turn it to the wrong side of the blanket to bind the edge of the flannel. Fold the thin fabric at the corners at a 90 degree angle. Then, pin and tack the hem in position before working small slip stitches (see page 33) along the hem to secure. The stitches should not penetrate the flannel nor show on the right side. Finally, carefully remove all tacking stitches.

Enlarge by 200%

Enlarge by 200%

Enlarge by 200%

Enlarge by 200%

BABY'S PATCH BLANKET KEY

DMC coton perlé no. 5

Closed herringbone stitch in 899

Closed herringbone stitch in 963

Closed herringbone stitch in 761

Closed herringbone stitch in 368

Closed herringbone stitch in 472

Closed herringbone stitch in 341

Closed herringbone stitch in 747

— *Running stitch in 437*

Note: You will need 1 skein of each shade.

Silk shading

Silk was discovered by the Chinese over 5,000 years ago, but the details of how it came to be produced and used in other countries are shrouded in mystery. However, there were undoubtedly many embroiderers, among both monastic and secular communities, working in silk in England by 900 AD. They were highly skilled, having trained for eight years before they were allowed to work professionally. Silk threads worked in split stitch were used extensively for drawn figures, their expressive faces and subtle shading of the garment draperies. This work, known as opus anglicanum, was produced for the next 600 years but was at its finest between 1250 and 1350.

Opus anglicanum was exported all over Europe but the earliest documented and best preserved examples are the Anglo Saxon stole and maniple from the tomb of St Cuthbert in Durham cathedral. Inscriptions on the design record that they were commissioned by Aelfflaed, wife of Edward the Elder, for Bishop Frithsan of Winchester between 909 and 916. They depict named figures of saints and prophets worked in stem and split stitch, with the ground covered in couched gold threads.

Court dress

Expensive silk embroidery was not restricted to work for the Church, but throughout history has also added status to the dress of the wealthy. The formal court dresses of the early 18th century had wide skirts supported on whale bone hoops and trains that provided an ideal maximum surface on which to display elaborate silk embroidery. Those worn at royal birthdays and weddings were particularly splendid, although courtiers had to be careful not to be too ostentatious as this was frowned on as a sign of 'impertinence and vanity'.

Decorative aprons, too, enjoyed a lot of favour and those embroidered on silk between 1710 and 1750 are particularly charming. They are short but wide to cover the skirts and are gathered at the waist. Usually of white or cream silk, but occasionally other colours, the floral embroidery designs often incorporate swags or scrolls and silver gilt metal threads. The flowers, leaves and twining stems were worked in long and short, stem, split and satin stitches.

Later in the century, men's suits worn on ceremonial occasions outshone the women's. Velvet coat fronts, collars, cuffs, pocket flaps and waistcoat fronts were exquisitely worked with subtly shaded multicoloured sprays of flowers. Attention was even lavished on the buttons which were embroidered in fine silk to match.

Needle painting

At the end of the 18th century, needle painting using twisted silk threads was introduced. Great skill was required for reversible colifichet embroidery worked in floss silk through thick paper or parchment. These small embroideries of flowers, portraits, shepherds or religious subjects, rarely more than 15cm (6in) long, were framed with glass on both sides. This technique probably came from China during the 17th century and was practised in Ursuline convents until the early 19th century. Other larger pictures were

Left: Leek embroidery, Ajunta design by Thomas Wardle, 1880s. Silk threads on linen in long and short stitch worked with couched gold threads.

Below: Mantle of the Virgin, detail, Whalley Abbey Dalmatic, 15th century.

Opposite page: Detail of a waistcoat pocket, possibly French, circa 1780. Floss silk embroidery on satin in split, stem, satin and straight stitches and French knots.

With the introduction of Berlin woolwork, silk embroidery lost its appeal, but enjoyed a revival later in the century.

Thomas Wardle, a silk dyer who worked extensively for William Morris, discovered a method of bleaching Indian wild silk, 'tussore', which made it commercially viable. He dyed fine floss silk threads with vegetable dyes to produce subtly coloured lustrous threads. In 1879 or 1880, Elizabeth, his wife, devised a method of working the floss threads on a block-printed tussore silk ground. The printed pattern on the silk dispensed with the need for a transfer and the design was worked in a variety of simple stitches including long and short, stem, buttonhole and French knots and greatly enriched by the addition of couched gold threads. Elizabeth and her friends formed the Leek Embroidery Society and promoted this form of art needlework through exhibitions that were given considerable coverage in women's magazines.

Due to the prevalent criticism of the poor standard of British design, great care was taken to use only high quality designs. Liberty's imported Oriental textiles and greatly influenced public taste, which encouraged the Leek Society to use designs derived from Indian art. Thomas Wardle visited India in 1886 and returned with designs taken from the 2,000-year-old Buddhist rock paintings in the Ajanta caves near Bombay. The Ajanta design of exotic flowers and birds was adapted for embroidery and became the most famous of the Leek Society's designs. It was worked in deep blue, terracotta and moss green on a cream ground with gold highlights. Wardle took ideas from Persian, Coptic and Celtic art as well as historic embroideries and adapted them. Other designers, including William Morris, produced embroidery designs for the Leek school.

In 1883, Thomas opened a shop in New Bond Street, London, with a special department for Leek embroidery. Pieces could be bought ready-worked or as kits with a printed design and appropriate silk threads. By 1894, these kits were also available through the Liberty's catalogue. The Leek Society flourished for more than 20 years and some time before 1890, became a branch of the Royal School of Needlework. However, with the death of Elizabeth in 1902, it declined.

Art neeedlework inspired many artists and designers to explore the medium of embroidery. Phoebe Anna Traquair, an Irish woman living in Edinburgh, was an accomplished artist and designer and a leading light in the London-based Arts and Crafts Exhibition Society. She worked as a painter, illustrator, enameller and book-binder, and also produced illuminated manuscripts, large-scale

worked in imitation of paintings, the flat, smooth long and short and satin stitches reproducing brush strokes. The subjects were usually based on popular paintings and engravings by well-known artists; others depicted figures beside classical ruins that appealed to neo-classical and romantic taste. Commemorative mourning pictures worked in this technique were particularly popular in the United States. The designs were professionally drawn on white satin fabric and some details such as the sky, faces and hands were painted in watercolour and left entirely unstitched.

murals and outstanding embroideries. The most famous are a set of four panels entitled *The Progress of the Soul,* representing the four stages in the spiritual life of man and worked between 1893 and 1902; each worked in her spare time took two years to complete. Measuring approximately 188 x 74cm, they are in coloured silks and gold threads on linen in traditional stitches.

Revival of skills

In Glasgow, Anne Macbeth became Head of the School of Art's Embroidery department in 1908. She abhorred the slavish copying of popular painting in embroidery and blamed the stagnation of embroidery on Berlin woolwork. She regarded figure panels as the supreme challenge for embroiderers and introduced her own distinctive form of embroidery in which the modelling of figures and drapery were suggested by solid blocks of colour worked in satin stitch in lustrous floss silk threads. These were usually on cream or white satin and the direction of the blocks was changed to vary the reflected light and give substance to the form. She introduced vivid colours to her work and also combined a variety of techniques such as couched thick floss silk threads, appliqué, metal threads and a variety of simple stitches.

Chinese silk embroidery

Silk has always been expensive and therefore enjoyed high status, particularly when combined with precious metal threads. Nowhere was this more obvious than in the Far East, especially in the Imperial Court of China, where lavishly embroidered silk dragon and court robes were worn by the emperor, mandarins and other dignitaries. Dragons formed the main design with wave and cloud patterns around the hem and on the sleeves and cuffs. Symbolism was important in Chinese culture with the five-clawed dragon the supreme motif, the accompanying wisps of flame indicating its supernatural character. Flowers, birds, mythical beasts and heavenly bodies represent a vast number of attributes, seasons and religious beliefs. Colours too were symbolic, with yellow reserved for the emperor and his family. At court, there was a strict hierarchy and officials often wore panels or badges embroidered with motifs to denote their rank. Women at court also wore special embroidered robes as did children, priests and actors. In the late 19th and early 20th centuries, a large number of Chinese embroideries found their way to the West via the trading port of Shanghai. Small items such as pairs of sleeve bands or cuffs were often framed and hung in middle class drawing rooms.

Above: **King of the Jungle, by Melissa Cheeseman, 1996. The technique is natural silk shading worked with stranded cotton threads.**

Left: Pair of uncut sleeve bands, Chinese, 20th century. Silk with floss silk embroidery in satin, long and short, fly and back stitches and couching.

Opposite page, top left: The Victory, by Phoebe Traquair, 1902. Silk and gold threads on linen. This is the last of four panels from the series The Progress of the Soul.

Opposite page, top right: Obi, by Midori Matsushima, circa 1980. Incorporating long and short, Japanese holding and Japanese suga stitches and couching.

Opposite page, bottom: Detail from an Altar frontal, designed by Ann Macbeth, worked by Agnes E.P. Skene, 1909–10. Silk threads with gold and silver metal threads on corded silk. Worked in satin, knot, chain, stem, straight, long and short, running and daisy stitches with French knots and couching; decorated with seed pearls and glass beads.

169

Silk shading stitches and techniques

Silk shading is a way of creating realistic studies of natural subjects through the skilful use of long and short stitch and the subtle blending of colour. It has traditionally been worked in silk threads that, because of their lustre and despite being laid flat, give the embroidery vitality and a three-dimensional quality. Practise the basics given here and gain the confidence to stitch your own beautiful images.

Fabrics

Silk fabrics give a richness which complements the technique and are available in a wide range of colours, textures and weights. The lightweight Habotai silk is not suitable for this technique as it is too flimsy. Dupion silk, on the other hand, is excellent as long as it does not have too many slubs in the weave. Furnishing silks can also be used: generally, the lighter the fabric the more it is recommended to use a backing cloth under the silk to give a firmer surface on which to stitch.

Needles

Use a crewel needle for long and short stitch as the longer eye will accommodate more strands of thread. The size of the needle will depend on the number of threads used for the design. Sizes 9 and 10 are generally suitable for a single strand of thread. Note that it is preferable to use a needle that is too large rather than one that is too fine, as the thread will not wear as quickly.

Threads

Silk threads were traditionally used and beautiful ranges of stranded silks are still available today. However, they are not always easy to get a hold of and are quite expensive. For this reason, stranded cotton is often, and successfully, substituted. It is a considerable advantage to be able to choose the number of strands to use and mix the shades in the needle.

Silk shading techniques

A fine outline is needed for this technique so to transfer the design, use either the prick and pounce method or dressmakers' carbon paper (see page 31).

Preparing the fabric

The embroidery must be stretched on a frame and a fine silk fabric should be mounted on a backing cloth (see page 17). The two fabrics must lie flat on each other, so stitch them together around the outlines of the design. This will prevent the fabrics from buckling when the heavy, long and short stitch is worked on top.

First, pin the top fabric to the backing cloth. Thread a fine crewel needle with a single strand of cotton sewing thread to match the silk fabric. Secure the thread and stab the needle vertically up and down through both layers of fabric to make a tiny straight stab stitch.

Pin the silk to the backing fabric then stab stitch around the design lines.

Repeat all around at about 1cm (½in) intervals just inside the outlines of the design.

Make sure the stab stitches are worked just outside the outline.

Planning the stitching

It is a good idea to try out your ideas for the colour shading of your design on paper first. Trace the design outlines onto paper and fill in the areas with coloured pencils to help you decide how many colours and shades you will need to use in the final design. Use the pencils to shade the different areas in the same direction that you plan to stitch them, to check your ideas work and to use as an extra guide later.

Mark the sequence in which you are going to stitch the areas onto your design. Always work the areas in the background first, starting with the bottom areas and working upwards. This sequence gives a sense of perspective to the embroidery.

Finally, with a dressmakers' chalk pencil or hard lead pencil, lightly mark the direction of the stitches, following the contours of the subject, within each area. Also, mark the colour changes onto the design in order to give you guidance as you stitch.

Defining the outlines

Before embroidering, the outlines of the design must be worked with split stitch, to give each shape a crisp, distinctive edge. Do not work split stitch around all the areas at once. Outline one shape, then fill with long and short stitch.

Perfecting the shading

Long and short stitches are worked in two different ways. If you stitch them all in the same direction, with the grain of the fabric, you will create a smooth area of colour that is useful for large areas and backgrounds.

To shade the subject, you need the stitches to look more natural and enhance the shapes of the design. To do this, adapt the long and short stitch to give it direction and create natural shading. It is better to start stitching on a wide area of the design, such as the outer edge of a petal, and working down,

decrease the number of stitches into a narrow area, such as the base of a petal, rather than the other way around.

Start on the top edge in the centre of the shape and work the first row of stitches towards each side in order to establish a smooth pattern. Work the first row alternating long and short stitches, bringing the needle up within the design area and taking it down over the split stitch edge. Always stitch in the direction

of your guidelines. Keep the stitches as close together as possible, without overlapping them. If you make a good, solid first row of stitches in the correct direction, the following rows should be easy to work. Your main aims are to keep a smooth surface and to subtly graduate the shades. Remember to bring the needle up through the previous stitches and stagger where you start them to avoid making stripes and ridges.

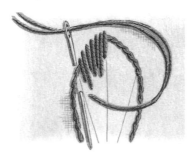

Use short stitches as wedges to help you follow the direction and the long stitches to create the smooth finish.

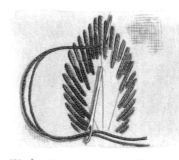

Work subsequent rows, making sure the stitches split the stitches of the previous row.

SPLIT STITCH

USES: outline, line

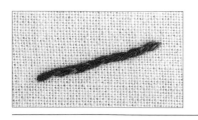

Bring the needle up through the fabric and then make a small stitch. Next, bring it up again, splitting the threads in the first stitch as you go and make a second stitch

of the same length. Repeat the sequence in order to complete the row of stitches.

Split stitch can be used in a functional way to define the edge of solid shaded shapes in both silk shading and crewel embroidery, where it will eventually become completely hidden. However, it is a useful stitch in its own right and can also be used decoratively in freer forms of embroidery. Worked

in simple lines, split stitch will emphasize both the linearity and movement in a design, or it can be closely packed to fill a shape.

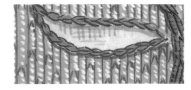

Work the split stitch around the outline of the shape, ready to cover it with natural shading.

LONG AND SHORT STITCH

OTHER NAMES: tapestry shading (shown here), natural shading (see above)

USES: filling, background

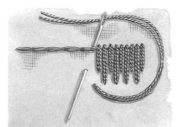

1 Come up in the shape. Make a stitch, at right angles to the edge, going down outside the outline. Work a short stitch close to the first. Repeat to finish the row.

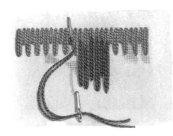

2 On the next row, come up through the ends of the stitches in the first row, splitting the threads. Make long, random stitches. Change colour as desired to fill the shape.

Long and short stitch shown in its two forms: tapestry shading and natural shading.

Autumn leaf and rosehip brooches

These brooches are a simple project with which to begin your journey into silk shading. Small enough to be completed quickly, they encompass the basics of long and short stitch in both tapestry shading and natural shading. When stitching is complete these little works of art are made up into brooches with a simple brooch pin. Alternatively, they could be mounted onto card and framed to hang on the wall. Designs by Samantha Bourne

Design area

5cm (2in) square

Materials

23cm (9in) square pre-shrunk calico

Embroidery threads (see diagram keys)

6cm (2½in) square each pale grey and pale blue craft felt

Equipment

Tracing paper and pencil

Dressmakers' carbon paper

15cm (6in) embroidery hoop

Size 7 and 9 crewel needles

Embroidery scissors

Needles, pins and thread for making up

Sewing threads to match felts

2.5cm (1in) brooch bar

Autumn leaf

1 Trace the design from the diagram below using tracing paper and a pencil. Make sure to include the directional arrow on the background and the square outside edge of the design. Lay the calico on a flat surface and place the dressmakers' carbon on top. Then, place your traced design on top of the carbon so the directional arrow runs along the grain of the calico. Using the pencil, draw over the design carefully. Lift off the tracing paper and the carbon paper to reveal a clear outline of the design.

2 Stretch the piece of calico in the embroidery hoop, pulling as tight as you can in order to achieve a firm surface.

3 Start the embroidery by stitching the background. Use two strands of the pale blue stranded cotton 828 and a size 7 crewel needle to stitch a line of split stitch around the square perimeter of the design. Continuing with two strands of the pale blue thread, fill in the background of the design with tapestry shading. Start at the top centre of the design and work the first row of stitches out from the centre to the sides.

stitches vertical as you work around the leaf shape. Leave a thin line for the leaf stalk.

4 With a pencil, draw the direction lines for the shading, referring to the diagram. Using a single strand of mid-brown stranded cotton 920 and a size 9 crewel needle, split stitch around the outer edge of the leaf. Work the leaf in two halves on either side of the central vein. With one strand of the mid-brown thread, start on the central tip of the leaf and work the first row of stitches around the edge down one side, following the direction lines. Fill the area of mid-brown and then repeat on the other side. Complete the shading in golden brown stranded cotton 729 by working the centre of the leaf in two halves, meeting along the central vein.

5 To complete the leaf, add a stem stitch (see page 206) vein and stalk with two strands of dark brown stranded cotton 801 and a size 7 crewel needle.

6 Cut the finished work out of the calico, leaving a 1cm (⅜in) border all around. Fold this excess to the back, pin and slip stitch into place (see page 33).

7 Trim the 6cm (2½in) square of pale grey craft felt until it covers the reverse of the brooch. Stitch the brooch bar to the back of the felt using a matching sewing thread. Then, pin the felt to the reverse of the brooch and carefully stitch the two together using small, neat slip stitches.

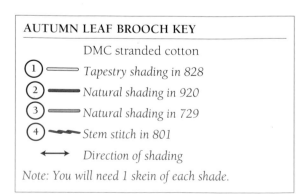

AUTUMN LEAF BROOCH KEY	
DMC stranded cotton	
① ▭	*Tapestry shading in 828*
② ▬	*Natural shading in 920*
③ ▬	*Natural shading in 729*
④ ∿	*Stem stitch in 801*
↔	*Direction of shading*

Note: You will need 1 skein of each shade.

Rosehip

1 Transfer the design from the diagram below in the same way as for the autumn leaf, using tracing paper and dressmakers' carbon paper. Stretch the calico drum tight in the hoop.

2 Start by stitching the background. Use two strands of the mid-turquoise blue stranded cotton 3766 and a size 7 crewel needle to work a line of split stitch all around the square perimeter of the design. Fill in the background for the design with tapestry shading. Start at the top centre of the design and work the first row of stitches out from the centre to the sides. Continue to cover the background, keeping the stitches vertical as you work around the rosehip and leaf shapes. Leave a thin line for the stem.

3 Referring to the diagram, trace the direction of the shading in pencil onto the calico. Stitch the leaves first, then the stem and finally the rosehip, working split stitch around the edge of each shape and then filling it with natural shading before moving onto the next one. Start with one strand of the darker green stranded cotton 987 in the size 9 crewel needle and outline the two small outer leaves on the rosehip. Fill in the leaf shapes with long and short stitch, using a single strand of the same colour, starting at the tip of each and working downwards.

4 Work the other leaves on the top of the rosehip and the other two on the stem, outlining them in split stitch with a single strand of the pale green thread 3364. Begin to shade the leaves in with a single strand of the pale green thread, changing colour to the dark green thread 987 at the base.

5 Work the stem with two strands of dark green, stitching along its length. Add a short row of stem stitching (see page 206) from the base of the stem halfway up to create a thicker line.

6 Now go on to stitch the rosehip. First, outline it with split stitch using a single strand of the russet brown thread 355. Start the shading at the tips of the rosehip in a single strand of the russet brown. Follow the diagram, making the colour changes to incorporate the inner areas of red and orange as you work down to the base of the rosehip.

7 Take the work out of the hoop and trim the calico, leaving a 1cm (⅜in) border all around. Fold the excess fabric to the back, pin and slip stitch it in place. Trim the square of pale blue felt to the same size as the brooch and stitch the brooch bar onto the back with matching thread. Pin the felt on the back and slip stitch it in position.

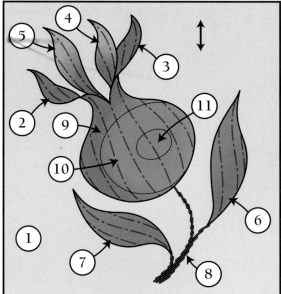

Work the split stitch outlines and then shade in each area of the design, once the background is complete.

ROSEHIP BROOCH KEY

DMC stranded cotton

①	——	*Tapestry shading in 3766*
②③	——	*Natural shading in 987*
④-⑦	≡	*Natural shading in 3364* *Natural shading in 987*
⑧	⟞⟞	*Stem stitch in 987*
⑨	——	*Natural shading in 355*
⑩	——	*Natural shading in 817*
⑪	——	*Natural shading in 900*
	⟷	*Direction of shading*

Note: You will need 1 skein of each shade.

INSPIRATION AND DESIGN:
subtle colours of nature

The natural beauty of flowers has inspired many embroiderers, as well as other artists and designers in all countries and cultures throughout the centuries. The variety of their shapes and exquisite shades of colour makes them a treat to work in many styles of embroidery, but no technique is more appropriate than silk shading, especially when it is stitched in real silk: the sheen of the threads catches the light, the petals sing out and the embroidered flower literally comes to life.

You will have your own personal favourites with special significance in your life, but the original idea for the pansy panel on the following pages came from the design on the tiles surrounding a Victorian fireplace. The Victorians gave meaning to many flowers, but they loved the humble pansy with its smiley face, as a symbol of happiness and friendship. It was therefore found in abundance in the decoration of their homes and, of course, in their gardens. The symmetrical design reflects the Arts and Crafts influence with the slightly crisp, stylized flowers and leaves on curvaceous stems. You could take your inspiration from all sorts of similar items around the home or found on rummages through antique shops, including the designs on tiles, china or fabric. Alternatively, look for images of flowers in magazines

or plant catalogues that will give lots of detailed information about the shapes and colours, or take your own close-up photographs.

You do not have to be able to draw to design for silk embroidery. Instead, trace around your favourite images. Transfer them onto paper and arrange a composition to your liking. Using real flowers and a photocopier will also give some exciting results. Make sure the copier glass is clean, lay the flowers on top and press them down gently under a sheet of paper. Experiment with the toner to give the clearest results and print them out to make your composition. You could also try scanning real flowers or images of them onto your computer, printing them out in colour to work with or editing your design on screen.

With the image of your chosen flower in front of you, you have all the information you need to decide on the colours and the way in which the design should be stitched. Observe the tiny veins on the petals and leaves as these will show you the direction for the shading on each part of the design.

Deciding on the colours is the next exciting stage. For a realistic effect, you will want to reflect the colours that nature gave to your flower. Pansies probably come in more different colour combinations now than when the Victorians grew them. However, after looking at lots of different images of the flower, a reminder of the classic combination of golds and reds on an old seed packet was the deciding factor in choosing the colour scheme for the pansy panel. Pick out the threads which follow your colour scheme and check that they will work well together.

Choosing the fabric for the background is just as important. A medium weight pure silk always works well, but it would also be worth experimenting with textured and rough silks or mixtures with other fibres. Even though it will be less easy to transfer the design onto a textured fabric, the contrast with the threads may make it worthwhile. Painting, printing or dyeing the background fabric before stitching also opens up other avenues and would take the embroidery to another level of creativity.

Pansy panel

This simple design is brought to life using a palette of vibrant silk threads, which are shown off to their best advantage on the parchment-coloured silk fabric. Natural shading is the perfect way to enhance the shape of the petals and leaves. Bullion knots add texture to the flower centres and stem stitch is used for the stems and veins. The embroidery makes a beautiful panel or a top for a special box. Design by Samantha Bourne

1 Trace the design from the diagram on page 180 and reduce it by 75 per cent. Lay the silk on a flat surface and secure with masking tape. Then, place a piece of dressmakers' carbon paper on top of the silk and lay the traced design on top, keeping it square to the grain of the fabric. With the pencil, draw over the design. Lift off the tracing paper and then the carbon paper to reveal a clear outline of the pansy design.

2 Place the piece of calico onto a flat surface and then lay the piece of silk fabric on top, smoothing out any wrinkles.

3 Stretch the fabrics into an embroidery hoop, and pull tight to achieve a firm surface, taking care to keep the tension on both fabrics even. To bond the fabrics and prevent movement, stab stitch around the design in a matching sewing thread.

4 With a size 7 crewel needle and two strands of green silk thread 107, stem stitch (see page 206) along the stem lines, excluding the veins in the leaves.

5 To begin each leaf, split stitch around the outside of the leaf with a single strand of the pale green silk 190 and a size 9 needle. Then, draw on the direction lines using a pencil. To begin each leaf, split stitch around the outside of the leaf with a single strand of the pale green silk thread 190 and a size 9 needle. Then, draw on the direction lines using a pencil. When shading with long and short stitch, work each leaf in two halves. Start each leaf at the very tip and, with one strand of the pale green silk, work the first row of stitches down one side following the direction lines as closely as possible before repeating on the other side. Continue shading the rest of the leaf in two halves following the colour changes shown on the diagram to incorporate the mid-green 191 and dark green 192 threads and meeting along the line of the central vein. Work the calyx around the flower bud in the same way using the same shades of green. Finish off the leaf design by stem stitching the central veins using two strands of the grass green thread 107 and a size 7 crewel needle.

6 The flowers and flower bud are all worked using a single strand of the silk. Follow the diagram for the sequence of working the petals, remembering to split stitch around each petal in an appropriate colour before you work the long and short stitch over it. Do not work the split stitch outlines around all the flower shapes at once. Instead outline each shape and complete the shading before you go on to the next, as this will give the shapes more definition and ensure a crisper result. To finish the two open flower faces, work long straight stitches in a single strand of the black silk thread 089 to create the stamen. Then, work two bullion knots side by side on each flower to create the centres, using a single strand of the pale green 190 silk thread.

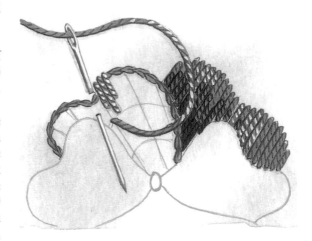

Complete the shapes at the back before working up to the ones on top and follow the directional lines.

7 Carefully remove the embroidery from the hoop and, if necessary, gently iron on the reverse of the work to remove any wrinkles. Trim a piece of stiff card to fit the aperture in the frame and stretch the embroidery over it, ensuring the design is correctly positioned and lacing the fabric on the back (see page 32). Choose a mount to complement the colours in the embroidery and assemble it with the embroidery in the frame.

Design area

11.5 x 19.5cm
(4½ x 7¾in)

Materials

30cm (12in) square parchment-coloured Dupion silk

30cm (12in) square pre-shrunk calico

Embroidery threads (see diagram key)

Equipment

Tracing paper and pencil

Masking tape

Dressmakers' carbon paper

25cm (10in) embroidery hoop

Sewing thread to match fabric

Size 7 and 9 crewel needles

Embroidery scissors

Stiff card for stretching embroidery

Strong thread for lacing

Mount board and frame of your choice

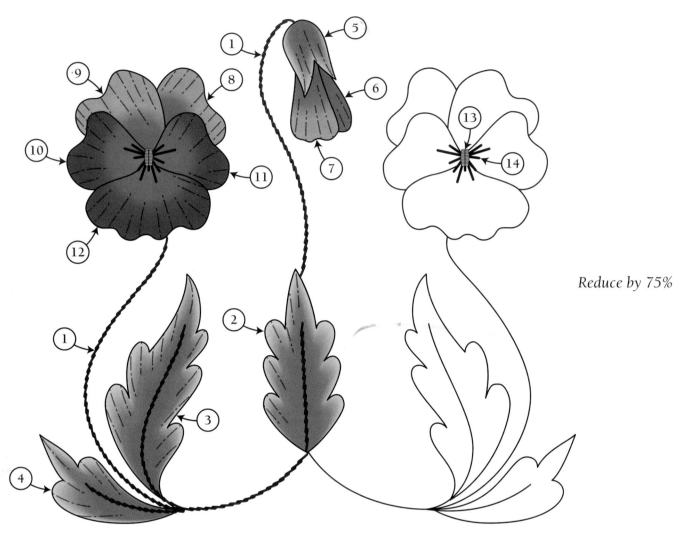

Reduce by 75%

PANSY PANEL KEY

DMC stranded cotton

① ━━━   *Stem stitch in 107*

② – ⑤ ≣   *Natural shading in 190, 191, 192*

⑥ ━━   *Natural shading in 181*

⑦ – ⑨ ≣   *Natural shading in 153, 155, 181*

⑩ – ⑫ ≣   *Natural shading in 155, 181, 065, 038*

⑬ ━━━   *Straight stitch in 089*

⑭ ▬   *Bullion knot in 190*

— ·— ·   *Direction of shading*

Note: You will need 1 skein of each shade.

Crewel work

The term crewel work refers to any coloured embroidery worked with crewel wool, a lightly twisted two-ply, worsted yarn usually sold in hanks or skeins. This strong yarn has been available to embroiderers since before the Middle Ages and is still in use today. The yarn is stitched with a crewel needle, which eases its path through the fabric. The term crewel may be derived from the Saxon word cleow meaning a ball of thread – the Norman victory over the Anglo Saxons celebrated in the Bayeux Tapestry is not only one of the most famous embroideries in the world, but the earliest complete surviving example of crewel work.

Commissioned by William the Conqueror's half brother Odo, Bishop of Bayeux (1036–1097), the Bayeux Tapestry tells the story of the events leading up to the Battle of Hastings and the defeat of King Harold in 1066. Measuring 70m long and 50cm wide (230 x 2ft), the embroidery is worked in terracotta, yellow, buff, blue and green crewel wools on linen, mainly in laid work and couching with stem and outline stitches. The lively pictures have a real sense of movement and the strong contrasts between the stitched and unstitched areas, between light and dark tones, add to the lively narrative. Latin inscriptions help to explain the events and characters. However, there is no use of perspective, with sailors, soldiers, their ships and horses all on the same scale. Yet they are shown in great detail with expressive gestures and faces and it is this detail, from a period when so few artefacts survive, that makes this embroidery such an important historical document. It was made in eight sections to allow several people to work on it at the same time and the pieces were joined when the embroidery was complete. It is believed to have been made in Kent between 1076 and 1086.

Such narrative hangings were used to decorate large rooms, but embroidery with wools was also used in churches. For example, the 11th century 'Creation' hanging in Gerona Cathedral, measuring 3.6 x 4.5m (12 x 15ft), is entirely covered with wool embroidery in couched work stem, chain and some satin stitch. In the centre is Christ surrounded by scenes of the Creation, rivers of Paradise and, in the border, the four seasons, the months, the sun and the moon. Scandinavian and Icelandic church wall hangings from the 14th to 16th centuries are worked in the same way. At a time when most people were illiterate, narrative images such as these were an important method of conveying religious information and ideas.

East meets West

At the time of the formation of the Dutch and English East India Companies in 1597 and 1600 the focus of trade was on pepper and spices, but gradually small quantities of exotic textiles were imported to Europe from India and China. These included woven and embroidered silks and muslins, and painted and printed calicoes known as palampores. The latter had great novelty value, but their white designs on a coloured ground did not appeal to European decorative taste and the agents encouraged the Indian textile merchants to adapt traditional designs to suit the European market.

Embroidery as an art

During the 1660s, designs were sent from England for the Indian printers to copy but as they were unfamiliar with the plants and animals, the designs became an amalgam of eastern and western elements. The resulting bold, colourful designs of printed calico had a great influence on English embroidery and by the late 17th century such embroidered designs were in great demand for bed hangings, covers and window curtains.

Above: Detail from the Bayeux Tapestry, Bayeux, France, 11th century. The embroidery is worked on linen fabric using yellow, terracotta, buff, blue and green crewel wools.

Opposite page: Exotic Bird, designed and embroidered by Phillipa Turnbull.

Right: Curtain, English, circa 1700. The linen twill fabric is embroidered with crewel wools in an extensive range of stitches. The flowering tree motif featured here dominated crewel work design from the mid-17th to the late 19th centuries.

Right: **Hares,** *designed by William Blake and worked by Mrs Thomas Butts, early 19th century.*

During the 18th century a taste developed for more delicate design and crewel embroidery was overshadowed by silk embroidery, although fine wool was used for needle painting as an alternative to silk. Among the most successful exponents was Mrs Mary Knowles who reproduced well-known paintings. Her remarkable self-portrait is part of the Royal Collection and can be seen in Kew Palace. Another celebrated embroideress was Mrs Butts, a friend and patron of the artist William Blake who is known to have drawn her two designs to work.

Crewel embroidery enjoyed a revival when William Morris (1834–1896) reacted against gaudy Berlin woolwork and, after his marriage in 1859, began to design embroideries to decorate his own home, Red House at Bexleyheath, Kent. He appreciated the importance of embroidered furnishings to interior design and his aim was to encourage a sense of beauty in the home. He taught himself, his wife Jane, his daughters and others embroidery stitches by unpicking late 17th-century embroideries and studying historic examples in the newly founded South Kensington Museum, now the Victoria and Albert. He liked the sense of movement that could be achieved with crewel embroidery. He also preferred the soft colours of the natural vegetable dyes of the 17th-century hangings to the garish aniline dyes introduced during the 1850s. Crewel work lent itself to both large and small scale work and by the 1870s the embroidery department became one of the most successful at Morris and Co. Embroiderers could purchase kits, including wools and small naturalistic designs traced on linen, or designs with small sections worked to indicate colour and stitches. Such embroidery was more refined than Berlin woolwork; it became known as Art Needlework and was to be the craze of the late 19th century.

Among the many examples of Morris's inspired crewel embroideries are the crewel work bed furnishings and coverlet at his new home, Kelmscott Manor. Embroidered between 1891 and 1895 by his wife, his daughter May and others, the trellis design is based on a wallpaper design by Morris. The valance is worked with one of his poems and the coverlet includes a quotation from another.

A number of needlework organizations were established in the 1870s to promote better design, but the most prestigious was the Royal School of Art Needlework founded in London in 1872. Its aims were to promote embroidery as an art and to provide employment for poor gentlewomen. Crewel work formed the basis of the teaching as it was regarded as the best training in surface stitchery, and quantities of crewel embroideries were produced for sale. Designs were commissioned from highly regarded artists such as William Morris, Burne-Jones and Walter Crane. By the 1880s, agencies were established in both Philadelphia and Boston as well as in major cities around Britain including Glasgow.

The Glasgow School

It was at the Glasgow School of Art between 1894 and 1908 that the ideas of William Morris were to be developed in a most innovative and influential way through the teaching of Jessie Newbery. She encouraged a strong sense of design in her students, fostering an essentially linear style. She liked the contrast of straight lines to curved, of horizontals to verticals, and tried to make beautifully shaped spaces that she believed were as important as the pattern. She used stylized plant forms such as pea-pods, pea-flowers and roses worked in crewel wools on unbleached linen in satin, long and short, and stem stitches. These were worked on cushions, curtains and door curtains, often including lines from poems, and combined with needleweaving. The colours used at the Glasgow School of Art differed from those used elsewhere. They preferred pearly greys, silvers, pinks and lilacs, but most distinctive was their use of green, white and violet. Jessie Newbery and many of her students were militant suffragettes and were aware that the initial letters of these colours represented the slogan 'Give Women Votes'

In the 1920s, in the aftermath of the First World War, there was a desire in Britain to preserve the status quo and a suspicion of anything foreign including new ideas in architecture and design. This led to a revival of Tudor and Jacobean styles in houses, furniture and embroidery. Many 'Jacobean' patterns for crewel work were published and kits for cushions were widely available, but these had neither the liveliness and colour of the 17th century designs nor the originality of Morris's designs. The standard of embroidery technique had also declined and crewel work lost favour in Britain. However, in America where it continued to be worked to a high standard and was generally influenced by traditional English patterns, the design was often less densely worked with more ground showing, giving a lighter effect. In recent times, crewel work has been combined experimentally with canvas work, appliqué, beadwork or machine embroidery.

Left: Cushion cover, designed and worked by Jessie Newbery, circa 1900. The linen fabric is worked with wollen threads in satin, long and short, and stem stitches with a border of needleweaving. The inscription 'Under every grief and pine runs a joy with silken twine', is a verse by William Blake.

Crewel work stitches and techniques

The beauty of crewel work is that it is a technique in which even the wary stitcher can become an artist and progress amazingly quickly once the basics are mastered. Sumptuously subtle colours of soft wool are used with long and short stitch to provide realistic shading to stylized images from nature. This soft shading is enhanced with other outline and filling stitches to give a richly coloured and textured piece of work.

Design your own

• *Study an historical piece of crewel work and note the stitches, colours and subjects that were used.*

• *Design with three or four shades of a cool colour such as mint green and the same number of a warm colour such as terracotta; then add one strong accent such as scarlet.*

Fabrics

To work crewel embroidery in the traditional way, you will need a special linen twill fabric, which is often called 'Jacobean'. For more adventurous work, you should use other upholstery weight fabrics, but they must have a dense weave, like the linen twill, in order to support the heavy wool embroidery.

Needles

Use a size 2 crewel needle. Its sharp point and fat body will ensure that the needle makes a hole in the fabric large enough for the wool to pass through without becoming fluffy, which would spoil the finish of your work.

Threads

Crewel embroidery is worked with two-ply crewel wool that should never be split.

The range is extensive, offering very closely graduated shades of soft and antique colours. These are quite difficult to distinguish between, so just select the colour you want to work with at any one time and keep all your threads well organized and labelled.

Additional tools

A hoop or frame is essential and it is useful to have a free-standing one, so you can work with one hand above and one below the fabric. This, and stabbing the needle through at 90 degrees to the linen, will help you develop a

steady rhythm and therefore keep your stitches neat. Make sure the fabric is drum-tight on the frame and re-tighten it as necessary. You do not need to remove the work from the frame between stitching sessions because the linen is extremely robust, but do loosen the tension slightly in order to let the fabric relax and then tighten it again before use.

Some crewel work designs are quite large, so if you are using a hoop, you will need to use white tissue paper to protect the embroidery. Place tissue paper over the stitched area before you replace the outer ring, then tear away any tissue covering the new working area.

Crewel work techniques

Long and short stitch (see page 171) holds the secret of gradual colour blending, which is so characteristic of crewel work. You should therefore become familiar with this stitch in order to obtain full enjoyment from your design.

Soft shading

The basic long and short stitch is used in exactly the same way as for silk shading (see page 171). A shape is filled with two or more rows of long and short stitch, the boundary between the rows being random and indistinct, allowing the shades to merge into one another. The softly shaded

effect is created by changing to a slightly different shade of the same basic colour for each row of stitches. In this way, you can graduate from light to dark shades of a colour in only three or four rows and without any visible colour boundaries.

To enhance the effects of this soft shading, remember to stitch up through the stitches on the previous row and take the stitch down into the unstitched area. The very first row is worked in the opposite direction, bringing the thread up within the shape and taking the stitch down over the edge of the shape.

You can, of course, blend two completely different colours using this particular stitch, but bear in mind that subtle changes are always easier to work.

Transferring the design

The best way to transfer a design onto the linen twill is by using a light box (see page 30). You need to make sure the design has a strong outline that will show through the linen fabric and go over the outlines with a pale coloured pencil.

Securing the thread

To start stitching with a single thread, secure it initially with a waste knot (see page 28) within a shape to be stitched over later. Then, work a few small straight stitches, or seeding, in order to anchor the thread more firmly, so you can cut off the waste knot after you have made a few of the stitches on the design.

If you need to use a double length of thread, start with a loop (see page 28). To finish the thread off securely, either make a few seeding stitches in an unworked area or weave through the back of stitches as appropriate.

Choosing a starting point
You can start anywhere on the design, but work the background areas first and choose one of the simpler shapes. On a simple background, the stitches are all worked in a vertical direction, like tapestry shading. Start at the top edge of the shape, placing the first stitch midway along the highest part. Then, continue to stitch the first row of long and short stitch towards the nearest end of the shape, adapting the length of the stitches to follow the contours of the edge. Vary the length of the stitches, keeping them parallel and close enough to hide the pencilled outline.

When you have reached the end of the shape, return to the starting point and then travel in the opposite direction to complete the first row of stitches.

Work the first stitch and travel to the left; return to the start and travel to the right.

To work the next row, thread the second shade of wool and start next to the original stitch on the first row. Bring the needle up through the stitch above and down in the unstitched area, so the colours blend together. Work

in the same sequence as before, first to one end and then to the other end of the shape from the starting point, making the stitches in random lengths. Continue to stitch subsequent rows with different shades in order to cover the bottom edge and complete the shape.

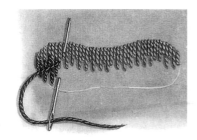

Bring the needle up through the stitches on the previous row.

Moving on from soft shading a simple shape
Once you have mastered the technique for simple areas worked in one direction (usually towards the base of a hill or the stem of a flower or leaf) develop your skills with the curving shapes described below.

Start with the first stitch at the top point and then work the first row down on the outside edge to the base. Use long stitches to establish the direction of shading and short ones as wedges to fill the gaps as the direction changes. Repeat on the other side.

Use the long and short stitches to direct the shading within the shape.

For the next row, choose a different shade. Bring the first stitch up through the first stitch on the previous row.

Remember to come up through the stitches on the previous row.

Work stitches of random length towards the centre in one half of the shape. Repeat on the other side, taking the stitches down along the same line, to fill the shape. On the last row, take the stitches down along the natural centre line, like a leaf vein.

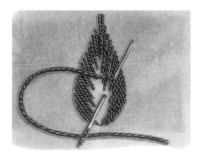

Work the last row of stitches down along the centre line.

Working more complex shapes
Some shapes need more practice. Work the first row as an outline from the tip down each side of the shape in turn. Where the shape curves out, add extra short stitches to fill the spaces and allow the long stitches to converge into the decreasing space.

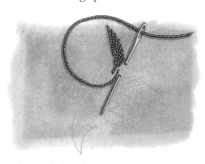

Short stitch to fill a convex curve, allowing the long stitches to converge.

Tips

• *Begin with an easy stitch – a blank fabric is always daunting and it is good to see a few areas done.*
• *If your wool is going fluffy or wearing thin, your wool is too long.*
• *Measure your wool from your elbow to the tip of your little finger, once for single and twice for double, and it will be an ideal length.*

Where a shape curves inwards, splay the stitches out a little on the inside of the shape, bringing the thread up a little way from the previous stitch. Make sure that the stitches are still very close together on the outside edge of the shape.

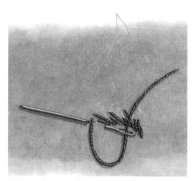

Splay the stitches out on the inside to fill a concave curve.

Laid and couched work

Another characteristic of crewel work is the filling often seen on the "hummock" shapes at the base of a traditional design. These look complicated, but are simple if approached systematically.

Long, straight stitches are first stitched in criss-cross fashion. These are then couched down with stitches. The couching stitches can be tiny straight ones or little crosses and the spaces between the laid threads can be filled with stitches such as French knots. Combine colours and stitches to suit your design.

Four shades of blue create a three-dimensional effect, contrasted with yellow couching.

Two grids create a rich texture of squares and diamonds in two greens under the couching stitches.

Crewel embroidery is a true feast of textures and you will need other stitches in order to achieve the raised effects with your designs.

Linear stitches are used to make flowing lines: take a look at stem stitch (see page 206), split stitch (see page 171) as well as chain stitch (see page 205). Other textural stitches, such as bullion knots (see page 146), buttonhole stitch (see page 98) and ermine stitch (see page 206), will also enhance your work.

SATIN STITCH

OTHER NAME: Gobelin stitch (see page 78)

USES: solid shape

Long and short stitch is not the only one that can be used to fill in blocks of solid colour in crewel work. Satin stitch is also characteristic of the technique, is simple to work and uses just one colour in any small shape. It can be worked flat, raised over a split stitch edge (see page 145) or padded (see below) and is useful in other techniques such as Hardanger, whitework and free embroidery. Always keep the stitches smooth and at an even tension.

1 Always make the first stitch across the centre of the shape to establish the direction. Come up on the inside edge of the design and make a straight stitch to the outside edge.

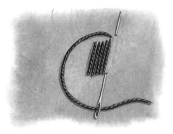

2 Start the second stitch close to the first. All stitches must be side by side to cover one side of the shape then the other. Stitches can be worked at an angle if kept parallel to each other.

PADDED SATIN STITCH

USES: solid shape

1 Make a first satin stitch across the centre of the shape far enough inside the design to allow for further layers of stitches. Work parallel stitches in one direction, then the other to cover.

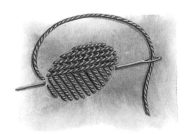

2 Work another layer at a 45 degree angle to the first, again starting in the centre of the shape. Start and finish the stitches just outside the first layer of padding and inside the design line.

3 Add a third layer of padding at an angle to the last, then the final layer in the direction you want to be on show. Make sure the final stitches cover the design line.

PISTIL STITCH

USES: filling, detail

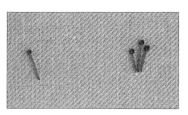

Pistil stitch is really a French knot on a stalk. This particular stitch could be used in a mass in order to produce stylized petals or more individually to make flower stamens for crewel embroidery designs. Of course, pistil stitch can be used more freely in experimental work if desired. It will probably help if you practise a few ordinary French knots (see page 205) before you actually have a go with pistil stitch itself.

1 Bring the thread up through the fabric where you want the base of the stalk to be. Then, wrap the working thread twice around the needle.

2 Turn the needle down where you want the knot to rest, near the starting point. With just the point in the fabric, pull the wool to tidy the knot. Take the needle through.

SEEDING STITCH

USES: filling

Bring the thread up and make a tiny straight stitch in any direction. Repeat to make similar stitches of the same size, working them in clusters or scattering them to fill an area.

BASIC COUCHING

USES: line

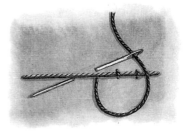

Bring a thread up and lay it on the fabric. Bring another thread up and make a stitch at right angles to the laid thread. Repeat at intervals. Take the laid thread to the back.

CLOSED FLY STITCH

USES: filling, line, single motif

Basic open fly stitch (see page 205) is a simple looped stitch that can be worked in many ways in crewel work and other techniques. Use it singly, as a scattered filling or work in a line as a filling. The closed fly stitch explained here, where individual loops are worked very closely together, is an attractive variation. It makes leaf shapes that look like satin stitch with a central vein that grows as you complete each loop.

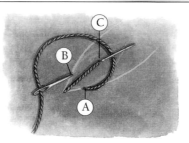

1 Make a straight stitch along the design centre line. Come up at A, down at B and up again at C, without drawing the needle through. Wrap the thread under the needle point.

2 Pull the needle through and secure the V-shaped loop with a short stitch along the centre line. Make the next V the same width and close to the last. Repeat to the end of the centre line.

SIMPLE LAID AND COUCHED WORK

USES: open filling

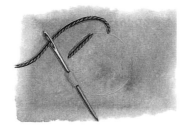

1 Make the first laid stitch at one end of the shape, straight from one side of the outline to the other. Come up on the outside edge and work parallel stitches across the shape.

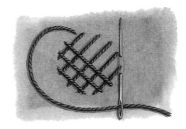

2 Repeat, working parallel stitches in the opposite direction at right angles to the first layer. Start each stitch on the same side of the shape as the end of the last stitch.

3 Work straight stitches down the line of thread junctions on one side of the shape. Work up along the next line and continue to complete the shape. Embellish with French knots.

The Glamis stag

This historic design was inspired by the set of bed hangings in Glamis Castle, Scotland, which was stitched in 1683 by the Third Countess of Strathmore for King Malcolm's bed. The design is worked in two traditional stitches, long and short stitch in soft shading and French knots, which will introduce you to the special qualities of crewel embroidery. Design by Phillipa Turnbull

Design area

18cm (7in) square

Materials

28cm (11in) square
  Jacobean linen twill

Embroidery wools
  (see diagram key)

Equipment

Pale coloured pencil

Hands-free frame (either
  floor or seat frame)

Size 2 crewel needle

Embroidery scissors

Pins

Wooden box with 20cm
  (8in) square recess

Strong thread for lacing

1 Transfer the design onto the linen fabric using a light box (see page 30). Draw over the outlines with a pale coloured pencil. Make a distinction between the heavy lines on the diagram, which denote the hard edges around different parts of the stag, and the lighter lines, which show where one shade merges into another. Stretch the fabric on the embroidery frame.

2 Thread a 30–38cm (12–15in) length of two-ply yellow wool 693 and start working on the hummock in the background. Make a single knot and take the needle down through the linen. Bring the thread up 2.5cm (1in) away from where you wish to begin, within the shape to be stitched, and make three small seeding stitches to secure the thread. Make the first stitch, 1.5cm (⅝in) long, at A in the centre top edge of the hummock in front of the stag's back legs. Start the stitch within the shape and take it down to cover the outline.

3 Continue the top row of random long and short stitches to the left of the first one, filling the top band of the hummock as shown on page 187. When the stitches reach the outline of the hummock in front, make satin stitches to complete the shape you are working. Start again to the right of the first stitch and complete the top row to the stag's hoof.

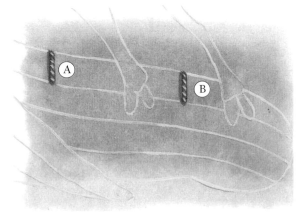

Start at A and complete the top row of stitches in front of the stag's legs, before moving on to start again at B.

4 Now, start stitching again at B in the centre of the area between the stag's back hooves. Fill the top band of the hummock with long and short stitch in the same way as previously. Finally, complete the shape to the right of the stag's last hoof.

5 Once the first row of stitches has been completed, re-thread your needle with the mint green wool 353. Start the second band of colour directly under the first stitch on the first row, coming up through that stitch and making the new stitch approximately 1.5cm (⅝in) long. Continue the second row to the left, working stitches of random length until they become satin stitches again to go along the edge of the hummock in front. Complete the row to the right of the first stitch, working around the stag's hooves.

6 Complete the next two bands of colour using first the lighter green wool 643 and then the darker green 157, in the same way as the second colour. When you work the bottom band, always make sure you bring each stitch down on the outline in order to give the lower edge a crisp finish. Then, work the front hummock in the same way, using the same combination of colours.

7 Now, start stitching the back of the stag, using the darkest brown wool 905. Position the first stitch in the middle of the back of the stag's neck, to help you establish the angle of the stitch on a straight section before you start encountering more awkward curves. Note the direction of the shading shown on the diagram and then angle your stitch in this way. You may find it quite helpful to draw faint pencil lines on your fabric to show you the shading direction to follow. Continue to complete the first row of random long and short stitches all along the stag's back and down onto his tail, altering the angles and positioning the stitches to work around the shape. Work more rows in the same colour in order to complete the first band of shading.

THE GLAMIS STAG KEY

Appletons crewel wool

1 ▬ Soft shading in 905

2 ▬ Soft shading in 766

3 ▬ Soft shading in 901

4 ▬ Soft shading in 693

5 ▬ Soft shading in 353

6 ▬ Soft shading in 643

7 ▬ Soft shading in 157

8 ◉◉ French knot in 901 and 766

9 ▬ Soft shading in pupil in 905, over eye in 901

10 ▬ Straight stitch in 905

‑ ‑ ‑ Direction lines for long and short stitch

Note: You will need 1 skein of each shade.

8 Proceed to the stag's head, flanks and legs, which are all worked in the ginger wool 766. Bring the stitches up through the existing ones on the previous row and vary the length of the new stitches. Keep the stitches on the second row random where they will blend into the next colour and finish them on the outline when they fill the shape of the design.

9 Complete the main parts of the stag's body by working the chest, stomach and inside legs, using the fawn wool 901.

10 Cover the hoof area with the dark brown wool 905, making sure that the effect is slightly raised by using a large number of densely packed stitches.

11 To make the eye of the stag, work satin stitch over the shape, using the fawn wool 901. Complete the eye with a pupil, stitching a few straight stitches in the dark wool 905.

12 Proceed onto the stag's mouth, which is worked with one straight stitch using dark brown 905. Work two small straight stitches on the tip of the nose in the same colour. The stag's face is now complete.

13 To make the antlers, use the ginger wool 766 and work French knots (see page 205) along the lines of the antlers. Then, surround these lines with a single row of French knots using the pale fawn wool 901.

14 Remove the finished embroidery from the frame. Block the fabric, with the embroidered design uppermost, to straighten it (see page 29). Spray the fabric with distilled water. Do not be worried about using too much water and make sure that the fabric is thoroughly soaked. Allow it to dry naturally, which will take approximately three days, and you will find the linen straightens up to a perfect finish.

15 Trim the fabric so it fits the board in the aperture of the wooden box, with an extra allowance for lacing. Stretch the embroidery over the board and lace it securely across the back. Insert the embroidery panel into the aperture on the box following the manufacturer's instructions carefully. A padded box lid would be particularly complementary to the crewel embroidery.

INSPIRATION AND DESIGN:
timeless images

Country houses and castles provide a perfect source of inspiration for new crewel work designs. There is no need to be a well-known embroiderer or a studious researcher to be allowed near most beautiful examples of past skills, as they survive on bed hangings and other furnishings in many places that are open to the public. Looking at the wealth of material on show, you feel transported back in time. You start wondering about the lifestyles of the original designers and embroiderers and how their surroundings and other influences in their lives shaped the gorgeous images they created, to produce embroidery that has been admired for the past 300 years.

Crewel work in its traditional form has appealed to fabric and wallpaper designers ever since William Morris was inspired by it. Contemporary embroiderers are also attracted to the colour, texture, stitch variety, beauty and timeless quality of the original work.

The medium of embroidery has taught us that there is much we share with our predecessors – a deep love of nature and natural shapes that is so strong that it is realized in tangible form through stitching. Our fascination with the variety afforded by different stitches, textures and unusual colour combinations all serve to underline our distinct empathy with fellow embroiderers

over the centuries and our admiration for their work. The Tree of Life panel designed for this section brings together some of the most beautiful and striking images encountered throughout the years. They are mostly drawn from the first half of the 17th century, and assembled in a style typical of historic crewel work, yet pleasing to the modern eye. Placed around the oak tree are Roman vines, hanging with ripe grapes; delicate wild flowers; a carnation, which symbolized support for Catholicism in the 18th century; acanthus leaves, representing the influence of images from India; and finally, the leaves and acorns of the English oak for strength.

The panel also features a lurcher dog and a couple of hares. A hunting scene in full flight would have seemed much too restless compared with the tranquillity of the other images, so instead the dog is pictured distracted by the scent of a flower. The hares, however, remain alert and ready to flee.

So, when you find an historic piece of work that inspires you, study it as closely as you can and then see if there are any postcards of it that you can take home with you. Broaden your ideas by collecting together any other related images from old engravings, greetings cards, gift paper or even photographs of your family pets. Take particular note of how the colours in your source of inspiration are combined, so that you can translate these into the rich array of crewel wools that are available.

The historic images that were chosen for the panel are intended to convey any given moment in an otherwise timeless story. Leaves and flowers have and will always blow in the wind; dogs have and will always chase hares. Trees live for hundreds of years, as has crewel work, and the panel reflects what is most typical of this particular type of embroidery: a compilation of 'Jacobean' and other designs through the ages, as relevant today as it was all those years ago.

Tree of Life panel

This beautiful panel displays some typical images of traditional crewel work. The legendary Tree of Life rises out of a landscape of rounded hummocks and bursts into life with stylized leaves and flowers. A hunting dog and hares are also caught in the still moment of time. This firescreen panel is extremely evocative in the depth of its strong colours and balance of delicate and solid shapes. Design by Phillipa Turnbull

1 One of the great joys of crewel work is that it allows you the pleasure of deciding which part of the design you want to stitch first. First, stretch the linen on a frame, wrapping it around one side of the frame if necessary (see pages 16–17).

2 Decide where you want to start, bearing the following guidelines in mind. It is advisable to start in a top corner on the opposite side to your dominant hand, in order to avoid resting your hand on stitched areas of the design. Start with the background areas and work up to those on top. Also, make sure you start with an easy stitch such as the stem stitch (see page 206) on the vine stems so you can start to establish the design quickly.

3 A recommended order of work would be to stitch the stems and leaves on the background vines, and then complete the grapes. Work the star-like blue flowers after you have stitched their stems and leaves, and complete them with the French knots (see page 205) in the centres.

4 Work down the design, making sure that you stitch the stems before the leaves and acorns that lie on top. Put in the filling stitches in the flowers before you work the outlines around them. Add the finishing touches of eyes, noses and French knots after the rest of the relevant animals, acorns and flowers have been stitched.

5 When all the embroidery is complete, remove it from the frame. Block the fabric, with the embroidered design uppermost, to straighten it (see page 29). Thoroughly soak the fabric and allow to dry naturally.

6 Trim the fabric to the size of the board, which has been cut to fit the aperture in the frame, adding an ample allowance for lacing. Centre the embroidery and then stretch it over the board, making sure to lace the fabric securely on the back. Assemble the embroidery in the frame and bask in its glow and the sense of achievement.

Design area

43 x 58cm (17 x 23in)

Materials

60 x 75cm (24 x 30in) Jacobean linen twill

Embroidery wools (see diagram key)

Black beads (see diagram key)

Equipment

Hands-free frame (either floor or seat frame)

Size 2 crewel needle

Embroidery scissors

Board for stretching embroidery

Strong thread for lacing

Firescreen or other frame and mount of your choice

Enlarge X 170%

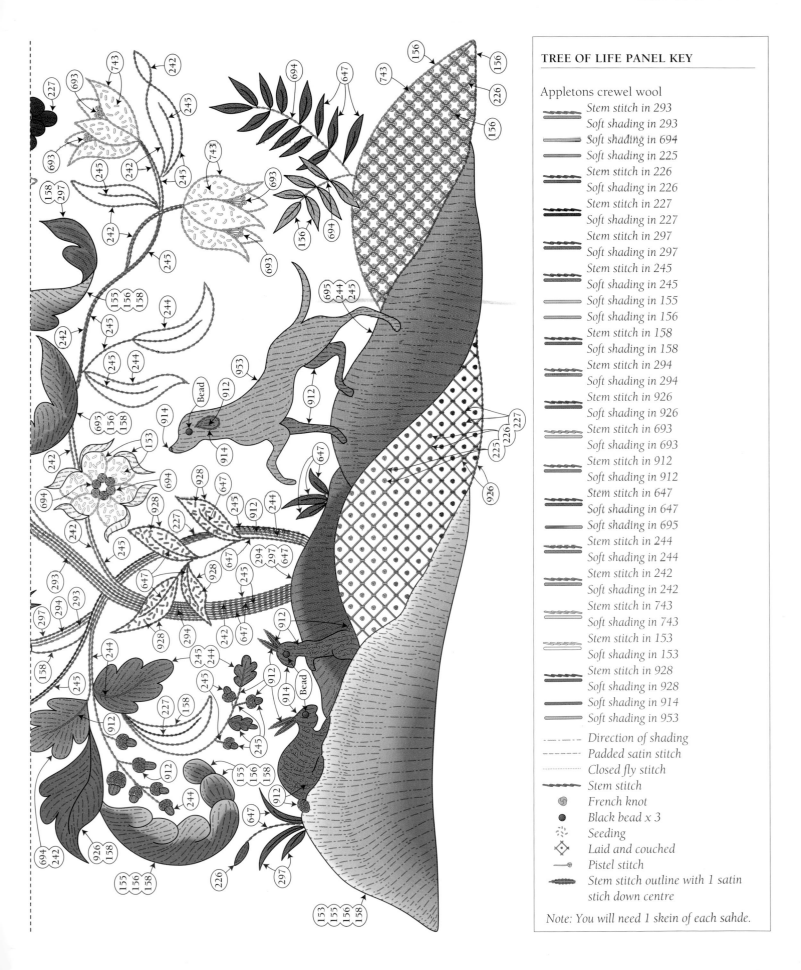

TREE OF LIFE PANEL KEY

Appletons crewel wool

Stem stitch in 293
Soft shading in 293
Soft shading in 694
Soft shading in 225
Stem stitch in 226
Soft shading in 226
Stem stitch in 227
Soft shading in 227
Stem stitch in 297
Soft shading in 297
Stem stitch in 245
Soft shading in 245
Soft shading in 155
Soft shading in 156
Stem stitch in 158
Soft shading in 158
Stem stitch in 294
Soft shading in 294
Stem stitch in 926
Soft shading in 926
Stem stitch in 693
Soft shading in 693
Stem stitch in 912
Soft shading in 912
Stem stitch in 647
Soft shading in 647
Soft shading in 695
Stem stitch in 244
Soft shading in 244
Stem stitch in 242
Soft shading in 242
Stem stitch in 743
Soft shading in 743
Stem stitch in 153
Soft shading in 153
Stem stitch in 928
Soft shading in 928
Soft shading in 914
Soft shading in 953

-·-·-· Direction of shading
- - - - Padded satin stitch
.... Closed fly stitch
~~~~~ Stem stitch
🌀 French knot
● Black bead x 3
⁖ Seeding
◇ Laid and couched
⊶ Pistel stitch
🟫 Stem stitch outline with 1 satin
stich down centre

Note: You will need 1 skein of each sahde.

199

Free embroidery

Free embroidery can be thought of as the opposite of counted techniques and has been used throughout history. For example, Peruvian embroideries made between 500 BC and 200 AD, long before the Incas, from burial sites in Paracas caverns used embroidery stitches freely. They incorporate fine chain stitch in rows that look like knitting, contrasted with textured areas of twisted chain and loop stitches. The multicoloured wools were worked on cotton cloth in different directions to create double-headed snakes, figures and birds. However, it is with the work from the 20th century that free embroidery is most usually associated.

In Britain, in the years immediately after the First World War, there were none of the vigorous fine art developments that occurred on the Continent, where the war seemed to give the impetus to a new style of architecture and design. Although this Modern Movement eventually had an impact on British design, initially its new ideas were viewed with suspicion in Britain where there had been no political disruption as there had been in Europe and there was a desire to return to the idyllic days of the Edwardian era. The result, in Britain, was a nostalgic continuation of the Arts and Crafts tradition established by William Morris. In embroidery, this took the form of an almost total reliance on both Elizabethan and Jacobean styles, particularly among amateur embroiderers. Among professional embroiderers, ideas were changing gradually and there was concern about the poor quality of design. The efforts of individuals such as Mary Hogarth and Rebecca Crompton, Head of Embroidery at Croydon School of Art, to remedy the situation, were to have an effect by the 1930s when stitchery was being used in a new way to enhance the design.

A fresh approach

Rebecca Crompton devised a radically new approach to embroidery as a creative art in the early 1920s. This free approach abandoned imitation of historic styles or copies of other work and relied on stitches worked in a spontaneous way. In her *Plea for Freedom* published in 1936, she stated that her aim was 'to dispel certain ideas on design especially as taught in some schools and to encourage more liveliness and vitality in the work done by children and others.' In this she was reacting against technical precision, as she believed that technique or skilful work was only one aspect of embroidery that, without design, becomes sterile. She also believed

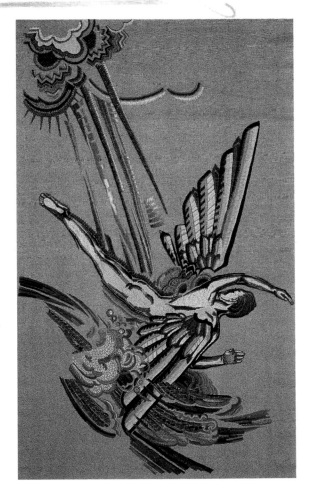

that embroidery should reflect modern life and in this she was supported by many published articles that pointed out that the best work of the past did not imitate the work of earlier periods.

An Exhibition of Modern Embroidery was held at the Victoria and Albert Museum in 1932. It brought new ideas to the public and, in a period of severe economic depression, encouraged people to provide their own decoration in the home and also

Left: Icarus, *by Kathleen Whyte, detail, 1932. This piece is worked in a variety of stitches including Romanian and herringbone, which are used for the wing feathers. Darning suggests the body contours and the brightly coloured wools are in gradations of tone.*

Opposite page: Glimpses, *by Dorothy Tucker, 2000. Freestyle hand embroidery worked in silks inspired by a buttercup field glimpsed between the timbers of an old shed.*

emphasized the need for good design. Rebecca Crompton's piece, entitled 'Creation of Flowers' was a practical example of the idea that technique should be governed by design. She described it as 'an experiment in textures, tones and colours built up without previous drawing.' The ground was of open canvas with a variety of applied fabrics including spotted linen, silver tissue, green wool, white satin, scarlet Vyella, velvet ribbon and net with silver buttons and braid. On this foundation were boldly worked simple stitches in grey and black. These included couching, tacking, detached chain, satin, whipped running and Cretan stitches.

Of the exhibits, Rebecca Crompton's piece in particular provoked lively debate and outraged traditionalists. She encouraged people to break the rules and work stitches informally and quickly. As more women sought paid employment outside the home and therefore had less leisure time, she saw a need for a faster method of embroidery. Although machine embroidery was gradually making an impact, hand stitching was still highly regarded. Many of her students adopted this liberating method of working, although some aspects of the style that developed in the 1930s became a cliché. The stitches were frequently worked on a shape of overlapping nets as a slipped outline with bold diagonal lines. The colours used were often fairly drab but with accents of shocking pink and yellow.

Right: Parable, *by Lilian Dring, 1941. This piece features mainly couched work with blanket, fly and running stitches. The materials of the ground are joined by herringbone stitch. Woollen, silk and white cotton threads, braid cord, bugles, beads, sequins, buttons and applied leather, net and linen are all used to picture the aeroplanes, bursting shells and barrage balloons above houses.*

In the 1950s, freely worked stitches were used in simplified, almost graphic forms, in which figurative images are centrally placed. Another distinctive design common to this period that exploits the free use of stitches is the exploding circle. Although some examples of this were based on directly observed natural forms, such as dandelion clocks, others were based on images of microscopic analysis. This idea can be linked to new scientific developments in microbiology and perhaps seen as a reflection of the concern over nuclear test explosions.

A time of change

The 1960s brought more abstract design based on seedheads or cross sections of fruit and vegetables, exploring their geometric and asymmetrical qualities. More interesting vegetables and fruit were now available in much greater variety due to increased air transport and travel. The resulting designs were often spiky, like the patterns on printed fabrics and drawings in the many new books offering design help to the inexperienced. Combinations of orange, pink and browns or dirty olive greens became popular.

Demarcations between techniques and different art forms were gradually breaking down. The concept of embroidery widened to include more inventive uses of threads and materials and absorbed more influences from fine art. Yet, at the same time, increased experimentation brought with it more investigation into the fundamentals of the embroidery medium, in other words, stitches.

Embroiderers were increasingly encouraged to investigate the potential of a single stitch through repetition and distortion, varying the scale and tension in an attempt to develop new relationships between the thread and ground. As threads can create different qualities of line and stitches, they explored the characteristics of threads: texture, suppleness, smoothness, roughness or the degree of twist. Such an exploration can be seen in Kathleen Whyte's 'White Waves', 1968, in which she freely worked rosette chain, crested chain and cable chain stitches in a variety of white yarns including rough spun linen and nylon knitting yarn to create fluid movement. The ground is of orange Donegal hopsack. In this work the affinity between the use of threads in embroidery and drawing or making marks on paper with crayons, pencil or pen is clear. The design was based on a chalk sketch and was built up in white tissue paper on brown paper. Such creative work uses rhythm, harmony and balance as well as contrast. During the 1960s and 1970s the sources of ideas became limitless: the repetitive rhythm of trolleys in a supermarket, fossils, reflections in a puddle, patterns of scaffolding, groups of birds on a beach, or notes of music all provided inspiration.

During the 1970s and 1980s, free stitchery was often used to create atmospheric landscapes, especially when worked on a painted or space-dyed fabric ground which was allowed to show through the texture of the stitches. Sometimes, the ground also had frayed or burnt edges. However, stitch alone continued to be used effectively as demonstrated in Veronica Togneri's small panel *On the Dunes*, which suggests the movement of ripples in sand through freely worked straight stitches.

More recently, freely applied small fragments of transparent fabrics, lace, paper or silk have been combined with machine and freely worked hand stitches to create texture. Although it sometimes appears that machine embroidery has taken over, the pleasure of hand stitching remains important for all embroiderers, experienced or novice. The satisfaction of working with texture and colour in rhythmic stitches is a powerful incentive to further exploration. The potential of the stitch is endless.

Above: On the Dunes, *by Veronica Togneri, 1979. This piece is worked on linen using both silk and woollen threads.*

Left: Shawl, northern India, 19th century. This shawl is embroidered with various stitches, including chain stitch in a design depicting women and hunters on horseback. During the 19th century, Kashmir shawls were freely decorated in dense swirling patterns worked in cross stitch. Today, many of the designs are still freely worked in a continuous chain stitch using a fine hook or ari, a technique similar to European tambouring.

Free embroidery stitches and techniques

Free embroidery is a relatively modern term which refers to the working of stitches by hand freely across the fabric. Almost any stitch from other traditional techniques can be used, but often just a few very simple ones will be most effective. Explore the stitches for the qualities that they give to your work whether that is a sense of movement, a regimented or scattered pattern, or a sudden burst of accent colour.

Tip

To remedy a twisted working thread, turn the work upside down in order to let the needle and thread dangle and unwind.

Fabrics

A large number of good-quality fabrics are suitable for freestyle embroidery. These range from fine, near-transparent materials such as lawn and muslin, to denim and heavy linens. Even felt can be an appropriate choice.

A plain fabric will give you the freedom to add colour as a wash, pattern or detailed background design before you start stitching. Undyed cottons and calico fabrics make a good starting point.

The weight and strength of the fabrics may not be sufficient on their own to take the embroidery threads and you may have to use a backing fabric behind the top fabric. Fine white cotton is usually best, as it provides strength but does not give bulk. Sometimes, however, it is more effective to use a double layer of the chosen fabric, for example, to retain the semi-transparent quality of a sheer fabric.

Needles

Generally, crewel needles are used for this technique. The eye of the needle should be large enough to take the thread with ease and allow a double thread to pass through the fabric easily.

Threads

Almost any thread can be used in free embroidery, as long as it can be threaded through a needle and will be suitable for the fabric.

The effect of the stitches can be altered by varying their size and changing the weight and type of thread – experiment to see the effects. The choice of thread largely depends on how the work is to be used. Pieces that require frequent washing should be stitched with cotton thread that launders well, whereas purely decorative pieces could be stitched with silks or fine wools.

Additional tools

Always use a frame or hoop to hold the fabric taut and keep the tension even while stitching. It is most important to use one big enough to allow plenty of fabric around the embroidery design and never to move the frame or hoop over any of the stitches.

Free embroidery techniques

Make sure the fabric is pressed and smooth before transferring the design. Whichever method you choose (see pages 30–31), always transfer the whole of the pattern before starting to stitch.

Starting to stitch

It is always a good idea to work in a continuous flow rather than starting in different places, to help provide continuity and rhythm throughout the stitching.

A thread should be no longer than 50cm (20in) or it may twist and knot. Start the stitching at the front with tiny running stitches (see page 63). Never use a knot to secure a thread, instead leave the thread in the finished embroidery. Isolated stitches such as French knots can pose a problem in this respect, especially as you should not run a thread across the back of an area that is to be left unstitched. This could spoil the tension and show through the finished work. Instead, leave a waste length of thread until you have finished the stitch and then run the waste thread back and forth through the threads of the stitch on the reverse before trimming it off.

Finishing the stitching

To finish a thread, either make a few tiny stitches that will be covered by the next thread or turn the work over and run the thread under a few stitches at the back. Before removing the embroidery from the frame, make sure all the design lines are covered and cut off threads once they are secured.

The stitches shown in this section range from simple outline and edging stitches to more intricate fillings and decorative ones. They are only a starting point, and can be adapted and combined in different ways. Other stitches, such as seeding (page 189), bullion knots (page 146), back stitch (page 49), satin stitch (page 188) and leaf stitch (page 80) can also be used in free embroidery to great effect.

CHAIN STITCH

USES: outline, filling

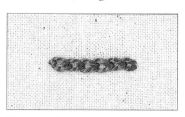

1 Bring the thread to the surface. Insert the needle into the same hole and back up one stitch length away. Do not pull the needle through but wrap the thread under the point.

2 Pull the needle through and repeat, starting the next stitch in the last hole. A detached chain stitch can be worked by anchoring a loop with a small straight stitch.

FRENCH KNOT

USES: filling, detail

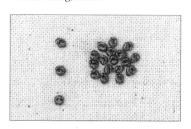

1 Bring the thread to the surface. Hold the needle in one hand and the thread taut with the other. Wrap the thread around the needle twice or more for bigger knots.

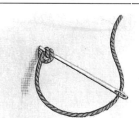

2 Insert the needle into the starting hole (or the next hole to prevent the knot slipping through). Pull through to form a knot and secure it with a small stitch on the back.

FLY STITCH

USES: border, filling, single motif

1 Bring the needle up at A, then down at B, making sure not to pull the needle through the fabric. Come back up at C, over the thread of the first stitch and pull through.

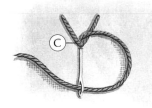

2 Ease the tension to make a V-shaped loop down to C. Make a short vertical stitch to anchor the loop. Fly stitch can be worked singly or as closed fly stitch (see page 189).

FEATHER STITCH

USES: line, border

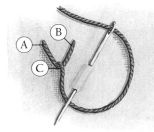

1 Working from the top, go up at A and then down at B. Keep the thread loose. Come up at C an equal distance below. Pass the needle over the loop of thread and pull it down.

2 The next stitch, worked in the same way, will naturally fall to the right of the first. Continue, lining further stitches up under the first two, and working downwards.

Design your own

• Look at straight lines, repeating curls and circles and see how effective they are at varying distances, grouped together or meandering across your design sheet.

• The spaces between the shapes are just as important as the shapes themselves.

• For inspiration, look at winter branches against the sky, ripples left by waves or a snake's trail left in the sand.

• Choose a simple shape such as a leaf or petal and experiment with working around the outlines in different stitches and then using different filling to add texture and contrast.

• Try different colour combinations – fresh, clear colours can look modern whereas rich, muted shades will convey a more traditional effect.

STRAIGHT STITCH
OTHER NAME: isolated flat stitch

USES: line, detail

Straight stitch is the easiest of all stitches and also forms the basic component for many other stitches, including cross stitch (see page 49). Simple straight stitches can be made at any length and can be placed overlapping, vertically, horizontally or diagonally, or even grouped in different ways in order to create simple shapes. They are versatile and you can work a whole design very effectively using just straight stitches.

1 To work circle shapes, bring the working thread up at any point on a circle of any size and make a straight stitch on the surface radiating out. Repeat stitches at regular intervals.

2 Straight stitches can be worked more randomly, in different lengths creating freer forms. Worked closely, they also form satin stitch (see page 188), which will fill solid shapes.

STEM STITCH
OTHER NAME: crewel stitch

USES: line, outline

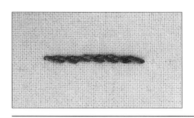

Work a straight stitch from A to B. Hold down with a finger. Come up at C halfway along the first stitch ready to make the next. Continue, keeping the stitches the same length.

WHIPPED STEM STITCH

USES: line, outline

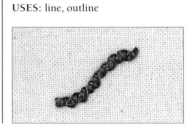

Work a line of stem stitch. Bring a contrasting thread up under the end of the stitch. Pass the needle down under it without catching any fabric, whipping the thread over regularly.

WHIPPED RUNNING STITCH
OTHER NAME: Cordonnet

USES: line, outline

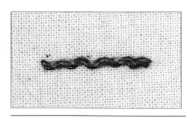

Work a row of running stitches (see page 63). Bring a contrasting thread up at the end of the first stitch. Go through the fabric below the first stitch, whipping the thread over it.

LACED RUNNING STITCH

USES: outline, border

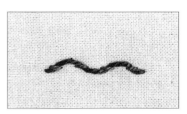

Working right to left with a round-pointed needle, weave contrasting thread up and down through a row of running stitches (see page 63). Adjust the tension to make loops.

ERMINE STITCH

USES: filling, single motif

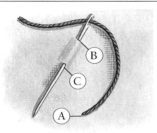

1 Come up at A and make a long vertical stitch to B, holding the stitch down with a finger. Bring the thread up again at C, about a third of the distance diagonally down to the left.

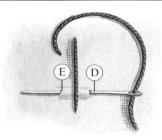

2 Make a long diagonal stitch, over the top of the first vertical one, to D. Bring the needle out again at E, straight across to the left of D and vertically down from C.

3 Make the final long diagonal stitch over the others to F, on the same level as C and directly up from D. This makes one isolated stitch, which you can repeat to make a filling.

ROSETTE CHAIN

USES: outline, border, filling

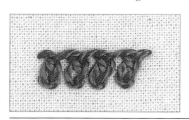

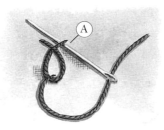

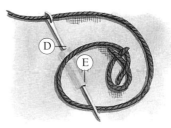

1 Bring the needle up at A and down at B. Bring the needle point up at C below but do not pull it through. Wrap the working thread across the needle and then under the point.

2 Now, pull the needle through in order to form a twisted loop. Then, slip the needle under the thread, between the twist and A, making sure not to pierce the fabric.

3 Pull the thread through and adjust the tension. Insert the needle at D one stitch width away and bring the point out at E, ready to make the twisted loop for the next stitch.

CHEVRON STITCH

USES: border

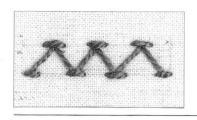

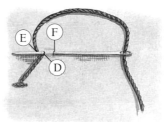

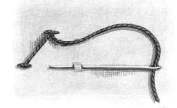

1 Work from left to right on two parallel lines. Make a stitch on the lower line from A to B. Come up at C halfway along the first stitch. Stitch diagonally up to D. Come up at E.

2 Make a second small horizontal stitch along the top line to F. Come up at D, in the same hole as the end of the first diagonal stitch. Keep the needle below the horizontal stitch.

3 Make another diagonal stitch to the lower line, as a mirror image of the first. Continue the same sequence as before, keeping all the stitches the same length and the same angle.

FISHBONE STITCH

USES: filling

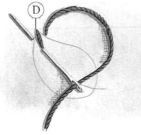

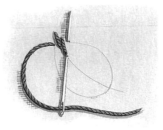

1 Come up at A, typically at the tip of a leaf shape. Make a short straight stitch along the centre line of the shape to B. Bring the needle up again at C, along the outline from A.

2 Make a sloping stitch back down to just beyond the centre line of the shape and just below the first stitch. Bring the needle up again at D, along the other side of the outline from A.

3 Make the sloping stitch on this side of the shape in the same way, finishing it just beyond the centre line. The stitches start to overlap each other slightly down the centre line.

WHEAT EAR

USES: line, border

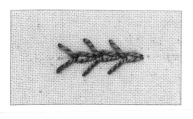

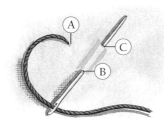

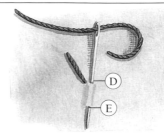

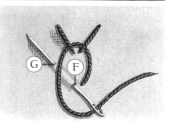

1 Bring the working thread up at A and make a straight stitch diagonally down to B. Bring the needle up at C, on the same level as A and the same distance away from B.

2 Pull the thread through and work another straight stitch diagonally down to D, so it completes a slightly open V shape at E, directly below B. Pull the needle through.

3 Without piercing the fabric, pass the needle and thread under the two straight stitches. Insert at F and bring out at G directly below A. Continue to complete more stitches.

Leaf spray cushion

This stylish design, with its simple spray of leaves in natural colours and emphasis on the textures of thread and linen, captures a modern spirit of design. The soft cream and slight sheen of the perlé thread could be stitched on any colour of fabric or you could try dark on light for a dynamic transformation. The design is quick to embroider and the perlé threads are easy to use, an ideal project for a beginner. Design by Lesley Teare

Design area

21 x 19cm (8¼ x 7½in)

Materials

1 x 0.5m (1 x ½yd) linen fabric

25cm (10in) square fine white cotton fabric

Embroidery threads (see diagram key)

35.5cm (14in) square cushion pad

Equipment

Dressmakers' scissors

Pale-coloured pencil

Stretcher frame

Size 3 or 9 crewel needle

Embroidery scissors

Pins

Needle and matching sewing thread for making up

1 Cut the linen fabric to give a 50cm (20in) square for the embroidery. Reserve the other piece for the back of the cover. Transfer the design onto the centre of the linen fabric using your preferred method (see pages 30–31). Then, back the linen with the white cotton fabric (see page 17) and stretch the two fabrics onto a stretcher frame, ensuring that the fabric grains remain straight.

2 For all the embroidery, use 45cm (18in) lengths of thread to avoid tangling. Start by working the chain stitch on the larger leaves. Note the direction of stitching shown on the diagram and stitch the large leaves from the base to the tip on each side.

3 Once all these leaves have been finished, stem stitch along the main branch from the base to the tip. Then, work out from the main branch along the other branches to the tips of the leaves just as they would grow. Always keep the stem stitches as even as possible and work into the flow of the design line.

4 Next, embroider the smaller leaves with satin stitches (see page 188) worked closely together. Following the direction lines from the diagram, make sure to keep all the stitches parallel. At the tips of the leaves, the point of the needle can be placed just under the previous stitch in order to give a tapered appearance.

5 Finish the stitching by working the French knots. As the coton perlé is quite bulky, it should just be wrapped once around the needle.

6 Remove the fabric from the stretcher frame and iron gently if necessary, always following the manufacturer's instructions. Make up as a simple cushion cover following the instructions on page 33, insert the cushion pad and finally slip stitch closed.

LEAF SPRAY CUSHION KEY	
DMC coton perlé no. 5	
———	*Satin stitch in 746*
- - - - -	*Stem stitch in 746*
●●●●●●	*Chain stitch in 746*
◉	*French knot in 746*
⟶	*Direction of stitching*
- - - ->	*Direction of shading*

Note: You will need 1 skein of each shade.

Poppy panel

This colourful panel captures the fleeting beauty of a summer meadow full of delicate poppies, daisies and cow parsley. Just a few simple embroidery stitches are used on a painted calico background to create this picture that will always remind you of glorious sunshine and happy summer days. You could also adapt this idea to stitch a panel of flowers from your own garden or favourite place in the country. Design by Lesley Teare

1 Cut a square piece of the calico fabric that is large enough to stretch over your choice of frame.

2 Trace the design from the diagram on page 213, including the grey broken lines, which indicate the main zones of paint colours. Transfer the broken lines and the main poppy shapes onto the calico, using a pale coloured pencil.

3 Stretch the calico onto the embroidery frame, making sure that the grain of the fabric remains absolutely straight.

4 Place the cyan 13 and primary yellow 01 paints in separate saucers, reserving one to mix the two together. Before starting to paint directly onto the calico, test the colours on a spare piece of fabric. Apply the colours to the fabric, a few drops at a time, so that you can see how strong the colours are and how far they spread across the fabric. Try diluting the colours with water and mixing them together, and paint them onto your sample piece. Remember that you can always strengthen the colour if it is too pale but, once on the fabric, it cannot be removed.

5 Before you start painting the background for your panel, take a note of the zones for the paint colours. The broken lines already traced from the diagram give very basic guidelines of the areas for the sky, the middle ground and the foreground. Apply the colours so they merge together between the zones and then soften the edges. As a final preparation, lightly dampen the calico in the design area, but make sure to avoid dampening the flower.

6 Start painting the sky in a shade of pale blue. Bear in mind that cyan is a very strong colour, so dilute a tiny amount with water and test it on spare calico. As you apply the paint, leave some calico without colour to give the impression of clouds. Then, paint the middle distance using primary yellow. You can use this paint undiluted, as it will soften on the damp calico.

7 Next, paint the foreground, applying different shades to give a mixture of merging soft colours. Use a basis of diluted primary yellow and add tiny varying amounts of cyan and iris violet 10. Once the background painting is completed, dry the calico with a hairdryer.

8 Mix a few drops of gitane 12 paint into diluted primary yellow in a saucer and then add a tiny drop of iris. Check the colour by testing it onto a spare piece of calico. Next, add the impression of grass in the foreground and trees at the top of the design, making sure that you retain light and dark areas. The calico can be dampened at any stage during the painting in order to achieve a softer feel and you can add more yellow or blue paint to vary the shades.

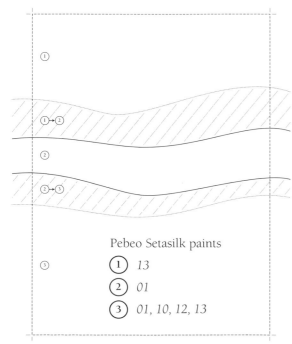

Pebeo Setasilk paints
- ① 13
- ② 01
- ③ 01, 10, 12, 13

Divide your panel into the various painting sections.

Design area

17.5 x 12.5cm (7 x 5in)

Materials

50cm (20in) unbleached calico

Fabric paints (see paint and stitch diagram keys)

50cm (20in) fine white cotton fabric (optional)

Embroidery threads (see diagram key)

Equipment

Dressmakers' scissors

Tracing paper and pen

Pale coloured pencil

Embroidery frame

Three saucers to mix paints

Paint brushes

Size 3 or 9 crewel needle

Stiff card for stretching embroidery

Strong thread for lacing

Mount board and frame of your choice

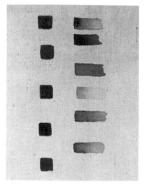

Make tests on spare calico.

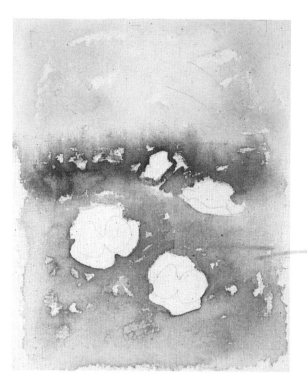

Paint the background then proceed onto the details.

9 Dilute the pearl red paint in a little water for the poppies. Build up layers like a watercolour painting. Leave to dry thoroughly, then add a tiny amount of the yellow over the red to make orange on areas of the petals for subtle variations. Although not essential, you can place dabs of yellow where the daisies will be stitched. Use a fine paintbrush to paint more grass if needed. Use the texture of the calico to try out effects.

10 When you are happy the background is complete, proceed on to fixing the dyes. To do this, iron on the reverse side of the calico for a couple of minutes, making sure to follow the manufacturer's instructions.

11 If you need to back the calico, remove it from the frame and tack the fine, white cotton fabric in position (see page 17). Stretch the two fabrics back onto the frame and proceed with the stitching.

12 Following the diagram opposite, use one strand of the red 854 thread and work tiny back stitches around the edges of the poppy flowers in order to outline the painted shapes. Add the poppy centres with a few straight stitches in one strand of the green 1058 thread. Finally, work stamens around each centre with straight stitches and French knots using the metallic 5287 thread.

13 Embroider the grasses that are under the daisies in fly stitch, using one strand of green 988 or 1058 stranded cotton and vary the size and angle of the stitches to add realism to the landscape design.

14 Work the daisies in straight stitches using two strands of yellow 3821 stranded cotton for the centres and two strands of blanc for the petals.

15 Using one strand of the green 988 stranded cotton, work the small leaves using fishbone stitch. These stitches can be worked as closed or open as you find attractive.

16 You can easily adapt this design by making your own decisions on exactly which colours and threads to use where. As a general rule, use lighter tones against a dark background and the darker shades against a light background. The exact mixture of matt, shiny or metallic threads can also have an impact on the effect of the finished panel.

17 Work stem stitch in two strands of green 988 stranded cotton for the stems of the poppies and add the tall grasses on the right with fly stitches in one strand of yellow 165 cotton.

18 To form the stems of the cow parsley, work tiny running stitches using one strand of yellow 165 stranded cotton. Then, work tiny stab

POPPY PANEL KEY

Stab stitch in DMC stranded cotton in 165

Straight stitch in DMC stranded cotton in blanc

Straight stitch in Anchor Marlitt in 1058

Straight stitch in DMC stranded cotton in 3821

Tiny running stitch in DMC stranded cotton in 165

Tiny straight stitch in DMC stranded cotton in 988

Fly stitch in DMC stranded cotton in 165

Fly stitch in DMC stranded cotton in 988

Fly stitch in Anchor Marlitt in 1058

French knots in DMC stranded cotton in blanc

French knots in DMC stranded metallic in 5287

Fishbone stitch in DMC stranded cotton in 988

Running stitch in DMC stranded cotton in 165

Back stitch in Anchor Marlitt in 854

Stem stitch in DMC stranded cotton in 988

Pebeo Setacolour Pearl in 46 and Setasilk in 01

Note: You will need 1 skein of each shade.

stitches with two strands of the same colour to make the seed and flowerheads. Alternatively, you can use tiny beads to represent the seeds and centres of flowers. Finally, add French knots in two strands of blanc for the distant daisies.

19 Make sure that you have finished the design before removing it from the frame. You could follow the diagram explicitly or take the freedom of this technique to alter it slightly. The main aim is to create a composition that is pleasing to the eye, so build up the areas of grasses and flowers to keep an overall balance, using the spaces but not overcrowding the surface.

20 When you are satisfied with the end result, remove the embroidery from the frame. If necessary, iron it with a warm iron on the reverse. Stretch the embroidery over a piece of card cut to fit the aperture of your chosen frame and lace securely on the back. Choose a complementary mount and frame the embroidery.

Machine embroidery

The introduction of machines capable of embroidery is comparatively recent. The earliest was invented by Josue Heilmann in 1828 and the patent was purchased by Henry Houldsworth, who became the main producer in Britain. Other industrial machines were developed in Switzerland in the 1840s and, although the embroidery was criticized for its repetitive motifs, with good-quality fabric and work it became popular. In 1865, the Schiffli machine was invented and led to the decline of hand-produced whitework. The word Schiffli was borrowed from the German for shuttle, which was by then fully automated and producing many different effects on Jacquard looms.

By 1900, the Cornely was produced in France and was later followed by Singer's 'Irish' machine. Both offered innovative wide zigzag stitches and have been in common use ever since.

These industrial machines were mainly used to make trimmings for fashion garments, although during the First World War a serious economic depression affected the Swiss industry. Cotton organdie was introduced in about 1913 and the Swiss began embroidering postcards on it. The designs were simple with flowers or the allied flags, and some had pockets with a flap to contain messages. They were sent by the troops to their families and many still treasure these mementoes.

Innovation and scepticism

Hand embroidery had stagnated after the war and was more concerned with the technical perfection of stitching worked from transfer patterns that were predominantly based on historic designs, than with innovative ideas or good design. However, there was a creative drive to express modernity in the fine and decorative arts and architecture during the 1920s. Embroidery too was affected by the new importance placed on contemporary design and the need to find a fresh means of expression. It was at this time that the idea of using machines for creative embroidery developed among a few hand embroiderers. This was the machine age: machines were celebrated in painting by the Futurists and in graphic art, so there seemed no more appropriate way to express ideas quickly in embroidery than by using the sewing machine. However, machine embroidery continued to be associated with commercial products, its use seen as a threat to traditional hand-craft, and it remained a controversial technique for many years.

Early in the century, the Singer Sewing Machine Company advertised their machines by reproducing paintings in machine embroidery and through

Left: Tea cosy designed by Rebecca Crompton, possibly worked by Dorothy Benson, 1938. Machine embroidery in black, green and pink cotton thread on white silk in a design of a horse and flowers.

decorative fans and garments that were made by their highly skilled employees in the embroidery department. They published a manual in 1911 and also provided classes for amateurs who were keen to learn the decorative possibilities of the machine. These were treadle-operated straight stitch machines but with practise could be used to good effect. At first, traditional hand techniques such as drawn threadwork and Hedebo were imitated but gradually more adventurous effects were attempted.

One of the first to excel in its use and to promote machine embroidery was Dorothy Benson, who went to work in the embroidery department at Singer aged 14 in 1916 and remained there until her retirement in 1962. She later worked in the education department where teachers were trained in the use of the domestic machine, which could imitate 47 stitches and methods of embroidery and 41 varieties of handmade lace without the use of special attachments. She produced many works designed by others, on organdie or voile, which show the delicate linear stitchery well. She also instructed Rebecca Crompton in machine use and often worked with her, demonstrating the machine's potential at her lectures. There was considerable resistance to

Opposite page: **Loutro Diagonal,** *detail, by Jan Beaney, 1997. Inspired by landscapes in Crete, worked on soluble fabric with hand stitches.*

Top: **Madonna and Child,** *by Peggy Thomas, 1952. Machine-embroidered black and green silk threads on white artificial silk organza.*

Bottom: **The Adoration of the Magi,** *by Susan Riley, 1961. Gold lamé ground, applied gauze and nylon with machine embroidery in cotton and woollen threads and gilt cord.*

machine embroidery as it was seen as a threat to hand stitching. Later, in the 1940s and early 1950s, both women published books on machine embroidery encouraging amateurs to regard it as an additional valid technique that could enhance their work and be used in conjunction with hand techniques.

Growing enthusiasm

One of the research projects undertaken by the Needlework Development Scheme in the late 1940s was to study ways in which sketched designs could be interpreted in embroidery most successfully. It was discovered that machine interpretations best maintained the spirit and detail of the design. The flexibility and speed of the machine in the hands of an experienced embroiderer were able to capture the spontaneous line of the drawings. In 1950, these were included in an Arts Council of Great Britain touring exhibition. An accompanying publication entitled *Experiment in Embroidery Design* included photographs of both designs and finished work.

Throughout the 1950s, there was an increased interest in the use of machine embroidery, either on its own or combined with hand stitching and appliqué. Free embroidery on the machine, also known as free darning, offers the best opportunity for creative work. Pulled and cutwork effects can be produced on organdie or scrim and with a tight lower and loose upper tension, the looped threads can be seen through the transparent fabric as shadow work. Practice is essential to control the machine, which creates a more continuous line than a pen. However, straight stitch can be a very effective drawing tool and many fluid linear designs were produced. Most of these were for decorative panels rather than furnishings, as interior taste had changed to a more streamlined, uncluttered Scandinavian look that banished unnecessary textiles such as antimacassars.

During the 1960s and 1970s, embroiderers such as Joy Clucas produced books on technique and design that stimulated wide interest. Among the most influential was Christine Risley, who taught at Goldsmith's College, London, where innovative work was done. The rising number of publications, together with the introduction of a domestic sewing machine with a swing needle, increased the popularity of the technique. The swing needle increased the potential of the machine embroidery and reduced the emphasis on line. Satin stitch could be worked more quickly, the width of stitch could be varied with ease to form blocks of solid colour or spiky effects if stitched at angles and couched threads and cords became a possibility. As machine embroidery became more widespread, a greater range of suitable threads, including synthetics, became available. The introduction of dissolvable fabric such as spun alginate or vanishing muslin further extended the scope. Machine embroidery on a ground that is dissolved to form a new fabric requires a machine running stitch to hold it together, but areas of zigzag can also be introduced to vary the texture. In this way, delicate, lace-like effects were achieved by artists such as Robin Giddings, working in the late 1970s. Vanishing muslin has been superseded by water-soluble fabric that dissolves in hot and cold water without leaving a sticky residue, while more recently, thermoplastic is machine stitched and used to create three-dimensional shapes.

Fascination with surfaces

During the 1980s, as interest in surfaces grew, embroiderers continued to experiment. Machine whip stitch or layers of randomly worked machine zigzag create a textured ground quickly and, by varying the tension between top and bottom thread and blending different threads, a rich texture and subtle effects are achieved. Working areas so heavily that they become almost three-dimensional can also add to the effect. Artists such as Alice Kettle work freely and intuitively without the constraint of fabric stretched on a frame, or always confined to a geometric format. This allows the rhythm of stitch

created by moving the fabric backwards and forwards under the needle to distort the fabric into soft, yielding forms. Her life-size figures are not hard-edged but built up in sections in this direct way.

This absorption with surfaces encouraged the introduction of other materials, most notably felt and paper, which are easy to control in combination with machine stitching. Paper-making courses were popular and a wide variety of handmade papers became available, ranging from fine tissues embedded with flower petals to thick, heavily textured recycled paper. Embroiderers became preoccupied with textured surfaces in nature such as lichen or moss-covered rocks, or on man-made objects such as peeling, flaking paint on old doors, or rusting metal. When a piece worked on vanishing muslin is complete, it is ironed, causing the ground muslin to disintegrate and crumble. As fragments of the crumbled muslin stick to the machine stitches, the surface texture is further enhanced and embroiderers exploited this property to create 'distressed' surfaces.

Technological advances continue and now textile artists and students use computer-aided design, explore the potential of electronic machines programmed to produce particular stitches and can combine these with digitally printed images. The best results, as with all techniques, continue to be highly individual statements that balance excellent technique and good design.

Below: **Little Egrets' Song,** *by Linda Miller, 2000. Densely worked machine embroidery in a variety of threads.*

Bottom: **Life Cycle,** *detail, by Alison King, 2000. In this mixed media triptych inspired by standing stones, handmade paper and felt are combined with batik, machine stitch and acrylic paint to create a vivid panel.*

Machine embroidery stitches and techniques

People often think that machine embroidery merely consists of using automatic patterns or that you need an expensive, computerized machine. Neither is true and every electric sewing machine, whatever its make or age, will produce beautiful machine embroidery. With a little practice, you will be thrilled at the different effects you can achieve with your own machine.

The machine

Always keep your machine in a warm room and make sure it is clean and oiled, referring to the instruction manual. After oiling, stitch on a scrap of fabric in order to remove any chance of excess oil spoiling your embroidery. Also, make sure your machine is regularly serviced.

If you are lucky enough to be choosing a new machine, the following are a few tips to bear in mind if you want to machine embroider. Consider an electric machine with straight and zigzag functions. This particular type can sometimes be called a swing needle machine. You also need to be able to lower or cover the feed dogs and adjust the bobbin tension. Also, look into built-in patterns, as some will prove really useful. Finally, you may want to investigate computerized pattern design. This is not really necessary, but you may like it for lettering or working built-in motif designs.

Bobbins

Although some bobbins will have been supplied with your machine, you will also need some extra ones. To store all your bobbins, a specially designed box, available from most machine retailers, is a good investment.

Never be tempted to wind one thread on top of another and always wind an empty bobbin for each new colour.

Needles

Unlike hand embroidery needles, machine needles blunt quickly and can cause the machine to skip stitches. Fit a new needle after about every five hours of stitching and discard old needles safely. Keep a supply of sizes 90, 100 and 110 (sometimes sold as jeans needles), as well as twin needles and special large-eyed needles for metallic threads.

Feet

Make sure you check whether you have a darning foot for your machine. Some models supply one as standard but you can also purchase one from your machine supplier. There is a wide range of extra feet available to produce special effects for most machines.

Threads

There is an extraordinary range of beautiful machine embroidery threads available that can literally transform your stitching. The majority are rayon threads, which give a shiny effect, but there are also shaded, variegated and metallic threads.

Fabrics

A firm, not too tightly woven fabric, such as medium-weight calico or cotton, is ideal for your first pieces of embroidery. As you become more confident, you can explore and experiment with the many other exciting fabrics that are available.

Frames

You will need an embroidery hoop to keep the fabric taut while stitching. Use a narrow wooden hoop that will slide under the needle or a metal spring hoop that is made specifically for machine embroidery.

Basic techniques

A good knowledge of your machine is the key to success so always read the manual if you are unsure about any feature.

Start stitching by trying the effects that you can create using the machine in the normal way, that is with the presser foot in place and the feed dogs up. In this situation, you do not need to use an embroidery hoop. Thread the machine, bringing the bobbin thread to the surface of the fabric, as usual. With the machine set up in this way, you are restricted to only straight or slightly curved lines of stitching, but you can achieve a variety of attractive effects.

Although cotton or calico is recommended for practice, try stitching on other types of fabric as well. On velvet for example, the stitches 'sink' into the pile, whereas a completely different effect will be achieved by stitching on an open weave or sheer fabric. Before you start machining, make sure you are familiar with the stitch length control and how it is operated on your machine.

Straight stitch

Work lines of straight stitching, changing the stitch length from very short to the maximum length.

To vary the effect of straight stitching, work massed lines, changing the stitch length in areas and also the top thread in order to give different blocks of colour.

Using thicker threads

Change the needle to a size 110 and also reduce the top tension a little. Then, thread the machine with a thick thread, such as a thin wool, an untwisted rayon floss, a fine crochet thread or even a three-ply metallic thread. Stitch slowly.

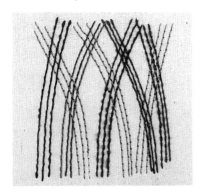

Zigzag stitch

Choose a size 90 needle and then select the zigzag function on your machine. Start stitching several lines, changing the stitch width from the narrowest to the maximum width as you stitch. Repeat but this time changing the stitch length. On a large number of sewing machines, you can change the needle position too, which will provide a different effect to your stitching.

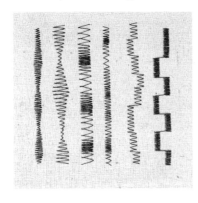

Using automatic patterns

The majority of sewing machines have a range of built-in utility stitches, as well as a selection of decorative patterns.

Try forming attractive patterns on the fabric by, for instance, laying torn strips of organza on top of calico before you start the actual stitching.

Work through some of the patterns, first as single lines, and then adding one pattern on top of another. Change the stitch width or length for one of the patterns or, alternatively, you may want to change the colour for the second pattern.

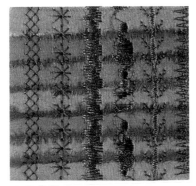

Effects with a twin needle

Every machine will take a twin needle and they are a lot of fun to stitch with. Check in your manual for guidance on how to thread the machine and adjust the tensions in order to achieve a pin-tucking effect. Try stitching a grid with the lines of stitching holding little squares of metallic mesh in place.

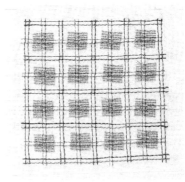

Using the braiding foot

A braiding foot has a hole through which you can thread either a ribbon or thicker yarns. This will enable you to couch them down onto your choice of fabric using either straight stitch or a narrow zigzag stitch.

Straight lines of tailor tacking

A tailor tacking foot is usually used for making tailor tacks in dressmaking, but it can also be used most effectively for embroidery.

Loosen the top tension a little and select a short stitch length. Work straight lines of stitching. Then, if you cut the loops of thread, a lovely spiky effect is obtained, but you must brush a little PVA adhesive on the underside stitching to stop it from unravelling. Try using a rayon thread, then change to a metallic thread for added effect. Or, you can thread the machine with two threads on the top by taking both threads through the threading guides and the needle together. This will give a much thicker pile of stitches and blend the two colours together.

Free machine embroidery

With a darning foot and the feed dogs lowered, your machine will be all the more versatile. With the machine set up in this way, you will be able to stitch in any direction and following any pattern you wish.

Before you start stitching, stretch the fabric in a hoop and thread your machine as normal.

Remove the presser foot and replace it with a darning foot. Then, lower or cover the feed dogs. Make sure to check in your instruction manual if you are unsure how to do this.

Set the machine for straight stitch, with the stitch length and width set at 0. Place the frame under the needle, with the fabric touching the bed of the machine, and lower the presser foot. Bring the bobbin thread to the surface by turning the fly wheel towards you so the needle goes down into the fabric, and back up to its highest position. As the needle starts to come down, the lower thread is brought to the surface.

Next, start to run the machine at a medium speed, making sure that you move the frame quite slowly. It takes a while to get used to the fact that you are controlling how and where you stitch but, very soon, you will realize that it is great fun.

Free running stitch

With the machine set up in this way, move the hoop towards you and then away from you, making short lines of running stitches. Try to move the frame smoothly, making the stitches quite small. With a little more confidence, try a pattern of curves.

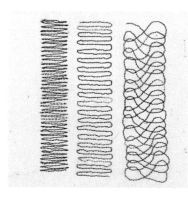

Free zigzag stitching

Set the machine to the zigzag function with a medium to wide stitch width. Then, move the hoop towards and away from you, overlapping the stitching. Moving the frame slowly, you will build up a concentrated patch of satin stitch. Working in curves gives a very different pattern. Try moving the hoop slowly from side to side to give an impression of grass or water.

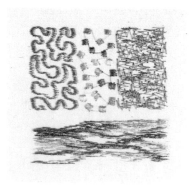

Vermicelli stitch

Vermicelli stitch is a meandering pattern of free running stitch where the lines do not cross each other. To work this stitch, first set the machine to straight stitch and the stitch width to 0. Then, using a fusible bonding web, apply little squares of organza to a piece of calico. Practise vermicelli stitches around the square shapes and then cover the background area. Use a shaded or variegated thread in order to obtain an even more effective look.

Whip stitch

This particular stitch is a heavier, more textured line of free running stitch. Whip stitch is achieved by tension alterations that bring loops of the lower bobbin thread to the surface, completely covering the top thread. Thread the machine with a different colour on the spool and bobbin and start stitching, moving the frame even more slowly and running the machine at a faster speed.

By gradually increasing the top tension on your machine, the colour of the thread in the lower bobbin will eventually come to the surface. On a large majority of sewing machines, this method is enough to achieve a perfect whip stitch. However, if you find that this does not result in a complete line of the lower bobbin colour, it may then be necessary to loosen the lower or bobbin tension.

Cable stitch (straight)

Wind a thicker thread such as coton perlé no. 5, thin wool or crochet thread onto the bobbin by hand. Thread the machine with a normal thread on top. Remember that your work is upside down, so the underside of the fabric shows the embroidery. Work a line of stitching so the thicker thread is couched onto the fabric lying underneath.

Loosen the bobbin tension a little and then try another line of stitching. Little bobbles will begin to appear and the looser the tension, the more bobbles. Do not loosen the screw too much or it may come out. For a more textured effect, it may be possible to bypass the tension on the bobbin but remember to stitch very slowly and stop if the machine seems to protest.

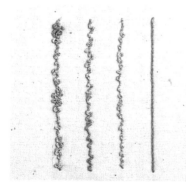

Cable stitch (curved)

Lovely patterns can be made with cable stitch, by simply varying the lower tension and combining it with whip stitch and free running stitch. First, work the cable stitch. Then, take

the fabric out of the hoop and turn it over. Re-stretch it in the hoop and then add lines of stitching in curves.

Couching threads

First, set the machine for free running stitch with normal tensions on the spool and the bobbin. Place a thick thread on the surface of the fabric and then hold it in place at the back and in front of the machine. Next, lower the needle into the middle of the thread and stitch along its length. Change to a zigzag setting, with a medium or wide stitch width, and couch the thread onto the fabric, the stitches going over the thread.

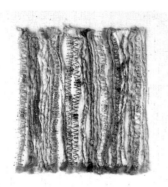

Couching ribbons

Narrow ribbons and braids are widely available and come in a lovely array of colours. To couch them onto a fabric, use free running stitches. As a means of further embellishment, try using metal mesh, painted paper and organza placed on calico with thin gold ribbons forming a grid pattern.

Dissolvable fabrics

There is a large number of dissolvable fabrics available (see page 23), but the most popular is probably a cold water one, which looks like thin plastic. Once the fabric is dissolved, the remaining embroidery resembles a lace-like web of stitching.

Position the dissolvable fabric in the hoop, thread the machine and then set it for free running stitch. Remember as you stitch to link or connect every line of stitching over one another. Otherwise, when the fabric is dissolved away, the stitching will unravel as well. A square grid can be an excellent starting point, filling some of the spaces with little overlapping circles of stitching.

When the embroidery is finished, remove it from the hoop and then cut away the soluble fabric to just outside the stitching. Next, place the fabric in a flat bowl of tepid water and leave it for about 10 minutes to dissolve the fabric. Remove it, rinse it with cold water and place it on kitchen paper to dry.

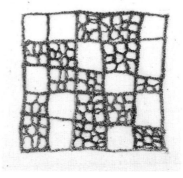

Altering bobbin tension

Locate the tension control screw on the bobbin case and make a note of the angle of the slot in the screw head, so you can always return the tension to normal. To tighten the tension, turn the screw clockwise and to loosen it, turn the screw anti-clockwise.

221

Velvet cushion

This rich and luxurious cushion, which uses velvets and beautiful stitched automatic patterns, will suit the beginner to machine embroidery. Of course, you can choose the colour scheme to complement your own décor. Velvet is not difficult to use in this way and you may have scraps left over from making curtains. The addition of your own machine-made braids adds that touch of originality. Design by Pamela Watts

Design area

28cm (11in) square

Materials

Furnishing velvet in two or three shades of red, to give 16 x 7cm (2¾in) squares

40cm (16in) square calico

Machine embroidery threads in matching colours and metallics

Thicker embroidery threads in matching colours, such as coton perlé, wools and metallics

30cm (12in) square cushion pad

Equipment

7cm (2¾in) square card template

Pencil or fabric marker pen/pencil

Dressmaking scissors

Pins

Embroidery scissors

Needle and matching thread for making up

1 Place the card template on the back of the small pieces of velvet and draw around the shape with a pencil or fabric marker pen. Remove the card and cut the fabric to the drawn shape. Make a total of 16 squares, using different-coloured velvets. Bear in mind that the direction of the pile will alter the colour so, with only two or three velvets, you can achieve a variety of colours. Arrange the squares in a 4 x 4 grid on the calico backing fabric with the edges just touching and pin temporarily in place.

2 Thread the machine with a matching colour and then straight stitch around each square of velvet, as close as possible to the cut edge. Then, practise some of the utility and automatic patterns on your machine on a spare piece of calico.

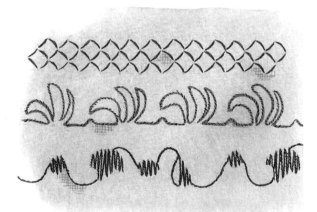

Practise different automatic patterns on a spare piece of fabric before you make a choice.

3 Having selected your patterns, stitch a curved vertical line over four of the velvet pieces. Repeat three more vertical lines on the adjoining pieces.

4 Choose another pattern and a different colour thread, and stitch over the same pieces of velvet in vertical lines, varying the pattern of the curves. Then, changing pattern and thread colour again, work similar curved lines in a horizontal direction.

Stitch two vertical and two horizontal lines across every square of velvet.

5 To make the decorative braids, you should first select the triple zigzag utility stitch on your machine and then thread the machine with a matching thread.

Select the triple zigzag pattern on your machine to couch down the braids.

6 Next, choose a selection of thicker embroidery threads that are in harmony with the velvets. Place four or five threads, depending on their thickness, side by side on the bed of the machine. Then, holding them firmly at the back of the machine and in front, stitch with the triple zigzag setting in order to secure them into a braid. Plan to make ten braids, with each braid measuring 30cm (12in) in length. In practice, you will find it

much more convenient to make longer lengths of braid and then cut them to the appropriate size after the stitching is completed.

Zigzag stitch the thicker embroidery threads to secure them into a braid.

7 Place one of the braids over the raw edges of the velvet pieces, between two lines of the squares. Then, stitch down the centre of the braid using straight stitch. Apply a length of braid along all the inner lines of the grid pattern and then stitch additional lengths around all four outer edges of the design. The front of the cushion cover is now complete.

8 To make up the cushion, you will first need to make two lengths of braid as described above, each braid measuring 1.25m (1⅓yd) in length for the edgings. Then, either tack or pin one of the braids on the front of the cushion cover, positioning it edge to edge with the braid that is already there. Zigzag stitch the two together, turning the ends of the braid under and then joining them neatly.

9 Measure the dimensions of the front of the cushion cover and then transfer these to the square of velvet to be used for the back cover. Next, either tack or pin the second braid in position along the inside edge of the outline. Secure in place with straight machine stitch, tucking the ends of the braid under in order to join them neatly.

10 Turn the seam allowance under on the front and back of the cushion cover and by hand, slip stitch the braids on each piece together. Leave an opening on one side and

then insert the cushion pad. Finally, slip stitch the remaining opening together in order to close the cushion.

11 When you need to dry clean the cushion, unpick a portion of the slip stitching to remove the pad. Then, replace the pad and re-stitch to close the cushion again.

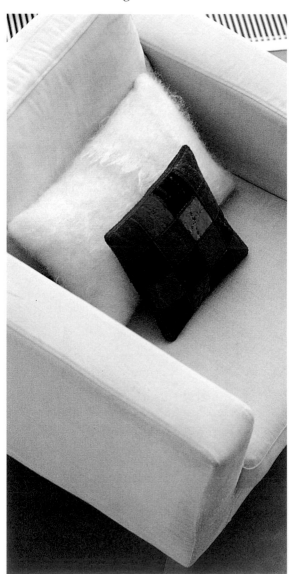

Evening purse

This delightful little evening purse demonstrates the exciting technique of stitching on dissolvable fabric. The delicate, lace-like embroidery is backed with black dupion silk and edged with beads to provide it with an air of sophisticated elegance. It will accessorize any special evening outfit perfectly, so make sure you choose a colour scheme that suits your favourite evening dress. Design by Pamela Watts

1 Make your selection of organzas, threads, braids and ribbons in complementary shades. You can choose shades that are quite bright for the fabric and the threads as the colours tend to become less intense and merge. A mixture of bright and soft pinks, purples and turquoises with silver were used on the purse shown here. If you are in any doubt about your choice of colours, always work a small sample piece first.

2 Fold the piece of dissolvable fabric in half, without cutting it, to make a 20 x 20cm (8 x 8in) square.

3 Trace the template for the purse from the diagram on page 227, including the vertical lines of the bands of lace. Cut around the outline to make a paper pattern. Place the pattern under one side of the dissolvable fabric and then trace all the lines with a felt-tip pen.

4 Cut small scraps of organza fabric in different colours and place these in between the two layers of dissolvable fabric, within the three pattern bands. Then, place the layered fabrics in an embroidery hoop.

5 Prepare the machine for free straight stitching, replacing the presser foot with a darning foot and lowering the feed dogs. Then, thread the spool and bobbin of the machine with one of your chosen colours of machine embroidery threads.

6 Work areas of free running stitch in a random, meandering pattern of circles and loops, connecting or overlapping each line of stitching with one another within each of the three bands of lace. Make sure you stitch a little more densely around the edges of the purse in order to keep its shape. Change the colour of thread in the top spool at regular intervals, and integrate one area of colour into the next. It is highly recommended to keep the same colour on the bobbin throughout the stitching.

7 Decide if you want to make another piece of machine-embroidered lace for the back of the purse. This could be a repeat of the three vertical bands or, alternatively, you could make one piece of lace to fit the purse shape exactly, using the outline of the pattern on page 227. You will need another piece of the dissolvable fabric, measuring 40 x 20cm (16 x 8in) if you decide to make a second piece of lace.

8 Once you have removed the lace from the hoop, cut away the excess dissolvable fabric, close to the stitching. Then, place the pieces of dissolvable fabric in a flat dish of tepid water and leave for about 10 minutes. Remove the pieces of lace and then rinse them thoroughly under the cold tap. Ease them back into shape, checking this against the pattern, and place them on kitchen paper to dry.

9 Place the paper pattern on the black silk fabric and trace around the shape with either a fabric marker pencil or white pencil. Then, cut out the fabric, making sure you add an allowance of 1cm (³⁄₈in) all around the traced outline. Prepare a second piece of silk to be used for the back of the purse in the same way.

10 Turn the fabric under all around the outline and tack the hem to the wrong side on both pieces of silk. When the lace is dry, slip stitch each piece into place on the silk, easing them to fit up to the edges of the purse shape. If little holes appear in the lace, these can be invisibly stitched or caught together, securing the lace to the silk backing.

11 To make the cord handles, select eight lengths of thicker embroidery thread, fine braid or ribbon. Cut each length to measure approximately 60cm (24in) long.

12 Set the machine for free zigzag stitching and thread it with one of the colours that was previously used in the lace. Then, start

Design area

11 x 10.5cm (4½ x 4in)

Materials

40 x 20cm (16 x 8in) cold-water-dissolvable fabric

Scraps of organza in various matching colours

Machine embroidery threads in matching colours and metallics

30cm (12in) square black dupion silk

Thicker embroidery threads and thin braids or ribbons in matching colours

Size 10 or 11 beads

Equipment

Tracing paper and pencil

Paper scissors

Felt-tip pen

Embroidery hoop

Darning foot

Kitchen paper

Fabric marker pencil or white pencil

Tacking thread

Paper-backed fusible web

Baking parchment or non-stick silicone paper

Size 10 embroidery needle and matching sewing thread for making up

stitching along the length of each embroidery thread, braid or ribbon in turn, bearing in mind that you will have to ease the thicker thread through under the needle.

13 Gather all the cord handles and knot them together, about 10cm (4in) from each end. Secure the ends of the cords to the inside hems on the purse, oversewing them by hand, one bundle of cords to the left-hand side of the front and the other bundle to the right-hand side of the back section of the purse.

14 Place the paper pattern on a piece of the same organza used in the lace embroidery, and draw around the shape with a soft pencil. Then, cut out the organza, making sure you add an allowance of 1cm (³/₈in) all around the outline. Prepare a second piece of lining in the same way.

15 For greater neatness and stability, cut another two pieces of black silk, this time a little smaller than the paper pattern and, using paper-backed fusible web, iron these onto the wrong side of the organza lining. Protect the fabric by covering it with a sheet of either baking parchment or non-stick silicone paper.

16 Turn the organza hem allowance over the edges of the black silk and tack in place. Repeat on the second lining piece, Then, place one of the two linings on the wrong side of the front of the purse, sandwiching the ends of the cord handles between the two layers. Slip stitch in place. In the same way, join the second lining to the back of the purse then remove the tacking stitches.

17 Tack the front and back of the purse together, lining sides together, so they match exactly. Choose a selection of little beads in one or a variety of the colours used in the lace embroidery. Then, with the embroidery needle, oversew the edges of the two parts of the purse together, adding a bead with every second stitch and finishing off the threads securely.

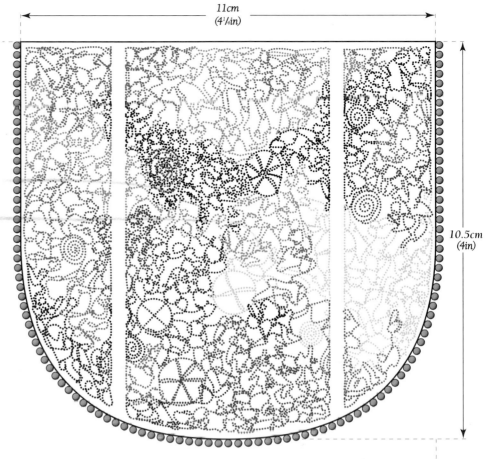

11cm
(4¹/₄in)

10.5cm
(4in)

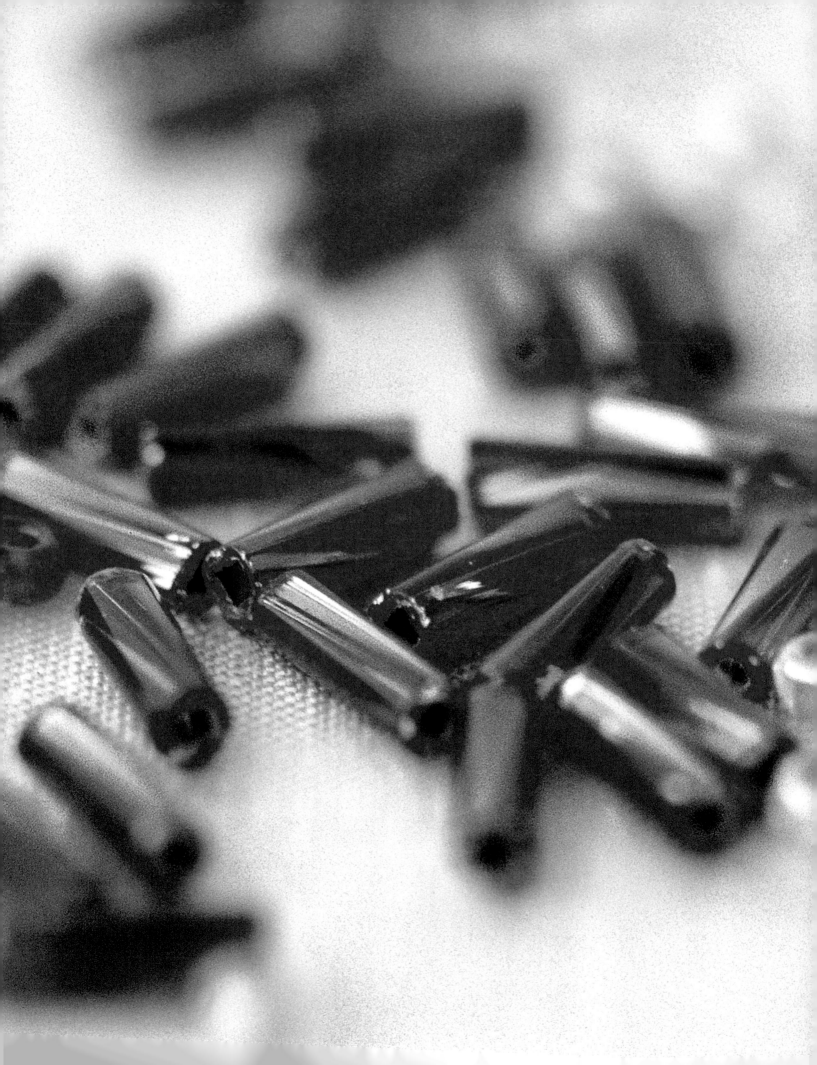

EMBELLISHING
THE SURFACE

Stumpwork

The exact origins of stumpwork are unknown, but it emerged as a peculiarly English form of three-dimensional embroidery in the 17th century. It was domestic, not professional, embroidery, stitched by wealthy young gentlewomen, most notably during the period from about 1650 to 1680. This work typically embellished practical items for the home, such as caskets and mirror surrounds, but was also intended to display the very best of a young lady's needlework skills, incorporating elaborate embroidery techniques and the most exquisite, finely worked needlelace.

Above: Thimble holder, English, late 17th century.

Raised or embossed work, which is better known as 'stumpwork' – a term that only came into use in the 19th century – was often the culmination of a girl's needlework training. To achieve the high standard of embroidery prevalent during the 17th century, training began at an early age and was a most important part of a young lady's education. Girls were sometimes taught embroidery at school but many daughters of the aristocracy were taught at home by a governess. The first exercise was a long narrow sampler of horizontal bands worked in simple stitches with patterns for borders, alphabets and numbers. This format was established by about 1630 and although the usual shape later changed to a square, this set the standard for almost 200 years. Often, initials and occasionally a name was included, but before the middle of the 17th century only rarely a date.

Several pictorial panels would be drawn out on one piece of fabric, usually white satin that, when complete, would be sent to a cabinet maker to be made up into a cabinet or casket. Each picture for the sides, top and drawer fronts would be mounted separately onto the wood and the edges hidden with silver gimp or braid. Finally, silver lock-plates and handles, and silvered wooden feet were fitted. The top was hinged and inside were divisions for perfume bottles or an inkwell and pen-tray. Sometimes, a mirror was fitted under the lid and, on quite rare occasions, the representation of a three-dimensional garden. The surviving boxes or caskets are of similar construction and many have the same secret drawer. The earliest dated example is in the Whitworth Gallery, Manchester, and it contains a letter written by Hannah Smith in 1657 recording the making of her cabinet. 'I was almost 12 years of age; when I went I made an end of my cabinette, at Oxford… and my cabinette was made up in the year of 1656 at London.' Although sometimes worked in laid silk threads, many of these caskets were predominantly of stumpwork.

Caskets of excellence

Stumpwork images would be made individually, first cut out in linen, stitched over card and padded with wool, horsehair, linen threads or whatever was available. Paper was pasted on the back to prevent fraying and the figure then slip stitched to the ground. Faces were of padded silk or embroidered satin glued over carved boxwood, or sometimes modelled in wax. The hands were usually of wood, painted or covered with satin, although they could also be made of wire wrapped with thread. Legs were covered in needlelace stitches for stockings and garments were either pieces of fabric exquisitely embroidered or made in detached needlepoint lace. The detailed figures were often embellished with real hair and lace, and seed pearls, coral beads, silver purl and feathers were added as contrasting textures. To create a greater sense of depth and perspective, the outline of the figures was occasionally worked in laid silk before the stumpwork figures were added.

Opposite page: Back of casket, English, circa 1650–1680. The man is holding a bible, the child a bird of carved wood and the woman a flower. Raised and padded work with silk and metal threads, metal purls, beads and lace.

Below: Panel, English, second half of the 17th century. Raised and padded work on satin ground. The various heraldic symbols around the man and woman suggest that this may have been worked as a betrothal panel or to celebrate a marriage.

Right: Apple Orchard, by Salley Mavor, late 1980s. This panel has a child-like quality and was originally created as a book illustration.

The ground was haphazardly covered with motifs, many, especially the caterpillars, butterflies and other insects, in stumpwork. Flowers, especially roses, could also be three-dimensional, the petals worked individually in detached buttonhole stitch and then applied. Various techniques were often combined in a single piece, and the variety is described by John Taylor in his poem 'Prayse of the Needle', which was the introduction to *The Needle's Excellency*, a small volume of embroidery patterns published in London in 1631.

> *For Tent-worke, Raised-work, Laid-worke, Froste-work,*
>   *Net-worke,*
> *Most Curious Purles, or rare Italian Cut-worke,*
> *Fine Ferne-stitch, Fisher-stitch, Irish-stitch, and Queen-stitch,*
> *The Spanish-stitch, Rosemary-stitch, and Mowse-stitch,*
> *The smarting Whip-stitch, Back-stitch, and the Crosse-stitch,*
> *And these are good, and these we must allow,*
> *And these are everywhere in practise now.*

Rural and classical subjects were used, but the main ones were biblical as the Bible was central to life, especially the Protestant ethic. The first readily available English translation of the Bible was authorized by James VI and published in 1611,

although many illustrated bibles were imported earlier from northern Europe following the Reformation. These provided the source of many embroidery designs and the importance placed on fidelity and the family is reflected in the choice of subjects.

Other decorative pieces

Some girls chose to work panels for a mirror frame rather than a casket. Mirror glass was very expensive and had begun to appear in wealthy homes. The frames are sometimes of tortoiseshell and the stumpwork is often divided into small compartments at the top and bottom. On either side were figures in fashionable dress that bear a remarkable resemblance to Catherine of Braganza and Charles II, who returned from exile in 1660. Some mirrors were fitted with feet and laid flat on the dressing table. To protect them, they had padded hinged covers that were sometimes decorated with beaded stumpwork.

Picture panels on white satin were also popular at this time and often show a man and woman in a pleasure garden. The man frequently carries his hat and the woman is usually holding a book or bible, or offers him a flower. In the distance, there may be a country house or a castle with shiny transparent mica for windows and they stand on either side of an elaborate fountain and grotto, fashionable elements of garden design. Sometimes, there is an arbour with sweet-smelling plants and the couple is surrounded by flowers and beasts with symbolic meaning. Such panels may celebrate a betrothal or marriage with the couple shown in a garden of love, but the garden may also represent paradise. Layers of meaning were everywhere and readily understood by the educated at the time.

Stumpwork details were also often added to canvas work panels. In some cases the motif, such as a lion, would be secured in place, the stitches concealed by a couched cord outline. Or, if a simple, less raised shape such as an apple was desired, the fabric would be slit at the back and the padding packed into the space before the slit was stitched up. Completely three-dimensional pieces were also made. A few birds survive, their padded bodies covered in buttonhole stitch with wing feathers worked separately and applied to form a drawstring pocket to hold a thimble. The legs were of wire wrapped with thread.

20th-century revival

During the 1950s and 1960s, new approaches to needlework were explored as a reaction to the rigours of war time, including three-dimensional work in embroidery, appliqué and soft sculpture. There was also an interest in figures that ranged from miniatures to life size, but it was not until the mid-1980s that there was a revival of interest in early stumpwork techniques and traditional needlelace stitches.

There have been several embroiderers of note who have made distinctive use of stumpwork. For example, in America, Salley Mavor is inspired by folk art and creates deceptively simple domestic rural scenes. These are colourful and highly textured through extensive use of wool and linen upholstery fabrics and direct use of simple stitches. The clarity of design and use of contrasting colour enhances the technique. In Britain in the 1980s, Barbara and Roy Hirst re-awakened interest in the technique through their writing, teaching and work that is humorous and careful in its attention to detail. They make particularly effective use of needlelace stitches worked over padded shapes in subject matter that ranges from historical scenes to modern pastimes.

Top: **Mr Brassica and Friend,** *by Barbara and Roy Hirst, 1995. This piece, worked on dyed calico, combines traditional stumpwork with overall free machine embroidery.*

Bottom: **Fishing for the Stars,** *by Jane Rowe, 1998. In his dreams, the fisherman casts his net of silver and gold needlelace from a leather shoe. Painted herrings laugh in the beaded needlelace waves.*

Stumpwork stitches and techniques

Stumpwork is a three-dimensional embroidery world into which you can introduce people, flora and fauna, and many other elements from our own environment. The raised components can be made in a variety of ways and are then added to a flat, embroidered background, so planning the order of work is important to prevent damage to delicate pieces. Learn the basic techniques and let your imagination run riot.

Fabrics

A strong fabric such as calico or silk is ideal to support the weight of the raised work and wired free-standing elements that are characteristic of stumpwork.

It is a good idea to back silk with muslin and treat the two fabrics as one. Colouring the background with silk or iron-on paints will help to set the scene.

Needles

Work the needlelace with a ballpoint or tapestry needle to avoid splitting the threads. You will also need embroidery and sharp needles for techniques that pierce the fabric.

Threads

A wide variety of threads can be used, but for needlelace, the best results are obtained with a closely twisted thread such as 100/3 silk or dentelles 70/80.

Additional tools

Work on your main design and the separate slips in either a hoop or a frame, but you should work needlelace fillings on a needlelace pad in the hand. You will need felt, craft interfacing and wadding for padding shapes and pointed tweezers will be quite helpful to do this. You will also need lengths of sugarcraft wire for constructing some shapes and beading wire for some of the needlelace edges. Always use heavy, good-quality tracing paper when tracing the needlelace outlines.

Padding techniques

You should work as much of the flat background stitching as possible before applying raised shapes and other delicate elements that may get damaged.

Applying embroidered slips

Outline the shape on calico and then work densely packed textured stitches such as French knots (see page 205) inside the outline. Cut out the shape with a turning allowance. Stab stitch it in place, turning the edge under, coming up through the background fabric and stabbing down into the slip. Work a few more knots in order to conceal any untidy edges.

Apply to the slip with stab stitch, tucking the edges under.

Padding raised slips

First, cut a piece of felt to the required shape and position it on the fabric. Attach with stab stitch, stabbing down through the felt, leaving a small opening for the stuffing. Then, insert the desired amount of stuffing and close the opening with stab stitch. An embroidered slip or a piece of leather can now be added. Cut the piece slightly larger than the original shape in order to cater for the stuffing. Then, attach with a series of stab stitches as before.

Secure the felt with stab stitch and insert stuffing.

Padding low shapes

Tack a piece of calico onto the wrong side of the fabric. Next, outline the required shape in running stitch and then trim the calico. Turn the work over, cut an opening into the fabric and insert the stuffing. Finally, stitch up the opening and then embroider over the shape in order to add texture.

Insert the stuffing and then stitch the opening closed.

Padding hard-edged shapes
Cut out the desired shape in craft interfacing. Paint the shape to blend with the background. Attach the shape in position with satin stitch (see page 188).

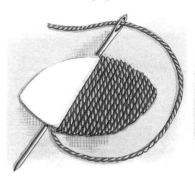

Satin stich to cover the firm shape.

Making faces
Cut an oval piece of calico slightly larger than the face you require. Run stitches around the edge and gather them so the edge turns over. Finish both ends of thread securely. Insert the stuffing into the shape. Stab stitch the face in position on the background. Stitch facial details in a fine, dark thread. Finally, add strands of thread for hair and stitch down in the desired hairstyle.

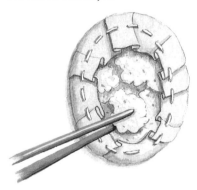

Insert the stuffing into the face and stitch to the background.

Wrapping techniques
These are useful to create finely detailed, linear shapes, such as hands and personal accessories.

Wrapping threads
This particular technique looks like a bullion knot but can be worked where the knots are difficult to achieve. Make a long straight stitch of the desired length and then evenly wrap it with the working thread without piercing the fabric. Finally, secure the wrapped thread with tiny couching stitches (see page 189).

Wrap straight stitches, then couch them down with tiny stitches.

Making hands
Evenly wrap five separate 5cm (2in) lengths of sugarcraft wire for 2cm (¾in). Lightly glue each wrapped fingertip. Wrap four wires together to start the hand and then add the fifth wire to make the thumb. Wrap the hand and arm to the desired length.

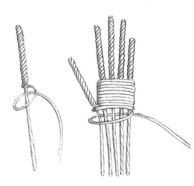

Bind five wrapped wires together for fingers and a thumb.

Needlelace techniques
These techniques produce a lacy fabric in various patterns that can be made to fit a required shape. The lace is made on a specially, but quite easily made pad. When finished, the lace is removed from the pad by cutting the couching stitches between the layers of calico fabric and then stitched into position on the embroidery.

Making a needlelace pad
Cut a 25cm (10in) square piece of calico. Fold it in half and then stitch the edges together. Trace the shape onto a sheet of tracing paper with a suitable drawing pen. It is possible to use a simple rectangular shape to practise the stitches, but there will be specific shape requirements for a real design. Tack the paper to the calico pad.

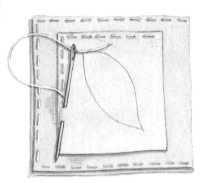

Tack the traced shape onto the calico.

Double up a length of thread long enough to go all around the traced outline. Place the looped end where it will eventually be covered by stitches then, starting here, couch the thread down at about 2mm (⅛in) intervals with tacking thread. When the outline has been completed, take both couched ends through the loop and divide them. Couch them down for 2cm (¾in).

Couch in a double thread around the outline and secure neatly.

Starting and finishing threads
Needlelace is worked from one side to the other, starting at the top of the shape. Secure the first thread by twisting it up the side of the couched outline. If you wish to introduce a second colour, secure that thread in the same way on the side from which it will start to work.

Working with two colours is possible when the stitch is corded. Work the cord and the working thread separately on two needles.

Secure a second colour to use as a cord across the lace.

Once the shape has been completed, you can then proceed to wrapping the working thread over each loop on the last row as well as on the bottom outline. Secure the working thread by looping it through itself and then twisting the cut end around the outline. Remember that all the ends will eventually be covered by edge stitching.

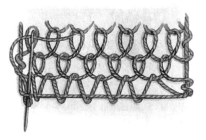

Attach the lace to the outline and finish securely.

Filling an irregular shape
It is likely that the shape you wish to make is either curved or has wider or narrower parts.

Here, you must increase or decrease stitches in order to fill the shape neatly.

To increase, make an extra stitch at the widening side of the shape. If the shape is raised and also expands outwards, you must add stitches into the loops along the row.

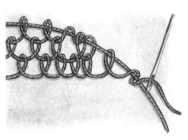

Add extra stitches along the row and at the edge.

To decrease, miss a stitch at the narrowing side of the shape and if the shape diminishes quickly, miss out some of the loops when you stitch the next row.

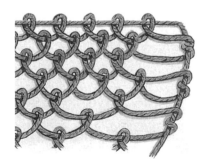

Miss stitches on the row and at the edge.

Edge stitching
Before removing the needlelace from the pad, you must finish the edges. To do this, lay a double length of thread that is long enough to go all around, along the outline. Then, using a sharp needle, closely buttonhole stitch (see page 98) all around the edge, picking up the outline and the padding threads with every stitch. You can also include a length of beading wire in the padding in order to mould the edging if you wish.

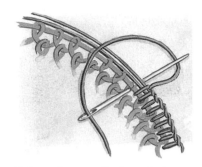

Using a sharp needle, buttonhole stitch all around the edge.

To join a new thread, start in the last knot, continue stitching over the new and old thread ends for about 2cm (¾in) and then cut them off. Buttonhole stitch all around and cut off the excess padding threads. Link the last stitch to the first and leave the thread for applying the lace to the background later.

Organizing your work
It is advisable not to remove the needlelace pieces from the pad until you are actually ready to apply them to your embroidery project, as it is very easy for them to be mislaid. You may also find it convenient to work several pieces of needlelace, provided they will fit, together on one pad, especially if they are related shapes on the same project.

Take time to re-appraise work in progress. Compare your original ideas on your master plan with the actual work as it evolves. You may consider developing part of the design, perhaps bringing in an additional detail in order to enhance the scene, re-positioning another component or even eliminating it altogether.

The following page features a selection of both needlelace and textural stitches that will start you off. There are many more stitches to explore and you will probably want to use surface embroidery stitches from other techniques on the backgrounds of your designs.

SINGLE BRUSSELS STITCH

USES: open filling

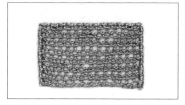

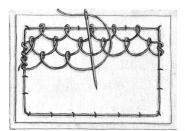

Work evenly spaced buttonhole stitches (see page 98), left to right, on the top outline. Twist around the side support and return, reversing the stitch, with one in each loop above.

HOLLIE POINT

USES: light filling

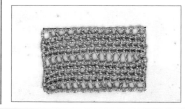

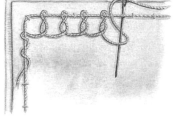

Working left to right, go over and under the top outline, then over and under the loop of thread. Pull taut. Continue, working rows in alternate directions as for single Brussels stitch.

PEA STITCH VARIATION

USES: open filling

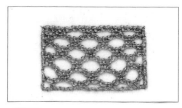

Work a row of single Brussels stitch. On the next, stitch into two loops then miss two. Next, make one stitch between the two loops and three on the long loop. Repeat last two rows.

SINGLE CORDED BRUSSELS STITCH

USES: dense filling

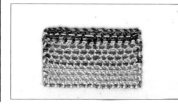

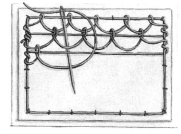

Work a row of single Brussels stitch. Take the thread back to the left, twisting it around the outline on each side. Repeat, working over the loops and the returned cord.

NEEDLEWOVEN PICOT

USES: textured detail

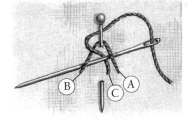

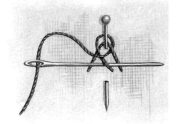

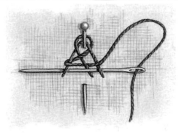

1 Insert a pin into the fabric. Come up at A, behind the pin and down at B. Come up at C. Take the thread behind the pin. Weave under thread A over the central one and under thread B.

2 Needleweave back in the opposite direction, going over, under and over the foundation threads. Pull the thread through towards the point, retaining the triangular shape of the picot.

3 Continue to weave back and forth, keeping threads closely spaced until you reach the fabric. Even the tension: too loose and the picot will be untidy, too tight and it will be misshapen.

PENDANT COUCHING

USES: texture, uncut or cut and trimmed

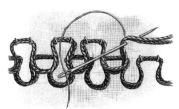

Starting at the bottom of the shape, form rows of loops by couching down one or more threads onto the background fabric. Add more rows to form a looped pile.

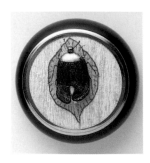

Beautiful beetle

This gorgeous beetle introduces two important elements of stumpwork: raised padding and needlelace. He sits, with his padded gold leather body, on a painted leaf background delicately outlined in stem stitch and decorates the lid of a bowl for special trinkets. If you carefully raise his glistening, wired needlelace wings, he looks as though he might just fly away. Design by Jane Rowe

Design Area

5 x 7cm (2 x 3in)

Materials

Transfer paints
(see diagram key)

20cm (8in) square
silk tussah

15 x 8cm (6 x 3¼in)
beige felt

5cm (2in) square
gold leather

Embroidery threads and
bead (see diagram key)

Small amount of wadding

25cm (10in) dark green
or brass beading wire
34 gauge

Equipment

Tracing paper and pen

Paper scissors

Baking parchment

Tissue paper

Pins

Sharp needle

Tacking thread

12.5cm (5in) embroidery
hoop

Embroidery needle

Embroidery scissors

Beige sewing thread

Needlelace pad
(see page 235)

Ballpoint needle

Round bowl with
8.5cm (3½in)
diameter aperture

1 Trace the leaf outline from the diagram on page 240 and transfer it onto a piece of paper. Brush the transfer paints on the reverse of the shape to give a pleasing effect, taking the colours beyond the outline. Cut out the leaf shape and transfer the paint onto a spare piece of fabric. Place the transfer, colour side down, onto the fabric, protect both with a piece of baking parchment and fix the colour with a warm iron following the manufacturer's instructions. If you are happy with the colour, repeat the process on the silk fabric.

2 Trace the body and the leaf outline onto the piece of tissue paper. Then, pin the tissue in place and tack around the body outline. Once this is completed, tear the tissue away.

3 Stretch the silk fabric in the hoop. With one strand of cotton 734, stem stitch (see page 206) around the leaf shape and add small, straight stitches radiating from the body to the edge of the leaf.

4 Cut a 15 x 2.5cm (6 x 1in) strip of felt, roll it up tightly then secure with a few stitches (see below). Next, cut the body shape out of felt. Position in the tacked outline on the silk fabric, then stab stitch around the edge with beige sewing thread. Leave an opening and insert first a little wadding around the edges and then the felt roll. Continue the stitching in order to close the opening, stuffing around the felt roll, until the shape is evenly filled. Next, remove the tacking stitches.

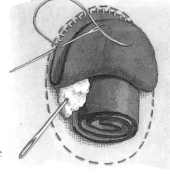

5 Cut a slightly larger body shape out of the piece of gold leather and then stab stitch this over the body, making sure you cover the felt completely.

6 Now make each leg. Working with thread 482 and referring to the diagram, make a straight stitch for each segment of each leg and then wrap each stitch. Couch the wrapped stitches down in the same thread.

7 Trace the wing-case outline onto good-quality tracing paper and tack this onto the needlelace pad. With a sharp needle and tacking thread, couch down the outline with a double length of dark green silk W585, starting on the top collar line.

8 Work the wing-case, using a ballpoint needle, silk W585 for single corded Brussels stitch and Astro 2 for the return cord. Start the first row of stitches at A on the diagram and work down to B. Also add the return cord at A. Continue, decreasing stitches to fit the shape and spacing the rows so that the last one ends on the centre line at X. Add any new threads on the collar edge.

9 Work the other half of the wing-case in the same way, starting at C and finishing the first row at D. When you finish this side, whip the two halves of the wing-case together and finish off neatly.

10 Shape the beading wire around the wing-case outline (see below). Take the ends through the needlelace pad at A and C to avoid them catching on threads. Lay a double length of dark green silk W585 alongside the wire. Edge stitch using the silk thread W585 and incorporating the couched outline, the wire and the padding threads around the A, B, D, C outline. Continue edge stitching along the collar edge which is not wired. Leave the ends of threads for attaching to the silk fabric later.

11 Remove the wing-case from the needlelace pad. Attach the first 1.5cm (⅝in) of the wings onto the silk in order to stabilize them. Then, take the wire and thread ends through to the reverse and fasten securely under the body.

12 Now finish the beetle's head. Make two antennae in the same way as the legs, adding a French knot (see page 205) at the tips in stranded cotton 734. Securely stitch the bead in place for the head.

13 To position the finished beetle onto the bowl, follow the mounting and framing instructions from the supplier.

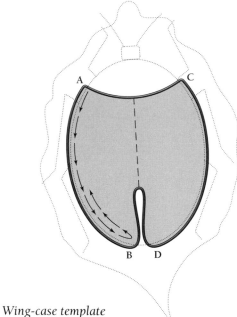

Wing-case template

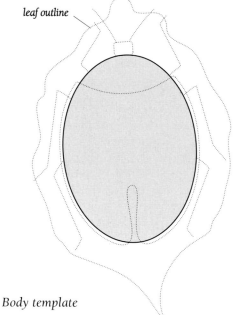

leaf outline

Body template

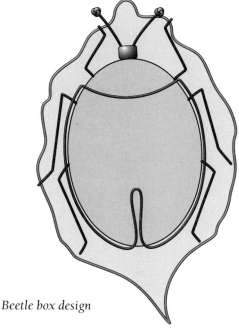

Beetle box design

BEAUTIFUL BEETLE KEY

Wrapped stitch in Madeira 40 in 482

Outline of wing-case in Mulberry silk in W585

Stem stitch in DMC stranded cotton in 734

French knots in DMC stranded cotton in 734

Mill Hill pebble bead 05081

Body shape

Direction of stitching in wing-case

Single corded Brussels stitch in Mulberry silk W585 and Madeira Astro in 2

Painted leaf in Deka Iron-on paints in 471, 483, 485

Note: You will need 1 skein of each shade.

Peaceful lagoon panel

Three elegant wading birds, a stilt and two egrets, are quietly feeding in this very peaceful lagoon. Blend a variety of threads – rayon, cotton and silk – for a lightly textured calm background leading down to a richly embroidered lakeside. As you become more confident about designing your own stumpwork you could choose your own colour scheme and create additional texture. Design by Jane Rowe

Design area

17 x 18cm (6¾ x 7in)

Materials

Transfer paints
 (see diagram key)

25cm (10in) square calico

6 x 7cm (2½ x 3in)
 grey felt

Small amount of wadding

6 x 5cm (2½ x 2in) pale
 grey leather

Embroidery threads
 (see diagram key)

10cm (4in) square
 pelmet stiffening

25cm (10in) square
 white felt

15cm (6in) beading wire
 34 gauge

1 length of sugarcraft wire
 30 or 32 gauge

Equipment

Tracing paper and pen

Baking parchment

Masking tape

Water-soluble pen

Embroidery frame

Paper scissors

White and grey sewing
 threads

Embroidery and
 ballpoint needles

Embroidery scissors

Tacking thread

Needlelace pad
 (see page 235)

Pins

Firm card for stretching
 embroidery

Strong thread for lacing

Mount and frame
 of your choice

1 Trace the main elements from the diagram on page 245, including the panel outline, the shapes for the birds, the mountains, the small islands, the areas of blue water and the main areas of vegetation. Keep this tracing as a master copy to use for making notes.

2 Trace over the design again, this time including just the two most distant mountains and the areas of blue water, and transfer this image onto a piece of paper. On the reverse side, paint these elements of the design with transfer paint. Dilute the brown and green to give a faded image for the distant hills and dilute the azure for the water.

3 Test the image by placing the transfer, colour side down, onto a spare piece of fabric, protecting both with a piece of baking parchment and fix the colour with a warm iron following the manufacturer's instructions. If you are happy with the colour, repeat the process on the calico background fabric.

4 Tape your master diagram onto a window or light box and then tape the calico background over the top. Mark the outlines for the nearer mountains, islands, birds and corners of the panel on the fabric with a water-soluble pen. Stretch the calico on the embroidery frame.

5 Make separate tracings of the two nearest mountains and cut them out. Cut the shapes out of the grey felt and then stab stitch them in position on the calico, padding them with wadding. Eliminate the pen marks as you apply the shapes. Cut out the shapes again, this time slightly larger, in the pale grey leather and stab stitch these in position over the felt with one strand of cotton 3072.

6 Make patterns for the two islands in the middle distance and cut these out of the pelmet stiffening. Position these over the outlines on the calico with two or three long tacking stitches.

7 Thread an embroidery needle with one strand of each of the stranded cottons 370 and 644 and the rayons 30503 and 30739. Work satin stitch (see page 188), blending the tones, over the padded mountains. With silk thread S611, work deep shadows under the mountains in straight stitch.

8 Make patterns for the felt body shapes from the templates on page 244. Cut these shapes out of the white felt and stab stitch them in position on the calico, padding them with wadding and, on birds 1 and 2, leaving openings for the insertion of wire legs later. With the padded felt bodies in position, it is easier to gauge the placing of stitches for the water.

Start to shape the body of bird 3 with felt, padded with wadding.

9 Add the main lines of surface stitches in the distance. With one strand of the rayon 30503, work 10 or 11 straight stitches below those already in place under the mountain on the left. Continue in a zigzag fashion to just above the island below. Now work on the other side of the design, making about 20 straight and long fly stitches (see page 205) to just above the island on the right. Add a zigzag on the edge of the blue water area. All these stitches must be horizontal in order to keep the calm mood of the design.

10 Now add more subtle shading to intensify this distant area by adding straight stitches in one strand of stranded cottons 370 and 644, and rayon 30739, with reference to the diagram.

11 Using the relevant pattern, cut out a body shape for bird 3 in grey leather, slightly larger than the felt shape. Stab stitch the leather over the felt, using one strand of stranded cotton 3072 and eliminating the pen marks. Then, wrap straight stitches using two strands of silk W777 for the legs and toes. Leave stitching the details on the head until later.

12 Satin stitch over the islands with silk F823 and with the same thread, work straight stitches for the clumps of reeds and a few French knots (see page 205) as shown on the diagram. Work more straight stitches in silks R143, F433 and S558 around both islands. Add straight stitches and French knots in flower thread 2907 to complete the raft of reeds for the bird.

13 Now complete the ripples of water in the foreground. To do this, use one strand of rayon 30503 and work straight stitches in a zigzag sequence almost down to the shoreline. Intensify the effect by adding straight stitches with silk S558 and fly stitches with silk W819. More stitches can be added later, when some of the shoreline detail is in place.

14 Prepare a needlelace pad for the wings and remaining body shapes. Trace all the templates ready for use and attach the paper to the pad, noting that the bodies are upside down for easier working. Couch down the outline with stranded cotton 3072, starting at X on the template. Work the shape in single corded Brussels stitch in dentelles 120, starting along the top edge of the template from A to B, decreasing on the left to form the back and increasing on the right to shape the head. Miss out a stitch in the middle of the shape if necessary in order to accommodate the curve. There is no need to stitch the upper part of the body shape as it will be covered by the wing later. Edge stitching is not required for the body shapes.

15 Couch the outline for bird 1 with silk 275. Complete the body shape in the same way and continuing with the same thread.

16 In the same way as step 15, proceed onto stitching the wings for each bird in single corded Brussels stitch. Use silk W777 for bird 1 and dentelles 120 for birds 2 and 3. Make sure to start along the upper edges from A to B, decreasing at each end.

17 The edges of the wings are finished in different ways before the shapes are removed from the pad. Simply edge stitch around the wing for bird 3 using one strand of stranded cotton 3072. The lower edges of the wings for birds 1 and 2 are part-wired from B to T. Cut a length of beading wire slightly longer than the distance from B, around A, to T on the template for bird 2. Edge stitch around the shape in stranded cotton 3072, incorporating padding threads also of 3072, the outline and the wire in the appropriate place. Part-wire and edge stitch the wing for bird 1 in the same way, using silk W777.

18 Cut the sugarcraft wire to length for the legs for birds 1 and 2, allowing extra to protrude into the bodies. Bend the wire into the appropriate shapes. Wrap the legs for bird 1 with one strand of stranded cotton 3706 and for bird 2 with silk W702, leaving longs ends of thread to secure the legs.

19 Fasten the wrapped legs in position by inserting the top end of the wire through the open edge of felt, under the wadding and finishing off the loose thread securely. Take the bottom end of the wire through the calico and secure. Couch the legs down at regular intervals with tiny stitches in the same thread. Wrap straight stitches in the same thread to make four toes on each leg. Secure and complete all the legs in the same way.

Insert the wrapped wire legs under the body and secure.

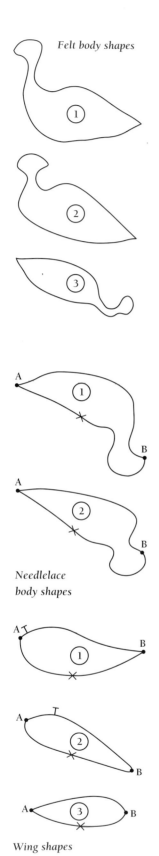

Felt body shapes

1

2

3

A

B

1

A

B

2

Needlelace
body shapes

A

B

1

A

B

2

A

B

3

Wing shapes

20 Remove the needlelace shapes from the pad and pin the bodies in position on each bird. Attach to the calico, using matching thread. Stab stitch into every loop along the edges that will be seen, but lightly attach the upper edges that will be hidden. Attach the upper edges of the wings in the same way, securing the wire ends on the reverse.

21 Trace the shapes of the mounds in the foreground from the diagram. Make the three slips, embroidering them on calico with French knots in flower thread 2907 and one strand of stranded cottons 3862, 731, 2841 and rayon 30469. Put the slips aside until later.

22 Now stitch the shoreline foreground, building up dense texture. Starting on the left, add horizontal straight stitches blending rayon 30841 and one strand of stranded cottons 470, 731, 734 and 2841. Work straight stitches for clumps of reeds in one strand of stranded cottons 469, 731 and 2841. With the same threads, wrap the nearest reeds to achieve greater definition.

23 On the left side, weave three picots in silk S558 and two picots in S4200 directly onto the calico. Stitch the two smaller slips in position and work clusters of French knots in S558 and S4200 at the base of the reeds.

24 On the right side, weave two picots in silk S4200 and a third in one strand of stranded cotton 2841. Attach the third slip, adding French knots in one strand of 731 and 2841. Work more French knots in S4200 under the bird's foot.

25 Complete the head of each bird, stitching three straight stitches for the beaks and a French knot for the eyes in W702. Add feathers on the top of the heads of birds 2 and 3 with straight stitches in dentelles 120. Add more straight and fly stitches to the lagoon between birds 1 and 2 in silks S558 and W819.

26 Remove the finished embroidery from the frame. Cut the board to fit the aperture of your chosen frame and pad it with a layer of felt before you lace the embroidery over it. Assemble the panel in the frame, without glass, or take to a professional framer.

PEACEFUL LAGOON PANEL KEY

Deka Iron-on paint in 483 and 485	— DMC stranded cotton in 644	● — DMC stranded cotton in 734
Deka Iron-on paint in 479	— Mulberry silks in S611	● — DMC stranded cotton in 469
Grey leather DMC stranded cotton in 3072	— Mulberry silks in W777	● — DMC stranded rayon in 30841
DMC stranded cotton in 370, 644 and stranded rayon in 30503, 30739	◎ — Mulberry silks in F823	● — DMC stranded cotton in 470
	— Mulberry silks in R143	◎ — Mulberry silks in S4200
DMC special dentelles 120 and stranded cotton 3072	◎ — Mulberry silks in F433	◎ — Mulberry silks in W702
Grey leather and DMC stranded cotton 3072	◎ — Mulberry silks in S558	------ Direction of stitches
	● — Flower thread in 2907	
Mulberry silks in S275	◎ — Mulberry silks in W819	Note: You will need 1 skein of each shade.
Mulberry silks in W777	— Mulberry silks in S275	
— DMC stranded cotton in 3702	— Dentelles in 120	
— DMC stranded rayon in 30503	— DMC stranded cotton in 3706	
— DMC stranded rayon in 30739	◎ — DMC stranded cotton in 3862	
— DMC stranded cotton in 370	◎ — DMC stranded cotton in 731	
	◎ — DMC stranded cotton in 2841	
	● — DMC stranded rayon in 30469	

245

INSPIRATION AND DESIGN:
lively embroidered stories

Nature in all its forms, from flowers to scenery on a grand scale, has inspired embroiderers for hundreds of years. A river estuary may seem an unlikely source of inspiration but, as often happens, it pays to wait and that was how the idea for the Peaceful Lagoon design came about. At first, all appeared to be deserted, but soon, a few wading birds could be spotted quietly feeding.

The impression was one of peace and serenity, and many of the elements in it seemed ideal for interpretation in stumpwork. However, a different setting would strengthen the sense of tranquillity, so it was decided to place three birds in a lagoon, with distant mountains lending a sense of place.

The next stage was to make a rough design that would form the basis for a satisfactory composition. Some research was needed to get certain features right and in this case, bird books and magazines provided much information on stance, habits and habitat. As the mood of tranquillity was a main concern, too much clutter was avoided. The areas of embroidery and raised work were decided and the order of work planned, accompanied by a master drawing with notes about textural interest and threads.

Stumpwork comprises a variety of elements and styles, many of which can be worked at any time. However, an overall scheme is essential to plan the

order in which they can be made and safely applied without damage. As the embroidery progresses, the master plan will be your point of reference and will probably include notes about the threads and components you wish to include, as well as any ideas that come to mind that may enhance the design.

Getting started on a stumpwork embroidery can be rather daunting and off-putting. An exciting approach is to look for an inspiring image, so start collecting cards, illustrations and magazine cuttings about the kind of subject that interests you.

To many, design is something to be avoided. If you feel that drawing is not your forte, cut out shapes of the important elements in a piece of work. Alternatively, make several tracings; these can be moved around until you are satisfied with their arrangement, avoiding constant rubbing out and potential dissatisfaction with the whole process.

Once you have the basis of an embroidery, concentrate on what you want it to say and take

steps to prevent the design becoming stiff and lifeless. Think of it as a story without words, just as some photographs or cartoons do not need words. For example, in a project featuring people or creatures you will want them to look as life-like as possible, so it helps to give them something to do. Include elements that add to the story being told. For example, in a garden scene, add tools and flower pots as well as shrubs and plants. Sometimes, a certain amount of research is necessary for authenticity. If the subject is engaged in a specialist skill, find out all you can about the equipment used, the working environment and so on.

The embroiderer new to stumpwork will find that the little artefacts to be included in a piece of work can be rewarding to make because of their miniature scale. Not only do they intrigue the viewer, but the final assembly, when all the components are stitched and put in position, is very satisfying and well worth the effort.

Ribbon embroidery

Since the late 15th century, silk ribbons have had a variety of uses. At first, ribbons were extremely expensive and produced mainly in France. Raw silk was imported from Italy by 'silk women' who wove it into ribbons. It was a specialized form of weaving, worked on a very narrow loom until the process was speeded up in the early 17th century, with the invention of a loom with 12 parallel shuttles to weave multiple ribbons. In London, the silk women were concentrated in Cheapside where jewellery and decorative clothing could be bought. Outside the main towns, ribbons were sold by pedlars and petty chapmen who travelled around selling haberdashery and textiles.

Gloves were an important item of clothing for both men and women and were frequently decorated with ribbons. They symbolized friendship and loyalty and were given as New Year gifts in reward for service or to guests at weddings. During the 16th and first half of the 17th centuries, the cuff or gauntlet was deep and usually heavily embroidered; the seam where it joined the glove was often hidden with either lace or ruched silk ribbons. From 1660 until the early 1670s, great use was made of colourful looped silk ribbons on short gloves with only a narrow cuff. These sometimes had raised ribbon rosettes stitched to the fingers and back of the hand.

These fine silken things

During the middle of the 17th century, ribbons were used in profusion to trim men's petticoat breeches. The breeches were short, very wide, floppy trousers with as much as 230m (250yd) of tiered ribbon loops around the waist and hems of the legs. Caricatures show exaggerated images of men wearing these breeches with very short doublets and additional ribbon rosettes hanging from locks of hair. John Evelyn, the diarist, described the fashion having seen 'a fine silken thing… that had as much ribbon on him as would have plundered six shops and set up twenty country pedlars: all his body was dres'd like a may-pole.' Earlier, Charles I tried to prohibit the wearing of gold and silver lace and ribbons during the Civil War, but the legislation was ignored.

However, it was not until the Huguenot weavers spread out from Spitalfields in London to areas such as Macclesfield and Coventry that silk ribbon began to be produced in large enough quantities for most people to be able to afford it. In the early 18th century, Daniel Defoe, on his tour of the country, reported that 'Coventry drove a thriving trade in tammies (a type of silk weaving) and in the weaving of ribbons.' By 1821, almost a quarter of the town's population were ribbon weavers. By this time, both plain and Jacquard looms were being used to produce a range of ribbons that is quite unimaginable today.

Opposite page: Man's waistcoat, circa 1835–1845.

Left: Man's gloves, 1660s–1680s.

Above left: Letter case or pocket book, 1780–1800. This piece is made of paper covered with white silk crêpe, embroidered with laid cord, pink silk ribbons and spangles. The central image is a drawing of a classical urn.

Above right: Detail of a bag, circa 1835. The silk moiré fabric is ornated with silk areophane flowers in red and cream. The stems are worked using silk chenille ribbons.

During the 18th century, ribbons were used to trim bonnets, dresses, fans and bags. The most usual form of ribbon embroidery was on ladies' 'workbags' of cream satin embroidered with the swags and floral sprays typical of rococo design.

A rise in popularity

But it was during the 1820s and 1830s that ribbon embroidery became most popular. Narrow silk ribbons, called 'chinas' in the trade, in bright colours shaded across the width were introduced. These could be used on canvas instead of woollen thread to give additional texture, in which case a tapestry needle was used. The ribbon, which was 3mm (⅛in) wide, was used for small flowers such as rosebuds, bluebells and forget-me-nots, or ears of corn, with chenille thread and 'penny ribbon' for the leaves.

Ribbon embroidery was included in the *Handbook of Useful and Ornamental Amusements,* which was published in 1845. It was a form of fancy work, a term introduced in the 1840s for the huge repertoire of applied decoration, including needlework items made by women of the leisured classes.

As Berlin work became the dominant craze, ribbon work declined, but was revived during the 1880s for domestic furnishings. Switzerland became a major centre of automated ribbon production and, with increased competition, many new ribbons were introduced. Silk ribbon embroidery became known as 'rococo work' from the 18th century designs that continued to predominate. The 1882 edition of *The Dictionary of Needlework, an Encyclopaedia of Artistic, Plain and Fancy Needlework* gives instructions for the work which it describes as 'when worked in small patterns it has a quaint old-fashioned look it cannot retain when enlarged.' China ribbons were also used for plaited ribbon work and China ribbon work was described in the Dictionary as: 'A modern name given to a kind of drawn work, into which coloured China ribbons are run instead of crochet cotton. It is suitable for any linen or cotton materials, coarse enough to allow of their threads being drawn out easily, and is useful for tablecloths and chair backs, and very simple in execution.'

In America during the late 18th century, native American Indians also used the craft of ribbon embroidery. The Woodlands, Plains and Great

Lakes tribes all employed European appliqué techniques in silk ribbons with their own designs. They used these to decorate blankets, leggings, moccasins and dance costumes with geometric or floral designs.

Ribbons enjoyed a revival in America in the 1920s with the publication of *Ribbon Art: How to Make Hundreds of Dainty and Practical Things of Ribbons*. Babies were not neglected, with ribbon decorations for baskets, blankets and bonnets while among the new introductions were head-bands and boudoir items. Lingerie was also included with camisoles, bloomers, an early brassiere made entirely of ribbon and 'gay garters' of ruched ribbon with bows and rosebuds. However, there was little embroidery skill needed as the items only required simple manipulative skills and glue was suggested as an alternative when making a more complex parrot decoration for a hat or frock.

At the same time in England, the Manchester School of Embroidery revived the traditional form of the embroidery in an issue of their publication *Needlecraft*. In the introduction, some of the newly available ribbons were described, including 'The Picotee', which was patented by Wm Briggs & Co. of Manchester. This particular ribbon had only one serrated edge and was available in three colours: white with a serrated scarlet edge, pale yellow with a crimson edge and blush pink with a deep ruby edge. These ribbons were ideal for working flowers and instructions with information on colours and the types of stitch – mainly satin, stem and French knots – were included. In addition were diagrams and illustrations for working various flower designs based on clover, roses, violets, cornflowers, snowdrops, poppies, fuchsias and tiger lilies that retain the delicacy of the early 19th-century work.

Below: **The Rose,** *by Ann Cox, 2001. The rose is worked in ribbon stitch using pale cream silk ribbon, then painted over with silk paints.*

Ribbon embroidery stitches and techniques

You do not have to be an experienced embroiderer to work ribbon embroidery as even a complete beginner can create amazing results. This technique has a quality of its own – your unique touch will make the ribbon twist and fold in a way that is personal to you. The ribbon lends itself particularly well to flowers and there are limitless effects you can achieve simply by altering the width of the ribbon or the tension of the stitch.

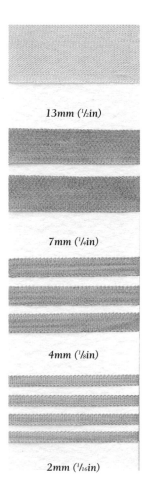

13mm (½in)

7mm (¼in)

4mm (⅛in)

2mm (¹⁄₁₆in)

Fabrics

Any fabric that allows the needle to pass through may be used for ribbon embroidery, from the finest silk to leather and even card. However, as silk ribbon comes from a natural fibre, it feels most compatible with others such as linen, cotton and wool.

Needles

Chenille needles are best suited to ribbon embroidery. Sizes 13, 18 and 24 are recommended for use with the widest to the narrowest ribbon.

Ribbons

Pure silk ribbon is the best to use for this technique, although cheaper polyester is available. The silk has a softness that makes it easy to coax into the shapes you want and a sheen that adds a luxurious finish to your work. Silk ribbon is available in a variety of colours. Four widths are most suitable for embroidery (see left).

The ribbon is stitched in a similar way to thread using traditional embroidery stitches. However, because of its width, the ribbon creates a different look to thread and covers more fabric. The design develops more quickly, creating a three-dimensional effect to almost any depth.

Silk ribbon is colourfast and may be laundered with care. It is important to consider the end use of your embroidery before you decide on the stitches. For items needing frequent laundering, smaller stitches with a firmer tension will be more suitable. For items that receive little wear, a greater variety of stitches and ribbon widths, worked with a looser tension, may be chosen.

Other threads

You will need a good selection of embroidery threads to add a variety of texture and colour to your designs. Choose different threads to reflect the qualities of the subject and blend threads to create more realistic shading. A strand of matching embroidery thread is also needed to secure the ribbon on the back.

Equipment

An embroidery frame or hoop is essential and a free standing one is useful to leave two hands free to manipulate the ribbon, provided it does not encroach on the design area. You will also need a small pair of very sharp scissors for cutting the ribbon.

Embroidery techniques

You do not always need to iron the ribbon before you start. If necessary, press a medium hot iron onto the silk as you pull the ribbon quickly through.

The silk ribbon is very fine and deteriorates quickly as you stitch so work with a length of 30cm (12in) or less. Cut the ribbon at a 45 degree angle to prevent the ends from fraying.

Securing ribbon

For the two narrower widths, tie a knot at one end and take the ribbon through to the front of the fabric. For the wider widths, take a very short end through from the front to the back of the fabric.

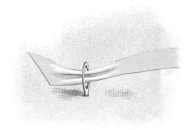

Take the end of a wide ribbon to the back of the work.

Secure the end of wide ribbon underneath the place where the first stitch will be worked, with a few stitches in one strand of matching thread. Finish off all widths of ribbon in the same way. Do not take the ribbon across the back of the work: this will show on the front and also cause problems as you try to stitch the rest of the design.

Secure the ribbon end to the back with a matching thread.

Working with ribbon

The secret of success is to get a feel for the appropriate amount of tension. If stitches are pulled too tight, the entire effect is lost. To avoid this, place a finger lightly on the finished stitch as you pull the ribbon back through to the surface ready for the next stitch. You will be able to feel any pull on the stitch as soon as it starts to happen. Occasionally, you can ease the stitch back with the point of a needle, but it is not always easy to correct.

It is essential to take the ribbon through the fabric in one direction at a time, stabbing the needle. Never scoop the needle in an attempt to rush. This will twist the ribbon so much that it will be useless and the only remedy will be to cut it and start again.

The ribbon will be damaged if it is stitched through, as with ribbon stitch, and should be pulled through to the back and secured behind another stitch or cut away, ready to start again.

Avoid bringing the needle up through a ribbon on the back of the work. As the ribbon for the new stitch is pulled through, it will drag all the previous stitches and spoil them. Come up through a gap between stitches.

Controlling the ribbon

When the ribbon comes to the surface of the fabric, it has to curl to get through the hole. Use this to advantage, coaxing it to curl into the ideal shape. The edges of the ribbon must curl downwards in a domed, convex shape.

The ideal shape with the edges of the ribbon curled down.

If the edges curl upwards in a dished, concave shape, you will need to turn and flatten it.

Ribbon with the edges curling up needs to be turned.

Turning and flattening the edges

Turn the ribbon over to lay it flat on the fabric. Hold the end of the ribbon firm and use the eye of a second needle to stroke the underside of the ribbon.

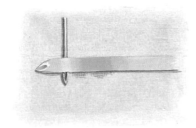

Stroke the ribbon with a needle down to the fabric.

Stroke towards where the ribbon emerges from the fabric. This has the effect of ironing it flat and the edges will turn down.

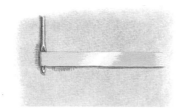

The ribbon will flatten to where it comes through the fabric.

Straightening twists

Sometimes the ribbon becomes twisted as it is pulled through the fabric. If this happens, use the eye of a second needle under the ribbon in order to flatten it from the correctly curled end, towards the twisted end.

Use the eye of another needle to flatten the twisted ribbon.

Hold the needle so it keeps the ribbon taut. With the other hand, pull the ribbon through to the back until the twists have been taken through and the stitch lies as you wish it to.

Pull the ribbon to the back of the fabric with the eye of another needle.

Ribbon stitch

While any traditional embroidery stitch may be used for this particular technique, ribbon stitch is unique to silk ribbon embroidery and is without doubt the most versatile.

A large number of embroidery stitches can be adapted for ribbon work, although you will achieve different effects. A selection of the most useful – including ribbon stitch, which is unique to this type of work – are explained on the following two pages.

Your designs will probably also need enriching with stitches worked in thread. Some of the simplest embroidery stitches, like straight stitch (see page 206), couching (see page 189), fly stitch and French knots (see page 205), will act as an effective contrast to the ribbon.

BASIC STRAIGHT STITCH

Bring the ribbon up. Flatten and lift it slightly with the eye of a second needle. Take the ribbon down through the fabric a short distance away, keeping it taut over the needle.

STRAIGHT STITCH LOOP

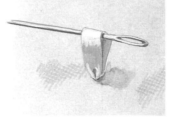

Bring the ribbon up and keep it taut over a second needle, as for the basic stitch, but take it back down close to, not through, the original hole. You can vary this by adding one twist.

CENTRE RIBBON STITCH

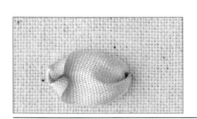

Ribbon stitch is unique to silk ribbon embroidery. It is also, without doubt, the most versatile stitch of all as the ribbon can go back down through itself, thereby creating a variety of different shapes at the end of the stitch. Taking the ribbon down in the centre or to the left or right will create slightly different pointed ends. If desired, you can also make a less pointed end with a curved edge ribbon stitch (see opposite).

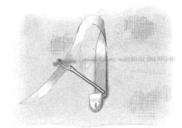

1 Bring the ribbon up. Flatten and lay the ribbon on the fabric, allowing it to retain a slight lift. Insert the point of the needle in the centre of the ribbon width and pull it through.

2 Once the needle is at the back, hold the ribbon close to the fabric and slowly pull it through, stopping just as the ribbon begins to curl in on itself.

LEFT RIBBON STITCH

Make this stitch in the same way as the centre ribbon stitch, but take the needle and ribbon through the left selvedge of the ribbon to the back of the fabric.

RIGHT RIBBON STITCH

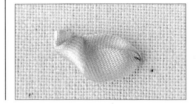

Work this stitch in the same way as the centre ribbon stitch, but take the needle and ribbon through the right selvedge of the ribbon to the back of the fabric.

RIBBON CHAIN STITCH
OTHER NAME: lazy daisy

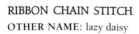

1 You can vary this stitch by altering its size and by choosing different widths of ribbon. To start, bring the ribbon to the surface and take it back down close to the original hole.

2 Allow the ribbon to sit on the surface of the fabric, creating an untwisted loop that forms the basic shape and length of the finished stitch.

3 Bring the ribbon back up where you want to end the stitch. Take it over the existing loop and, holding it flat with the eye of a second needle, pull it through to the back.

CURVED EDGE RIBBON STITCH

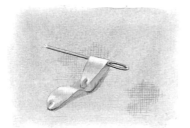

Work as centre ribbon stitch. With the eye of a second needle, hold the ribbon straight and taut. Pull the ribbon to the back until tight around the needle and remove the needle.

French knots worked in ribbon can vary in size from the tiniest dot to a knot as large as a thumbnail, depending on the width of ribbon chosen, the number of loops worked and the tension. You can wind the ribbon around the needle any number of times, to obtain different and attractive results. The photograph shows French knots worked with one, two and three loops (bottom to top row) in the four different widths of ribbon (from left to right).

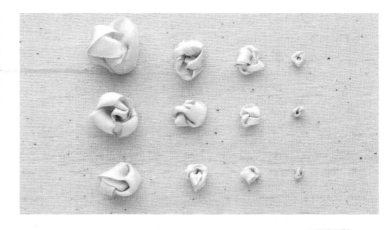

FRENCH KNOT

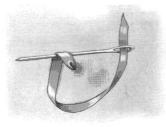

1 Secure the ribbon and bring it to the surface. Hold the needle above and slightly beyond the hole where the ribbon emerged. Keep the ribbon straight and wrap around the needle.

2 Hold the ribbon on the needle and insert the point of the needle close to the original hole in the fabric. Pull the needle through to the back without pulling the knot through.

3 As the ribbon goes down, place your index finger on it, close to the knot to keep it in place. Gently continue to pull the ribbon through until the knot is the right size.

FRENCH KNOTS WITH TWO KNOTS OR MORE

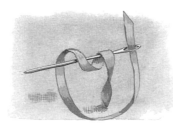

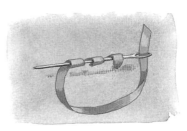

1 French knots can be made with more than one loop, but need extra care. Bring the ribbon to the surface and hold it straight. Then, turn the ribbon once clockwise.

2 Hold the working needle in the same position as for the basic knot and wrap the ribbon twice or more. Take the needle and ribbon through and finish the knot in the usual way.

3 Avoid wrapping the ribbon neatly around the needle as it will telescope and not make a knot.

Rosebud cot blanket

A delicate trellis of sweet rosebuds and forget-me-nots is the gentlest way to cocoon your baby in sleep. The prettily coloured pastel silk ribbons are worked in tiny stitches that cannot be pulled with baby's fingernails. Worked with just two ribbons and a few embroidery stitches, this cosy blanket is a relaxing way to begin ribbon embroidery and ensure your little sleeping beauty gives you lots of peaceful nights. Design by Ann Cox

Design area

6 x 8cm (2¼ x 3in)

Materials

78 x 107cm (30½ x 42in)
   pure wool white
   blanket fabric

Ribbons and
   embroidery threads
   (see diagram key)

Stranded cotton threads
   to match ribbons

78 x 107cm (30½ x 42in)
   cotton fabric

4.5m (5yd) satin blanket
   binding

Equipment

Pins

Contrasting tacking
   threads

Size 8 crewel needle

Embroidery scissors

Tracing paper and pencil

10 x 12cm (4 x 5in)
   thin card

Large needle

Long ruler

Quilting hoop

Size 18 and 24
   chenille needles

Matching sewing thread

1 Place the wool fabric on a clean, flat surface. Fold it across one diagonal, mark the line with a few pins and then tack along the line in contrasting thread. Fold the fabric across the opposite diagonal and tack along the line as before. Using a different coloured thread, sew a line of tacking stitches 10.5cm (4⅛in) on each side of the tacked diagonals.

Establish the baselines (pink) and guidelines (green) for the design.

2 Remove the tacking for the first diagonal baselines. Continue to tack lines at 21cm (8in) intervals, working out to each corner from the four original guidelines.

3 Cut a length of coton perlé 25cm (10in) longer than the longest guidelines, secure it at the end and lay it along one of the central lines. Thread one strand of matching cotton thread in the crewel needle and, with stitches at a slight angle, couch

(see page 189) the coton perlé down along the length of the guideline. Fasten the ends of thread securely. Repeat until all the guidelines have been couched over, then remove all the tacking stitches.

4 Trace the design from the diagram on page 259 and transfer it onto thin card to make a template. Using a large needle, make a hole through the card in the centre of the open briar rose and at the tip of each petal. Mark the top and bottom of each rosebud and the centre of each forget-me-not in the same way. Mark the lines for the trellis in pencil to the edges of the card.

5 With the wool fabric on a flat surface, position the template so that the pencil lines for the trellis match up exactly with one intersection of couched thread on the blanket. Using a pin, check the centre of the briar rose on the template is exactly where the couched threads cross. Keeping the template in the same position and using a fine sharp pencil, make a dot through the holes in the template to mark the tip of each of the six rose petals.

6 Place the fabric in the quilting hoop, tensioning it enough to keep it firm without stretching it too much. The wool fabric is delicate, so remove the hoop whenever you put the embroidery to one side.

Briar rose

7 Thread a size 18 chenille needle with the 7mm (¼in) pink ribbon. To make the petals, bring the needle up very close to the centre each time, but not through the same hole. Work six centre ribbon stitch petals with a curved edge, taking the needle down at each dot marking the petal tip. Fasten off all the ribbon securely on the back of the work.

8 Using the 4mm (⅛in) yellow ribbon, work a French knot (see page 205) with two loops into the centre of the rose. Fasten off. With one strand of the pale yellow stranded cotton, work tiny French knots with one loop around the ribbon French knot to complete the stamen.

Rosebuds and stems

9 Replace the template over the embroidery and mark the top and bottom of each rose bud on all four sprays onto the fabric.

10 Thread a size 18 chenille needle with the 4mm (⅛in) pink ribbon. Work three centre ribbon stitch buds and fasten the ribbon off after completing one spray.

11 With the green coton à broder, make a straight stitch stem from the briar rose to the base of the top bud. Work a straight stitch from the base to the centre of the bud and then a fly stitch (see page 205) to cup the bottom edge of the bud and finish the calyx.

12 Bring the green coton à broder to the surface again just to the left of the main stem, below the next bud down. Slip the needle under the main stem and make a straight stitch for a side stem to the base of the second bud, pulling the thread of the main stem slightly over to the left. Make the calyx for this bud in the same way as for the first.

Pull the thread gently to each side in order to create a realistic stem.

13 Make the stem and calyx for the last bud on the spray in the same way, pulling the main stem slightly over to the right. Repeat the whole process to complete the other three stems of buds.

Forget-me-nots

14 Replace the template over the embroidery and make a dot on the fabric for the centre of each forget-me-not. Work the stems, couching down two strands of the green coton à broder with one strand.

15 Thread a size 24 chenille needle with first the 2mm (¹⁄₁₆in) blue and then the 2mm (¹⁄₁₆in) pink ribbon in order to work one-loop French knots. Then, make a circle of five French knots for three whole flowers and a triangle of three knots for the small flower on each stem. Work three tiny straight stitches using the blue ribbon at the end of each stem. Finish the centres of each individual flower with one French knot with two loops using two strands of the pale yellow stranded cotton.

16 Embroider a cluster of the same flowers at each intersection of the couched trellis on the fabric. When you have finished all the embroidery, make sure all the tacking is removed and there are no untidy ends of ribbon or thread on the back of the work.

17 Place the finished embroidery right side down on a clean, flat surface. Then, press the cotton fabric for the lining and position it on top of the wool fabric. Working from the centre outwards, stitch rows of large tacking stitches at 10cm (4in) intervals through both layers of fabric.

18 Turn the fabric so the embroidery side is facing you. Starting at the end of one of the short sides, pin the satin binding along the edge, making sure to leave a 8cm (3in) length overhanging at the corner. Attach the widest side of the binding, which is purchased already folded, to the fabric.

19 When you reach the other end of the first edge, keep the binding flat and insert a pin 5mm (¹⁄₈in) beyond the long edge of the fabric. Fold the binding up at right angles to make a 45 degree mitre. Press the fold.

Fold the binding to start the mitre at the corner of the blanket.

20 Remove a few of the pins along the edge. Open the binding out and then fold it right sides together at right angles to the point that you pressed for the mitre. Pin both layers of binding together along the centre crease. Next, machine stitch along both sides of the fold lines, starting and finishing with a few stitches at an angle on the waste side of the seam in order to provide added strength. Fasten off the threads securely and then trim the seam.

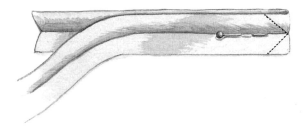

Pin both layers of binding together along the centre line, ready to machine stitch the mitre.

21 Press open both sides of the mitred seam, taking care not to flatten the original crease along the length. Turn the binding right side out and press the mitred corner again.

22 Place the mitred binding over the corner of the blanket and pin in position along the next long edge. Make another mitre in the binding in the same way as you work around to the next two corners.

23 To mitre the last corner, pin the binding along both edges, and insert a marker pin and fold both ends of binding as before. Check the binding has not been twisted anywhere. Press the mitre folds, open out the binding and match the marker pins so the mitre lines are exactly on top of each other. Machine stitch and finish the mitre as before.

24 Lay the blanket on a clean, flat surface right side up. Next, position another layer of binding, right side up, over the edges of both fabrics. Pin each corner in place and then tack just the right side of the binding to both fabrics. Machine stitch the top layer of satin to the wool fabric, very neatly along the selvedge of the binding. Turn the blanket over and slip stitch the other edge of the binding to the machine line on to the lining (see page 33). Finally, remove any tacking stitches that remain.

ROSEBUD COT BLANKET KEY

YLI silk ribbon 4mm (⅛in) x 1.5m (1⅔yd) in 14

YLI silk ribbon 4mm (⅛in) x 5m (5½yd) in 05

YLI silk ribbon 7mm (¼in) x 4m (4½yd) in 05

YLI silk ribbon 2mm (¹⁄₁₆in) x 8m (8¾yd) in 163

YLI silk ribbon 2mm (¹⁄₁₆in) x 1.6m (1¾yd) in 26

French knot in stranded cotton in DMC 727 or Anchor 292

Straight stitch in coton perlé no. 5 to match blanket fabric

Straight stitch in coton à broder size 16 in DMC 38140 or Anchor 214

Note: You will need 1 skein of each thread.

Spring flower panel

It is amazing how easily silk ribbon can be formed to look like a myriad of different blooms and this beautiful panel could be the start of an addictive adventure, with its eight specially chosen flowers. Explore your creativity by following the simple steps to paint a background garden, and the tulips, irises and daffodils will emerge in silken folds with all the grace and delicacy of the real thing. Design by Ann Cox

Design area

20 x 25cm (8 x 9¾in)

Materials

35 x 40cm (14 x 16in)
  medium-weight calico

Ribbons and
  embroidery threads
  (see diagram key)

Stranded cotton threads
  to match ribbons

Equipment

Tracing paper and pencil

Embroidery frame

Large and fine paint
  brushes and palette

Fabric paints in red, blue
  and yellow

Tacking thread

Silver gutta

Silk paints in red, blue
  and yellow

Coarse natural sponge

Size 8 crewel needle

Size 18 and 24
  chenille needle

Embroidery scissors

Card for stretching
  embroidery

Strong thread for lacing

Mount and frame
  of your choice

1 Photocopy the template on page 265, enlarging it by 250 per cent. Transfer the template onto paper and then cut around the outer border. Place the template on the straight grain of the calico and pin it in position.

2 Using a large needle, make holes through the paper along the lines of the stone wall in the design. Next, mark the fabric through the holes with a very fine, sharp pencil. Once the marks are completed, remove the template and, with the same pencil, lightly draw in the stone wall on the calico.

3 Press the calico carefully and then stretch it taut on an embroidery frame. Dilute some of the blue fabric paint in water to make a pale blue. Next, moisten the calico with clean water and a large paintbrush. With the same paintbrush and the pale blue paint, start at the top of the fabric and brush a wash of colour to approximately a quarter of the way down. Then, clean the brush and, with clean water, go over the blue wash in order to dilute the colour in patches and fade out areas of the sky completely.

4 Now, mix quantities of yellow and blue fabric paint with clean water to make a light green. Wash a band of about 2cm (¾in) of the green across the design area above the level of the stone wall. Then, dilute the wash with clean water and fade it out towards the sky.

5 Mix a slightly darker green and then, making sure the calico is still damp, paint a line under the base of the wall. Fade the colour out along the bottom edge as before. Allow the calico to dry naturally or, alternatively, you can speed up the process with a hairdryer.

6 Re-position the template accurately over the calico, matching up the marks for the wall. Then, tack a guideline around the outside edge of the template.

7 Practise with the gutta on a piece of waste fabric. Then, paint around each stone in the wall, making sure there is no break in any of the lines. Allow the gutta to dry. Mix the three silk paints to make grey and then dilute some of it to make it paler. Moisten each stone with water and then partially paint each one with the two shades of grey. Leave the calico to dry.

8 Mix the blue, yellow and a tiny spot of red fabric paint to make two shades of green. Wet the sponge and squeeze out the excess water. Using both greens to create light and shady areas, sponge in the background greenery for the climbing clematis.

9 Using the same greens and a finer brush, lightly paint in grass at random for the back of the flower border. Finally, to add extra depth, sponge the green along the base of the border and the top of the wall. Leave the calico to dry completely and fix the colours with an iron following the manufacturer's instructions.

10 You are now ready to start the embroidery. Remember to start and fasten off the ribbons securely after you have made each component in the design.

Clematis

11 Position the template over the design area and mark the start and ends of the clematis stems on the calico. Cut two strands from each of the brown stranded cotton 829, 854 and 856 in 20cm (8in) lengths. Twist the strands together slightly to blend the colours and then fold the length in half. Place the loop of the thread at the base of the clematis stem and secure with a pin.

12 Carefully twist the two lengths of six strands for about 9cm (3½in) until the stems split. At this point, divide each bundle into two more, each with three strands. Place these thinner branches in position for a short distance.

Then, split the strands again into one and two and pin these in place. Couch (see page 189) the branches in place with a matching thread.

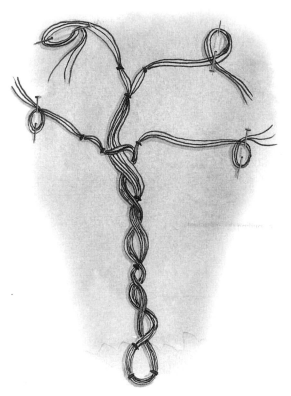

Keep dividing the strands of thread in order to make thinner branches.

13 Work the clematis flowers at random along the branches using the 4mm (¹⁄₈in) pink ribbon in shades 05 and 08. Thread the ribbon in the size 18 chenille needle, secure it with a knot, and bring it up in the centre of each flower. Work four evenly spaced ribbon stitch petals. Secure the ribbon on the back and start again if the next flower is more than 1cm (³⁄₈in) away.

14 Finish each flower, using one strand of the pale yellow stranded cotton 745. Make one French knot with two loops in the centre, surrounded by a random cluster of one-loop French knots. To finish the clematis, work the leaves in ribbon stitch with the 4mm (¹⁄₈in) green ribbon in shades 20 and 72.

Foxgloves

15 Replace the template and mark the top and bottom of each foxglove stem. Using the moss coton à broder 3346, position the first stem working from the base to the tip. Bring the thread back up outside the design area and place the needle into the calico. Wrap the thread around the needle to keep it taut.

16 Work the underlying petals up the foxglove stem with the deep mauve ribbon 179. Bring the ribbon up close to the stem and work a straight stitch, making a straight edge with the eye of a second needle. Go back down at the base of the petal. Continue to work up the stem, alternating from side to side and making each pair of stitches slightly smaller than the previous one, finishing about 1.5cm (⁵⁄₈in) from the tip of the stem.

Regulate a straight edge on the first petals to go up the stem.

17 Embroider a layer of ribbon stitch petals on top of the first using the pale mauve ribbon 178, again starting at the bottom and working up. Bring the ribbon up between the stem and the existing petal. Work a shorter curved edge centre ribbon stitch over the base petal. Continue up the stem until almost all the base petals are covered. Cover the rest with the same pale mauve ribbon and smaller straight stitches to make buds. Fasten off after each flower is worked.

Cover the base petals with smaller stitches in a paler colour.

18 Release the thread for the stem and pull it through to the back. Bring it up just below the top of the stem and then work a straight stitch to look like an unopened bud. Work another bud on the other side of the stem just above the first mauve bud. Using the same thread, work a small straight stitch up through the top of each flower and take it back down through the stem to make a calyx for each one. Make the rest of the foxgloves in the same way.

Make the tiny calyces all down the stem with straight stitches.

Irises

19 Replace the template and mark all the tips of the irises and the base of their stems, where the darker petals meet. Start on the iris on the furthest left of the clematis stem, working a loop with the pale blue ribbon 126. Secure the loop at the top with a ribbon chain stitch.

20 Using the soft green coton à broder 3814, make a single straight stitch from the base of the blue petal to the base of the stem.

21 To finish the petals, refer to the diagram and bring the deep blue ribbon 117 to the surface at the tip of the petal falling on the right of the iris. Take the ribbon, without pulling too tight, behind the loop of the chain stitch and down at the tip of the petal on the opposite side. Use the eye and the needle to prevent snagging. Pass the ribbon behind the chain stitch and back down at B. Bring the ribbon back up just above the top of the stem and through the loop of the chain stitch. Make a central petal of similar length to the others and take the ribbon back down at the tip. Fasten off.

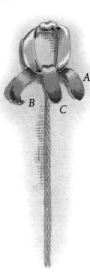

The iris looks effective in two shades of blue.

22 To make the leaves, work three or four long straight stitches with the narrower soft green ribbon 33. Allow the ribbon to twist once, and occasionally twice, to give added texture. Complete the remaining irises in the same way, working the ones at the back first and those at the front last.

Hyacinths

23 Replace the template and mark the top and bottom of each one of the five hyacinths. Start the three darker hyacinths, using the deep blue ribbon 45. Work a row of six or seven French knots with two loops, one above the other. Then, work a row of French knots with one loop all around, keeping them close to the first row. Complete all three flowers. Work the remaining two hyacinths in the same way in the mid-blue ribbon 46. Fasten off after each flower is worked.

24 Make the hyacinth stems with one straight stitch in coton à broder 3346 for each flower. Work the leaves in the narrower deep green ribbon 21 with straight stitches of varying lengths radiating out from the base of each stem.

Tulips

25 Replace the template and mark the base of the stem and the top and bottom of flowers on all the tulips. Take a short end of pale cream ribbon 156 from the front through to the back and secure at the bottom of the flower on the furthest left. Work a centre ribbon stitch, taking the ribbon back down at the tip of the flower. Make the rest of the tulip flowers, making sure to fasten off after each flower is worked.

26 Next, make stems for all the tulips, each with a straight stitch in the pale green coton à broder 369. Work the two leaves for each tulip using the wider soft green ribbon 33. Anchor the ribbon at the base of the stem and work a centre, left or right ribbon stitch as best suits each flower, pulling the stitch tight.

Daffodils

27 Replace the template and then mark the positions for all the petals on the daffodils and the bottom of the stems. Using the pale yellow ribbon 13, come up to the surface at the tip of each petal and go down at the centre of the flower, but not through the same hole.

Make four yellow petals, regulating the ribbon with a second needle.

28 Next, take a short end of the wide deep yellow ribbon 145 through the centre of the daffodil and secure at the back. Rethread the ribbon on the surface and take the needle down at the tip of the trumpet. Use the eye of a second needle to pull the ribbon over and make a flat edge.

Make sure the trumpet of the daffodil has a flat edge.

29 Work the stems of the daffodils with a straight stitch in the soft green coton à broder 369. Make the leaves in the same way as for the iris, using the narrower moss green ribbon 20. Complete all the daffodils, fastening off after each flower is worked.

Primulas

30 Make the leaves of these flowers first. Replace the template and mark the centre point for each plant and the end of each leaf. Anchor the wider moss green ribbon 20 at the back of one of the centres. Work five to seven leaves on each plant in straight stitch, using the eye of a second needle to pull the ribbon over from the centre to the end of each leaf.

31 Work a French knot with two loops in the 7mm (¹/₈in) pale yellow ribbon 72 for each of the flowers on the left-hand plant and in 7mm (¹/₈in) gold ribbon 46 for the flowers on the other plant. In order to give a smoother surface to the flowers, use the eye of another needle to keep the ribbon flat on the fabric as it is pulled through to the back.

32 Using three strands of the yellow stranded cotton 745, make a French knot with three loops into the centre of each ribbon knot. With a single strand of green 937, work a straight stitch stem from each flower to the centre of the plant.

Aubrietas

33 These leaves, placed at random to create a background, are also worked before the tiny flowers. Make a mixture of ribbon and straight stitches with the 4mm (¹/₈in) deep green 21 and the deep moss green 72 ribbon, tucking the leaves around the bases of the other flowers.

34 Work the flowers in 4mm (¹/₈in) ribbon in clusters of either the fuchsia pink 145, deep mauve 177 or blue 117 narrow 4mm (¹/₈in) for each plant. To make each flower, work a straight stitch loop, lifting the loop with the eye of a second needle as high as the width of the ribbon. Using two strands of pale yellow stranded cotton 745, make a French knot with one loop into the centre of each ribbon loop, pulling it tight to the fabric. Fasten off after each flower is worked.

Grass and moss

35 With one strand of green stranded cotton 937, stitch a few straight grasses behind the hyacinths. Work a few more along the base of the wall using dark and moss green.

36 To complete the design, add small patches of moss between the stones. Make French knots with one loop in single strands of a random selection of the green threads.

37 Remove the finished embroidery from the frame. Then, remove the tacking thread. Ensure that there are no loose ends at the back of the work then press the fabric, avoiding the embroidery. Stretch and lace it over a piece of card cut to fit the aperture of your chosen picture frame.

SPRING FLOWER PANEL KEY

1. YLI silk ribbon 4mm (¹/₈in) x 1.5m (1²/₃yd) in 20
2. YLI silk ribbon 4mm (¹/₈in) x 1.5m (1²/₃yd) in 72
3. YLI silk ribbon 4mm(¹/₈in) x 1.4m (1¹/₂yd) in 05
4. YLI silk ribbon 4mm (¹/₈in) x 1.4m (1¹/₂yd) in 08
5. YLI silk ribbon 4mm (¹/₈in) x 1.5m (1²/₃yd) in 179
6. YLI silk ribbon 4mm (¹/₈in) x 1.5m (1²/₃yd) in 178
7. YLI silk ribbon 4mm (¹/₈in) x 1m (1yd) in 126
8. YLI silk ribbon 4mm (¹/₈in) x 1m (1yd) in 11
9. YLI silk ribbon 2mm (¹/₁₆in) x 2m (2¹/₄yd) in 33
10. YLI silk ribbon 7mm (¹/₄mm) x 60cm (²/₃yd) in 156
11. YLI silk ribbon 7mm (¹/₄in) x 1m (1yd) in 33
12. YLI silk ribbon 7mm (¹/₄in) x 70cm (²/₃yd) in 15
13. YLI silk ribbon 7mm (¹/₄in) x 70cm (²/₃yd) in 54
14. YLI silk ribbon 7mm (¹/₄in) x 70cm (²/₃yd) in 20
15. YLI silk ribbon 4mm (¹/₈in) x 1.5m (1²/₃yd) in 145
16. YLI silk ribbon 4mm (¹/₈in) x 1.5m (1²/₃yd) in 177
17. YLI silk ribbon 4mm (¹/₈in) x 1.5m (1²/₃yd) in 117
18. YLI silk ribbon 4mm (¹/₈in) x 2m (2¹/₄yd) in 21 and 72
19. YLI silk ribbon 4mm (¹/₈in) x 2m (2¹/₄yd) in 46
20. YLI silk ribbon 4mm (¹/₈in) x 3m (3¹/₃yd) in 45
21. YLI silk ribbon 2mm (¹/₁₆in) x 1m (1yd) in 21
22. YLI silk ribbon 7mm (¹/₄in) x 40cm (¹/₂yd) in 15
23. YLI silk ribbon 4mm (¹/₈in) x 1.4m (1¹/₂yd) in 13
24. YLI silk ribbon 2mm (¹/₁₆in) x 1.5m (1²/₃yd) in 20

- French knots in stranded cotton in DMC 745 or Anchor 292
- French knots in stranded cotton in DMC 744 or Anchor 295
- Coton à broder in DMC 3346 or Anchor 262
- Coton à broder in DMC 3814 or Anchor 214
- Coton à broder in DMC 369 or Anchor 260
- Stranded cotton in DMC 522 or Anchor 859
- Stranded cotton in DMC 937 or Anchor 268
- DMC stranded cotton in 829, 854, 856
- Wall outlines

Note: You will need 1 skein of each thread above and a selection of stranded cottons in light and dark moss greens for the grass and moss on the wall.

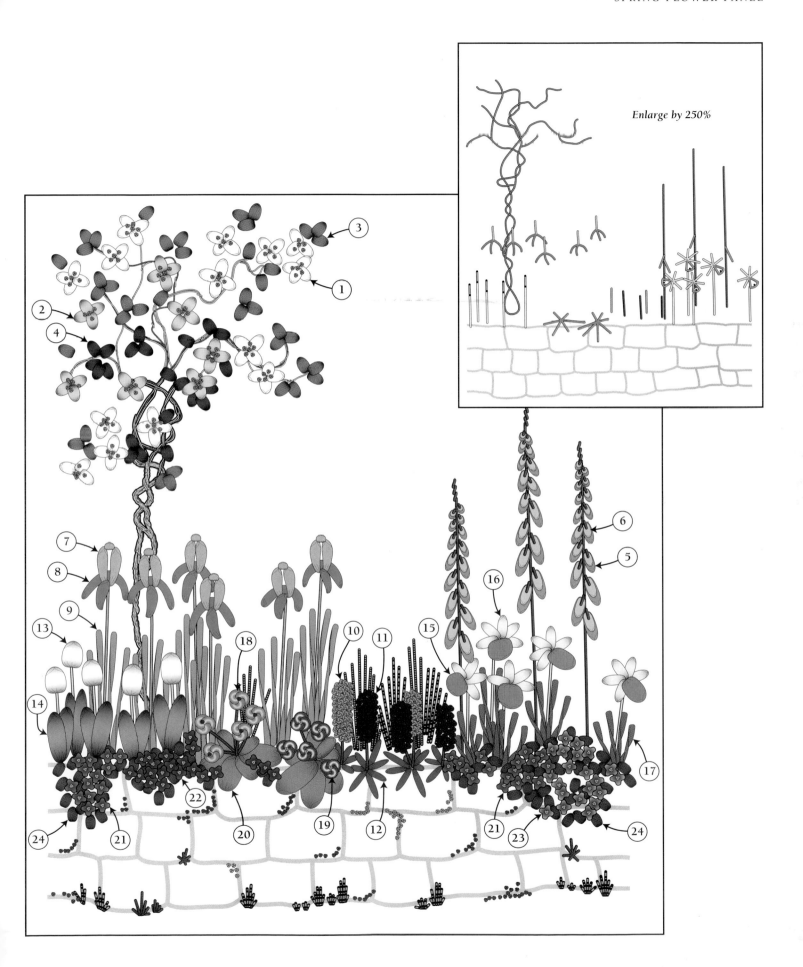

Enlarge by 250%

Goldwork

Gold has long been regarded as a symbol of wealth and power. Textiles worked with gold were a highly desirable status symbol and had an important role in international diplomacy. Gold was discovered early and first used as pure beaten metal in thin strands or cut into shapes and stitched onto fabric. Apart from its cost, it was appreciated in embroidery because, unlike silver, it does not tarnish. First used in the East and in Egypt, Assyria and Babylon, the Old Testament describes gold cut into wires to work on coloured linen. From there, goldwork techniques were brought to Greece and Rome. The main centre was Tyre, now Beirut, where the Byzantines controlled gold embroideries.

Below: Detail of St Peter from the maniple of St Cuthbert, Durham, England, worked between 909 and 916.

The ability to work gold thread was highly prized and craft skills were handed down through the generations of individual families. Aristocratic women also did goldwork. In the 11th century, the daughter of Canute's second wife rejected marriage and retired to a convent at Ely where she and her maids devoted themselves to gold embroidery. The earliest surviving examples of English work are the stole and maniple of St Cuthbert in Durham Cathedral on which the pure metal is couched, five threads per millimetre. This technique may have originated in Persia, now Iran, and reached its peak in *opus anglicanum*.

Supreme embroidery and design

Opus anglicanum is characterized by the use of underside couching, which enabled large areas to be covered fairly quickly. The silver gilt or gold thread for the background was usually laid vertically, parallel to the warp thread of the linen. The strong linen couching stitch was taken over the gold thread and returned through the same hole, taking a small loop of gold thread to the back of the fabric. This means that little of the gold was wasted on the back of the fabric, the couching stitch is invisible and, because it is protected, is durable. Through the careful arrangement of stitches, subtle patterns such as chevrons, diaper or bricking could add richness to the ground, creating facets that would reflect the candlelight when the vestments were worn. This technique also has the important advantage of creating a flexible textile. Couched silk threads were frequently combined with goldwork. Although seen at its best in *opus anglicanum,* underside couching was also worked in Sicily, France and Italy.

The work was time consuming and expensive. For example, the accounts of Westminster Abbey record payment for an altar frontal in 1271. The costs involved £36 for the wages of four women working for 3¾ years and more than £220 for gold and silk thread, pearls, enamels and garnets set in gold and silver plaques. Unfortunately, much of this work was destroyed, either to recover the semi-precious stones and precious metals or during the Reformation.

In order to maintain high standards, there were strict conditions controlling embroiderers producing goldwork. They could only work professionally after completing an enforced apprenticeship, were not allowed to work by candlelight, only daylight, and workshop owners were restricted in the number of apprentices they employed to ensure proper training. Gold workers were prohibited from using inferior quality gold and risked the work being burnt if they did so. They were also permitted to work in silk. From illustrated manuscripts we know that fabric to be worked was stretched within wooden frames and held taut by strong stitches with the frame supported on trestles. Unfortunately, no needles survive because they were so thin.

Apart from the high quality of stitchery, *opus anglicanum* is special because of the quality of the design, the fine drawing of the figures and the arrangement of fabric, particularly copes (semi-circular ecclesiastical outer garments), which were the most important. Professional artists were employed by wealthy patrons from the Church, nobility and merchant classes to design embroideries. Where the stitches have worn away it is sometimes possible to see the original drawing. It has been suggested that manuscript illustrators also designed *opus anglicanum*. Sometimes velvet, the most expensive silk fabric, was used for backgrounds and this created problems, so the designers often drew the design on white linen or silk which was applied to the velvet and worked over.

Opposite page: Detail of the Whalley Abbey Dalmatic, English, circa 1415–1430. The opus anglicanum orphrey band is worked with a scene from the life of the Virgin. The ground is patterned with couched gold threads and the figures embroidered with silk.

Above: Jeanne D'Arc, *by Doris Taylor, circa 1914. Couched gold, silver and silk threads mix with silk embroidery and applied beads.*

Right: Court dress, English, 1740s. The ribbed red silk is embellished with silver embroidery.

Below: Daniel in the Lions' Den, *by Mhairi McIver, 1956. This work features machine embroidery, appliqué and goldwork.*

Regalia

Metal thread embroidery was also used to decorate regalia such as heraldic banners and tabards, and is still used today on court dress and military uniforms. Court dress of the late 17th and 18th centuries made lavish use of such embroidery. While a man's suit made of brown wool embroidered with silver and dating from the 1720s can be seen in the Bath Costume Museum, the most magnificent dress in the collection of the Victoria and Albert Museum is a red silk and silver mantua worn at the court of George II during the 1740s. Its wide skirt with side hoops is heavily embroidered with almost ten pounds weight of silver in a Tree of Life design with exotic fruits and flowers. The embroidery was worked by members of a Huguenot family that had emigrated to London from France. Another dress of green silk worn by the Duchess of Bedford was described as being 'embroidered very richly with gold and silver and a few colours; the patterns were festoons of shells, coral, corn, corn-flowers, and sea-weeds.'

Survival in religious use

Although goldwork went out of fashion on dress at the end of the 18th century, it continued to be used for church work throughout the 19th century. With the revival of interest in Gothic architecture encouraged by Augustus Pugin, architect of the Houses of Parliament, new stained glass and embroidered hangings were introduced in churches. Many new societies were established to provide these furnishings and especially important was the Ladies' Ecclesiastical Embroidery Society founded in 1855. They produced work influenced by contemporary secular art and during the 1860s, the design was of a more romantic medievalism akin to the work of Edward Burne-Jones.

During the 1950s, there was a new interest in goldwork among embroiderers. Goldwork techniques were included on decorative panels as new and cheaper synthetic metallic threads and materials became available. Embroidery design for churches adapted the techniques to the new synthetic substitutes and also experimented with combinations of techniques in an innovative way. Today, great use is made of symbolism and bold design in keeping with church architecture, in order to provide a focal point for contemplation even when viewed from a distance. Vivid colour is often combined with goldwork techniques. Three-dimensional effects and fine stitchery add textural variety and more detail when viewed closely. Beryl Dean, Kathleen Whyte and Hannah Frew Paterson are the most renowned embroiderers to have produced innovative work during this time.

Left: Detail of an altar cloth, by Hannah Frew Paterson, 1993. Commissioned for St Margaret's Chapel in Edinburgh Castle, the piece is worked with linen, silks, leather, gold kid, freshwater pearls, silk, gold, silver and metal threads.

Below: **Birth,** *by Midori Matsushima, 1999. The fabric used is silk kimono and the eggs are made of felt padding ornated with twisted gold threads.*

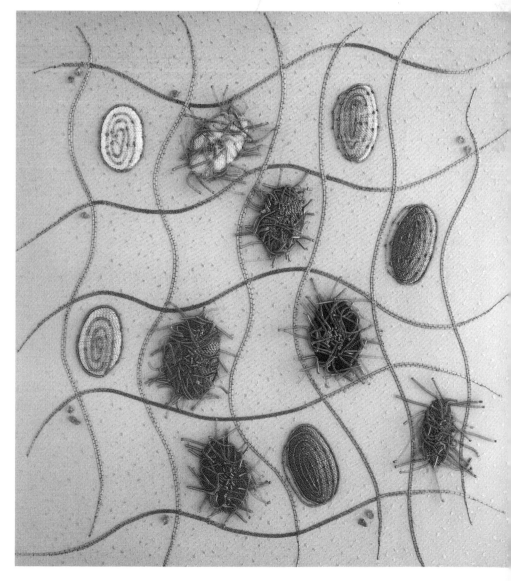

Couching circles

These can be worked using single or double metal threads. For a perfect circle, start in the centre and work out, couching the threads carefully to keep the edge neat. If using double threads, plunge the ends singly to achieve a smooth edge to the circle.

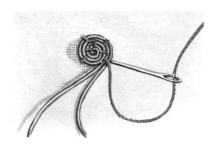

Start in the centre and then work outwards to ensure a perfect circle.

Couching check thread

Stitch check thread down in single lines, mixing alternate rows of smooth passing and check thread in order to show off the qualities of both types.

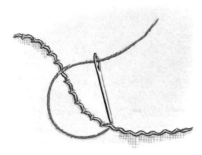

Couch the passing thread in single lines.

Stitching down twist threads

Twist threads can be stitched down using a couching stitch or sewn through using very small stab stitches in a matching sewing cotton thread.

Leave a short tail of the twist thread beyond the end of the design and bring the sewing thread through the fabric on the line. Work a tiny stab stitch into the gold thread and go back through the fabric. Repeat but plunge the tails later.

Sew the twist thread to the fabric using very small stab stitches.

Plunging couching threads

Once you have finished stitching an area of metal couching threads, you will need to plunge the tails to the back of the work. Use a large chenille needle as this has a big eye that will take the thread.

Pass the tail of the thread through the eye of the needle, then carefully pull it through the fabric. Plunge only one thread at a time. When all the tails have been pulled through, turn the work over and secure them down with a few small stitches in sewing thread. Stitch into the couched area or the layer of calico, making sure these stitches do not actually come to the surface of the work. Finally, trim the ends of the passing threads to neaten.

Plunge the tail of the passing thread through the fabric.

Stitching down pearl purl

Pearl purls are most often used around the edge of areas of couched passing threads to neaten them. There is no need to plunge the ends of the pearl purls – just leave them neatly cut on the surface of the work.

Use a single length of waxed sewing thread to attach the pearl purls, starting both at the end of the design line. Hold the pearl purl in place on the line with one hand and couch over the metal thread with the sewing thread. As you pull the thread tight, insert it through one of the bobbles on the pearl purl so the couching stitch is hidden in the metal thread. Continue working along the line, couching down the metal thread in about every third bobble, making sure all the stitches are hidden and couch the metal thread. Sharp corners and turns can be achieved by bending the pearl purl with tweezers.

Couch the pearl purl down between the bobbles.

Adding colour to pearl purl

To add even more interest and colour into metal threadwork, pearl purls can be stretched out and a coloured thread added as a central core. With this particular technique, you should only use half the usual amount of thread. Pull the pearl purl out to twice its original length. Stranded silk or cotton threads usually work well as a core yarn. You will need to experiment in order to obtain the exact number of strands required for the size of pearl purl thread.

Wrap the core yarn around the stretched pearl purl, leaving a tail at both the beginning and the end. Then, couch down the pearl purl using one or two strands of the same thread. When the couching is completed, plunge the ends of the core yarn to the back of the work and then neaten them in the same way as for the couching threads.

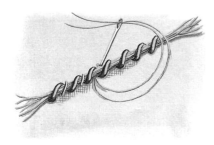

Couch the pearl purl down using a strand of matching thread.

Attaching chips of purl thread

You should use bright check purl threads for this technique, as the smooth purls will not look as effective. Carefully cut chips in 2–3mm (⅛in) lengths and thread onto the needle, letting them slip down to the base of the sewing thread. Then, take the needle carefully through the fabric to secure the purl chip down, just as you would to secure a bead. Sew the chips down randomly using a double length of waxed sewing cotton, aiming to fill the entire surface of the design area without crushing the purls.

The finished filled shape should be smooth, with no little ends of wire sticking out that could catch. Using a mixture of coloured purls such as silver, copper and gold also creates an interesting effect.

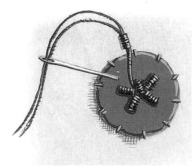

Fill the area generously, but without crushing.

Applying purls over felt

Lengths of purl thread will look rather effective when stitched over craft felt padding, as the light catches the higher surface of the purls. Smooth, rough and

bright check purl threads are all suitable for this particular technique and mixing them together will provide different finishes to the work.

Carefully cut the purl thread to the required length, taking extra care not to damage it. Thread it onto a double length of waxed sewing thread. Then, take the needle down through the fabric and manoeuvre the purl into place. Make sure to keep a firm tension on the sewing thread, but do not pull too tight as this will distort the padding and create unsightly undulations.

You will find that the final effect is very similar to satin stitch. The purl threads need to sit snugly against one another. However, make sure they are not squashed, otherwise they will start to buckle over themselves, which is far from being the desired effect.

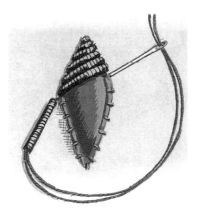

Make sure the purls are the correct length and fit snugly together.

Applying purls over string

Short lengths of purl threads, whether they are smooth, rough or bright check, can be stitched over string padding. The string provides a hard surface to lay the purl threads on and they should therefore not distort. Purl threads can be sewn over the string padding either at a right angle or diagonally. Make sure to keep the threads snug against the string in order to create a crisp line.

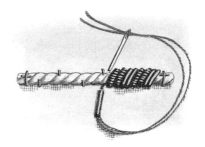

Sew the purl thread over the string either at a right angle or diagonally.

Applying metallic leather

Trace the relevant area from your design and then make a paper pattern, allowing a little extra all around if the padding is to be very high. Cut out the shape in leather. Position the leather over the padded shape, but do not use pins to secure it as they will leave holes.

Use large tacking stitches right across the leather at intervals of approximately 1.5cm (⅝in). Avoid pulling these stitches too tight, however, as they can easily mark the leather. Using a single waxed sewing thread and a fine sharp needle, stab stitch down into the leather in order to attach it to the fabric. You can also use a leather worker's needle if the leather is very firm. Once you have completed this, you can remove the tacking stitches. If desired, you can add an edge of couched threads to hide the stab stitches. Be aware that it is preferable to attach the leather shapes before commencing any of the metal threadwork.

Work long tacking stitches over the leather shape to secure it in place.

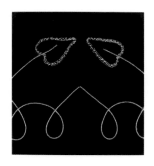

Evening wrap

This elegant wrap is very quick to stitch and make up. The sumptuous black silk velvet fabric sets off the simple entwined design to perfection. The wrap is lined with the same velvet in order to enhance the draping quality of the fabric. The swirling stems and hearts are couched using pearl purl, smooth and check threads to provide a varied texture to the design. Design by Samantha Bourne

Design area

35 x 8cm (13¾ x 3¼in)

Materials

2m x 90cm (2¼ x 1yd) black silk velvet

50 x 30cm (20 x 12in) grey medium-weight iron-on interfacing

Metal threads (see diagram key)

Equipment

Black and grey sewing threads

Dressmakers' scissors

Tracing paper and pencil

Prick and pounce tools

Fine paintbrush and white watercolour paint

50cm (20in) roller frame

Size 10 crewel needle

Size 18 chenille needle

Embroidery scissors

Block of beeswax

Pins

Tacking thread

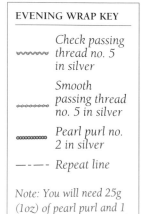

EVENING WRAP KEY

~~~~~ *Check passing thread no. 5 in silver*

·-·-·-·- *Smooth passing thread no. 5 in silver*

──────── *Pearl purl no. 2 in silver*

─ ─ ─ *Repeat line*

Note: You will need 25g (1oz) of pearl purl and 1 reel of each thread.

---

1 Fold the velvet fabric in half along the length and cut it carefully down the centre line. Bind the edges of both pieces of velvet and put one piece to one side. Fold the remaining piece in half along the length and then insert two or three long pins at each end to mark the centre line, taking care they do not crush the pile.

2 Trace the design from the diagram below and make a pattern, carefully lining up three repeats of the motif. Next, rule a pencil line 6cm (2½in) under the motifs to help you position them accurately on the fabric.

3 Place the velvet on a flat, firm surface and transfer the design onto both ends, using the prick and pounce method (see page 31). Line the pattern up with the centre of the middle motif on the centre line of the fabric and the ruled line along the short edge of the fabric. Draw the design onto the velvet with a fine line of white paint.

4 Cut the interfacing in half along the length and iron it onto the reverse of the velvet under both design areas. Using a cool iron and following the manufacturer's instructions, iron the velvet, right side down, on top of another piece of velvet so as not to crush the pile. Stretch the fabric on the embroidery frame.

5 Using a single strand of the grey sewing thread and the size 10 crewel needle, start with a waste knot (see page 28) near one end of the design. Unreel some of the pearl purl thread, without cutting it, and lay it along the first part of the stem before the loop at one end of the design. Start to couch it down, gently bending it around the entwining loops until you reach the centre of a heart shape. Cut the pearl purl only when that length is securely couched in place. Make sure you have also couched the end of it down securely. Finish off the ends of the sewing thread on the back of the work.

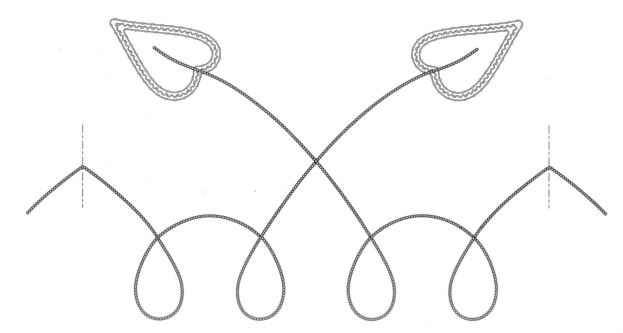

6 Couch down the rest of the pearl purl along the design lines in the same way, only cutting it in the centres of the heart shapes and laying one line over another where the stems cross.

7 For the heart shapes, couch a single line of smooth passing thread around the design line. Then, couch down a single line of check passing thread and finally another line of the smooth one. Leave a tail at both ends of each of the threads until they are all couched in position. When this is completed, plunge each thread to the reverse of the fabric, spacing them carefully so they make holes no bigger than necessary in the velvet. Secure the passing threads on the back with the sewing thread and then trim to neaten them.

8 Repeat the same design on the other end of the velvet fabric. Then, remove the finished embroidery from the frame.

9 If necessary, press the velvet as before with a very cool iron, avoiding the design area. Then, place the two pieces of velvet, right sides together. Pin and tack them in position. Machine stitch a 2.5cm (1in) seam around all four sides of the wrap, leaving an opening on one long side. Remove the tacking and trim the seam allowances to about 1.5cm (⅝in).

10 Turn the velvet wrap right side out. Finally, slip stitch (see page 33) the opening by hand in order to close it.

Art Nouveau panel

The elegant flowing lines of Art Nouveau designs lend themselves perfectly to gold threadwork. The intense colours of enamelled jewellery inspired the use of coloured threads, which intensify the gold without being too overpowering. The gold threads chosen have varied textures to enhance different parts of the design, with padding to create more interest. This beautiful panel is sure to be treasured. Design by Samantha Bourne

1 Trace the design from the diagram on page 279. Iron the silk with a cool iron and lay it on a flat surface, taping it down. Place a piece of carbon paper face down on the silk and lay the traced design, centrally, on top of this. Carefully trace over the lines of the design.

2 Lay the calico on the flat surface and place the silk fabric on top, smoothing out any wrinkles. Secure the backing to the silk (see page 17), matching the grain, and stretch both so they are drum-tight in the embroidery hoop.

3 To give greater stability to the fabrics, stab stitch just inside the design lines using a matching sewing thread.

4 Pad all the enclosed shapes on the design with craft felt, stitching all the layers in position with matching sewing thread, before you go on to the gold threadwork. You will need one layer of felt for the circles within the curls at the bottom of the vertical stem and for each outer petal on the flowerhead. Use two layers for the heart shapes, the central flower petal and for the three parts of the calyx. Finally, you will need three layers for the scroll shapes on both sides of the design.

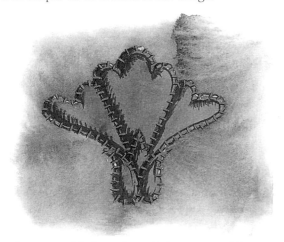

Apply separate felt shapes for each distinct part of the flower and secure them with matching thread.

5 First, stitch the central vertical stem on the design, using a 10cm (4in) length of the no. 3 pearl purl thread. Stretch the pearl purl out until it measures the length of the stem. Then, take all six strands of the paler peacock silk thread 119 and wrap them around the pearl purl, taking care not to divide them and leaving a 2.5cm (1in) tail at each end of the metal. Couch the pearl purl thread down along the design line using two strands of the same silk thread. When the metal is firmly attached, take the silk threads to the back of the work and finish them off securely, leaving the pearl purl on the surface.

6 Use the no. 1 pearl purl to make the two curls at the base of the stem now in position and then couch it down securely with matching thread. Fill in the padded circles within the curls using tiny chips of the no. 6 bright check purl thread, stitching them down randomly in order to cover the felt.

7 Next, couch the no. 1 pearl purl down with matching thread around the outer edges of the padding in the curved scroll shapes on both sides of the design. Make sure you create smooth, flowing lines. Then, couch shorter lengths of the pearl purl along the inner edges of these shapes in the same way, cutting the pearl purl so all the lines look continuous.

8 Fill in the centres of these scroll shapes by couching down the no. 5 smooth passing thread. Remember to couch down two lengths of thread together. Using the paler peacock silk thread 119, start the first line on the outside of the curve. Make your stitches closer together than usual to create an area of denser colour. Instead of turning the threads at the corner, cut them off and leave tails at the end of each line. As you get nearer to the inside edge of the shape, change to the darker peacock 117A. When you have finished couching all the threads, plunge them individually to the back of the work and secure them with the silk thread.

Design area

10 x 19cm (4 x 7½in)

Materials

30 x 40cm (12 x 16in) pale olive dupion silk

30 x 40cm (12 x 16in) pre-shrunk calico

Pale olive sewing thread

20cm (8in) square yellow-gold felt

Yellow-gold sewing thread

Embroidery and metal threads (see diagram key)

Equipment

Tracing paper and pencil

Masking tape

Dressmakers' carbon paper

25cm (10in) embroidery hoop

Matching sewing thread

Block of beeswax

Size 10 crewel needle

Size 18 chenille needle

Embroidery scissors

Pins

Firm card for stretching embroidery

Strong thread for lacing

Mount and frame of your choice

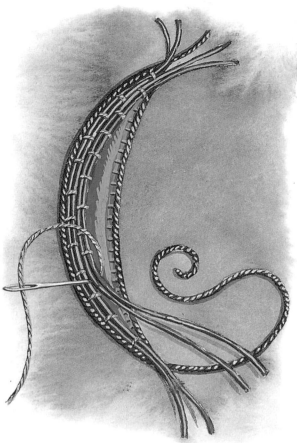

Couch down pairs of passing thread with close stitches of peacock thread.

9 Outline the heart shapes in the no. 1 pearl purl thread and then fill them with tiny chips of no. 6 bright check purl, sewn down randomly to cover the felt.

10 Couch the stems of the hearts in the medium twist, hiding the matching sewing thread. Apply the twist in short lengths to the points where the line is interrupted by pearl purl and then leave tails. When all the lengths of twist are securely in position, plunge the tails to the back of the work and secure them there.

11 The flowerhead is the last area to complete. Start by couching down a single strand of no. 5 smooth passing thread in order to make the two curls of stamen on top of the flower. Then, work a line of stem stitch (see page 206) along the outer edge of the gold using the paler peacock silk 119.

12 Fill the petal shapes, working the two outer ones first and the middle one last. Couch alternate rows of double smooth passing threads

and single check passing thread. Begin on the outer edge and, following its contours, work in towards the centre. Leave tails on every row and plunge and secure these when the whole of each area is complete. When all three petals are finished, couch a line of no. 1 pearl purl thread all around the centre petal and then around the remaining edges of the outside petals.

13 Continuing with the pearl purl, outline the three parts of the calyx at the base of the flower. Start and finish at the point of each outer shape and couch an upside down V shape for the middle one. Fill in all these areas with cut lengths of the no. 6 smooth purl thread, taking your time to ensure the threads lie flat next to each other and look like satin stitches.

14 Carefully remove the finished embroidery from the frame. If necessary, iron out any wrinkles on the silk, following the manufacturer's instructions. Lay the work face down on a soft towel and avoid the stitched areas at all costs when ironing.

15 Cut some stiff card to the size of the aperture in your chosen frame. Then, lace the silk over the card. Make sure you do not choose a frame that is mounted with glass as this could damage the golden threads. Assemble the embroidery within the mount in the frame and admire your beautiful work.

ART NOUVEAU PANEL KEY

Pearl purl no. 3 x 10m (11yd) in gold with Pearsall's Filoselle stranded silk in 119

Pearl purl no. 1 x 2m (2¼yd) in gold

Bright check purl no. 6 x 2m (2¼yd) in gold

Smooth passing thread no. 5 in gold

Pearsall's Filoselle stranded silk in 117A

Pearsall's Filoselle stranded silk in 119

Medium twist x 1m (1yd) in gold

Check passing thread no. 5 in gold

Smooth purl no. 6 x 1m (1yd) in gold

Note: You will need 1 skein of each silk shade and 1 reel of each passing thread.

INSPIRATION AND DESIGN:
fluid lines of gold

The Art Nouveau era was a magical time for arts and crafts. This outpouring of creativity has left us with an inexhaustible supply of inspiration and it also encourages the desire for us to emulate the superb workmanship of the men and women of that age.

The jewellery and metalwork pieces of this period are the perfect start for designing gold thread embroidery. Studying the work of René Lalique, among others, will provide a great many fascinating ideas. Lalique is widely known for his work on glass, but further research will show that he also used his incredible talents in the design and production of jewellery. Many of his designs are typical of Art Nouveau, with strong fluid lines linking flowers and other organic shapes, and can be easily translated into designs for embroidery in gold threads, like the panel design on pages 276–279. All the information you would require in order to create a goldwork design can be found in his sumptuous pieces of jewellery.

The raised areas on the metalwork can be translated into goldwork and given another dimension by using felt padding under the gold threads. With so many different textured threads available, it is possible to copy every texture from the original metalwork, whether it be smooth or hammered.

The coloured enamels employed in Lalique's work and other jewellery of this period open the mind to possibilities of adding colour to the gold. A large embroidered piece entirely worked with gold thread can seem a little too brash and the introduction of colour will relieve that impression. Colour can also be used to create shadows and highlights to intensify the final look.

Beautifully illustrated, copyright-free books are available for the designer to use as a starting point. Photocopying or tracing the designs will give you the basis of your design for gold embroidery. Keep the design as simple as possible until you become confident with the threads, the padding and the endless possibilities of this technique.

Pewter and metalwork of this period are also interesting avenues to explore. If you have a piece of original metalwork from this time, you may find that making a rubbing of the piece with a soft crayon, charcoal or pastel stick will give you a good image to use as a design source.

Museums with collections of Art Nouveau treasures are worth a visit to appreciate the colours and textures of original pieces of jewellery and textured metalwork and silver-smithing.

Once a design has been finalized, choose a fabric for the background to complement the metal threads. Then, the fun of creating the embroidery begins. First, decide which areas are to be padded, because these need to be worked before the gold threads are applied. The padding creates a lot of fluff, and this fluff needs to be removed before it comes in contact with the gold. The next decision is which threads to use and, with so many available, this can be a difficult task. It is best to think 'less is more' and use a limited number, applying them in different ways. Pick out the dominant lines of the design and use continuous lengths of thread in order to retain the original fluidity. Then, enjoy the satisfaction of stitching down the gold and purl threads to fill the padded areas and complete your design.

Beadwork

The word bead comes from the Middle English 'bede' meaning prayer, after the rosaries used to count prayers. Decorative beadwork probably began with the use of shells, seeds, bone, wood and pebbles – all frequently used as amulets to protect the wearer from harm. For example, by tradition in western society, children wore coral necklaces to guard against evil and illness. Beads have also been highly valued and used as barter and currency. They have been made of many materials, including clay and porcelain, turquoise and lapis lazuli in ancient Egypt, and granulated gold in ancient Greece. However, the most widely used beads were made from glass.

Left: Beadwork basket, English, circa 1675. This work is said to have been made by Elizabeth Clarke (1655–1699) when she was about 20 years old.

Glass was reputedly discovered about 5,000 years ago in Mesopotamia. It was an important commodity in the Middle East and exported through Alexandria. By the 11th century, the Venetian glass industry was established on the island of Murano, where it remains. Glass workers were banished to the island because of the fire risk to the city. As the making of glass beads spread from Venice to Bohemia and northern Europe, so the technique of using them in embroidery spread to convents and private houses.

17th-century popularity

Beadwork is particularly associated with the second half of the 17th century, although the choice of colour was restricted, with blue, yellow and green being most widely used. Red is found less frequently as it was the most expensive. Beadwork was often combined with other techniques in the working of the same designs as those used for silk threads. On picture panels depicting King Solomon and the Queen of Sheba with motifs of

Opposite page: Detail of a state evening dress, by Sir Norman Hartnell, English, 1957. Shows ornate decoration of gold and silver pearls, with various flowers and a bee motif. The dress was worn by HM the Queen in 1957.

*Above: Beadwork purse,
French, late 18th century.*

*Right: Side of a box,
English, late 17th century.
Worked entirely in beads,
the design is derived from a
traditional medieval figure.*

*Opposite page, top:
Banner firescreen, English,
mid-19th century.*

*Opposite page, bottom:
Contemporary design
by Lynn Horniblow.
The motifs were stitched
on an automatic sewing
machine and further
enhanced by hand with
beads and sequins.*

14th century and there are early references to flowers made of tiny pearls or beads accompanied with silk leaves.

By the early 17th century, glass bead production had extended to the newly established colony at Jamestown, Virginia, where Venetian craftsmen were making pea-sized beads for trading with the local Indians. Before the arrival of the settlers, native American Indians used beads of shell and clay, but immediately took to the colourful glass beads. They used a bow-loom to weave sashes and belts, sometimes entirely of beads. An alternative method was to string the beads and interweave the string at intervals to make a pattern of beads on the surface of the woven cloth. Embroidery with glass beads became more popular than the older methods of working with moose hair and porcupine quills and was used to decorate moccasins, waistcoats and head-bands. This embroidery work was influenced by the Spanish and French nuns in the convent and missionary schools and European floral designs were combined with traditional geometric patterns. The most usual embroidery methods were either to stitch the beads individually or to arrange them on strings that were couched down at intervals, a quick method known as 'lazy squaw'. Beads continued to be used as trade goods in North America until the middle of the 19th century. Large irregular opaque china beads were imported from Venice and then transported to the Plains Indians until about 1840 by pony pack trains and became known as pony beads.

High fashion

In France, during the middle of the 18th century, there was a fashion for particularly fine sablé beadwork purses. The name sablé means laid or covered with sand and suggests that the beads were as small as grains of sand as there were usually more than 165 tiny beads per square centimetre. When complete, the purses were lined with silk and a drawstring was added. In keeping with French tastes the designs were often floral, although scenes were sometimes depicted including the first balloon flight in 1783.

Glass and steel beads were also used for less exquisite purses and reticules made by amateurs during the early 19th century. The beads could be bought in small glass bottles or boxes from haberdashers or Berlin wool repositories. Those used on canvas were sold by weight and called pound beads. Their popularity increased considerably in Britain and America when it became fashionable to enhance Berlin woolwork with beads, particularly of faceted cut steel. Around

birds, animals and flowers, the beads are stitched to a satin ground. However, although beads do not fade, extant pieces of beadwork are often in poor condition because both the weight and hardness of the glass have abraded the supporting fabric and threads.

More complex in construction were embroidered wire baskets. These baskets had a satin-covered base decorated with beadwork and sides covered with three-dimensional beadwork flowers, fruit or exotic animals such as leopards, giraffes or camels. For solid forms, each bead was threaded individually and looped to the bead in the row above and secured over a padded shape. These were then fixed to a wire in order to support the free-standing shape. Smaller details such as flowers and leaves were threaded together before the outline was wired and then fixed to the side of the basket. Caskets also occasionally had three-dimensional beadwork gardens concealed under the lid. Schoolmistress Mrs Hannah Woolley, who wrote the *Gentlewoman's Companion* in 1675, described the technique as 'All kinds of Beugle Work upon wires or otherwise'. In Italy, glass beads had been threaded and used in relief since the

1860, a distinctive form of pictorial beadwork appeared called grisaille. This monochromatic style, worked on a canvas ground, used mainly grey, white and black beads, although sometimes a colour was added. The weight of the beads restricted their use to small items such as tea cosies or banner firescreens and mantel borders which were frequently finished with a bead fringe.

Tambouring was also used for attaching beads to fabric making an attractive decoration on clothing as the beads reflect the light as the wearer moves. The fabric, wrong side uppermost, is stretched across a frame and the beads are threaded onto a continuous thread. A tambour hook is held in one hand above the frame and the other under the frame controls the thread and beads. The thread is pulled through the fabric in loops forming chain stitch on the wrong side, each stitch anchoring one bead to form a line of them on the right side.

Jet beadwork on clothes was very popular during the late 19th century, but coloured beadwork is most usually associated with the flapper dresses of the 1920s. Evening dresses of fine net and silk were completely worked with beads and sequins, and although apparently flimsy they were very heavy and subsequently disintegrated. During the 1930s, beadwork was confined to collars, shoulders and hip yokes for day wear. Although hand-beaded fabrics continue to be made for the couture market, notably by the prestigious Paris firm Lesage, which works for all the major fashion houses including Schiaparelli, Dior and Yves Saint Laurent, most are now made either by hand tambouring in India or by machine.

Beading pastimes

There were all kinds of novelty beads made as a hobby during the late 19th and early 20th centuries. For example, the petals from dark red, perfumed roses were used. They were ground to a pulp, left to dry and pulped again, before being moulded into beads. If left unvarnished, they would retain their perfume. Pearl buttons have also been used like beads, most notably to create exuberant patterns on the clothes of the pearly kings and queens of the east end of London.

In modern embroidery, beads continue to be used, but during the mid-1960s found objects were added. These objects could be washers, ring pulls from cans, plastic straws or even watch parts. Today, beads are often combined with other embroidery techniques such as cross stitch, machine embroidery or smocking for instance. However, they are equally popular for three-dimensional and woven pieces worked entirely in beads.

Beadwork stitches and techniques

Beads are so well loved that they have found their way into many types of embroidery and other crafts. They can be applied freely and effectively to give small areas of texture to techniques such as cross stitch and free embroidery. Or, they will fill the whole design area, on plain weave or counted fabrics. However you use them, do it with discretion so they do not become overwhelming.

Fabrics

Most fabrics can be used for beading. Use silks, velvet and lace for evening and wedding wear. Wool, felt and even leather can be used to create a more ethnic appeal. Fine fabrics will need the support of a muslin or fine cotton backing to help with the considerable weight of the beading.

Needles

A betweens or quilting needle size 10 will be adequate for the majority of your beadwork. If you are stringing beads for couching, use a beading needle, as some of the holes in the beads are very small. Beading needles are long and bend easily, and will deal with all beads. They start with size 10, which is the most used, and go up to size 16, which is a very fine needle.

Threads

A variety of threads can be used for sewing beads to fabric. When choosing a thread, always make sure it is strong, as it will have to take the weight of the bead and hold it to the fabric. Also, you should use the heaviest thread that will pass through the hole in the bead, bearing in mind that with some stitches, it will have to pass through more than once. If you choose to use transparent beads, be aware that the thread will show.

Normal synthetic sewing threads are strong and excellent for work with beads.

Quilting threads are also available in a variety of colours and are ideal to achieve strong, knot-free beading. There are also threads designed especially for stringing beads. These are strong but also fine enough to make threading them through the small eyes of fine beading needles easier. Unfortunately, they are available only in a limited range of colours.

Additional tools

Always support your embroidery on a frame or hoop to help keep the tension even and avoid the weight of the beads dragging the fabric while you are working.

A small pair of pliers will be useful to pull a needle through a bead that has become stuck.

Use beeswax to help strengthen threads and prevent knotting. Coat the thread with wax before threading the needle. It will also protect the thread from the sharp edges of bugle beads, and prevent it from being cut.

You will need a controlled surface on which to spread out your beads, or you will lose most of them to the vacuum cleaner. Use a small, flat plate or lid and line it with a piece of dark-coloured velvet. The beads will lie quite safely on this surface and will be much easier to scoop up onto a needle.

There are various plastic boxes, jars and containers available for storing beads, so invest in some to keep your beads safe. Another option is to regenerate packaging such as old roll film containers. Whatever you choose, make sure the lids fit tightly as beads have a habit of escaping. If you store them in plastic bags for any length of time, the plastic will crack and the beads will be lost.

Beads

Look for the most economical way to buy your beads. Small pre-packed quantities are the best buy if you need relatively few beads in any one colour, but if you need a lot, it is better to buy them by weight.

Beads are made from various materials and come in many shapes, sizes and finishes. The finishes are beautiful and some of the most popular are opaque or transparent ones, iridescent beads with a matt or shiny surface, those with white hearts or silver linings along the holes, matt frosted or shiny and metallic lustred beads, and not forgetting the innocent milk look of the pearl (or Ceylon).

The following is just a general guide for starting with beads, and it is by no means exhaustive. Be warned – buying beads will become very compulsive!

Glass beads

Small, round glass beads are sometimes known as rocailles or seed beads. This type of bead comes in many finishes, colours and sizes. The common sizes for beading fabric are 8, 10 and 11 – the higher the number, the smaller the bead.

Another variety of glass bead is a bugle. These look like tiny tubes and are available in a variety of lengths, which start at 2mm and can be as long as 50mm. The shortest length, 4mm and 6mm are the three most popular for sewing onto fabric and the longer ones are generally used for fringing. Bugles, however, have very sharp edges and can therefore easily cut threads.

Metal beads
These beads generally come in gold, silver, pewter and bronze effects. They come in a number of sizes and novelty shapes. The small drops and balls are mostly used for sewing onto fabric.

Sequins
Sometimes known as spangles, sequins are either flat or cupped and their diameters vary from 2mm to 10mm. Quite a range of novelty shapes are available, including flowers, stars and leaves. Brightly coloured and iridescent, sequins proclaim their presence loudly.

Glass embroidery stones
Stones, or gems, have a faceted surface, which is highly reflective. They come in a large number of shapes such as stars, squares, hearts, rounds and drops. Most shapes come with two holes to sew onto the fabric. Glass embroidery stones are available in gemstone colours.

Pearl beads
These come in a limited range of sizes suitable for embroidery from P2 to P4.5. They are available in a natural milky tone or can be dyed in soft shades.

Explained on the following pages are the stitches used to attach beads and the techniques to combine them to create small areas of texture or whole designs.

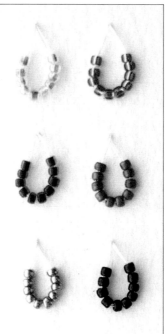

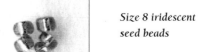

Size 11 transparent iridescent seed beads

Size 11 silver-lined seed beads

Size 11 transparent lined seed beads

Size 11 matt seed beads

Size 11 metallic seed beads

Size 11 shiny lustre seed beads

Size 9 silver-lined seed beads

Size 8 iridescent seed beads

Size 7 iridescent seed beads

Size 5 silver-lined seed beads

Size P2 pearls

Size P3.5 pearls

4mm bugles

5mm bugles

6mm bugles

10mm bugles

SINGLE SEWN BEADS

USES: filling, texture

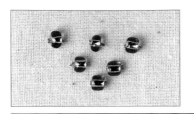

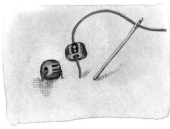

Bring the working thread up in the position for the bead. Thread one bead. Take the thread back through the fabric, one bead width away. Repeat to attach beads close by.

STITCHED SEQUINS

USES: filling

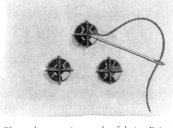

Place the sequin on the fabric. Bring the working thread up close to the sequin and take it back down in the centre hole. Make three more stitches at 90 degrees to each other.

RIBBON BUGLES

USES: border

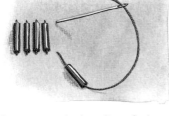

Come up on the base line of where you want the band. Thread one bugle. Take the thread down, one bead length away. Repeat, attaching the bugles at regular intervals.

LAZY STITCH

OTHER NAME: bead satin stitch

USES: filling

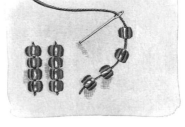

Bring the working thread up on the base line. Thread up to four beads. Take the working thread back down to allow the beads to lie flat and secure. Repeat to complete.

BEADED BEAD

USES: filling

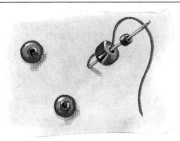

Come up and thread one big, then one small bead. The small bead must not fit into the hole in the big bead. Return the needle through the big bead and the hole in the fabric.

BEAD AND SEQUIN

USES: filling

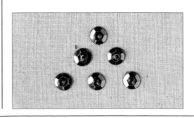

Bring the working thread up and thread one sequin, then one bead. Take the thread back through the sequin and back through the hole in the fabric.

BEAD AND SEQUIN DANGLE

USES: edge, fringe

Come up through the fabric. Thread alternate beads and sequins for about 1.5cm (⅝in). Take the working thread back through the original hole to form a loop.

BUGLE TRIM

USES: edge, fringe

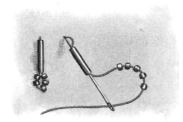

Bring the working thread up. Thread one bugle and five seed beads. Take the thread back through the bugle and the hole. Do not pull too tight as the beads will stick.

COUCHED BEADS

USES: outline

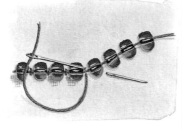

Bring one working thread up and string the beads on. Bring the other thread up and couch down the beads. Take both working threads through to the back and fasten off.

RIBBON SEQUINS

OTHER NAME: back stitch sequins

USES: outline, filling

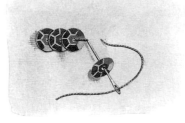

Come up half a sequin width from the end of the design line. Thread one sequin from top to bottom. Take the thread back down on the end of the design line. Repeat and secure.

RIC-RAC BUGLES

USES: border

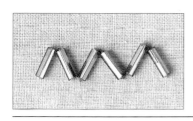

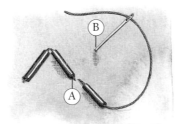

Bring the working thread up at A on the base of the design line and thread a bugle. Position the bead on the diagonal and take the thread back down at B.

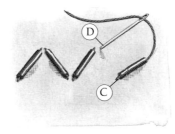

Bring the thread up at C on the base line. Thread the next bugle and position it to form a V shape with the previous one. Take the thread down at D, as close to B as possible.

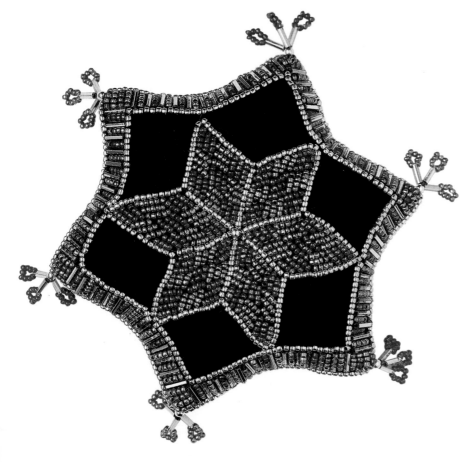

The central six-pointed star on this decorative pin cushion is filled with metallic beads in two different colours, worked in lazy stitch. The outer border alternates bugles with strings of beads, and three bugle trims make up the tassels to finish off each point of the star.

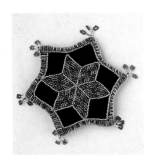

Star pin cushion

Pin cushions were made by Victorian ladies for their work baskets. Their designs would probably have included a quote from the Bible or a few sentimental words, and have been trimmed with ribbons. This one, based on the idea of a snowflake but with a bold choice of colour, uses the contrast of velvet and beads for maximum impact. It is extremely tactile and a joy to hold. Design by Lynn Horniblow

Design area

13cm (5in) diameter

Materials

2 x 24cm (9½in) squares
   dark purple velvet

2 x 24cm (9½in) squares
   white muslin

Beads (see diagram key)

Quilting thread to
   match velvet

2 handfuls of toy stuffing

Equipment

Tracing paper and pen

Tissue paper

Tacking thread

Matching sewing thread

Embroidery hoop
   or frame

Size 10 between
   or quilting needle

Beading needle

Dressmakers' scissors

1 Trace the design from the diagram below and make a pattern on tissue paper. Next, lay the two pieces of muslin fabric on a flat surface and then place the velvet, wrong side down, on top. Tack the two sets of fabric together and put one aside to use later.

2 Pin the pattern onto the back of one of the muslin pieces and velvet square, and transfer the design, tacking with matching thread (see page 31). Tear the tissue paper away. The tacking will probably be covered with beads or must be removed later.

3 Stretch the velvet in an embroidery hoop or frame. If using a hoop, it must be big enough for the whole design to avoid crushing the fabric.

4 Start beading the inner star at point A on the diagram. Couch down a string of the silver 602 beads, with matching threads, all around the inner star shape and return to A.

5 Now couch down strings of the same beads across the centre of the inner star, from B to C, D to E and F to G. This will divide the star into six diamond shapes.

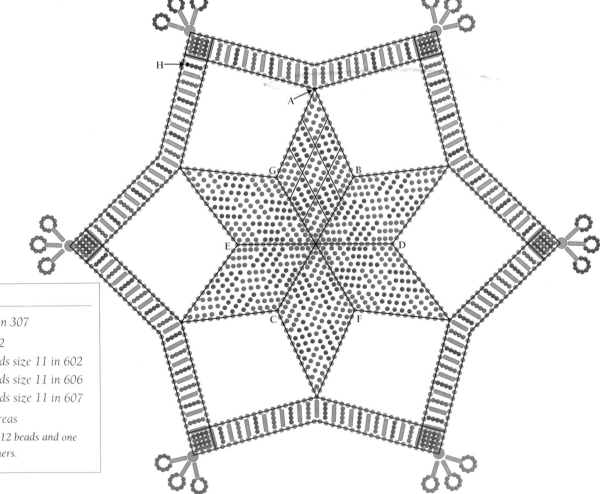

PIN CUSHION KEY

▬ *DMC bugle beads 7mm in 307*

● *Beadcraft M12 beads in 2*

· *DMC metallic lustre beads size 11 in 602*

· *DMC metallic lustre beads size 11 in 606*

· *DMC metallic lustre beads size 11 in 607*

── *Outline for bead-filled areas*

Note: You will need 10 of the M12 beads and one tube or packet of each of the others.

9 Bring the thread up again and secure the mauve beads in position with tiny couching stitches. Fill as much of the space as you can with the roundels touching each other, then add more single mauve beads in any remaining spaces to completely cover the silk fabric in these areas.

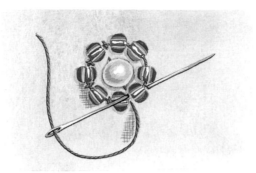

Couch down the circles of mauve beads and fill the spaces with roundels.

10 Stitch down a line of ribbon sequins around the inner edges of the beaded area, keeping them flat and back stitching them securely in position close to the row of mauve beads and pearls.

11 Finish the embroidery by working the roundels of pearls and mauve beads in the same way as before in the inner panel of the design. Follow your marks from the diagram and make sure they are in straight lines, to give the most attractive result.

12 Turn the work face down in the frame on a towel in order not to crush it and lightly steam the back of the embroidery. The steam will set both the stitching and the fabric. Remove the work from the frame.

13 Lay the embroidered silk right side down on a flat surface. Pin the interfacing on top, within the tacked outline, and tack in position. Fold the 2cm (³⁄₄in) seam allowance on the silk over the interfacing. Mitre the corners neatly and slip stitch in place (see page 33). Secure the edges of the silk to the interfacing with an open herringbone stitch (see page 158).

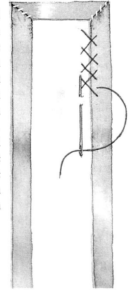

Turn the silk over the edges of the interfacing and herringbone in place.

14 Cut another piece of silk dupion measuring 17 x 51cm (7 x 20in) to be used for a lining. Turn under and tack a 1cm (³⁄₈in) hem all around. Then, place the lining centrally on top of the embroidered silk, wrong sides together, and slip stitch the pieces together.

15 Place the silk fabric face down with the embroidered end furthest away from you. Fold the silk over along the first tacked guideline in order to make the inside front. Make sure the cord is a comfortable length and cut if necessary. Slip the ends of the cord between the layers at the fold and then stitch them down securely.

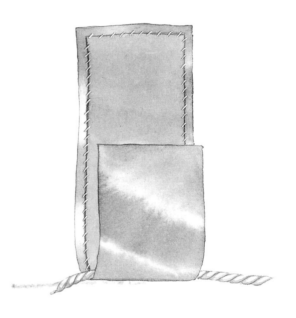

Fold the silk to make the bag shape, securing the ends of the cord.

16 Slip stitch up both sides of the bag, working several stitches over each other at the top to strengthen the bag at the open end. Finally, slip stitch the cord in position up each side of the bag and fold the front flap over, ready for use.

In the beaded areas, make sure you stitch down the beads closely together so the fabric does not show through.

USEFUL
INFORMATION

Glossary

Aida
A stiff embroidery fabric with clearly defined blocks and holes, particularly suitable for cross stitch.

acid-free
Paper or board that will not react with the materials touching it and damage them over time.

acrylic paint
Water-soluble, thick paint in a wide range of colours.

air-soluble pens
(also light-soluble pens)
Used for drawing a design onto fabric – the marks will fade in time.

analogous colours
Closely related colours, such as orange and red.

appliqué
Stitching cut-out fabric motifs onto background material for decorative effect.

Assisi work
Single colour cross stitch in which the outline and background are filled in, with the design left blank.

Ayrshire work
Fine, lace-like whitework produced in the early 1800s in Scotland.

backing cloth
Plain material (such as cotton sheeting) stitched to a delicate fabric to strengthen it, or used to enable a small or irregular-shaped piece of work to fit in a frame.

ballpoint needle
Sewing needle with a smooth, round end.

Bargello (Florentine work)
A distinctive style of canvas work characterized by straight stitches worked in steps, often in zigzags or angular flame shapes. The design is emphasized by bands of colour.

beadwork
Embroidered or woven items created entirely or mainly from beads.

beading needle
Long, fine, flexible needle designed to pass through the hole of a tiny bead and hold a number of beads at a time.

bed of the machine
This is the base plate of a sewing machine.

Berlin woolwork
Simple form of canvas work very popular in Victorian times, using soft, untwisted, silky wool in order to work a wide range of commercially produced designs.

between needle
(or quilting needle)
A short needle designed for fast, even stitching.

bias binding
Narrow strips of material cut with the grain running diagonally, most commonly used in hemming to obtain a smooth result.

birchbark embroidery
See *Naversom*.

blackwork (or Spanish work)
Precise, delicate stitchery of fine black threads on white evenweave linen.

blanketing wool
Firmly woven wool fabric.

blending filaments
Fine metallic or lustrous threads designed to be mixed with other threads in order to obtain special effects.

blocking
A method for squaring up distorted work, particularly canvas work, by dampening and pinning into position on a cloth-covered board until thoroughly dry.

blocking board
Cloth-covered board marked with a grid onto which distorted work can be eased back into shape.

bobbin
Small reel onto which thread is wound ready for use.

bobbin thread
Basic thread for the reverse side of machine stitching.

bodkin
Big, blunt-ended, large-eyed needle used for drawing cord or elastic through a hem.

booboo stick
Brush-ended gadget used for careful unpicking.

braid
Long, ribbon-like lengths of decorative, textured material.

braiding foot
Sewing machine attachment used to attach ribbon or thick yarn onto the surface of fabric.

broderie anglaise
A form of cutwork or eyelet embroidery, featuring white cotton thread outlining holes cut in white cotton fabric.

bugle beads
Small tubular glass beads.

calico
Plain cotton fabric that is often sold unbleached.

canvas work
Term for embroidery on canvas, usually cross stitch.

chart
Reference sheet, mapping out the design in a square grid, with each square representing one stitch.

charted designs
Designs for counted thread work printed on a square grid where each square equals one stitch.

check thread
Ribbed metallic thread used in goldwork.

chenille needle
Needle with a sharp point and large eye, designed to allow thicker thread to pass through fabric without being flattened.

chenille thread
Thread with a velvety pile and soft sheen.

Chikan work
Similar to Dresden work, a style of whitework where different thicknesses of threads provide a contrast between lacy areas and opaque fillings.

Coggeshall work
Floral whitework using white cotton thread on white muslin.

colourfast
This refers to when colour is permanently fixed into a material, so will not run out when wet.

complementary colours
Colours giving greatest contrast, such as blue and orange.

congress cloth (or coin net)
Fine mono canvas, with 24 holes to the inch.

coton à broder
Smooth embroidery thread with a gentle sheen.

coton perlé
A twisted, invisible embroidery thread with an attractive sheen.

cotton
Natural fabric available in many weights, from fine lawn to heavier poplin and piqué.

couched
Thick thread or similar material held onto the fabric surface by stitches looping around it at regular intervals.

count
The number of threads per inch of fabric.

crewel needle
(or embroidery needle)
Sharp, pointed needle with
a large eye, designed to carry
thick thread through material
without damage.

crewel wool
Strong, lightly twisted, two-ply
worsted yarn usually sold in
hanks or skeins.

crewel work
Any coloured embroidery using
crewel wool.

cutwork
Style of embroidery in which
parts of the fabric are cut away
in order to emphasize the design.

cyan
Printer's term for the primary
shade of blue.

damask
A self-coloured patterned
linen fabric.

darning patterns
Way of creating geometric
designs by weaving over and
under the base fabric threads.

darning foot
Sewing machine attachment that
is very useful for free machine
embroidery as it enables stitching
to be made in any direction.

Delsbo work
Style of Swedish embroidery
distinctive for its use of star and
heart motifs in blue and red on
white linen.

designer threads
Special 'bespoke' threads
available in a wide range of
colours, weights and textures.

dévoré
A technique used on velvet
where areas of the pile are
dissolved away in order to
create the design.

dissolvable fabric
Base material that can be
stitched onto and then dissolved
away, which then leaves the
stitching to stand alone.

doctor's flannel
Firmly woven wool fabric.

double canvas
Stiffened cotton evenweave
material where the mesh is
formed by double threads –
stronger than mono canvas
but more limited in the stitches
that can be worked.

drawn threadwork
Embroidery technique in which
some fabric threads are pulled
out and others are strengthened
and embellished.

Dresden work
Lacy shadow work developed
in Saxony in the 18th century,
which is worked on fine muslin.

dressmakers' carbon
transfer paper
Best tracing method for dark
or heavy fabric – when the paper
is placed between the fabric and
the design, drawing around the
design transfers it to the fabric.

dressmakers' marking pencil
Brush-ended pencil for making
removable marks on fabric.

embroidery hoop
(or tambour frame)
Two tightly fitting wooden or
plastic rings used to keep fabric
taut while it is being embroidered
– best for small projects.

embroidery scissors
Sharp scissors that cut right up
to the point of the blades.

evenweave fabric
Material with a regular number
of threads in both directions,
which is important in counted
threadwork techniques.

fabric pens
Used for drawing fine details
onto fabric.

fasten off
Finish off the thread, usually by
neatly weaving it through the
back of the last few stitches.

fat quarters
Pre-cut pieces of material
50cm (½yd) deep by half the
width of the roll.

felt
A non-woven, non-fraying fabric
with fibres matted together.

fix
Bond colour permanently to
material, usually by ironing with
a hot iron.

flexi-frames
Easy-use frames sold particularly for small embroideries.

floor stand
Adjustable stand for an embroidery frame, leaving both hands free to stitch.

floss silk (or Japanese silk)
A delicate, untwisted thread with a high shine that can be divided for very fine work.

flower thread (or Danish flower thread)
This is a fine, soft, matt, embroidery thread.

frame
A circular or rectangular holder used to keep fabric taut and at an even tension when stitching. See also *embroidery hoop, tambour frame, slate frame, rotating frame, stretcher frame, spring hoop, no-sew frame, seat frame, table clamp and floor stand.*

freestyle
Embroidery that is not constrained by counting stitches.

goldwork
Term that describes embroidery in gold or silver.

grain of the fabric
The direction in which the main threads of a fabric run.

grid method
A way of altering the size of a design by marking it out in a grid then copying each square onto another grid of the required size.

gros point
Term for cross stitch canvaswork worked on canvas of 16 threads per inch or less.

gutta
A water-resistant medium used to prevent colours running into areas where they aren't wanted.

haberdashery
Sewing goods and textiles.

Habotai silk
Lightweight silk.

Hardanger embroidery
Norwegian style of geometric openwork embroidery, characteristically all white, stitched on eavenweave fabric using cotton or linen threads.

Hedebo
Openwork technique from 18th century Denmark, which combines cut and drawn threadwork with surface embroidery, usually in geometric patterns.

hem
The turned-in and stitched or bonded edge of material.

interfacing
Non-woven, non-fraying material used to stiffen or back thin fabrics.

interlaced
Passed alternately over and under.

interlock canvas
Canvas with the threads locked in place, preventing slippage – however, it is not as strong or durable as single canvas.

Japanese silk
See *floss silk.*

Japan thread (or passing thread)
A fine gold thread usually couched on the fabric surface.

Jarvso work
Swedish embroidery similar to Delsbo work, but in rose-coloured thread on white or natural linen, often with added tassels.

kloster blocks
Small blocks of satin stitch that are used in Hedebo and Hardanger embroidery.

laid work
Surface embroidery.

lame
Fine metallic fabric that has a high gloss.

light box
Box containing a light under a sheet of glass, enabling designs to be traced directly onto fabric.

linen twill
Closely woven natural fabric with diagonal weave.

magenta
Printer's term for the primary shade of red.

mercerized cotton thread
Cotton thread that has been treated to give it a smooth finish.

metallic media
A range of metallic paints, sticks and powders that are used for special effects.

mica
Transparent silica that can be split into thin, pliable sheets.

mitring
This is the process of folding or cutting corners at a 45-inch angle for a neat finish.

moire taffeta
Stiff fabric made from natural or artificial silk, which has a strong sheen and watermark effect.

motif
A design element capable of standing alone.

mount
The inner card border added to a piece of work before it is put in a frame.

mounting board
Stiff, acid-free board onto which a piece of embroidery is stretched prior to being framed.

Mountmellick
Robust whitework embroidery of soft thick cotton thread on cotton sateen, which was produced in Ireland in the 19th century.

muslin
Fine soft cotton with open weave, which gives a gauzy effect.

Naversom (or birchbark embroidery)
Swedish drawn threadwork.

needlelace
A form of embroidery used to create a lace-like effect, usually across a cut hole in fabric or in stumpwork.

needlepoint
Simple stitching on canvas.

needlewoven stitches
Technique of weaving embroidery thread through existing base fabric threads, which is used in drawn threadwork.

net
This is a sheer, open material that is formed by knotted intersecting threads.

neutral colours
"Colourless" colours – white, grey and black.

non-woven backing (or iron-on interfacing)
A non-fraying material, useful for strengthening fine fabrics.

no-sew frame
Fabric is attached to this embroidery frame by clips, drawing pins or staples (see also *stretcher frame*).

nylon
Smooth, strong, closely woven, manmade fibre.

open work
General term for stitching that changes the structure of a fabric by cutting, pulling or removing threads.

opus anglicanum
Medieval English embroidery produced primarily for ecclesiastical purposes

organdie
This is a fine, plain weave, stiffened cotton.

organza
Fine fabric similar to organdie but made from silk or synthetics.

paint sticks
Large oil crayons used to draw permanent images on fabric.

paper-backed fusible web
A thin layer of glue attached to silicon paper, which is used to bond fabrics.

passing thread (see Japan thread)
Metallic thread, in a smooth or check (ribbed) finish, that is used in goldwork

pearl purl
Hard wire that is spun to form a spring-like structure resembling a row of beads or pearls. Pearl purl is used in goldwork

pelmet stiffening
Thick, sturdy interfacing.

perforated paper
An alternative background material that has regularly punched holes, and is suitable for surface stitching.

Persian wool
A three-stranded wool that can be separated into single strands.

petit point
Term for tent stitch canvaswork when it is worked on a canvas of 18 threads per inch or higher.

picots
Small stitched bobbles used to create a decorative edge to fabric.

pile
The textured, raised surface created by cut threads, giving a luxurious, furry effect (as in velvet or chenille).

plain weave fabrics
Material that has a tightly woven surface, which is suitable for surface embroidery.

plastic canvas
A more rigid material than cotton canvas, this is best used

tailor t
Sewing
designed
useful in

tambou
The te
continu
fabric o
hook res

tapestr
A wove
textile, l
often use
or needle

tapestr
Blunt-er
eyes, wh
wool eas
without

tapestr
Slightly
this is us
cannot b

tassel
Decorativ
threads
end form

templat
Master d
copied ag

tension
The stat
fabric un
to keep w

tpi
This stan
otherwise
the fabric

tracing (
A way o
laying thi
and draw

transfer
Drawn o
image for
ironed on

for creating structured pieces
such as boxes or bags.

point paper
Squared paper onto which Berlin
woolwork designs were printed –
one square represented one stitch.

polyester
Manmade fibre available as a
fabric that comes in a wide range
of finishes.

pounce
Powder made from charcoal
(black) or cuttlefish (white) or a
mixture of the two (grey) – used
to transfer designs onto fabric (see
prick and pounce).

presser foot
Standard sewing machine
attachment that is used for
straight stitching.

prick and pounce
Traditional method of transferring
designs onto fabric by pressing
powder through holes pricked
along the lines.

primary colours
Red, yellow and blue, these are
the three basic colours from
which – with the addition of
black and white – all other
colours are obtained.

printing blocks
Firm substance (such as wood,
rubber, lino or potato) with a
design cut out of it, which can be
linked and transferred repeatedly
onto the desired surface.

**pulled fabric work
(or open work)**
Where woven threads of the
fabric are pulled together to
create open, lacy effects.

purl thread
A hollow thread made of fine
wire that is wound tightly like
a spring. It can be cut and used
as a bead.

random-dyed thread
See *space-dyed thread*.

rayon
Manmade cellulose fibre.

rayon thread
A stranded embroidery thread
with a brilliant silken shine.
This thread is tricky to use as
it has a tendency to kink.

rebate
The inner depth of a picture
frame, indicating the maximum
thickness possible for the item
to be placed in it.

reweave
This refers to when a fabric
thread is woven back almost
invisibly into the fabric, as
in drawn threadwork.

Richelieu work
Form of cutwork that is similar
to broderie anglaise.

rococo
Highly ornamental style of
elaborate curves and scrolls
that was developed in 18th
century France.

rococo work
This is another name for silk
embroidery designs from the
18th century.

**rotating frame (also known
as a tapestry or roller frame)**
A frame with rollers onto which
fabric can be wound. It is most
suitable for use with larger pieces
of work.

rug canvas
Coarse canvas with a large mesh
of strong, glazed threads.

samplers
Designed both as exercises in
stitchery for young girls and
also as a way of recording a
range of stitches, patterns
and techniques.

scalloped
An attractive edging effect of
shallow curves.

scroll
Sweeping design of curving lines
that is used to create an elegant
framing effect.

sealed
Refers to a surface that has been
sprayed with fixative to prevent
drawn marks from smudging.

seam allowance
The extra margin of material
required to prevent stitching
being too close to the fabric edge.

seat frame
A height-adjustable embroidery
frame with a flat base that fits
under a leg when seated, to leave
both hands free

secondary colours
Orange, green and purple – these
are the three colours that are
obtained when primary colours
are mixed in pairs.

seed beads (or rocailles)
Small round glass beads, available
in many colours and sizes.

selvedge
The sealed, unfrayable edge on
each side of a roll of fabric.

Suppliers

The companies listed below are suppliers of tools, threads, fabrics and other embroidery materials, and may be contacted for information on local suppliers or mail order arrangements. All details are correct at the time of publication, but neither the publisher nor those listed can be held responsible for subsequent changes.

United Kingdom

Ann Cox
(YLI silk embroidery ribbon)
Craigers Cottage
Green Lane
Burridge
Southampton SO31 1BN
Tel: +44 (0)1489 582 484

Appleton Brothers Limited
(wool yarns, embroidery wools)
Thames Works
Church Street
Chiswick
London W4 2PE
Tel: +44 (0)20 8994 0711
Fax: +44 (0)20 8995 6609

Barnyarns
(Madeira machine
embroidery threads)
Brickyard Road
Boroughbridge
York YO51 9NS
Tel: +44 (0)870 870 8586
www.barnyarns.com

Benton and Johnson Limited
(goldwork threads)
19–21 Great Queen Street
London WC2 5BE
Tel: + 44 (0)20 7242 0471
Fax: +44 (0)20 7831 8692

Bits and Pieces
(fabrics)
4 Thorold Road
Bitterne Park
Southampton SO18 1JB
Tel: +44 23 80 55 33 34

Bogod Machine Company
(sewing machines)
50–52 Great Sutton Street
London EC1V 0DJ
Tel: +44 (0)20 7253 1198

Brother UK Limited
(sewing machines)
Shepley Street
Audenshaw
Manchester M34 5JD
Tel: +44 (0)161 330 6531

Coats Crafts UK
(Anchor and Kreinik embroidery
threads and tools)
PO Box 22
Lingfield Point
Lingfield House
McMullen Road
Darlington
County Durham DL1 1YQ
Tel: +44 (0)1325 394 394
www.coatscrafts.co.uk

Creative Beadcraft Limited
(beads and sequins)
Denmark Works
Sheepcote Dell Road
Beaumond End
Amersham
Buckinghamshire HP7 0RX
Tel: +44 (0)1494 715 606
Fax: +44 (0)1494 718 510
or 20 Beak Street
London W1R 3HA
Tel: +44 (0)20 7629 9964
Fax: +44 (0)20 7734 7989
www.creativebeadcraft.co.uk

Delicate Stitches
(wool blanketing fabrics, silk
ribbons, beads and other
embroidery fabrics and threads)
339 Kentish Town Road
Kentish Town
London NW5 2TJ
Tel: +44 (0)870 203 2323

DMC Creative World Limited
(fabrics, threads, beads,
waste canvas and tools)
Pullman Road
Wigston
Leicestershire LE18 2DY
Tel: +44 (0)116 281 1040
Fax: +44 (0)116 281 3592

ETP Sales & Agencies
(fine gloving leathers)
Goldcroft
Yeovil
Somerset BA21 4DT
Tel: +44 (0)1935 433 538
Fax: +44 (0)1935 706 874

Fabric Flair Limited
(linen and cotton fabrics)
Unit 3
Northlands Industrial Estate
Copheap Lane
Warminster
Wiltshire BA12 0BG
Tel: +44 (0)800 716 851
Fax: +44 (0)1985 846 849
mail@fabricflair.com
www.fabricflair.com

Framecraft Miniatures Limited
(frames, project accessories
and silk gauze)
372–372 Summer Lane
Hockley
Birmingham B19 3QA
Tel: +44 (0)121 212 0551
Fax: +44 (0)121 212 0552
www.framecraft.com

Fron Isaf
(hand-dyed yarns and fibres)
Llanglydwen
Hebron
Whitland SA34 0JX
Tel: +44 (0)1994 419 523

Golden Threads
(goldwork threads and kids)
Spotted Cow Cottage
Broad Oak
Heathfield
East Sussex TN21 8UE
Tel/fax: +44 (0)1435 862 810
www.goldenthreads.co.uk

Heffers Art & Graphics Shop
15–21 King Street
Cambridge
Cambridgeshire CB1 1LH
Tel: +44 (0)1223 568 495
Fax: +44 (0)1223 568 411

Inca Studio
(fabrics and other
embroidery supplies)
10 Duke Street
Princes Risborough
Buckinghamshire HP27 0AT
Tel: +44 (0)1844 343 343

John Lewis
(haberdashery)
Oxford Street
London W1A 1EX
Tel: +44 (0)20 7629 7711
jl_oxford_st@johnlewis.co.uk

Janice Williams
(goldwork threads)
Sheldon Cottage Studio
Epney
Saul
Gloucester GL2 7LN
Tel: +44 (0)1452 740 639

Leon Conrad Designs Limited
(blackwork kits and
freshwater pearls)
20 Courtenay Street
Kennington
London SE11 5PQ
Tel: +44 (0)20 7582 8213
Fax: +44 (0)20 7793 8339
www.lcdesigns.org

Macleod Craft Marketing
(Caron Collection threads)
West Yonderton
Warlock Road
Bridge of Weir PA11 3SR
Tel: +44 (0)1505 612 618

Madeira Threads UK Limited
(machine embroidery threads)
Thirsk Industrial Park
York Road
Thirsk
North Yorkshire YO7 3BX
Tel: +44 (0)1845 524 880

Margaret Beale
(silk, sheer and velvet fabrics)
28 Leigh Road
Andover
Hampshire SP10 2AP
Tel/Fax: (0)1264 365 102
margaret.beale@onet.co.uk

Mulberry Silks
(silk threads)
2 Old Rectory Cottages
Easton Grey
Malmesbury
Wiltshire SN16 0PE
Tel: +44 (0)1666 840 881
Fax: +44 (0)1666 841 028

Offray Ribbon
[contact Christine Kingdom,
their marking agent, at +44
(0)118 973 6796 for details]

Oliver Twists
(hand-dyed threads, fabrics
and fibres)
22 Phoenix Road
Crowther
Washington
Tyne and Wear NE38 0AD
Tel: +44 (0)191 415 3405
Fax: +44 (0)191 416 6016

Pearsalls Limited
(stranded silk threads)
Tancred Street
Taunton
Somerset TA1 1RY
Tel: +44 (0)1823 253 198
Fax: +44 (0)1823 336 824
www.pearsalls.co.uk

Pebeo UK Limited
(fabric paints)
109 Solent Business Centre
Millbrook Road West
Millbrook
Southampton SO15 0HW

Tel: +44 (0)2380 901 914
Fax: +44 (0)2380 901 916
www.pebeo.com

Rainbow Silks
(machine embroidery threads;
fabrics, including dissolvable)
6 Wheelers Yard
High Street
Great Missenden
Buckinghamshire HP16 0AL
Tel: +44 (0)1494 862 111

Ribbon Designs
(ribbons and braids)
PO Box 382
Edgware
Middlesex HA8 7XQ
Tel: +44 (0)20 8958 4966

Simply Scissors
(embroidery and
specialist scissors)
24 Walker Close
New Southgate
London N11 1AQ
Tel: +44 (0)20 8368 5596

Spangles (The Bead People)
(beads, beading needles
and beading thread)
1 Casburn Lane
Burwell
Cambridge
Cambridgeshire CB5 0ED
Tel/fax: +44 (0)1638 742 024

Steff Francis
(embroidery threads)
Waverley
Higher Rocombe
Stokeinteignhead
Newton Abbot TQ12 4QL
Tel: +44 (0)1803 323 004

The Bead Merchant
(beads and beading wire)
38 Eld Lane
Colchester
Essex CO1 1LS
Tel: +44 (0)1206 764 101

Index

First published in 2002 by Murdoch Books UK Ltd
Copyright © 2002 Murdoch Books UK Ltd

Picture credits: p44 V&A Picture Library; p45 Glasgow Museums; p46 *top* Glasgow School of Art, photo Andy Stark, *bottom* Glasgow Museums; p56 Manchester City Art Gallery; p57 *left* National Museums of Scotland, *right* Glasgow Museums; p58 *top right and bottom left* Burrell Collection, *top left* Leon Conrad; p59 *left* Jack Robinson, *right* Melissa Cheeseman; p72 Traquair House; p73 *left* V&A Picture Library, *right* Parham House; p74 Burrell Collection; p75 *left* Private Collection; p75 *right* Pamela Watts; p90 Embroiderers' Guild; p91 Glasgow Museums; p92 *top* Glasgow Museums, *middle* Glasgow School of Art, photo Andy Stark, *bottom* Blair Castle; p93 *bottom* Glasgow School of Art; p108 Jill Carter; p109 Glasgow School of Art, photo Andy Stark; p110 *left and right* National Museums of Scotland; p111 *left* Jill Carter, *right* Coats Viyella; p124 Burrell Collection; p125 Glasgow School of Art, photo Andy Stark; p126 *top* Glasgow Museums, *bottom* Jenny Adin; p127 Glasgow School of Art, photo Andy Stark; p140 Glasgow Museums; p141 Glasgow Museums; p142 *left* Paisley Museum & Art Gallery, *right* Glasgow Museums; p143 *left* Jenny Adin, *right* Folk Museum, Ulster; p154 Rosemary Campbell; p155 Embroiderers' Guild; p156 Private Collection; p157 *top* Glasgow School of Art, photo Andy Stark; p166 Private Collection; p167 *left* Glasgow Museums, *right* Burrell Collection; p168 *top left* National Galleries of Scotland, *top right* Midori Matsushima, *bottom* Glasgow Museums; p169 *left* Private Collection, photo Andy Stark; p182 Phillipa Turnbull; p183 The Bayeux Tapestry, by special permission of the City of Bayeux; p184 *top* Embroiderers' Guild, *bottom* Fitzwilliam Museum; p185 Glasgow Museums; p200 Dorothy Tucker; p201 National Museums of Scotland; p202 National Museums of Scotland; p203 *top* Glasgow School of Art, *bottom* Glasgow Museums; p214 Jan Beaney, photo Michael Wicks; p215 Glasgow School of Art, photo Andy Stark; p216 *top and bottom* National Museums of Scotland; p217 *top* Linda Miller, *bottom* Alison King; p230 Burrell Collection; p231 *top and bottom* Burrell Collection; p232 Apple Orchard © 1992 Salley Mavor; p248 Hampshire Museums; p249 Museum of London; p250 *left* Gallery of English Costume, Manchester, *right* Hampshire Museums; p266 Burrell Collection; p267 Durham Cathedral; p268 *top left* Private Collection, *top right* V&A Picture Library, *bottom* Glasgow Museums; p269 *top* Hannah Frew Paterson, *bottom* Midori Matsushima; p282 V&A Picture Library; p283 Burrell Collection; p284 *top* Glasgow Museums, *bottom* Burrell Collection; p285 *top* Glasgow Museums.

ISBN 1 85391 988 8
A catalogue record for this book is available from the British Library.

Senior Commissioning Editor: **Karen Hemingway**
Project Editor: **Carine Tracanelli**
Designers: **Tim Brown**
Consultant: **Vivienne Wells**
Managing Editor: **Anna Osborn**
Design Manager: **Helen Taylor**
Photo Librarian: **Bobbie Leah**
Picture Researchers: **Liz Arthur, Helen Stallion**
Photograper: **David Brittain**
Photographer's assistant: **Marc Kirk**
Stylist: **Claire Richardson**
Stylist's assistants: **Louisa Grey, Claire Morgan**
Illustrator: **Carolyn Jenkins**
Chart and diagram illustrator: **Ethan Danielson**

CEO: **Robert Oerton**
Publisher: **Catie Ziller**
Production Manager: **Lucy Byrne**
International Sales Director: **Kevin Lagden**

Colour separation by Colourscan, Singapore
Printed in China by Toppan Printing

Murdoch Books UK Ltd
Ferry House, 51–57 Lacy Road
Putney, London SW15 1PR
United Kingdom
Tel: +44 (0)20 8355 1480
Fax: +44 (0)20 8355 1499
Murdoch Books UK Ltd is a subsidiary
of Murdoch Magazines Pty Ltd

Murdoch Books®
Pier 8/9 23 Hickson Road
Millers Point NSW 2000
Australia
Tel: +61 (0)2 8220 2000
Fax: +61 (0)2 8220 2020
Murdoch Books® is a trademark
of Murdoch Magazines Pty Ltd